THE TITHE WAR IN ENGLAND AND WALES 1881–1936

Boydell Studies in Rural History

Series Editor
Professor Richard W. Hoyle

This series aims to provide a forum for the best and most influential work in agricultural and rural history, and on the cultural history of the countryside. Whilst it is anchored in the rural history of Britain and Ireland, it also includes within its remit Europe and the colonial empires of European nations (both during and after colonisation). All approaches and methodologies are welcome, including the use of oral history.

Proposals or enquiries are welcomed. They may be sent directly to the editor or the publisher at the e-mail addresses given below.

Richard.Hoyle@reading.ac.uk

Editorial@boydell.co.uk

Previous titles in the series are listed at the back of the volume.

The Tithe War in England and Wales, 1881–1936
A Curious Rural Revolt

John Bulaitis

THE BOYDELL PRESS

© John Bulaitis 2024

All Rights Reserved. Except as permitted under current legislation no part of this work may be photocopied, stored in a retrieval system, published, performed in public, adapted, broadcast, transmitted, recorded or reproduced in any form or by any means, without the prior permission of the copyright owner

The right of John Bulaitis to be identified as the author of this work has been asserted in accordance with sections 77 and 78 of the Copyright, Designs and Patents Act 1988

First published 2024
The Boydell Press, Woodbridge

ISBN 978 1 83765 187 0

The Boydell Press is an imprint of Boydell & Brewer Ltd
PO Box 9, Woodbridge, Suffolk IP12 3DF, UK
and of Boydell & Brewer Inc.
668 Mt Hope Avenue, Rochester, NY 14620–2731, USA
website: www.boydellandbrewer.com

A CIP catalogue record for this book is available from the British Library

The publisher has no responsibility for the continued existence or accuracy of URLs for external or third-party internet websites referred to in this book, and does not guarantee that any content on such websites is, or will remain, accurate or appropriate

For Mum and Dad

CONTENTS

	List of Illustrations	viii
	Acknowledgements	ix
	List of Abbreviations	xi
	Prologue: The Battle of the Ducks	xv
	Introduction	1
1	The 1836 Tithe Commutation Act	13
2	Hops, Pantomime and Martyrs, 1881–86	31
3	Wales and Southern England, 1886–91	49
4	Tithe after the Great War	81
5	The Settlement Unravels, 1927–31	115
6	The Bounty and General Dealers	147
7	English Agrarianism and Fascism	189
8	Pressures for a Settlement	225
9	The Royal Commission	259
10	Aftermath	287
	Conclusion: A 'Curious Rural Revolt'?	295
	Sources and Bibliography	301
	Index	315

ILLUSTRATIONS

Frontispiece: Map of the English Counties   xiii

Figures

1	'The Battle of the Ducks': front page of London *Evening Standard*, 5 September 1934	xiv
2	'A Modern Eden': cartoon published by the Liberation Society, c.1886	44
3	Troops of the 9th Lancers, police and bailiffs in Llanfair Talhaiarn, May 1888	52
4	'Lively Tithe Sales in Kent': Front page of *Daily Mirror*, 25 September 1931	139
5	Sir George Middleton	169
6	Police guarding trucks of cattle seized by General Dealers, Wortham, 22 February 1934	193
7	Fascists at Whitestone, 29 November 1933	215
8	Fascists at Wortham, early February 1934	219
9	Demonstration at a distraint sale near Wrexham, 22 February 1933	233
10	Effigy of 'Queen Anne' before being burnt at a tithe sale, 9 April 1935	270
11	Rev. Roderick Kedward addressing the crowd after the 'Great London March', 24 June 1936	282

Tables

1	Value of tithe rentcharge vested in Queen Anne's Bounty, 1 October 1933	4

Full credit details are provided in the captions to the images in the text. The author and publisher are grateful to all the institutions and individuals for permission to reproduce the materials in which they hold copyright. Every effort has been made to trace the copyright holders; apologies are offered for any omission, and the publisher will be pleased to add any necessary acknowledgement in subsequent editions.

ACKNOWLEDGEMENTS

This book began as a short project to find out more about the Battle of the Ducks, the episode with which it begins. Soon, however, attempts to contextualise the incident took the research far and wide, in terms of both geography and periodisation. Many people helped me navigate the territory, which was relatively unknown for an historian of modern France.

The following individuals provided invaluable help in finding sources: Jeremy and Judy Wilson (Elham) allowed access to the papers of their grandfather, Kingsley Dykes; Dr Susan Pittman (Crockenhill) shared her research into local farming families; Carol Twinch allowed generous access to the Mobbs Papers; Kinn McIntosh MBE shared the Doreen Wallace Papers and Elizabeth Finn (Kent Archives) pointed me in the direction of files relating to General Dealers.

Important local knowledge was shared by Dr Sheila Sweetinburgh (Canterbury), Tom Burnham (Staplehurst), Derek Boughton (Elham), Jim Weir (Westcourt Farm, Shepherdswell), Gill Bromley (Smarden), Andy Harris, Pam and Adrien Corder-Birch (Halstead and District Local History Society), Kaye Sowden (Pluckley) and Tom Burnham (Staplehurst), who provided biographical information about E. W. I. Peterson. Special thanks are due to Martin Woodward, great-great grandson of George Cooper, the 'Smarden Martyr'.

I received assistance from archivists and librarians at the following institutions: Berkshire Record Office, Bodleian Library, Canterbury Cathedral Archives, Churchill Archives Centre (Cambridge), Church of England Record Centre, Dorset Record Office, Essex Record Office, Hampshire Record Office, Kent History and Library Centre (Maidstone), Lambeth Palace Library, LSE Library, Museum of English Rural Life (University of Reading), National Archives, North East Wales Archives, Parliamentary Archives (Palace of Westminster), Suffolk Archives, University of Warwick Modern Records Centre.

The following students (now former students) acted as research assistants, all in an exemplary and professional fashion: Christian Cronin, Christina Dickens, Heather Stracey and Eli-Sian Wyllie. Canterbury Christ Church University contributed towards their wages and towards payments for copyright and reproduction of images.

Acknowledgements

I thank Rev. Harvey Richardson (Shepherdswell) and Dr Ralph Norman (CCCU) for imparting information on Methodism and Anglicanism, particularly useful for a lapsed Catholic, Dr Sonia Overall (CCCU) for discussions on effigies and Professor Michael Turner (University of Hull) for sharing his expertise on copyhold. Dr Paul Dalton and Dr Paula Simpson provided important knowledge on tithe through the ages. Professor Richard Hoyle (University of Reading) read the text and provided invaluable feedback. Special thanks for support and advice goes to Caroline Palmer, Laura Bennetts and Demi Wormgoor at Boydell & Brewer.

This project began after a talk given to the Shepherdswell and Coldred History Society. I admire its members for their passion for local history, particularly Carol Howell, Keith Roberts, Brian Flood, Steve Durbridge, Chris Gray, Jean Wooldridge and Steve Newman.

The idea for a book began to take shape after I was invited by the Brook Rural Museum to deliver the Nightingale Lecture on 'The Battle of the Ducks' in 2015. Subsequent invitations to talk about the 'tithe war' to numerous history societies, community groups, farming organisations and academic conferences helped to hone my research and arguments. Particular thanks go to Dr Mark Bateson for the invitations to speak at the Kent History and Library Centre. Dr Margaret Creear offered all kinds of support, including sophisticated feedback on the text.

Most of all, my heartfelt gratitude goes to Stella and Vincent Bulaitis. They have consistently inspired and encouraged me to finish what I mistakenly assured them was going to be a very short project.

ABBREVIATIONS

AgHR	*Agricultural History Review*
BUF	British Union of Fascists
BuFP	*Bury Free Press*
CAC	Churchill Archives Centre
CCA	Canterbury Cathedral Archives
CDI	Church Defence Institution
CDU	Churchmen's Defence Union
CERC	Church of England Record Office
ChCh	*Chelmsford Chronicle*
CLA	Central Landowners' Association
CPAC	Conservative Parliamentary Agricultural Committee
DE	*Dover Express and East Kent News*
DEx	*Daily Express*
DHe	*Daily Herald*
DiEx	*Diss Express*
DMa	*Daily Mail*
DWPap	Doreen Wallace Papers
EC	Ecclesiastical Commission
F&S	*Farmer & Stockbreeder*
FW	*The Fascist Week*
GPR	George Pitt-Rivers Papers
HC Deb	House of Commons Debate
HL Deb	House of Lords Debate
HRO	Hampshire Record Office
KE	*Kentish Express*
KG	*Kentish Gazette*
KHLC	Kent History and Library Centre

Abbreviations

KM	*Kent Messenger*
LAH	Lady Allen of Hurtwood Papers
LPL	Lambeth Palace Library
LU	Land Union
LW	*The Land Worker*
MERL	Museum of English Rural Life
NDJ	*North Devon Journal*
NFU	National Farmers' Union
NTA	National Tithepayers' Association
NUAW	National Union of Agricultural Workers
ODNB	*Oxford Dictionary of National Biography*
QAB	Queen Anne's Bounty
Royal Comm	Royal Commission on Tithe Rentcharge (1936)
SEG	*South Eastern Gazette*
SuRO	Suffolk Records Office
TNA	The National Archives
TQA	Tithe Question Association
TRC	Tithe Redemption Committee
WADA	Wessex Agricultural Defence Association
WG	*Western Gazette*
WMN	*Western Morning News*
WT	*Western Times*

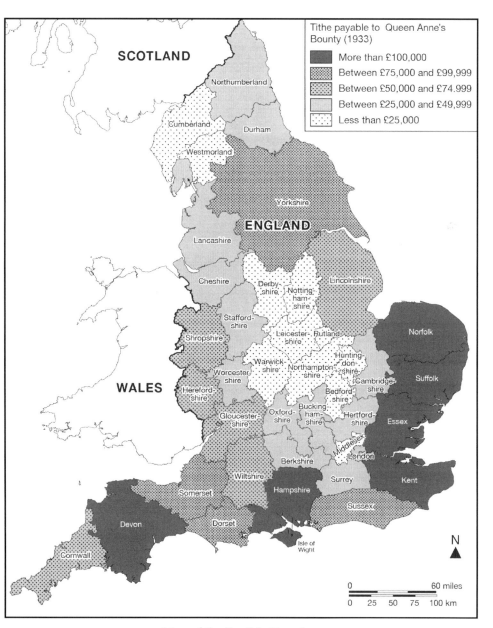
Map of the English Counties.

Evening Standard

CLOSING CITY PRICES — FINAL NIGHT

No. 34,332 — LONDON, TUESDAY, SEPTEMBER 4, 1934 — ONE PENNY

TITHE BATTLE OF DUCKS

150 Masked Men Raid a Kent Farm at Midnight

THEIR PASSWORD—"SOCKS!"

60 Ducks Seized, Reseized, and then Seized Again

An astonishing Battle of the Ducks is being fought in the Kent tithe "war."

Yesterday sixty ducks were seized under a tithe distress order at the farm of Mr. R. M. Kedward, at Westwell, Hothfield, near Ashford.

To-day, very early in the morning, 150 masked men drove up to the Ecclesiastical Commissioners' farm at West Court, Shepherd's Well, and reseized the ducks. They drove back to Ashford and put the ducks on Mr. Kedward's pond again.

A police superintendent, a sergeant and three policemen rushed to Mr. Kedward's farm to intercept the raiders, failed, and then spent six hours re-rounding up the ducks.

"RENDEZVOUS AT 12 WITH MASKS"

From Our Special Correspondent

ASHFORD (Kent), Tuesday.

THE countryside round Ashford is buzzing with tales of the amazing one-o'clock-in-the-morning raid on the Ecclesiastical Commissioners' farm.

Here is the full story of the exploit—masks, passwords and all—as told to-day by a member of the raiding party.

"I am being chased by the police, I suppose, for having been in a modern rustling expedition," he said.

"It was great fun.

MIDNIGHT MEETING ON DOVER ROAD

"Last night I was told that a raid was being planned to recover the stock seized from Mr. Kedward's farm. Would I take part? I said I would.

"A reconnaissance party was sent out to discover the lay of the land, and at about midnight I drove to the rendezvous that was arranged outside the halfway public-house on the Dover road.

"There I found about 150 farmers and their sons.

"Here I was given the password, 'Socks,' and the procession moved off slowly. We all wore masks. None of the 30 cars and two farm lorries carried lights.

"One of the lorries was empty. The other contained 20 of the toughest men it was possible to find.

"We arrived at Shepherds Well at about one o'clock. We had to pass through a wood and up a long farm lane. We stopped at the first farm cottage, and one of our men got out to cut the telephone wires, but we discovered that the farm was not on the telephone.

"We threw out a cordon right round the farm, and one of us knocked on the door of the cottage.

"An old man came to the door in his nightshirt. He was terribly frightened by our masks.

"'I am only a poor man,' he told us; 'I will show you what you want.'

FARM MANAGER HELD BY 3 MEN

"We asked him if the farm belonged to the Ecclesiastical Commissioners and he said, 'Yes.' We asked him where the manager was, and we took him, still in his nightshirt, and he showed us the farm manager's house.

"We rattled the door-handle, and a man put his head out of the window. 'What do you want?' he shouted. We called back, 'Where is the stock that was taken from Mr. Kedward's farm?' He said, 'I know nothing about it.'

"We told him we had got men all round the farm, and we said, 'We want those ducks.'

"He then rushed off and said he would fetch his gun, but he came down to the front door and three of our men held him. We had previously allowed the cottager to fetch his trousers, and he took us up to the farm buildings.

"He could tell where the ducks were because they were making a frightful commotion.

"About 50 of us went to the turkey run at the back of the farm and each seized a duck or two and loaded them in the farm lorry.

WOMAN CRIES FOR THE POLICE

"After this, we heard a shrill scream from the house, and we found it was the wife of the manager, seeing her husband held, shrieking for the police.

"As there were people living within a quarter of a mile, we thought it time to clear off.

"By following all the back roads we got back to Mr. Kedward's farm at Westwell. Here we backed the lorry with the ducks to the farm pond and with one long quack the ducks flopped back into their own pond.

"We had told the farm manager that we had plenty of men available and that we could have taken all the stock that we seized had we wanted to. We had three dogs to contend with at the farm, but these we quietened.

"It all went off very smoothly. We had only one real scare. That was just after we had started out. Two cars passed us going in the direction of Dover and we thought they were police cars.

"All the time, we were expecting to be met by the police when we arrived at the farm.

"Coming back the ducks made a terrible commotion. At one public-house which we passed the landlord put his head out of the window. We could only shout to him that everything was all right, for we were afraid he would telephone the police.

"The raid over, the party split up and (Continued on PAGE FIVE)

The DUKE OF GLOUCESTER, who left Hendon by air for Paris this afternoon on the first stage of his Australasian tour, saying good-bye to Mr. J. H. Thomas before boarding the airplane.

General Booth Will Remain An American

COMMANDER EVANGELINE BOOTH, the General-elect of the Salvation Army has already made two decisions.

They are that—

She will remain an American citizen, and not take up British citizenship again, and

There will be no relaxation of the ban on the youth of the Salvation Army attending cinemas or smoking.

On her determination to remain an American Commander Booth said it would be of advantage for her to continue for citizenship of the United States.

NO CHANGES

There would, she said, be no fundamental changes in policy. The General would have the same control as hitherto.

Explaining the regulations against smoking and attendance at cinemas, she said, "We build all the defences around youth that we can."

The General-elect said there would be no change in the style of the Salvation Army dress.

"In these days of changing fashions," she added, "when dressing is a perfect agony for most women, Salvation Army lasses have a distinct advantage with their trim blue uniforms and Army bonnets.

POLICE LEAVE STOPPED ON DAY OF FASCIST MEETING

A NOTICE was posted in all Metropolitan and City of London police stations this afternoon.

It read:—

All leave to officers of all ranks has been stopped for Sunday, September 9. Further instructions will be given when reporting for duty on Saturday and Sunday.

This notice is a sequel to conferences between Lord Trenchard, the Commissioner, Sir Hugh Turnbull, of the City Police, and the senior officers of both forces in connection with the proposed Fascist demonstration and counter-demonstrations which have been arranged to take place in Hyde Park on Sunday.

THE SPECIALS

The notice is an indication that the authorities are going to allow the demonstrations to proceed, but that they are recruiting the full strength of the police as a precaution.

The Chief of the Special Constabulary has been consulted. There is expected to be a full muster of these officers to take over traffic duties.

The whole of the Special Branch of Scotland Yard are to be on duty in Hyde Park.

Mounted police are to be considerably augmented.

Final police preparations will be made when the 24 superintendents of London's police divisions meet in conference at Scotland Yard to-morrow.

Surprise Banner Hung at Law Courts

A banner in red and white reading, "March against Fascism on September 9," was suspended from the top of scaffolding at the Law Courts to-day. It had been hung while workmen were at their dinner. The workmen on return took it down. The letters, red on white background, were two feet high.

LATE MR. F. C. GOODENOUGH

The funeral took place at Broughton Poggs Church, Oxfordshire, to-day, of Mr. F. C. Goodenough, chairman of Barclays Bank.

Mr. Goodenough, who was 66, died in a nursing home in London on Saturday, following an operation.

MAN KILLED BY TUBE TRAIN

The body of a man was found lying on the track in the tunnel between Marble Arch and Lancaster Gate tube stations to-day.

"Met a man yesterday who had never heard of Four Square."

"Must have been the man who thinks that an arpeggio is a group of islands."

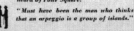

GEORGE DOBIE & SON LTD. (Manufacturers of Quality Tobaccos since 1809), Paisley, Scotland

FIGURE 1. 'The Battle of the Ducks': front page of London *Evening Standard*, 5 September 1934 (© Evening Standard).

PROLOGUE: THE BATTLE OF THE DUCKS

The Halfway House, so named to mark the mid-point on the road between Canterbury and Dover, has been the setting for several dramatic episodes in rural history. In October 1830, local landowners and magistrates convened there to organise resistance to 'the outrageous conduct of agricultural mobs of the lower classes going about demolishing the threshing machines of farmers', the first stirrings of the uprising that became known as Captain Swing.[1] By the early twentieth century, the seventeenth-century coaching inn had become a popular venue for family outings, as well as a meeting place for the local hunt. On the evening of 3 September 1934, it was the assembly point for a well-publicised skirmish in what contemporaries were calling the 'tithe war'.

Events are recorded in a substantial police dossier held at the National Archives. The gathering was of around seventy people, mainly male – 'there were three women' – and mostly young, though with older men directing operations. Most came from villages and hamlets in the nearby Elham Valley, though 'six or eight motor cars' carried contingents from villages surrounding the coastal towns of Sandwich and Deal. According to witnesses, this group had been organised by 'Solley of Sandwich', the sobriquet of George Christopher Solley, a well-known figure in east Kent political and cultural life. Solley was chairman of the East Kent Tithepayers' Association and had recently joined the British Union of Fascists. Those present represented a cross section of the rural community: farmers and farmers' sons, hired hands and cowmen, a gardener and undergardener, a driver's mate for a coal merchant, two lorry drivers, a local garage owner and mechanic in his employ; there was also a trooper in the King's Royal Hussars, lodging in an imposing residence in Lyminge to fulfil his duties as an officer's batman. After a briefing, the group formed a convoy of cars and two trucks – which were decorated with the words 'Terry, Elham' – and

---

[1] 'Outrages in Kent', *The Atlas*, 3 Oct. 1830.

Prologue: The Battle of the Ducks

travelled two miles down the Dover Road towards West Court Farm, on the outskirts of the village of Shepherdswell.[2]

West Court Farm was church property administered by the Ecclesiastical and Church Estates commissioners. That morning, its manager, Fred Grabham, had received a telegram from the Commissioners' agents instructing him to prepare for the delivery of one shorthorn bull, one sow, a Fordson tractor and fifty-six Indian Runner ducks. The stock arrived, along with a bailiff's 'possession man', and was secured on the farm.[3] It had been removed for non-payment of tithe rentcharge shortly after dawn from Beechbrook Farm, Westwell (near Ashford), a holding owned by Rev. Roderick Kedward, a methodist minister and former Liberal MP for Ashford (Kent). Kedward was president of the National Tithepayers' Association (NTA) and refusing to pay his tithe as part of the association's campaign against an 'unjust tax on agriculture'.

Tithe – etymologically a tenth – had been converted into a 'tithe rentcharge' by the 1836 Tithe Commutation Act. In place of a tenth of produce, the Act made tithepayers liable for a cash payment worked out by a complicated formula to the price of corn. Kedward owed tithe to the Ecclesiastical Commissioners and to Queen Anne's Bounty, an institution originally established in 1704 to provide funds for poorer sections of the clergy. Since 1931, he had on three separate occasions stymied applications for a distress order on his possessions. But on 20 August 1934 bailiffs arrived in Westwell with a warrant issued by Ashford County Court. They 'distrained' – in other words, confiscated – a field of oats, livestock (the bull, sow and ducks), and various items of machinery, leaving the goods under the watchful eye of a 'possession man'. The following week, the entire lot was sold to General Dealers Limited, a company established in December 1932 by Queen Anne's Bounty, the Ecclesiastical Commissioners and other titheowners with the specific aim of breaking the tithepayers' non-payment campaign.

Men employed by General Dealers arrived at Kedwood's farm on the morning of 3 September with orders to remove the distrained stock. A journalist described how their trucks 'found the lane blocked with motor cars belonging to neighbouring farmers' and 'the entrance to the farmyard was blocked by a wagon drawn across the roadway'. Further 'difficulties arose when they tried to load up a bull [and] in order to capture several dozen ducks on the pond, men had to wade waist deep into the water. A field of oats, the main item in the list, was left standing because of the rain.'[4] News of events spread through nearby

[2] Dossier, 'Kent Chief Constable: Tithe Sale Disturbances', 5 Sept. 1934, TNA, HO 144/19199.
[3] Statements from Frederick and Donald Grabham, 11 Sept. 1934, TNA, HO 144/19199.
[4] 'Tithe Dispute in Kent', *Kent and Sussex Courier*, 7 Sept. 1934.

Prologue: The Battle of the Ducks

rural communities and information leaked that the goods had been taken to West Court Farm. In the village of Elham (eight miles from Shepherdwell), officers of the Tithepayers' Association decided to make attempts to retrieve the stock and called on supporters to meet that evening at the Halfway House. The Elham Tithepayers' Association was one of the most active branches of the NTA in the country. In December 1932, it had successfully mobilised hundreds of people to thwart the seizure of distrained livestock from ten local farms. Legal proceedings arising from the affair had rumbled on throughout 1933.

On 3 September 1934, the convoy from the Halfway House arrived at West Court Farm at around 11.30 p.m. One of the farm's labourers described how he was woken to find twenty men outside his cottage. 'All the men were disguised. They had a handkerchief tied across their faces,' he told police.[5] After some commotion, the visitors were taken to the seized stock. Thinking better of trying to tackle the bull and sow, they rounded up the fifty-six ducks and put them into the back of one of the trucks. Accompanied by several cars, the truck sped back into the night, heading towards Beechbrook Farm to reunite the ducks with their pond.

Police were quickly on the trail. On receiving eyewitness descriptions of the trucks, officers visited a farm near Elham operated by John Terry. Police Constable Charles Riley reported: 'I found a lorry. The radiator and engine was still warm. I examined the interior of the lorry and noticed some fresh straw. Amongst the straw I found a quantity of brown and white duck feathers and some sprigs of fresh oak leaves.' The officer duly returned to West Court Farm to continue his sleuthing:

> I noticed a trail of brown and white duck feathers leading from the enclosure for about a hundred yards across the edge of a field. I took possession of a quantity of these feathers as they were similar to those found in Terry's lorry. In a lane, I found several freshly broken sprigs of oak leaves. I took possession of these as they appeared similar to those in Terry's lorry.[6]

Police officers were despatched to Rev. Kedward's farm. They reported: 'We saw on a pond a number of ducks. We reported the discovery and kept guard over them until mid-day. The ducks were then removed from the premises.'[7]

Newspapers highlighted these farcical aspects of the incident. 'Ducks "in Custody"', announced *The Daily Mirror*; 'Ducks Seized in Tithe Distress', reported *The Times*. 'Tithe Battle of the Ducks' was the front-page banner headline in the London *Evening Standard*: the incident

---

[5] Statement from Arthur Lee, 11 Sept. 1934, TNA, HO 144/19199.
[6] PC Charles Riley (4 Sept. 1934), TNA, HO 144/19199.
[7] Sergeant Purkiss and PC Hayden (4 Sept. 1934), TNA, HO 144/19199.

Prologue: The Battle of the Ducks

was, said the paper, an 'astonishing' story about which 'the countryside round Ashford is buzzing'.[8]

The authorities, in contrast, treated the affair with utmost seriousness. Frank Newsam, the most senior civil servant at the Home Office, wrote: 'At a time when the tithe question is so much a matter of controversy, a very serious view must be taken of such conduct on the part of opponents of tithe. It would be a good thing if the ringleaders could be brought to trial on a charge of conspiracy.'[9] Twenty-three police officers patrolled the perimeter of West Court Farm for several days to deter attempts to retrieve the remaining seized goods.[10]

On 6 September, General Dealers returned to Beechbrook Farm in order to remove the remainder of the stock, including the harvest of oats. They brought four trucks and a group of burly men, including a former army heavyweight boxing champion, and were accompanied by a large police presence, including 'mobile police on motor cycles'. This time, newspaper articles spoke of a 'pitched battle', 'a wild chase' and a 'struggle' before 'police dispersed the crowd'. *The Times* reported 'several free fights' between 'young farmers' and the men hired by General Dealers.[11]

Six hundred miles away, in a remote location in the Highlands, the archbishop of Canterbury was following events with some anxiety. His chaplain wrote to George Middleton, who as First Estates Commissioner was the Church's most senior lay official and responsible for the functioning of the Ecclesiastical Commissioners and Queen Anne's Bounty:

> His Grace […] keeps in touch with what is going on in the South of England by perusing newspaper cuttings. […] He has, therefore, become aware that Mr Kedward has declared that he intends to serve a subpoena on the archbishop of Canterbury in respect of some ducks […] For His Grace's peace of mind, are you in a position to assure him that this particular worry is not likely to confront him on his return to London.

'You may completely reassure the archbishop,' replied Middleton, 'the Commissioners are no wise implicated in […] the removal of the ducks [which were] sold to General Dealers by the Registrar of the County Court.'[12]

---

8   *Daily Mirror* and *The Times*, 5 Sept. 1934; *Evening Standard*, 4 Sept. 1934.
9   Note by Frank Newsam, 17 Sept. 1934, TNA, HO 144/19199.
10 Superintendent Webb, 11 Sept. 1934, TNA, HO 144/19199.
11 *DEx, DHe, DMa* and *The Times*, 7 Dec. 1934.
12 Correspondence between Alan C. Don and George Middleton, 13 & 14 Sept. 1934, CERC, ECE/SEC/TITHE/RC2/3.

Prologue: The Battle of the Ducks

Over the next few weeks, the police investigation identified many of the participants in the 'Battle of the Ducks'. Arrests began and on 29 October a special court session was convened in Dover Town Hall to hear charges of unlawful assembly and conspiracy to commit unlawful assembly. Nineteen men were committed for trial at the Kent Assizes.[13]

A piece of microhistory, the Battle of the Ducks reveals the essential themes and elements of the history outlined in the pages that follow. It illustrates how a controversy – ever-present in the popular media – posed a dilemma for government, a headache for the police and authorities, and a serious 'worry' for the Church of England. Shining a light on rural social relations, it reveals a bitter conflict, one with roots put down over centuries but conditioned by the context of the modern age. It indicates the character, strategy and tactics of the tithepayers' movement – politically, a rather strange coalition. Seizures of livestock and property raised the ire and resistance of farmers. But amongst the weapons deployed were wit and ridicule. Important, as well as entertaining, this story deserves to be told.

---

[13] 'The Shepherdswell Tithe Raid Charges', *DE*, 2 Nov. 1934.

Introduction

The renowned historian of twentieth-century English rural social history, Alun Howkins, described the tithe war of the 1930s as a 'curious rural revolt', a 'widely remembered but little studied' episode with 'complex and sometimes uncomfortable bits'.[1] It is an insightful observation, though the extent to which the conflict is 'widely remembered' is open to debate. Tithing is well known as a feature of life in the medieval world, its memory kept alive by imposing former tithe barns, now often restored as museums or wedding venues. Familiar also are humorous portrayals from the eighteenth century of portly parsons grasping their 'tithe pig', an image immortalised in pottery and poetry. Yet the fact that the Church and other non-clerical titheowners were still collecting tithe in England and Wales during the fourth decade of the twentieth century often comes as a surprise, even to those with a fair knowledge of history.

In 1934, around 70 per cent of land in England and Wales was subject to tithe, which had a total value of £3,100,000 (the equivalent of around £200 million in 2023).[2] Queen Anne's Bounty was responsible for collecting £2,091,000 on behalf of around 7,200 parochial clergy and a further £96,000 on behalf of forty-one ecclesiastical corporations, including Cathedral Chapters. The Ecclesiastical Commissioners collected an additional £274,000. In total, 310,000 tithepayers – for the most part, farmers – were liable to pay ecclesiastical tithe to either Queen Anne's Bounty, the Ecclesiastical Commissioners or – in a small number of cases – directly to local clergy.

A significant amount of tithe (around £550,000) was in the hands of secular institutions and private individuals.[3] The biggest proportion of this (around £100,000) was collected by Oxford and Cambridge university colleges: 14 per cent of the total income of the historic Oxford

---

[1] Alun Howkins, 'Review of Tithe War, 1918–1939. The Countryside in Revolt by Carol Twitch', *AgHR*, 53, 2 (2005), 260–1.
[2] W. G. Hannah, 'Tithe Rentcharge' (QAB report), 14 Apr. 1934, LPL, Lang 71.
[3] W. G. Hannah, 'Introductory Notes', 4 July 1936, LPL, Lang 72.

colleges (those founded before 1800) derived from tithe.[4] Other lay impropriators – as they were called – included historic public schools (Eton, Winchester, Charterhouse and Christ's Hospital – known as Bluecoat School), hospitals (including Guy's and St Bartholomew's) and almshouses (such as the St Cross Trust), ancient guilds, such as the Worshipful Company of Haberdashers, and insurance companies, including Norwich Union Life Assurance. Many aristocratic landowners also owned tithe, such as the earl of Malmesbury, a Conservative whip in the House of Lords, and Earl De La Warr (Herbrand Brassey Sackville), who in 1934 was parliamentary secretary to the minister of agriculture. In Wales, where the Church of England had been disestablished by the Welsh Church Acts of 1914 and 1919, tithe to the value of £210,000 was collected by the Commissioners of Church Temporalities in Wales and distributed to the University of Wales, the National Library of Wales, Welsh county councils and as life-stipends to clergy who had been in post and collecting tithe at the time of disestablishment. The separate history of the teind (tithe in the Scots language) meant that the conflict did not involve Scotland.[5]

While the above is a good summary of the situation, it should be noted that a major difficulty faced by those seeking to find a solution to the 'tithe problem' was the absence of precise information about titheowners and tithepayers. In 1936, the Royal Commission, which had been established to find a resolution to the conflict, felt it necessary to 'call attention to the absence of accurate statistical information as to many points of importance':

> No central register of tithe rentcharge showing the present day titheowners and landowners exists. Even when the tithe to land is registered – and a registered tithe to agricultural land is a very rare occurrence – the register contains no record of the existence or non existence of a liability to tithe rentcharge. [...] It has not been possible for us to give the exact figure which complete statistical information would have enabled us to produce.'[6]

---

[4] J. P. D. Dunbabin, 'Finance since 1914', in Brian Harrison (ed.), *The History of the University of Oxford, Volume VIII, The Twentieth Century* (Oxford: Clarendon Press, 1994), 660–1.

[5] A process of secularisation of teinds began in the sixteenth century, when the Church embarked on leasing out rights to private landowners. In the seventeenth century, major reforms allowed landlords to buy out teindholders, which meant for the farmer teinds and rents were fused, dissipating much potential acrimony. See research project, 'Agriculture and Teind Reform in Early Modern Scotland': http://teinds.shca.ed.ac.uk/.

[6] *Report of the Royal Commission on Tithe Rentcharge in England and Wales* (London: HMSO, 1936), 5.

Introduction

Similarly, registers of tithepayers were notoriously unreliable, failing to record when tithable land had been sold and tithe reapportioned. As a result, it was common for tithepayers to be chased for tithe attached to land that they did not own. Information exists, however, that shows the marked regional variations in tithe liabilities. Recording the value of tithe collected by Queen Anne's Bounty in each English county, Table 1 shows that the most highly tithed regions were in East Anglia and the south. In fact, large parts of the Midlands, Lancashire, Lincolnshire and Cumbria were effectively tithe free, titheowners having relinquished their rights during the parliamentary enclosures and being rewarded handsomely with additional plots of land.[7] In areas dominated by pastoral farming, tithe was relatively light, though grievances could still exist.[8]

Though grievances over tithe stretched back for centuries, the first shots of the conflict that reached a climax in the 1930s were fired half a century earlier, in the 1880s. The Tithe Commutation Act of 1836 had been an attempt to modernise an archaic institution, which was viewed as an obstacle to agricultural production and increasingly an 'inconvenience' to the Church. The Act secured relative peace for just over four decades, but as the 'golden age' of agriculture gave way to the 'great depression', agitation around tithe swept through southern England and Wales. In 1881, a movement against extraordinary tithe – a charge applied to hop and fruit production – broke out in Kent and parts of East Sussex. The Anti-Extraordinary Tithe Association co-ordinated a campaign of non-payment and mobilised crowds at auctions of seized stock. From 1886, the focus shifted to the iniquities of ordinary tithe and tithepayers' campaigns sprang up in southern English counties, most notably in Essex, Kent, Berkshire, Hampshire and Devon. The struggle was fiercest in Wales, where grievances over tithe fused with demands for radical land reform and calls from nonconformist communities for the disestablishment of the Anglican Church in Wales. Under pressure, on one side, from the Church hierarchy and its aristocratic 'friends' to take tough action against the tithepayers' movement and, on the other, from the agricultural lobby for measures to alleviate 'the burden' on landowners and farmers, Lord Salisbury's Conservative administration struggled with the 'tithe problem' for almost five years. Eventually, the government succeeded in passing the 1891 Tithe Act, which managed to calm matters in the short term.

---

[7] Roger J. P. Kain and Hugh C. Prince, *The Tithe Surveys of England and Wales* (Cambridge: Cambridge University Press, 1985), 22–4; Eric J. Evans, *The Contentious Tithe: The Tithe Problem and English Agriculture, 1750–1850* (London: Routledge & Kegan Paul, 1976), 94–114.

[8] Statement of Evidence submitted to Royal Commission by QAB, 381.

TABLE 1. Value of tithe rentcharge vested in Queen Anne's Bounty, 1 October 1933.[9]

Norfolk	197,335
Kent	148,515
Suffolk	136,376
Essex	134,705
Devon	110,103
Hampshire	102,880
Somerset	97,318
Sussex	88,050
Yorkshire	86,089
Lincolnshire	73,437
Wiltshire	71,178
Shropshire	63,396
Cornwall	57,934
Dorset	57,675
Gloucestershire	56,554
Herefordshire	52,683
Berkshire	45,753
Cambridgeshire	43,646
Worcestershire	40,057
Hertfordshire	33,213
Surrey	32,468
Lancashire	32,074
Staffordshire	31,741
Oxfordshire	31,240
Cheshire	31,006
Northumberland	27,976
Durham	25,710
Buckinghamshire	25,582
Northamptonshire	24,096
Warwickshire	23,815
Leicestershire	21,448
Derbyshire	21,426
Nottinghamshire	16,973
Cumberland	13,582
Bedfordshire	9,993
Huntingdonshire	7,710
Middlesex	7,482
Rutland	5,412
Westmoreland	3,299

[9] Statement of Evidence submitted to Royal Commission by QAB, 381.

Introduction

Tithe re-emerged as a political issue in the aftermath of the Great War. After negotiations throughout 1924 between the Church and farming and landowning interests, a new Tithe Act entered the statute book in 1925. But, as the agricultural depression deepened, the new 'settlement' quickly unravelled. Farmers belonging to tithepayers' associations began a campaign of 'passive resistance' in 1931, during the final months of Ramsay MacDonald's minority Labour government. Over the next five years, the battle would be waged outside farms, in meeting halls, in the law courts and in the wider court of public opinion. The geographical pattern of the conflict was uneven. The hotspots were the cereal-growing farming regions in southern and eastern England, particularly in Kent and the East Anglian counties of Suffolk, Norfolk and Essex. The conflict travelled south-westwards into Sussex, Hampshire, Dorset, Wiltshire, Somerset, Gloucestershire, Devon and Cornwall; north-westwards, it spread to Cambridgeshire, the Chilterns, the Cotswolds, and areas surrounding the Malverns in Shropshire, Worcestershire and Herefordshire. In Wales, the agitation reached Denbighshire, Cardiganshire, Pembrokeshire and Montgomeryshire.

The National Government initially adopted an uncompromising position towards the tithepayers' campaign. Stanley Baldwin, the Conservative leader, declared that he could not 'condemn too strongly the acts of violence [...] on the part of tithepayers in resisting the operation of the law', adding that the government could 'hold out no prospect of legislation on the question'.[10] Leaders of the National Farmers' Union (NFU) also attacked the 'unconstitutional methods' of the National Tithepayers' Association and argued that 'the time was not opportune' to reopen the tithe question.[11]

By 1934, however, ministers had recognised that facing down the farmers' movement was no longer an option. Sections of the judiciary were warning that the non-payment campaign had placed the county court recovery system in a 'precarious position'.[12] Walter Elliot, the minister of agriculture, realised that the tithe issue was threatening to undermine the corporatist partnership he was cultivating with leaders of the NFU, whose ambivalent attitude towards the conflict prompted criticism from amongst its membership. In May 1934, Elliot made a *volte face* and announced a Royal Commission to inquire into the entire question of tithe. While the Commission gathered evidence and deliberated during late 1934 and 1935, the Queen Anne's Bounty

---

[10] House of Commons Debate (HC Deb.), *Hansard*, 22 June 1932.
[11] *NFU Record*, Feb. 1932, 107.
[12] 'Statement of Evidence submitted by the Lord Chancellor's Office', Royal Comm, *Appendices to Minutes of Evidence*, 622.

and other titheowners stepped up attempts to break the non-payment campaign and the 'war' became increasingly bitter.

The Royal Commission reported in February 1936 and recommended that the state 'expropriate [...] titheowners by compulsory purchase', compensating them 'fairly' with government bonds. In place of tithe, tithepayers would pay a fixed annuity to the Inland Revenue for a period of forty years.[13] The proposal – albeit amended by the government to be less favourable for tithepayers – formed the basis of a new Tithe Act (1936) which, despite being opposed by the NTA and in parliament by the Labour Party, succeeded in bringing the tithe war to a close.

The first book devoted to this history was a contemporaneous account by Doreen Wallace. Published in 1934 by Victor Gollancz, *The Tithe War* sketches a history of tithe, outlines the grievances of farmers and charts the initial stages of the protest movement.[14] Married to a Suffolk farmer, Wallace wrote a series of novels that won plaudits for their astute observation of rural life. She also became a partisan of the anti-tithe struggle. In February 1934, bailiffs distrained fifteen bullocks and 134 pigs for tithe non-payment from two farms owned by her husband, Rowland Rash. Subsequent events received national publicity when nineteen members of the British Union of Fascists, who had joined pickets to prevent removal of the stock, were arrested and stood trial at the Old Bailey. In her book's preface, Wallace suggests – in somewhat tongue-in-cheek fashion – that 'someday when the war is over, someone must write a fully documented account of the whole matter: the sort of book which has quarter of a page of text to three-quarters of notes.'[15] As Howkins observed, historians have been reluctant to take up the suggestion.[16] Rather than the topic of a book weighed down by its scholarly apparatus, the tithe wars of the late nineteenth and early twentieth centuries have remained a footnote in the general histories of those years, as well as in more specialist studies.

The writing of England's social and political history has been conditioned by the nation's position as a pioneer of industrialisation. Rural social subjects that continued to exist in large numbers on the European continent – the small peasantry in France, landless labourers in Spain, Italy and parts of Germany, 'village communities' in Eastern Europe and Russia – seemed marginalised by the nineteenth century

---

[13] Royal Comm, 26–8.
[14] Doreen Wallace, *The Tithe War* (London: Victor Gollancz, 1934).
[15] Ibid., 3.
[16] Howkins, 'Review of Tithe War', 261.

Introduction

within the English social landscape. By the 1930s, only 6 per cent of the population was employed in agriculture, compared with 36 per cent in France, 29 per cent in Germany, 47 per cent in Italy and 35 per cent in Denmark.[17] General histories of the interwar years published towards the end of the twentieth century tend to 'have little to say about the countryside', suggesting that rural issues were 'not a major feature' of the social and economic history of the period.[18] Studies of politics also show 'almost overwhelming concern with urban political systems and industrial cleavages', which leads – in the words of three leading social scientists – to 'the study of rural politics [becoming] something of an intellectual backwater'.[19] Historians of social movements – perhaps influenced by Marx's characterisation of rural societies as 'a simple addition of homonymous magnitudes, much like […] a sack of potatoes' – have also focused on urban themes: trade unionism, strikes, unemployed workers' movements. As Howard Newby noted some decades ago, interest in social conflict in the countryside declines 'the more one moves from the Captain Swing riots'.[20]

Historians and social scientists began to correct these trends during the first decade of the twenty-first century. Martin Pugh's social history of the interwar years lends more weight to rural affairs. A volume edited by Paul Brassley, Jeremy Burchardt and Lynne Thompson highlights an 'energy at work in the countryside between the wars'.[21] Clare Griffiths traces the evolution of the Labour Party's rural programme and activity during the 1920s and 1930s.[22] By shining a spotlight on the tithe conflict, the current book also emphasises the political, social and cultural importance of the rural world during the first half of the twentieth century. While the numbers working in agriculture were in substantial decline, the rural population remained vibrant – in 1931, around 9 million people

---

[17] Laird Boswell, 'Rural Society in Crisis', in Nicholas Doumanis (ed.), *The Oxford Handbook of European History, 1914–45* (Oxford: Oxford University Press, 2016), 243–60.

[18] Paul Brassley, Jeremy Burchardt and Lynne Thompson (eds), 'Introduction', in *The English Countryside between the Wars: Regeneration or Decline?* (Woodbridge: Boydell Press, 2006), 3.

[19] Andrew Flynn, Philip Lowe and Michael Winter, 'The Political Power of Farmers: An English Perspective', *Rural History* 7, 1 (1996), 15.

[20] Howard Newby, *The Deferential Worker: A Study of Farm Workers in East Anglia* (London: Allen Lane, 1977), 23.

[21] Martin Pugh, *We Danced All Night: A Social History of Britain Between the Wars* (London: Vintage, 2008); Brassley et al., *English Countryside*, 249.

[22] Clare V. J. Griffiths, *Labour and the Countryside: The Politics of Rural Britain, 1918–1939* (Oxford: Oxford University Press, 2007).

within a total population of 45 million.[23] Perhaps more significantly, during the years following the Great War, an imagined vision of the countryside became an essential element of Englishness. The 'pleasant pastures', 'clouded hills' and 'green and pleasant land' – William Blake's words for the anthem *Jerusalem* – became embedded within the national psyche.

Politically, during the interwar years, the countryside remained a battleground for the three main parties. The Conservatives recognised their dependence on 'agricultural constituencies […] to maintain a working majority'; Liberals sought ways to prevent their party becoming 'extinguished in rural England' and the Labour Party increasingly recognised that gaining rural seats was 'the key to power'.[24] All this meant that the tithe conflict resonated widely. Stories of plucky 'yeoman' farmers, 'freemen' resisting authority to fight for English 'fair play', featured prominently in the right-wing popular press, including the *Daily Mail*, *Daily Mirror* and *Daily Express*, but were also carried by the Labour-supporting *Daily Herald* and even the Communist Party's *Daily Worker*.[25]

Tithe complicated attempts by the political parties to formulate strategies to mobilise the rural vote. For Conservatives, anti-tithe sentiments amongst the burgeoning class of owner-occupying farmers – viewed as a natural constituency – conflicted with the party's defence of property rights and its close ties with the Church of England. In some areas, the Tory Party's hostility to tithe reform helped open the door for support for fascism. The Liberal Party, facing crisis and decline, adopted contradictory positions on tithe. The party's 584-page report *The Land and the Nation*, prepared in the mid-1920s, did not mention tithe.[26] As for the Labour Party, its position on tithe evolved dramatically. In 1925, Labour MPs opposed a reduction in the level of tithe payments because, in the words of party spokesman Josiah Wedgwood, this would be 'a gift' to the 'landlord class' and 'deprive the parsons […] of what they are legitimately entitled'. Yet, in 1936, the party gave support to the tithepayers' movement and called for

---

23 Brassley et al., *English Countryside*, 3.
24 Conservative Party chairman J. C. C. Davidson to Stanley Baldwin, June 1927, cited in Michael Dawson, 'The Liberal Land Policy, 1924–1929: Electoral Strategy and Internal Division', *Twentieth Century British History*, 2, 3 (1991), 275; Lloyd George (1925), cited in Dawson, 'Liberal Land Policy', 273; Griffiths, *Labour and the Countryside*, 8–10.
25 *DEx*, 2 Aug. 1933; 'The English Yeoman Strikes!', *DHe*, 29 Sept. 1931; 'Farmers Storm London in Fight Against Tithes', *Daily Worker*, 25 June 1936.
26 Liberal Party, *The Land and the Nation: Rural Report of the Liberal Land Committee, 1923–25* (London: Hodder and Stoughton, 1926).

Introduction

'the extinction of a charge which cannot be justified under modern conditions'.[27]

The biggest challenge was, of course, reserved for the Anglican Church, struggling to reposition itself within an increasingly secular world. Publicity about seizures of stock from 'impoverished farmers' threatened its moral authority. In the hotspots, relations between clergy and rural communities became fraught. Doreen Wallace's husband, Rowland Rash, was just one of several churchwardens to resign their positions over tithe. The Church's strategy to deal with the tithepayers' campaign was devised and marshalled by leading lay figures, including Sir Frederick Radcliffe, the 'knight philanthropist' best known for his work with Liverpool Cathedral, and George Middleton, a former trade unionist and Labour MP who was in 1932 appointed chair of the tithe committee of Queen Anne's Bounty. Senior clergy, including the archbishop of Canterbury Cosmo Lang and the bishop of Norwich Bertram Pollock became embroiled in the affair.

Histories of tithe tend to focus on the medieval or early modern periods. Eric Evans (1976) provides an excellent account of the processes that led to the Tithe Commutation Act of 1836, but his narrative touches only briefly on events after 1850.[28] Important studies of rural politics in the late nineteenth and early twentieth centuries tend to overlook tithe, effectively leaving out an important piece of the jigsaw. Readman's account of 'the politics of land' between 1880 and 1914 makes no reference to tithe.[29] Andrew Cooper's study of Conservative Party agricultural policy between 1912 and 1936 does not include the word in its index.[30] Clare Griffiths' *Labour and the Countryside* – which devotes two sentences to the tithe conflict – shows how Labour's programme and activity changed from one aimed primarily towards agricultural workers towards a more 'pragmatic' policy 'designed to articulate the needs of the whole agricultural community'. Yet it fails to note that the party's policy towards tithe provides an excellent example of this process.[31] Historians of Church–societal relations also fail to examine the Church's embarrassing role

---

[27] HC Deb., *Hansard*, 18 June 1925; Albert Alexander, HC Deb., *Hansard*, 13 May 1936.
[28] Evans, *Contentious Tithe*.
[29] Paul Readman, *Land and Nation in England: Patriotism, Nation Identity, and the Politics of Land, 1880–1914* (Woodbridge: Boydell Press, 2008).
[30] Cooper links the 1936 Tithe Act to other measures introduced by Walter Elliot to stimulate agriculture, including marketing boards, import controls and subsidies, but makes no reference to the torturous path that led to it. Andrew Fenton Cooper, *British Agricultural Policy 1912–36. A Study in Conservative Politics* (Manchester: Manchester University Press, 1989).
[31] Griffiths, *Labour and the Countryside*.

in the conflict.[32] Even fictional writers seem to go out of their way to avoid the tithe war: the beautifully crafted *All Among the Barley* by Melissa Harrison, set in rural Suffolk during 1933–34, explores themes of tradition, landlordism, nationalism, fascist activity and memory, but completely ignores the tithe conflict – which would connect to the themes of the novel and was raging throughout the region at the time.[33] In 2001, Carol Twinch published an accomplished popular account of the tithe war, drawing from the archive of Albert G. Mobbs, a Suffolk farmer and major figure within the NTA.[34] Perhaps an over-reliance on the perspective of a single participant explains some factual errors and a tendency to avoid some 'uncomfortable bits' of the story. Yet it is instructive that the only full-length account of this significant social and political episode is not penned by a trained historian.

The chapters that follow chart the evolution of this 'curious rural revolt'. They offer a narrative account of events, explaining the strategies and activities pursued by the principal adversaries, while also attempting to unravel processes that gave rise to the conflict's 'complexities' and 'uncomfortable' aspects. The book's *dramatis personae* is made up of prominent politicians and personalities of the time – an indication of the significance of this history. It also contains relatively unknown historical actors: farmers, campaigners, families and communities who participated in the campaign at local and national level, and who deserve rescuing from the 'condescension of posterity'.

After outlining the pressures that led to commutation, Chapter 1 discusses why the 1836 Act not only failed to resolve the 'problem' of tithe but also created new contradictions and grievances. Chapters 2 and 3 examine the tithe conflicts of the 1880s and early 1890s, their scale and characteristics, as well as the challenges they posed for government and political parties. Chapters 4 and 5 discuss the post-war Tithe Acts of 1918, 1920 and 1925, which were based on the false assumption that prices of agricultural produce would remain relatively stable. They outline the growth of tithepayers' associations and the renewal of conflict. An important change was that the tithepayers' movement was made up primarily of owner-occupying farmers, many of whom had purchased their holdings in the aftermath of the Great War. Chapter

[32] See Edward R. Norman, *Church and Society in England, 1770–1970: A Historical Study* (Oxford: Oxford University Press, 1976), 346; Matthew Grimley, *Citizenship, Community, and the Church of England: Liberal Anglican Theories of the State between the Wars* (Oxford: Clarendon Press, 2004); Robert Beaken, *Cosmo Lang: Archbishop in War and Crisis* (London: I.B. Tauris, 2012).

[33] Melissa Harrison, *All Among the Barley* (London: Bloomsbury, 2018).

[34] Carol Twinch, *Tithe War 1918–39: The Countryside in Revolt* (Norwich: Media Associates, 2001).

Introduction

6 shifts the focus to the response of the Church, which recognised the 'genuine hardship' faced by many farmers but, simultaneously, sought to enforce its rights to tithe in the face of a campaign by 'agitators' and 'extremists'. It includes an account of the creation and functioning of 'the Company', camouflage in Church documents for General Dealers Ltd. The establishment of a secret instrument to break the tithepayers' movement is one of the most shameful episodes in recent ecclesiastical history. Chapter 7 discusses the relationship between the tithepayers' movement and the radical right, one of the 'uncomfortable bits' of the tithe war. Historians of fascism have traced the intervention by members of the British Union of Fascists in East Anglia and Devon.[35] A broader perspective is taken here, attempting to situate the tithepayers' movement within the surge of right-wing agrarian ideas. As well as the British Union of Fascists, the chapter discusses the politics of some prominent figures in the movement, including Viscount Lymington and George Pitt-Rivers, who – while not members of Mosley's movement – can be firmly located within the 'magnetic field of fascism'.[36] Chapters 8 and 9 outline the final stages of the conflict: first, the pressures on Walter Elliot to find a settlement, which led to a botched attempt at legislation in early 1934, and, secondly, the deliberations and recommendations of the Royal Commission, which led to the Tithe Act of 1936.

The book attempts an overview of the tithe controversy from the early 1880s to the late 1930s, drawing detail primarily from the southern and eastern English counties. While covering Wales during both the nineteenth and twentieth centuries, the account cannot do justice to the particularities of the conflict in that nation. The Welsh tithe wars still await their historian. In the exposition of events, the reader may notice a certain slant towards Kent. This can be justified. The methods deployed by the Anti-Extraordinary Tithe Association in the county in the early 1880s provided a template for subsequent campaigns, both later that decade and between the wars. In the 1930s, the campaign of tithe non-payment began in Kent and the first demonstrations to disrupt distraint auctions took place in the county. The NTA was based in Canterbury and its most prominent representative, Rev. Roderick Kedward, was a major figure in Kentish politics, sitting as MP for

---

[35] Andrew Martin Mitchell, 'Fascism in East Anglia: The British Union of Fascists in Norfolk, Suffolk and Essex, 1933–1940' (unpublished Phd thesis, University of Sheffield, 1999), 40–97. Available at: http://etheses.whiterose.ac.uk/3071/; Todd Gray, *Blackshirts in Devon* (Exeter: The Mint Press, 2006), 111–34.

[36] The classic phrase coined by Philippe Burrin in 'La France dans le champ magnétique des fascismes', *Le Débat*, 32 (1984/5), 52–72.

Ashford between 1929 and 1931.[37] Perhaps, however, some unconscious bias should be conceded. Research for this book was driven by a desire to find out more about the Battle of the Ducks, an episode that took place in the village where the author resides.

---

[37] Historians of Kent have also neglected the tithepayers' movement. An otherwise excellent study of Kentish agriculture and rural society in the twentieth century devotes only three sentences to the conflict. Alan Armstrong, 'Agriculture and Rural Society', in Nigel Yates (ed.), *Kent in the Twentieth Century* (Woodbridge: Boydell Press, 2001), 89.

1

The 1836 Tithe Commutation Act

Barham Downs, 1834

Barham Downs, near Canterbury, were for countless generations a rallying point for large gatherings and festivals. They are just over a mile from the Halfway House, the meeting point in 1934 for the 'battle of the ducks', the incident with which this book began. Almost exactly one century earlier, on 19 May 1834, 2,000 people assembled on the Downs to discuss the Tithe Commutation Bill recently introduced in parliament by Lord Althorp (John Spencer), the Whig chancellor of the exchequer. The meeting had been convened by the high sheriff of Kent at the request of members of the East Kent Agricultural Association, an organisation dominated by large landowners and large-scale tenant farmers, originally established to campaign in defence of the Corn Laws.

Althorp's bill was his second attempt to steer tithe reform through parliament in so many years. It proposed 'to abolish the collection and payment of tithes in kind throughout England and Wales'. Tithe would be commuted into a money payment linked to the value of land. The bill also encouraged the 'redemption' of tithe, an appropriately theological term used to describe a tithepayer buying out a titheowner. Under the bill, a tithepayer would be able to 'free himself' from tithe by making agreed payments over a twenty-five-year period.

A group of farmers within the East Kent Agricultural Association agreed to organise a petition in support of Althorp's proposed legislation. The decision provoked protests from aristocratic members of the association, including the earl of Guilford and the earl of Winchilsea. Given the controversy, it was agreed to petition the sheriff to convene a meeting of 'the agriculturalists of East Kent' so that a policy on the proposed legislation could be considered.[1]

The assembly on the Downs did not go as planned. To the dismay of the dignitaries gathered on the speaker's wagon, the meeting provided a voice to a third, more radical, argument about tithe. Proceedings began with a prominent member of the local gentry and future Whig MP, Edward Royd Rice, proposing a petition be sent to parliament in favour

---

[1] *KG*, 6 May 1834.

of Althorp's bill. Next, another Whig supporter of the bill challenged Tory opponents of the legislation to come forward to explain their case. Although the two MPs for the district – Sir Edward Knatchbull and John Plumptre – were in attendance, 'the Conservative party,' as the local newspaper put it, 'held entirely aloof' from the discussion. Instead, Edward Hughes, a farmer from Smeeth Hill who had made a name for himself as a champion of 'smaller growers of corn', climbed up on the speakers' wagon to move an amendment. It denounced the 'evils inflicted by the tithe system' and called for 'the abolition of the present system of tithes'. Rejecting both commutation and redemption of tithe, the amendment proposed a tax of two shillings in the pound on the rental price of land, which would 'be amply sufficient' to support the Church, 'which is now possessed of a most unwarrantable and injurious superfluity of wealth and emoluments'. Hughes's amendment was carried with 'a majority of about two-thirds'. Perturbed, Edward Rice argued that the vote had not been 'put in such a way as to be generally understood' and insisted on another show of hands. This time the 'majority in favour of the opponents to the ministerial measure was still greater'.[2]

By linking a replacement to tithe to the value of land, the resolution passed on the Downs was not a million miles away from some of the principles underpinning Althorp's bill. Yet observers had little doubt about the motives of those supporting it. The local newspaper condemned the activity of 'radicals', 'levellers' and 'revolutionaries' determined 'to support any proposition however monstrous, any measure however absurd and ridiculous, calculated to express a feeling of hostility to the upper classes of society'. It hoped that the 'respectable "liberal" gentry' would learn that an 'appeal to the "popular" voice' was as dangerous as 'trusting themselves upon the wide ocean to the mercy of the winds and the waves'.[3]

Lord Althorp's bill in 1834 failed to make it onto the statute book. So too did a tithe bill presented the following year by Sir Robert Peel, prime minister of the short-term Tory minority government. In all, between 1828 and 1835, five different bills to transform tithe into a cash transaction in some way or other were unsuccessful.[4]

[2] *KG*, 12 Mar. 1833 and 20 May 1834.
[3] 'The Barham Downs Farce', *KG*, 27 May 1834.
[4] As well as Althorp's two bills (1833 and 1834) and the bill proposed by Peel (1835), a bill was presented by Thomas Greene in 1828. The archbishop of Canterbury also presented a 'Tithe Composition Bill' to the House of Lords in May 1830. See Evans, *Contentious Tithe*, 115–35.

Grumbling hives of discontent

The parliamentary time devoted to tithe during these years reflects the pressure on the political elites to find an acceptable solution to the long-standing 'tithe problem', as well as the difficulties they faced in trying to do so. Landowners and the Church warned that compulsory or permanent commutation of tithe would endanger property rights and their 'vested interests'. In 1828, Sir Robert Peel, the Tory home secretary, said such measures would be 'pregnant with injustice to the Church of England'.[5] But, as the events on Barham Downs illustrate, the movement for tithe reform was itself divided into two distinct wings. The first – led by Whig politicians and capitalist farmers, such as those at the head of the East Kent Agricultural Association – sought to 'modernise' tithe. From the late eighteenth century, improved methods of crop-growing and stockbreeding, as well as a trend – accelerated in many regions by the enclosure acts – towards larger and more labour-intensive farms, had generated an increase in agricultural output, as well as the ascendency of 'the gentleman farmer'. This wing viewed tithe not only as an impediment to investment in new agricultural methods and techniques but also as grossly unfair. In contrast to farmers, factory entrepreneurs did not have to hand over a proportion of their output to a 'sleeping partner'. Although tithe payments had increasingly become money transactions, titheowners still possessed the right to demand payment in kind, including the right to enter a farm to stake a claim on particular produce. Moreover, cash payments in lieu of tithe (known as 'compositions' and 'moduses') were calculated according to local custom and practice, with wide variations between, and even within, different parishes. The big tenant farmers and their political representatives argued that tithe should be detached from yield, calculated consistently and be subject to nationally agreed and legally enforced regulations.[6]

The second wing of the movement was a rather unwieldy coalition of smaller tenant farmers, rural labourers, religious nonconformists and political radicals. It wanted a more far-reaching solution, though there were different ideas about what should be its precise nature. Some argued – as at Barham Downs – that tithe should be replaced with a tax on land, with the clergy funded through a stipend, rather than by tithe. Others urged outright abolition, which they linked to other radical measures, including the disestablishment and disendowment of the Church of England. The fourth of the fourteen 'reform propositions' in William Cobbett's *Manchester Lectures* (1831) was 'to abolish tithes of every description; to leave the clergy the churches, the church-yards, the parsonage houses and the ancient glebes; and, for the rest, leave

[5] HC Deb., *Hansard*, 17 Mar. 1828.
[6] Kain and Prince, *Tithe Surveys*, 6–27.

them to the voluntary contributions of the people'.[7] Variations of these two approaches to the tithe problem – a 'moderate' and a more radical wing – would re-emerge during the 'tithe wars' of the 1880s and 1930s. Their genealogy can be traced back to the sixteenth and seventeenth centuries, when a series of changes disrupted the medieval structure of agriculture, including the system of tithes.

Tithe was enshrined in canon law in the twelfth century. It possessed a certain logic in a society based on a largely subsistence, agrarian economy. The Church provided spiritual services to communities at key moments in the life cycle, as well as support for the needy. In return, it received a proportion of productive output, essentially agricultural goods collected from the peasantry but also with contributions from the secular ruling elite. Some endowments of tithes were granted to religious houses and educational institutions. In 1268, Edward I assigned the 'Church of Eleham [...] together with all its appurtenances and rights' to the college established by Lord Walter de Merton – which explains why, during the 1930s tithe war, farmers in Elham (Kent) were in conflict with Merton College, Oxford.[8] Three kinds of tithes existed: praedial tithes (drawn from produce of the soil), mixed tithes (from the produce of livestock) and personal tithes (drawn from the industry of humans). Tithes were also divided into 'great' and 'small', a designation originally linked to relative value (great tithes – such as grain – were usually due to the rector, while small tithes, such as potatoes, were collected by the vicar). Despite these complexities, the open-field system ensured that tithe collection was relatively straightforward. Though a coercive arrangement, supported by legal obligations as well as the fear of divine judgement, tithing served as the basis for a type of social contract underpinning the relationship between the Church, landed classes and peasantry.

Yet conflict was inherent in the system. The historian Norma Adams describes 'a long conflict between Church and State over tithes', which during the thirteenth and fourteenth centuries manifested itself as 'a border war' over the relative jurisdictions of ecclesiastical and secular courts in resolving disputes about tithe.[9] A more subversive challenge came during the fifteenth and sixteenth centuries from the Lollards, dissenters associated with the teachings of John Wycliffe, who advocated that tithes be withheld from priests not performing their duties and given to the poor

---

[7] William Cobbett, Manchester Lectures in support of his Fourteen Reform Propositions (London: Bolt-Court, Fleet Street, 1832), 2.

[8] 'Grant of the Church of Elham to Merton College, May 21 1268', in Edward France Percival (ed.), *The Foundation Statutes of Merton College* (Oxford: William Pickering, 1847), 8–9.

[9] Norma Adams, 'The Judicial Conflict over Tithes', *English Historical Review*, 52, 205 (1937), 1–22.

instead.[10] The growth of commerce and the rise of an urban merchant class – which generally did not pay tithe – encouraged resentment towards a system resting almost entirely on the agricultural population. Disputes arose over the cultivation of new areas of land – which had not previously been viewed as tithable – and over tithes on crops introduced for growing urban markets, such as potatoes and turnips. Further tensions arose as local clergy became transformed into an educated and professional elite, socially integrated into the gentry. Tithepayers began to begrudge handing over the fruits of their labour to maintain lifestyles often more privileged than their own.

Most significant were the changes at the Reformation. After the dissolution of the monasteries and other religious houses (1536–1540), Henry VIII transferred the rights to around one-third of the most valuable 'great tithes' into the hands of 4,000 'lay impropriators'.[11] This extension of secular ownership changed an essential characteristic of tithe, in that it was no longer almost entirely a system to provide resources to the Church. Tithe became a form of property that could be bought and sold or – as some clergy and cathedral chapters began to do – leased to 'tithe farmers'. It was, nevertheless, a particular type of property. Tithe was a claim on resources created on land to which someone else possessed the ownership deeds. Yet, in legal terms, it was classed as property. Titheowners were liable to pay rates for poor relief, in the same way as landowners, and tithe was inherited by the heir-at-law in the same way as other property.[12]

These changes in the quality of tithe had two major implications. The first was an increase in disputes between titheowners and tithepayers, which led to litigation in both the ecclesiastical and civil courts. A study by Paula Simpson of the position in Kent describes 'small-scale resistance', revealed in 'ritual and symbolic form'. During the period 1501–1600, the ecclesiastical courts in the diocese of Canterbury heard 6,304 cases relating to tithe – and the courtroom was just one of a number of 'strategies of resistance' deployed by tithepayers.[13] Examining the position in Leicestershire around a century later, Anne Tarver finds tithe

---

[10] Susan Royal, 'John Foxe's "Acts and Monuments" and the Lollard Legacy in the Long English Reformation' (unpublished PhD thesis, Durham University, 2014), 230–54; Susan Royal, *Lollards in the English Reformation: History, Radicalism and John Foxe* (Manchester: Manchester University Press, 2020).

[11] Laura Brace, *The Idea of Property in Seventeenth-Century England* (Manchester: Manchester University Press, 1998), 15–21, 45, 65.

[12] Eric J. Evans, 'Tithes 1640–1750', in Joan Thirsk (ed.), *Agricultural Change: Policy and Practice: 1500–1750* (Cambridge: Cambridge University Press, 1990), 216–32.

[13] Paula Simpson, 'Custom and Conflict: Disputes over Tithe in the Diocese of Canterbury, 1501–1600' (unpublished PhD thesis, University of Kent, 1997) and Paula Simpson, 'The Continuum of Resistance to Tithe, c. 1400–1600', in Robert Lutton and Elisabeth Salter (eds), *Pieties in Transition: Religious Practices and Experiences, c1400–1640* (London: Ashgate, 2007), 107.

disputes in 68 per cent of parishes, though in most cases a settlement was arranged between the parties before reaching court. Disputes arose over issues such as whether certain produce should be tithed, the calculations used to 'compound' tithe in kind into a cash payment and increased tithe demands from newly appointed incumbent clergymen.[14] Research indicates significant regional and local variations in the extent of this legal conflict as well as an increasing tendency through time to settle disputes through negotiation, especially those involving clerical tithe. Reports of visitations by the bishop to parishes in Norfolk during the 'long eighteenth century' indicate tithe disputes in only sixteen parishes (out of 579), though another study of the situation in the county describes 'grumbling hives of discontent'.[15] The downturn in the amount of litigation does not imply any lessening of tensions over tithe. Conscious of the need for good relations with parishioners, the clergy generally sought compromises. Farmers who were wealthy and literate enough to consider litigation were amongst the most influential laity in a parish, those in the best position to negotiate concessions from an incumbent clergyman and loath to instigate legal disputes that might poison relations between the Church and parish community.[16]

The second implication was that tithe became a stronger link in the chain binding the institutions of the Church, the state and the propertied classes. In consequence, demands for tithe reform posed the question of major political and social change. The link became explicit during the English Civil War. The radical wing of the parliamentary camp, the Levellers and particularly the Diggers, campaigned for tithe abolition. For Gerald Winstanley, the Digger leader, 'the paying of tithes [was] the greatest sin of oppression'.[17] In July 1653, controversy over tithe erupted in the parliament summoned by Cromwell (the Barebone's Parliament). Petitions arrived from around the country supporting the idea of tithe abolition and the voluntary maintenance of Church ministers. One from Kent attacked tithe as the continuation of 'Norman power', meaning the power of the royalist aristocracy. Simultaneously, large landowners and merchants dispatched petitioners to parliament to argue that opposition to tithe threatened the fundamental rights to property decreed in the Magna Carta. The conflict came to a head in December

[14] Anne Tarver, 'The Due Tenth: Problems of the Leicestershire Tithing Process, 1560–1640', *Transactions, Leicestershire Archaeological and History Society*, 78 (2004), 97–107.

[15] W. M. Jacob, *The Clerical Profession in the Long Eighteenth Century, 1680–1840* (Oxford: Oxford University Press, 2007), 137; Robert Lee, *Rural Society and the Anglican Clergy, 1815–1914: Encountering and Managing the Poor* (Woodbridge: Boydell Press, 2006), 13.

[16] Brace, *Idea of Property*, 25–8.

[17] Cited in Christopher Hill, *Change and Continuity in Seventeenth-Century England* (New Haven, CT: Yale University Press, 1991), 143.

when a report from a parliamentary committee upholding tithes failed to win a majority. Pro-tithe members walked out, urging Cromwell to dissolve the parliament. Tithe prompted, therefore, the crisis that led to Cromwell's protectorate and, in the longer term, strengthened the forces for monarchical restoration.[18] After 1653, the Quakers – continuing the legacy of the Lollards – became the 'vanguard of popular agitation against tithe'. As one adherent put it, tithe was the means by which a parasitic 'company of caterpillars' lived off the produce of labour.[19] Many Quakers suffered imprisonment or had possessions seized for tithe non-payment. Throughout the seventeenth century, the landowning classes waged an indefatigable defence of tithe. As Laura Brace explains, for them

> [tithes] had become so much part of the established order, of the structure of society, that to meddle with them was dangerous. Any attempt to dismantle them would bring the whole edifice of property relations crashing down. Rents, wages and other kinds of taxes and public dues would no longer be safe. Tithes must be defended if property itself was to survive.[20]

Pressure for reform

The ruling elites expressed similar fears when demands for tithe reform were raised in the first decades of the nineteenth century. The first concerted campaign for reform coincided with the onset of agricultural depression in the immediate aftermath of the Napoleonic Wars. Farming had prospered during the war years, but after 1814 prices of produce, particularly wheat, began to fall sharply – though never returning to pre-1795 levels. The Corn Law of 1815 helped to sustain prices and farmers sought to reduce their labour costs, squeezing the living standards of rural labouring families. Farmers complained that, while demands for tithe remained constant, the titheowners' share was in real terms increasing in relation to the value of produce and annual profits.[21] They drew support from economists, such as David Ricardo,

---

[18] Christopher Hill, *The World Turned Upside Down: Radical Ideas During the English Revolution* (London: Penguin, 1991); Margaret James, 'The Political Importance of the Tithes Controversy in the English Revolution, 1640–60', *History*, 26, 101 (1941), 1–18.
[19] Barry Reay, 'Quaker Opposition to Tithes, 1652–1660', *Past & Present*, 86 (1980), 106.
[20] Brace, *Idea of Property*, 18.
[21] Evans, *Contentious Tithe*, 67–82. Roger Kain, 'Tithe as an Index of Pre-Industrial Agricultural Production', *AgHR*, 27, 2 (1979), 73–81.

who described tithe as an 'unequal tax' that 'tends to discourage both cultivation and production'.[22]

In May 1816, the House of Commons established a select committee on tithe after two Whig MPs, Robert Newman and John Curwen, coordinated a petitioning campaign to 'express the general feeling of the agricultural interest' against 'an obnoxious mode of taxation'. Two years later, Curwen introduced a bill to amend some arcane aspects of tithe legislation dating from the reign of Elizabeth I.[23] A colourful character who once appeared at the House of Commons dressed as a Cumberland labourer carrying a loaf and cheese, Curwen was head of the Workington Agricultural Society and committed to an innovative form of 'scientific farming', which necessitated the 'modernisation' of tithe assessment and collection.[24] Curwen, Newman and their supporters stressed that they had 'no intention of invading the property' of titheowners, which was 'as much property as any other species of property'.[25] Yet their initiatives aroused vehement opposition from the Church, lay titheowners and their political spokespeople. John Smyth, the Whig MP for Cambridge University, attacked Curwen's proposed legislation for wanting to 'depriv[e] the clergy and other tithe-owners of that property to which they had as much right as any freeholder had to his land'. A statement from the university declared that the 'law of tithes' [was] interwoven with the Constitution, no less of the State than of the Church and has been guaranteed by every Charter of our Civil Liberties'.[26] When reporting the parliamentary debate on the tithe petitions received from farmers, *The Times* thundered:

> The very first step of the French revolutionists was to strip the clergy of their property. [...] They were plundered, persecuted, exiled, massacred [...] and when one species of property is attacked, every other is in no distant danger. After the property of the clergy fell in France, that of the landholders quickly followed, then of the merchants, then of the national creditor. The petitions which assume that the right of tithes is questionable ought to be wholly laid out of account.[27]

The refusal of titheowners to contemplate changes to even minor aspects of tithe law on the grounds that any change would contravene

---

[22] David Ricardo, *On the Principles of Political Economy, and Taxation* (Cambridge: Cambridge University Press, 2015), Chapter IX, 'Tithes'.
[23] HC Debs, *Hansard*, 19 Feb. 1818 and 16 Mar. 1818.
[24] J. V. Beckett (revised), 'John Christian Curwen (1756–1828)', *ODNB* (2007).
[25] Robert Newman, *Hansard*, HC Deb., 22 May 1816.
[26] HC Debs, *Hansard*, 22 May 1816, 19 Feb. and 16 Mar. 1818; Evans, *Contentious Tithe*, 116–17.
[27] *The Times*, 23 May 1816.

The 1836 Tithe Commutation Act

the right to administer their property as they saw fit meant that these first attempts at reform reached an impasse.

Alongside continuing pressure for tithe reform came calls for the review of other medieval laws acting as obstacles to agricultural advancement, particularly those relating to land tenure. In 1828, a Royal Commission – the Real Property Commission – began to consider 'a body of law that had evolved without any major review since the imposition of feudalism by the Norman Conquest'.[28] One form of tenure scrutinised was copyhold, under which tenants had held rights to their homes and land in return for military or labour services to the lord of the manor. Over time, such services had invariably been replaced by cash payments and 'fines' paid to the lord on the death of tenants. Yet, even in the early nineteenth century, there were complaints that the lord could still apply the custom of 'heriot', which permitted him 'the best chattel' after the death of a tenant.[29] Certainly, most new tenants remained subject to 'fines arbitrary', charges relating to the increased value of the property under the previous tenancy. Not only considered deeply unjust – the lord effectively forcing incoming tenants to pay for the labour and investments of the previous occupants – the system of fines arbitrary also deterred improvements on the land, such as irrigation or the renovation of buildings.[30]

Throughout the 1820s, broader demands for constitutional and social reform also continued to increase. The 1830 general election led to the resignation of the duke of Wellington as prime minister and an administration led by the Whig reformer Charles Grey (the second Earl Grey). The Church hierarchy demonstrated instinctive opposition to the reform movement, symbolised by the votes of bishops in the House of Lords against the Reform Bill in October 1831. Yet the Church was on the retreat, fearful that intransigence would give sustenance to arguments from radicals for restrictions to the Church's status and even disestablishment. In less than a decade, a series of measures redefined aspects of the Church's position as the religious and administrative arm of the state. Beginning in 1828 with the repeal of the Test and Corporation Acts (laws that allowed only members of the established Church to hold positions of State) and in 1829 with the Roman Catholic Relief Act (which allowed Catholics to sit in parliament), the legislation included the Irish Church Act (1833), the Marriage Act (1836) and the establishment of the Ecclesiastical Commission (1836), which aimed to ensure a more equitable distribution of church finances. In addition, the Poor Law Amendment Act (1834) removed administration of the Poor Law from vestry control

---

[28] Mary Sokol, 'Jeremy Bentham and the Real Property Commission of 1828', *Utilitas*, 4, 2 (1992), 225.
[29] Lord Cranworth, House of Lords Debate (HL Deb.), *Hansard*, 25 May 1852.
[30] I thank Professor Michael Turner, Emeritus Professor of Economic History, University of Hull, for sharing his expertise on copyhold.

and the Municipal Corporations Act (1835) ended the direct link between the Church and municipal corporations.

Against this background, the hierarchy drew the conclusion that tithe reform was not only inevitable but probably desirable, on condition that any new arrangement was favourable to the vested interests of the Church. Reports from local clergy about increased difficulties in collecting tithe encouraged this sentiment. Typical was the complaint by the vicar of Broxbourne and Hoddesdon that he was being 'defrauded by many [...] parishioners of various vicarial dues and rights to which the laws of heaven and earth entitle me'.[31] Others drew attention to the way tithe had soured relations with parishioners and was fuelling support for nonconformism. Methodism and other nonconformist denominations had developed a significant following in some rural areas, particularly amongst the rural poor. 'Dissenters' naturally resented having to fund the Anglican Church, though most did not adopt the position of the Quakers, who continued their refusal to pay tithe as a matter of principle.[32]

In 1830 the archbishop of Canterbury, William Howley, unsuccessfully proposed a Tithe Composition Bill in the House of Lords. It would have encouraged and given legal status to voluntary arrangements to 'compound' tithe into cash payments for periods not exceeding twenty-one years – legislation similar to the provisions of the Tithe Composition Act (1823) introduced for Ireland. The archbishop remained implacably opposed to any attempt to 'extinguish tithe', such as schemes that would substitute tithe with fixed cash payments or corn-rents (payments linked to the price of corn). Yet he conceded that the tithe system needed a major 'remedy'. It exposed the farmer to 'uncertainty' and 'prevented him from employing his capital to as much advantages as he would be enabled to do if some settled arrangement were adopted'. Even more worryingly, it was tending 'to destroy that harmony which should always exist between the pastor and his parishioners'.[33]

Radical opposition to tithe, which expressed itself in two mass movements, soon made 'a remedy' even more urgent. In 1830–31, tithe abolition became one of the demands of the Captain Swing movement. Beginning in Kent in late August 1830 and spreading through large swathes of southern and eastern England, Swing was at root a rebellion by agricultural labourers against threats to job security, working conditions and changes to poor relief. But the tithe question served to broaden the movement. Farm labourers sought to form pacts with tenant farmers by offering to take action to 'stop the tithes' in return for promises for

---

[31] Cited in Eric J. Evans, *Tithes and the Tithe Commutation Act 1836* (London: Bedford Square Press, 1978), 3.
[32] Eric J. Evans, 'Some Reasons for the Growth of English Rural Anti-Clericalism c.1750–c.1830', *Past & Present*, 66 (1975), 84–109.
[33] HL Deb., *Hansard*, 10 May 1830.

increased wages. At Wrotham (Kent), a crowd of around 500 people demonstrated outside the rector's residence and, with cries of 'bread or blood', demanded that he reduce his tithes to enable farmers to pay higher wages. In Lower Wallop (Hampshire), farmers collectively agreed to raise wages 'on the proviso that the labourers must go to the tithe proprietor and demand 30 per cent reduction on the threat of his house being set on fire if he refused'.[34] The alliance between labourers and farmers over tithe was possibly strongest in Norfolk, where clergymen reported confrontations with 'mobs' of labourers prepared to keep them 'in bodily fear' until agreeing a reduction in tithe.[35]

For the landed classes and larger tenant farmers, these were worrying developments. By the nineteenth century, rural social relations had evolved into a 'tripartite' system of landowners, tenant farmers and landless labourers, though this model hides a range of complexities and regional variations. A generally prosperous class of 'yeoman farmers' also owned land and were prominent in the local social and political hierarchy. Friction between landowners and farmers was common, including arguments over the level of rents, tenancy agreements and compensation for improvements to holdings. Yet in terms of social attitudes, the large-scale tenant farmers adopted the 'gentlemanly ethic' of the landlords – living in expensively furnished farmhouses and wearing the finest fashions. For them, farming meant primarily running a business, rather than personally working the soil or looking after livestock. A previously close, if unequal, relationship with their workers had become transformed into 'a simple cash-nexus'.[36] Yet the category of tenant farmer was far from homogeneous. The proportion of small farmers remained high. The 1851 census would find that, in England and Wales, 23.8 per cent of farmers worked the land without hired labour; a majority (52.4 per cent) employed two or fewer workers. In Suffolk, a bastion of agricultural capitalism in which one-fifth of farmers employed ten or more labourers, two-fifths of farmers still employed two or fewer workers.[37]

The large tenant farmers understood the necessity of a political alliance with the landlords, amongst other things to resist the repeal of the Corn Laws. They also sought leadership of the entire 'family' of

[34] Carl J. Griffin, *The Rural War: Captain Swing and the Politics of Protest* (Manchester: Manchester University Press, 2012), 87–95, 115–16, 143, 238 and 280–1.
[35] Eric Hobsbawm and George Rudé, *Captain Swing* (London: Phoenix Press, 2001), 152–9; Lee, *Rural Society*, 11–12; see the map of tithe protests during Captain Swing (1830–31) in Andrew Charlesworth (ed.), *An Atlas of Rural Protest in Britain, 1548–1900* (Abingdon: Routledge, 2018), 152.
[36] Howard Newby, *Country Life: A Social History of Rural England* (London: Cardinal, 1987), 53–8 and 34.
[37] Newby, *Deferential Worker*, 25–6.

farmers to pressurise the landlords and enhance their economic position. Yet, although smaller farmers often aspired to the social status enjoyed by their more privileged colleagues, the depression had hit them hard. Living in closer proximity to the rural poor, some could identify with or even openly collaborate with the labourers' movement against – as small farmers in Chilham (Kent) put it – 'the opulent farmer [able] to avail himself of every rise in the market'.[38]

An even bigger warning of the potential for tithe to become a catalyst for serious unrest came from across the water in Ireland. Beginning while the Swing movement was sweeping through the English countryside, entire farming communities – with support from the Catholic clergy – refused to pay tithes to the Church of Ireland, at times prompting a violent response from the authorities. Contemporaries described the conflict as a 'tithe war', the first time the term enters the vocabulary. The methods of struggle – mass non-payment, mobilisations to prevent seizures of stock, disruption of auctions – as well as the phrase coined to describe them, 'passive resistance', would be adopted by activists in later 'tithe wars' in England and Wales. The rebellion led to the Tithe Commutation Act for Ireland (1838) – which made landlords rather than tenants responsible for tithe – and speeded the disestablishment of the Church of Ireland (1869).[39]

The 1836 Act

In 1836, Lord John Russell, home secretary in William Lamb's Whig administration, succeeded in steering his Tithe Commutation Bill through parliament. With some minor exceptions, such as tithes on fish, the legislation 'commuted' the payment of tithe in kind into a cash payment, a 'rentcharge' linked to the price of grain (calculated through a formula of the average prices of wheat, barley and oats during the preceding seven years).[40] The Tithe Act should be viewed as part of the Whig reform programme of the 1830s. Russell was also the principal architect of the Representation of the People Act (1832), which gave more political power to the urban middle classes but also to farmers, who became the largest social group within most county electorates. The Factory Act (1833)

[38] Report of Royal Commission on Poor Laws (1834), cited in Paul Hastings, 'Radical Movements and Workers' Protests to c1850', in Frederick Lansberry (ed.), *Government and Politics in Kent, 1640–1914* (Woodbridge: Boydell Press, 2001), 112.

[39] David Patrick Reid, 'The Tithe War in Ireland, 1830–1838' (unpublished PhD thesis, Trinity College, Dublin, 2013); Noreen Higgins-McHugh, 'The 1830s Tithe Riots', in William Sheehan and Maura Cronin (eds), *Riotous Assemblies: Rebels, Riots & Revolts in Ireland* (Cork: Mercier Press, 2011), 80–95.

[40] For a detailed explanation see Geoffrey Alan Lee, 'The Tithe rentcharge: a pioneer in income indexation', *Accounting, Business & Financial History*, 6, 3 (1996), 301–13.

extended the jurisdiction of the state over some particularly rapacious aspects of capitalism, such as child labour. Other measures (see above) secularised institutions and laws that were previously the preserve of the Church. Far-reaching and of long-term historical significance, the reforms aimed to make the established order more acceptable and functional in the eyes of – what Whigs described as – 'the intelligent and independent portion of the community'.[41]

Whereas Althorp's bill in 1834 had prompted hostile petitions from the clergy, not a single clerical or episcopal petition was organised against Russell's proposed tithe legislation. Even the most conservative elements within the Church viewed it as an opportunity rather than a threat. In 1833, the bishop of Exeter had said that legislation to amend tithe law 'on any principle not applicable to property of other descriptions would be to violate the right, and shake the title, of all property whatever'. Yet, in 1836, he welcomed the possibility of a settlement that could 'for ever extinguish [...] heartburnings and jealousies' enkindled by tithe, while maintaining a guaranteed income for the Church.[42]

Russell secured broad support because his tithe bill was a compromise. Its text drew much from earlier unsuccessful pieces of legislation, most particularly those presented by two Tories, Thomas Greene (1828) and Sir Robert Peel (1835). Russell made concessions to entice the Tory opposition and the bishops in the House of Lords to accept compulsory commutation by proposing to accord significant responsibilities to the Church authorities in overseeing the whole process. The aim was, he announced, to 'produce as little disturbance as possible to existing interests [and] not to diminish violently or excessively any income now enjoyed by any titheowner'.[43] The compromises dismayed some on the Whig benches, but Russell was determined to secure cross-party support at almost any cost.[44] He warned that 'objections to tithe were felt so strongly that men were becoming every day more and more unwilling to pay what was legally due, and more and more anxious to see these payments altogether cease'. It was, he said, 'the duty of Government [...] to come to a settlement of it' before demands became 'so unreasonable as to render it impossible for Parliament at once to do justice and to give satisfaction'.[45]

A similarly cautious approach was adopted towards those aspects of medieval law pertaining to land tenure. Though favouring the abolition

---

[41] Norman Gash, *Aristocracy and People: Britain 1815–1865* (London: Edward Arnold, 1979), 147.
[42] Norman, *Church and Society*, 109.
[43] Lord John Russell, 'Commutation of Tithes – England', HC Deb., *Hansard*, 9 Feb. 1836.
[44] Evans, *Contentious Tithe*, 125–8.
[45] HC Deb., *Hansard*, 9 Feb. 1836.

of copyhold, in 1832 the Real Property Commission proposed a gradualist approach, fearing that 'a proposal for a code of property law [would] raise the fearful spectre of republican France'.[46] In 1841, the Enfranchisement of Copyholds Act – commonly referred to as the Copyhold Emancipation Act – introduced a voluntary enfranchisement (the buying out by copyholders of obligations to the lord) along with provisos that protected manorial rights. Despite further legislation during the nineteenth century (1852, 1858, 1887, 1894), the law of copyhold persisted into the early twentieth century.

Historians studying the 1836 Tithe Commutation Act tend to judge it favourably. According to Roger Kain and Hugh Prince, the fact that its essential elements remained on the statute book for a century showed it to be a 'remarkable' achievement that 'withstood the test of time'.[47] The Act certainly left an important legacy. Its implementation was overseen by a 'tithe commission' which headed up a large and expensive administrative machinery. Dividing the country into over 12,000 tithe districts (in most cases, parishes), an army of assistant commissioners and their clerks surveyed the ownership, occupancy and usage of every field in every district, a process that in some cases took a decade to complete. The resulting tithe maps and tithe apportionments (lists of landowners, tenants and fields, along with the rent charge apportioned to each) have been described as 'the most detailed and important national inventory [...] after the great Domesday Book of the eleventh century'.[48] They have proved an invaluable source for historians and genealogists. The Act's 'durability' can, however, be exaggerated. The Royal Commission, established in 1934 in response to the 'tithe war', noted that it had been necessary to amend the Act 'by no fewer than fifteen subsequent Acts'.[49] Using an analogy drawn from the Bible, one activist in the interwar tithepayers' movement described the legislation's history as 'the continuous patching of an old garment with undressed cloth [so that] there is little left of the original fabric [...] to be a serviceable garment'.[50]

The Act's aim was to keep the value of monetary payments by tithepayers at broadly the same level as the previous value of tithe in kind. The income of titheowners would also stay relatively constant, with the septennial average preventing sharp variations from year to year. To decide the level of rentcharge, parish meetings involving titheowners and tithepayers were convened to agree the gross average value of tithe collected in the district. If no agreement were possible, the commissioners would have powers to calculate a figure based on the average value of

[46] Sokol, 'Jeremy Bentham', 244.
[47] Kain and Prince, *Tithe Surveys*, 67.
[48] Ibid., 256.
[49] Royal Comm, 3.
[50] 'New Cloth on an Old Garment – 1836–1934', *Tithe*, 6, Oct. 1934.

tithe during the seven-year period of 1829–35. After deducting costs of collection, storage, threshing and other expenses, the total tithe was divided between the different plots of titheable land, apportioning an amount either to each farm or each separate field. This total was assigned a 'par value' of 100. Tithe would then fluctuate annually according to the average price of the three main cereal crops (wheat, barley, oats) – chosen as a determinant of the cost of living – during the preceding seven years.

This system of calculation ensured variations in tithe between and even within regions. Because of the relatively high price of grain – artificially inflated by the Corn Laws – rentcharge was highest in arable farming areas, particularly in East Anglia and the South East, while pastoral farming regions in the North remained lightly tithed. Moreover, as shown in a statistical analysis, the indexation of the cereal crops was arranged in such a way as to introduce 'an upward bias [...] favouring the owners at the payers' expense'.[51]

The Act also introduced an 'extraordinary tithe rentcharge' on orchards, market gardens and hop-growing fields, an additional tithe to take account of the higher profitability of their produce. This was another compromise – introduced on the behest of landowners concerned that the inclusion of fruit and hops would lead to a higher core value of ordinary tithe. It created another anomaly: ordinary tithe was attached to land, while extraordinary tithe was attached to a type of crop. Sixteen counties were liable for extraordinary tithe, but over half of it was paid by farmers in Kent and East Sussex.

Although the 1836 Act transformed tithe into a cash payment, its legal quality was unaltered. Tithe rentcharge remained a 'form of property', liable for rates and subject to laws of inheritance. As with tithe in kind, tithe rentcharge was not a personal debt on a tithepayer, but a charge 'issuing out of the lands'. Yet titheowners had extensive and severe powers in the event of non-payment. Tithe was due every six months. After twenty-one days of arrears, the titheowners were entitled to seek recovery through the machinery of distress. Without any judicial process, they or their agents could, after giving ten days' notice, 'distrain' – in other words, confiscate – produce and livestock on the lands liable for the payment, or on other land in the same parish occupied by the tithepayer. The only concession to tithepayers was that only up to two years' arrears could be recovered at any one time. In the event of goods of insufficient value being found, titheowners could sue for a writ of possession allowing them to take over the land for a temporary period with the right 'to receive' rents directly from tenants or to farm the land until the outstanding tithe was recovered.[52]

---

[51] Lee, 'Tithe rentcharge: a pioneer', 305.
[52] Clauses 81 and 85, Tithe Commutation Act, 1836.

By changing the nature of tithe from a charge linked to yield to a charge 'issuing from' the land, the Act created a series of new contradictions and potential grievances. First, it did not consider the impact of fluctuations in the value of land. If this were to fall, the tithe attached to a piece of land would increase relative to its value. The situation could – and indeed did – arise in which tithe on a plot of land reached or exceeded its value, making it virtually impossible to rent or sell the plot. Secondly, it made no allowance for the fact that the usage and output of land could change. Poor harvests, market conditions, or putting a field to grass could lead to big fluctuations in output, though make no difference to the demands of the titheowner. In some coastal areas, farmers lost land to the sea, but still faced liability for tithe – as in the case of a dairy farmer in Swalecliffe (Kent) during the tithe war of the 1930s.[53] Thirdly, the new system did not take into account that a sudden drop of prices would severely affect the income of the farmer, while his bills for tithe – because their calculation was based on a septennial average – would reduce more gradually. In fact, tithe demands could increase at a time the price of agricultural produce was falling.[54] Fourthly, it stipulated that tithe payments should be the responsibility of the landowner. In practice, however, many landlords wrote an obligation for tithe payments into tenancy agreements. Fifty years later, the Conservative prime minister Lord Salisbury would outline the problem this posed:

> Tithe is a very peculiar property. It is not a burden on the land; it is not a burden on the landowner; it is a burden on the produce of the land. But the produce of the land is in the hands of the occupier; while by law the person responsible with respect to the tithe is not the occupier but the owner. The result of that state of things is this – that in order to get at the produce of the land you must levy distraint upon the occupier. Yet the occupier, who is not the debtor, has to suffer the inconvenience of distraint for a debt that is not his own.[55]

The Act also side-stepped the issue of tithe 'redemption' – that is, a scheme allowing tithepayers to make payments to titheowners to 'extinguish' their liability to tithe (as proposed in Lord Althorp's 1834 bill). MPs on the Liberal benches would have favoured the inclusion of such a measure, which was viewed as an eventual path towards abolition of the charge. Yet Church leaders and Conservatives considered a mechanism giving tithepayers 'power to free themselves' from tithe as a potential challenge to property rights. In another concession to titheowners, Lord

---

53   The farmer was Mr C. D. Lyon. Report of 'Control Commission', 13 Apr. 1933, CERC, ECE/SEC/TITHE/GD/5.
54   Lee, 'Tithe rentcharge: a pioneer', 307–8.
55   HL Deb., *Hansard*, 23 Mar. 1888.

Russell recognised the need not to 'cumber' the bill with an 'additional difficulty', promising to return to the matter in the future.[56]

The principle of tithe redemption was introduced in a new Tithe Act in 1846.[57] Yet the legislation contained few provisions to encourage it. Tithepayers could only apply 'to redeem tithe' on relatively small plots of land (those with tithe below 20s) and received no automatic right to buy out a titheowner, as redemption required permission from the bishop or patron of a benefice. Tithepayers had to pay 'not less' than twenty-four times the par value of tithe – even if the annual value (linked to the price of corn) had fallen below 'par' – and, in several cases, bishops were to demand thirty years' purchase. Moreover, payment had to be by lump sum. Not surprising, by 1918 few tithepayers had engaged with the scheme, which led to only £73,000 worth of redeemed tithe.[58]

After 1836, the payment of tithes remained part of life for many farmers, in much the same way it had been previously.[59] Not surprisingly, tensions and conflicts over the charge continued during the decades that followed. Sometimes, unruly incidents involving tithe collectors and farmers reached the courts. In 1856, magistrates in Lichfield (Staffordshire) heard a case of assault after a bailiff had executed a distraint and seized two horses on behalf of Theophilus Guy, a lay titheowner. Attached to a plough at the time, the horses were owned by Henry Litherland, a local publican who also farmed sixty acres of land with the aid of two labourers. When the bailiff informed Litherland of his actions, 'the interview was not a friendly one' and the two men 'proceeded from words to blows, the blood flowing profusely from both sides'.[60] In 1873, John Flint, a farmer at Steeple Gidding, appeared before the county bench in Huntingdon (Cambridgeshire) charged with using 'threatening language'. The court heard that after his goods were distrained at the behest of the local rector, Rev. Henry Molyneux, 'the defendant went to the complainant [...], called him a dirty old rascal, scoundrel, and such like names' and told him that if his possessions were removed, '"I'll shoot you, as sure as you are a man".'[61]

In Mevagissey (Cornwall) a dispute over tithe on pilchards rumbled on throughout the 1860s. The local vicar claimed an annual cash sum from the fishing company Messrs Fox & Co, as well as one-twelfth of the money paid to the 'seaners' (fishermen who worked drift nets). As Quakers, the Fox family objected to tithe on conscientious grounds, and

---

[56] HC Deb., *Hansard*, 9 Feb. 1836.
[57] Tithe Act 1846, https://www.legislation.gov.uk/ukpga/Vict/9-10/73/enacted.
[58] Lord Prothero, HL Deb., *Hansard*, 15 Oct. 1918.
[59] Evans, *Contentious Tithe*, 128–60.
[60] 'The Sessions', *Staffordshire Advertiser*, 5 Jan. 1856.
[61] 'County Bench', *Peterborough Advertiser*, 27 Sept. 1873.

the fishermen were also increasingly creating 'difficulty' when demands for payments were made. A series of distraints of salt and pilchard oil were carried out but, as a local journalist put it, when the distrained goods were offered for sale at auction, 'so iniquitous do the Mevagissey people generally deem the proceedings to be, that few persons there can be found to bid for the goods'.[62] At a national level, the Society of Friends (Quakers) continued to resist tithes, its annual report for 1868 recording 155 distraints on property owned by members of the Society.[63]

In general, however, between 1840 and 1875, the provisions introduced by the 1836 Tithe Act functioned without serious difficulties. The value of tithe remained relatively stable, varying by over 10 per cent in only two years (1855 and 1861).[64] More significantly, for many farmers healthy profits tended to mitigate demands for tithe. Agriculture during the 1850s and 1860s entered a prosperous 'Golden Age' of 'high farming', underpinned by a buoyant urban market and technological advances.[65] But the illusion held by politicians and commentators that the tithe issue had been 'settled' would be rudely shattered in the 1880s.[66]

---

[62] 'Distraints for Fish Tithes', *Falmouth Packet & Cornwall Advertiser*, 14 May 1870.
[63] 'Quakers and Church-Rates', *Western Daily Press*, 12 Aug. 1868.
[64] Lee, 'Tithe rentcharge: a pioneer', 312.
[65] Newby, *Country Life*, 53–75.
[66] Tithe Assistant Commissioner Thomas Woolley, cited in Evans, *Contentious Tithe*, 161–2.

2

Hops, Pantomime and Martyrs, 1881–86

Organised and politicised agitation around tithe re-emerged in southern England during the winter of 1879–80. In many areas, it was animated by members of the Farmers' Alliance, an organisation seeking to represent, primarily, the interests of tenant farmers. The biggest and most significant movement during the first half of the 1880s took place in Kent and East Sussex. It focused on extraordinary tithe, the additional charge levied on fruit farming, market gardening and hop cultivation. Breaking out in 1881, the conflict became increasingly bitter until parliament introduced legislation to reform extraordinary tithe in 1886.

The beginning of anti-tithe agitation coincided with the end of agriculture's 'Golden Age' and the first stage of the 'Great Depression'. Heralded by a series of disastrous harvests and pressure on prices from, first, imported grain and, later, refrigerated meat, the depression marked a major decline in agriculture's position within the national economy – its share of gross domestic product shrinking from 14.2 per cent in 1875 to 6.4 per cent in 1901. Psychologically, the crisis stimulated anxiety about a 'rural exodus' and 'depopulation' of the countryside. While its impact on output varied between regions and types of farming, the depression was particularly severe in the arable farming areas of southern England and East Anglia.[1] At the time of tithe commutation in 1836, agriculture had been at its most prosperous in these regions and, in consequence, the par value of tithe was particularly high. Now, as prices of agricultural produce fell, tithe payments grew in proportion to rents and farming profits.

The depression disrupted an unstable social equilibrium within rural communities and, in places, reignited a dormant radicalism. On its eve, farm labourers had begun to organise trade unions to fight for improvements in wages and conditions, a revolt described by one historian as 'a sustained and considered assertion of human rights

---

[1] E. J. T. Collins, 'Rural and Agricultural Change' and M. E. Turner, 'Agricultural Output, Income and Productivity', 140, both in E. J. T. Collins (ed.), *The Agrarian History of England and Wales, Vol. VII, 1850–1914* (Cambridge: Cambridge University Press, 2000).

and dignity by an oppressed social group'.[2] Landowners and large-scale tenant farmers retaliated with sackings and evictions from tied cottages. In 1874, around 10,000 workers were 'locked-out' from farms in East Anglia and the southern Midlands, a five-month struggle that severely weakened the National Agricultural Labourers' Union, led by Joseph Arch. In the winter of 1878–79, Kentish landowners and farmers attempted to break the Kent and Sussex Agricultural Labourers' Union, a movement with 14,000 members under the leadership of Alfred Simmons, a Maidstone journalist.[3]

Simultaneously, tenant farmers became more outspoken over issues concerning their interests and conditions. Relations between farmers and landlords became fraught over game laws, security of tenure and compensation for improvements on rented land, particularly buildings and drainage. The Central Chamber of Agriculture had been formed in 1865 to fight for the 'common agricultural interest', but pressure grew for an independent voice for tenant farmers. In 1879 the Farmers' Alliance was launched and, during the next decade, gained a significant following in rural communities.[4] Though the Alliance stressed it was 'non-political', many of its leading members were Liberal Party politicians or activists.

The depression pushed agriculture and the land question up the political agenda. Less inclined to pay deference to the authority of landowners, tenant farmers became more wary of the Conservative Party, which – though claiming to be the 'farmers' friend' – defined itself primarily as the party of aristocratic propertied interests. Many farmers viewed Disraeli's Conservative government (1874–80) as having failed to act decisively in support of agriculture as the depression took hold. The subsequent Liberal administration, Gladstone's second, introduced limited reforms in the interests of tenant farmers, including the Ground Game Act (1880) and the Agricultural Holdings Act (1883). Conservatives and landowners complained that such measures were 'invasions' of the rights of property. But their biggest fear was the impact of the Irish Land Act (1881), which extended tenants' rights over rent, tenure and land sales. According to Lord Salisbury, soon-to-become Conservative leader, the Irish legislation threatened to start 'an earthquake wave [...] travelling towards the English landowner' and threatening other forms of property. Similar anxieties were expressed on the right wing of the Liberal Party. Possessing a social base amongst gentlemen farmers and

---

[2] Rollo Arnold, 'The "Revolt of the Field" in Kent, 1872–1879', *Past & Present*, 64 (1974), 72.
[3] Ibid.
[4] J. R. Fisher, 'The Farmers' Alliance: An Agricultural Protest Movement of the 1880s', *AgHR*, 26, 1 (1978), 15–25.

landowners, prominent Whigs spoke out against 'dangerous' attacks on property rights posed by a 'new radicalism' within the party.[5]

While Conservatives mobilised in defence of landed property rights, 'radical' Liberals sought a widening of rural property ownership. Despite launching attacks on 'indolent' landlords, their aims were socially conservative. The creation of a numerous class of small proprietors would promote social stability and thwart revolutionary agitation, while reversing rural depopulation and 'decay'. Jesse Collings, MP for Ipswich, promoted the model of France, where despite 'social and communistic doings' in the large industrial towns, the 'safety of the nation' was protected by the existence of five million 'owners of the soil'.[6]

Yet Liberals were radical in the sense that they challenged the idea that landowners had an absolute right over their property. They embraced a populist patriotism that viewed owners as 'custodians' of the land. In the words of Robert Arthur Arnold, MP for Salford, 'the soil of England was the inheritance of the English people': it belonged 'to the nation, to the State, to the people'. Land was, consequently, a special type of property and, if individual ownership conflicted with the wider interests of the population, the state had the duty to intervene in the national interest. This position fuelled campaigns during the 1880s around the Free Land League and the Commons Preservation Society, forerunner of the National Trust, as well as the Land Nationalisation Society and English Land Restoration League (both movements influenced by the American political economist Henry George).[7] It also underpinned the case for the reform of tithe law. Tithe should, argued Liberal campaigners on tithe, not be 'treated as private property of a permanent character' but viewed as 'national property', which meant that tithe should not only be subject to parliamentary scrutiny but also that the charge should benefit the whole community, rather than exclusively privileged sections, such as big landowners and the Church.[8] This was not an argument for tithe abolition. In fact, during the 1880s Liberals consistently defended tithe as a 'valuable national property that had long been misappropriated' by the Church and big landowners. They argued that the property should be

---

[5] Ewen Green, 'No Longer the Farmers' Friend? The Conservative Party and Agricultural Protection, 1880–1914', in J. R. Wordie (ed.), *Agriculture and Politics in England, 1835–1939* (Basingstoke: Macmillan Press, 2000), 150–6; E. H. H. Green, *The Crisis of Conservatism: The Politics, Economics and Ideology of the British Conservative Party, 1880–1914* (Abingdon: Routledge, 1995), 79–80 and 82–4.

[6] Readman, *Land and Nation*, 43–9; HC Deb., Hansard, 20 July 1883.

[7] Readman, *Land and Nation*, 21 and 110–19.

[8] T. H. Bolton, 'To the Editor of The Times', *The Times*, 3 Oct. 1881.

'preserved' with its benefits redirected towards 'really national purposes', particularly social welfare and public education.[9]

The election of Gladstone's second administration stoked anxiety within the Church. By the late 1870s, political nonconformism – expressed primarily through the Liberation Society – had become the 'most vocal of the sectional alliances' within the Liberal Party.[10] Nonconformist leaders believed that the political tide was flowing in their direction. The first Gladstone government (1868–74) had abolished Church Rates and religious 'tests' at universities. Most significantly, it had faced down strong Conservative opposition to pass the Irish Church Act (1869), which disestablished the Anglican Church in Ireland and removed many of its endowments, including its rights to tithe. The affair, which led to the refrain that the Church of England was 'the Conservative Party at prayer', ensured that the debate about the relationship between Church and state would be fought on party lines.[11] In 1880, the perceived danger of further challenges to ecclesiastical rights prompted the Church Defence Institution, an organisation of clerical and lay leaders formed in 1859 to resist political nonconformism, to step up its activities. At a 'conference' at Lambeth Palace in March 1881, Church and Conservative Party politicians, including Lord Salisbury, resolved to fight against the threat of disestablishment, described by one prominent participant as 'a movement against [...] property' pervaded by a 'strong current of communism and socialism'.[12]

Land policies secured big gains for the Liberals in rural constituencies at the 1885 general election. A year earlier, a majority of male agricultural labourers had been enfranchised by the Third Reform Act. In 1885, they gave enthusiastic support to Joseph Chamberlain's 'radical programme', which – popularised under the slogan 'three acres and a cow' – proposed state-sponsored provision of smallholdings. In many southern constituencies, Liberal candidates campaigned on the issue of tithe. In Woodbridge (Suffolk), the successful candidate, Robert Lacey Everett, a farmer and practising Baptist, prompted 'cheers and uproar' when he attacked the 'tithe-paid clergy' as 'the grandest support Toryism in this country has'. Tithes, he said, had 'awoken a sense of injustice' which should be harnessed for the wider aims of a 'second Reformation'.[13]

[9] Charles Morley, 'Liberalism at Shepton Mallet', *Western Chronicle*, 29 May 1891.
[10] Norman, *Church and Society*, 190–1.
[11] Ibid.
[12] Egerton cited in M. J. D. Roberts, 'Pressure-Group Politics and the Church of England: the Church Defence Institution 1859–1896', *Journal of Ecclesiastical History*, 35, 4 (1984), 573.
[13] 'Mr Everett's Address to the Farmers', *Ipswich Journal*, 12 Nov. 1885; Robert Lacey Everett, *Tithes: Their History, Use, and Future* (London: James Clarke & Co, 1887), 26 and 58.

Hops, Pantomime and Martyrs, 1881–86

Tithe and the Farmers' Alliance

As the depression deepened, farmers began to make collective requests to titheowners for reductions in tithe, along the lines of rent concessions offered by many landlords. In several cases, local clergy responded positively. The vicar of Leighton Buzzard (Bedfordshire) received fulsome praise in the local newspaper for his 'noble and substantial sacrifice', after offering a 25 per cent tithe reduction to the 'many small land-occupiers' of his parish. Generally, however, titheowners were intransigent. The same newspaper lamented the refusal by the Ecclesiastical Commissioners to show 'liberal consideration' to the tithepayers' plight.[14] A meeting between the rector and tithepayers in a small Hampshire village broke up in ill-temper after his 'refusal to abate any of the tithes due'.[15] In St Minver (Cornwall), farmers' demands were met with 'an obstinate refusal' from the titheowner's agent, prompting the meeting to 'unanimously agree [...] to defer payment' of tithe.[16] In March 1880, members of the Farmers' Alliance organised a protest rally in Reading Town Hall, which attracted farmers from every corner of Berkshire.[17] Speakers pledged not to pay tithe until 'forced to do so'. The following October, the Ecclesiastical Commisioners seized a quantity of corn from the farm (in the village of Hurst) of one of the campaign leaders, John Wingfield, a tenant farmer and Liberal Party activist. In December 1881, the Commissioner's agent returned to Wingfield's farm to impound nine cattle. A large meeting 'recorded a protest against the unfair working of the tithe law as it now oppresses the farmer', after which – according to a journalist – the agent was 'hustled and pushed into some water'.[18]

The campaign against extraordinary tithe in Kent and East Sussex began in 1881. Much of the preparatory work was laid by two individuals: Thomas Bolton, a talented solicitor who had been born into an East Sussex farming family and described himself as 'an advanced Liberal', and Albert Bath, secretary of the West Kent Farmers' Alliance, a radical Liberal and practising Baptist, who cultivated two farms with his brother near Halstead (Kent). In January 1878, Bath had chaired 'a large meeting of working men' organised by the National Agricultural Labourers' Union and addressed by Joseph Arch. Bath viewed the Farmers' Alliance

---

[14] 'The Tithe Rent-Charge', *Leighton Buzzard Observer*, 18 Nov. 1879.
[15] 'The Tithe Question – An Impromptu', *Hampshire Independent*, 26 Nov. 1881.
[16] 'St Minver Tithe Audit', *Cornish & Devon Post*, 20 Dec. 1884.
[17] 'Tithes in Relation to Agriculture. Meeting at Reading', *Reading Mercury*, 13 Mar. 1880.
[18] 'The Tithe Question and the Berkshire Farmers', *Reading Mercury*, 16 Oct. 1880; 'Seizure for Tithes at Hurst Anti-Tithe Demonstration', *Reading Mercury*, 24 Dec. 1881.

as a 'trade union of tenant farmers' and sought to forge a pact with agricultural labourers against the interests of landlords and titheowners.[19]

The Farmers' Alliance made no reference to tithe within its founding statement of aims. But at its annual meeting in December 1880 Bath and Bolton successfully moved that securing 'the redemption of the land from tithe charges' should be added to the Alliance's programme.[20] Bath argued that tithes 'should be transferred [to the state and applied] in the relief of the poor rate and in the relief of the education rate'. Only lay titheowners, particularly schools and universities, should be able to claim compensation if they 'could make out a good title for it'.[21] Bolton focused his critique on extraordinary tithe. He argued for its abolition through a redemption scheme, which would pay 'very little compensation' to the Church because 'most of the livings affected are otherwise amply endowed'.[22] Bolton said the Alliance 'might well take a lesson in organisation from the Land League in Ireland' – which at the time was waging a struggle against 'unjust rents' and mobilising demonstrations to prevent evictions by landowners.[23]

Bath and Bolton won enthusiastic support for a campaign against extraordinary tithe from hop and fruit growers in the Alliance's West Kent branch. But others in the Farmers' Alliance remained uncomfortable with their strategy. James Howard, Liberal MP for Bedfordshire and national chairman, warned that 'the Alliance recognised a property in the extraordinary tithe and could not allow it to go forth that they wished to do away with it without proper compensation'.[24] Even in Kent, prominent members of the Alliance expressed caution, arguing that farmers could 'gain the sympathy of both political partners [Liberals and Conservatives] by seeking to attain only that which was practicable and by being moderate'.[25]

Grievances over extraordinary tithe had been building for more than a decade. Farmers complained that the charge prevented them switching production to fruit and vegetables at a time when cereals faced increasing foreign competition. They pointed to substantial differences in extraordinary tithe between and within regions. In Kent, tithe on fruit orchards varied between 6s and 10s per acre and on hops between

---

19 'A Public Meeting', SEG, 12 Jan. 1885; 'Westerham', SEG, 12 Jan. 1878; 'The Farmers' Alliance' & 'The Farmers' Alliance in Kent', SEG, 21 Feb. 1881 and 7 Mar. 1881.
20 'The Farmers' Alliance', The Times, 9 Dec. 1880.
21 'The Farmers' Alliance in Kent', SEG, 20 June 1881.
22 T. H. Bolton, 'To the Editor of The Times', The Times, 3 Oct. 1881.
23 'The Farmers' Alliance', The Times, 9 Dec. 1880.
24 'The Farmers' Alliance in Kent', SEG, 21 Mar. 1881.
25 Charles Fitch-Kemp, a Conservative Party member who joined the Alliance. 'The Farmers Alliance in Kent', SEG, 9 Apr. 1881.

2s and 22s.[26] In 1873, a campaign by market gardeners had led the first Gladstone government to agree a limited reform. Legislation removed extraordinary tithe on newly established market gardens, while retaining it on land previously designated as such. Market gardeners continued to argue that extraordinary tithe hindered them from increasing production, particularly for the London market.

Hop farmers made a similar case. By the second half of the nineteenth century, hop cultivation had become part of a sophisticated industry. As well as requiring considerable investment, it was reliant on skilled labour as well as a large seasonal workforce, and linked to a network of maltsters, brewers and traders. Hop growing could be a very profitable concern, but a constant threat from pests and disease meant it was – as one Kent farmer put it – 'a bit like gambling on cards'.[27] By the 1880s, the industry faced several challenges, including competition from abroad and changing tastes in beer. Some smaller growers, particularly on the Kentish and Sussex Weald, went out of business. Yet farmers venturing into the industry were confronted with demands for extraordinary tithe as soon as they grubbed up fields for hops, before seeing a penny in return.[28]

The question of extraordinary tithe was taken up by Frederick Inderwick, Liberal MP for Rye. In October 1880, he made a widely publicised speech urging reform of the charge, while stressing the need to reject 'extreme' solutions.[29] He introduced a bill in parliament and was appointed chair of a select committee charged 'to inquire as to the expediency of abolishing extraordinary Tithe [...] upon equitable terms'.[30] Membership of the committee included James Howard (chair of the Farmers' Alliance) and three Kentish Conservative MPs. The committee presented a report in July 1881 and, shortly afterwards, Inderwick reintroduced a bill based on its recommendations. It proposed to extend the provisions of the 1873 legislation relating to market gardening to include hop cultivation. The bill also proposed a 'redemption' scheme with rates of purchase to be negotiated between titheowners and tithepayers, with a final decision in the hands of the tithe commissioners if agreement could not be reached. When suggesting criteria for compensation, Inderwick stressed that

[26] 'Report from the Select Committee on Tithe (Rent-Charges)', House of Commons, 22 July 1881, xii.
[27] B. A. Holderness and G. E. Mingay, 'The South and South-East', in Collins (ed.), *Agrarian History of England and Wales, 1850–1914*, 371.
[28] Celia Cordle, *Out of the Hay and into the Hops: Hop cultivation in Wealden Kent and Hop Marketing in Southwark, 1744–2000* (Hatfield: University of Hertfordshire Press, 2011).
[29] Frederick Andrew Inderwick, *Taxes on Agriculture: The Extraordinary Tithe on Hops, Fruit and Market Gardens: Speech at the Market Hall, Rye, October 1880* (London: National Press Agency, 1880), LSE Selected Pamphlets.
[30] HC Deb., *Hansard*, 2 May 1881.

extraordinary tithe was 'clearly [...] private property' whose owners 'have a right [to be] compensated for any loss'.[31] Hop and fruit growers in Kent immediately criticised the bill's limitations, particularly its failure to abolish existing extraordinary tithe, which would remain on all land originally designated for the charge. Bolton attacked Inderwick's characterisation of extraordinary tithe as private property as 'incorrect and misleading' and described the bill as 'quite worthless, [...] a most lame and most impotent proposition'.[32]

The extraordinary tithe war, 1881–86

Frustrated at events in parliament and equivocation from within the Farmers' Alliance, Bolton, Bath and members of the West Kent Farmers' Alliance announced the launch of the Anti-Extraordinary Tithe Association. Its first public activity was to mobilise an 'agricultural demonstration' at a distraint sale on one of the farms occupied by Bath and his brother, Colegate's Farm in Halstead (Kent). On the orders of the local vicar, 'a stack of excellent meadow hay' had been seized and put up for auction in lieu of £22 of extraordinary and ordinary tithe. On 15 August 1881, 200 farmers and their supporters turned up to the auction. Proceedings have been well described as akin to a pantomime. After several speeches, there were 'hisses and groans' on the entry of the 'villain' of the piece, the auctioneer, who introduced himself as 'probably not a very welcome visitor'. Yet the whole affair was good humoured. The 'farce' finished with 'cheers' when the lot was knocked down to a neighbouring tenant farmer, who purchased it on behalf of the Bath brothers.[33]

Five weeks later, the Anti-Extraordinary Tithe Association held its founding conference in a hotel adjacent to London's Borough Market (hub of fruit, vegetable and hop trading in the capital). Chaired by Bolton, it was attended by 300 farmers and hop growers, mostly from Kent and East Sussex, though others had travelled from Berkshire, Norfolk and Cambridgeshire. Some participants argued for a campaign to secure the abolition of all tithes, but the majority agreed to focus on the fight for abolition of extraordinary tithe – considered an achievable aim in the short-term. The conference set a deadline (1 October 1883) by which time abolition should have occurred. It advocated compensation for titheowners of around three years of par value of tithe, substantially below the figure of nine years signalled by Inderwick or the minimum

---

[31] F. A. Inderwick, 'To the Editor of The Times', *The Times*, 28 Sept. 1881.
[32] T. H. Bolton, 'To the Editor of The Times', *The Times*, 3 Oct. 1881; 'The Anti-Extraordinary Tithe Association', *SEG*, 26 Sept. 1881.
[33] Iain Taylor, 'Pressure Groups, Contested "Land-Spaces" and the Politics of Ridicule in Sevenoaks, Kent 1881–85', *Journal of Victorian Culture*, 21, 3 (2016), 329; 'Distraint for Extraordinary Tithe', *SEG*, 20 Aug. 1881.

of twenty-five years suggested by spokesmen for the Church. At the end of the conference, many attendees made a commitment not to pay their extraordinary tithe.[34]

The pledge led to a succession of distraint sales in Kent and East Sussex. Four geographical areas were particularly touched: the two Wealden districts around Staplehurst-Headcorn and Hawkhurst, the Darent Valley (including Crockenhill on the hills above) and the countryside around Sittingbourne. During 1882 and 1883, auctions took place on farms in Ticehurst (2), Crockenhill, Chart Sutton, Mersham, Boughton Monchelsea, Lower Halstow, Sutton-at-Hone and Southfleet. During 1884 and 1885, there were sales at Goudhurst, Crockenhill, Shoreham, Upchurch and on four farms at Leeds (near Maidstone). Stock auctioned included haystacks, hop poles, farm implements, wagons, horses, cattle and sheep.[35] Events at St Mary Cray in August 1882 were typical. At the behest of the local vicar, a cow 'gaily decorated with ribbons' belonging to a fruit grower was auctioned and the lot knocked down to Albert Bath, who promptly handed the cow back to the farmer. After 'an indignation meeting', during which several farmers expressed 'determination [...] not to pay' tithe, participants were 'invited to lunch, accompanied by fife and drum band, in a tent [...] erected on the land'.[36]

The Anti-Extraordinary Tithe Association's strategy was to use the auctions to mobilise farming communities and – through generating publicity – win public and political support for the abolition of extraordinary tithe. Bath described it as a campaign of 'passive resistance'.[37] As the campaign continued, the demonstrations grew in size and drew a broader layer of participants. Newspaper reports began to comment on the 'considerable number of labourers' in attendance.[38] Alfred Simmons, secretary of the agricultural labourers' union, pledged the 'support and concurrence' of farm workers and expressed the 'hope [...] that the farmers would persevere in this great work'.[39] Many farm workers saw a link between the campaign against tithe and their own bitter strike of 1878, which had faced resistance from landowners, large farmers and conservative sections of the clergy. Tradesmen and workers associated with the

[34] 'The Anti-Extraordinary Tithe Association', *SEG*, 26 Sept. 1881 and 17 Oct. 1881.
[35] *SEG*, 19 June 1882, 25 June 1882, 17 Sept. 1883 and 12 Jan. 1885; *Sevenoaks Chronicle*, 14 Sept. 1883; *Sevenoaks & Kentish Advertiser*, 24 Oct. 1884 and 18 Dec. 1885.
[36] *Bromley Record*, 1 Sept. 1882.
[37] 'The Extraordinary Tithe Agitation: Distraint Sale at Halstead', *SEG*, 5 Nov. 1883.
[38] 'Tithe Distraint: Riotous Proceedings', *Sevenoaks Chronicle*, 14 Sept. 1883.
[39] 'Extraordinary Tithes. Conference in London', *SEG*, 7 Aug. 1882; 'The Extraordinary Tithe Question', *The Standard*, 28 Sept. 1882; 'The Extraordinary Tithe Agitation', *SEG*, 5 Nov. 1883.

hop and fruit industries, including barrow boys at London's Borough Market, also mobilised. In November 1883, a distraint sale at a farm in Southfleet operated by a large fruit and hop grower (John Bartholomew) attracted 'upwards of 2000 persons'. According to a journalist: 'The rough element from the Borough [...] was exceedingly strong, and, had it not been for the persistent efforts of the distrained farmer [...], the auctioneer [...] would have been severely handled.'[40]

Indeed, the good humour on display at the earlier auctions had begun to evaporate. Journalists reported auctioneers being 'pelted with rotten eggs' or facing the humiliation of having their 'hat knocked off'.[41] According to one report, at a second distraint at the Baths' Halstead farm in November 1883: 'one of the parties [...] threw a small bag of soot, and the auctioneer's face was blackened. In the scuffle, [his] coat was torn and eventually reduced to shreds. In this condition he was advised to get off the farm.'[42] While, clearly, such accounts of disorder are exaggerated, they are an indication that the mood was hardening.

Several incidents led to court cases. In April 1882, magistrates at Hurst Green heard charges arising from an auction on a farm in Ticehurst (East Sussex). The auctioneer had arrived accompanied by ten sheriff officers to distrain four horses, a wagon and a stack of hop poles. His party was confronted by the farmer, John Tyman, and thirteen of his workers. Men on both sides were carrying 'sticks and hop poles in their hands'. Both the farmer and auctioneer were charged with assault. Charges against Tyman were eventually dropped, but the auctioneer was found guilty of striking the farmer's niece 'five or six times' and throwing her against a fence. The court was told that the vicar of Ticehurst, who ordered the distraint, had 'received a letter accompanied with a coffin and cross bones, threatening him with instant death if he continued the proceedings'.[43] In February 1885, Bromley Petty Sessions heard a case against James Stow, a fruit farmer in Farnborough (Kent), who was also charged with assaulting an auctioneer. After arriving at Stow's farm to sell a Berkshire sow seized for tithe non-payment, the auctioneer was confronted by demonstrators, who supposedly pushed him towards 'a pool of liquid manure' and 'hooted [him] out of the village'.[44]

[40] 'Scene at a Tithe Sale in Kent', *SEG*, 3 Dec. 1883.
[41] 'The Extraordinary Tithe Question', *The Standard*, 28 Sept. 1882; *Saint James's Gazette*, 25 Aug. 1885.
[42] 'The Extraordinary Tithe Agitation', *SEG*, 5 Nov. 1883.
[43] The case against Tyman was dropped at the Lewes Assizes, though not without the judge speaking of the need to ensure that in Sussex 'no similar attempt would ever again be made to resist the law by violence'. 'The Sussex Extraordinary Tithe Distraint Case', *SEG*, 10 Apr. 1882; 'Extraordinary Tithe', *The Times*, 6 Apr. 1882; 'The Extraordinary Tithe Assault Case', *SEG*, 15 July 1882.
[44] 'Extraordinary Tithes – At Bromley Petty', *The Times*, 10 Feb. 1885.

Hops, Pantomime and Martyrs, 1881–86

Conservative opinion denounced the farmers' campaign. An editorial in the London *Standard* spoke of the 'indecent eagerness' of those leading the movement 'to injure' the Church, landlords and the Conservative Party. 'The agitation has now almost ceased to be one against Extraordinary Tithes in themselves, and is fast drifting into a Radical crusade against Parsons, Establishments, Tories, and the possession of property,' lamented the paper.[45] Earl Stanhope, a prominent Conservative politician and Church Estates commissioner, characterised a crowd of 500 people at an auction in Orpington as 'a great rabble' and demanded that the Kent county constabulary should 'put down disturbances of the kind'.[46]

Initially, prominent figures within the Church adopted an intransigent approach. In May 1881, the Tithe Committee of the Lower House of the Convocation of Canterbury (assembly of clergy) described the relatively moderate reforms in Inderwick's bill as 'unjust' and 'an attack [...] on the weakest section of owners of rentcharge'.[47] Some local clergy viewed the whole affair as an assault on the Church instigated by nonconformists. The vicar of Crockenhill reported that 'his mission' had been seriously impeded by the agitation, 'not least because most labourers were Dissenters who bitterly opposed the Church, and seven of the eight employers were Dissenters and actively hostile'.[48] One of the most belligerent clergymen was Rev. Edwin Dyke, cousin of Sir William Hart Dyke, local landowner and Conservative MP for Mid Kent. In one case, bailiffs dispatched to seize stock on an orchard tenanted by William Dyke were unable to find enough produce to be sold. A court gave possession of the land to Rev. Dyke, who managed it until fruit had ripened and was ready for sale.[49]

Yet the clergy did not always present a united front. The vicar of Bearsted was amongst a number who offered a reduction in tithe to parishioners – in his case, 50 per cent.[50] In 1885, the vicar of Monkton agreed to remit a whole year's extraordinary tithe, and refund any monies already received, on account of the failure of the hop harvest in the region.[51] One clergyman openly sided with the farmers' campaign. Addressing a demonstration at the Baths' farm, Rev. J. L. Gardner described extraordinary tithe as 'a tax that could not be defended'. He 'knew that in taking up that position as a clergyman, he should incur the

---

[45] *The Standard*, 28 Sept. 1882, 4.
[46] 'Kent General Sessions', *Kent & Sussex Courier*, 13 Apr. 1883.
[47] 'Report of the Committee on Tithe, both Extraordinary and Ordinary', Convocation of Canterbury, Lower House, 11 May 1881, LPL, Benson 8.
[48] Susan Pittman, 'John Wood & Family: Fruit farmers of The Mount, Crockenhill, Kent' (Darenth Print & Design, 2020), 20–6; sources: LPL, Archbishop's Visitations, 1885, VG 3/7a, ff. 235–6 & 1889 VG 3/8a, ff. 238–9.
[49] Ibid. and *St James's Gazette*, 24 May 1883.
[50] 'Extraordinary Tithe – The Rev. F. O. Mayne', *The Times*, 25 Nov. 1882.
[51] 'Extraordinary Tithe', *The Times*, 7 Sept. 1885.

enmity of his brethren [but] he would be a coward and a renegade to his opinions if he did not come forward to render assistance.'[52]

As the Anti-Extraordinary Tithe Association's campaign broadened in support, senior figures in the Church sought ways to diffuse the conflict. In 1883, a paper read to the Diocesan Conference in Rochester rejected the suggestion that there was in 'the present system [of tithes] any great wrong or injustice to be redressed'. But it also recognised the hardship faced by many tenant farmers. The paper advocated the transfer of responsibility for payment of tithes to landlords along with a scheme to encourage redemption of the charge – proposals not far removed from those put forward by the Farmers' Alliance.[53]

The extraordinary tithe war reached its climax during the early months of 1886. In March and April, demonstrations took place at farms in Ticehurst, Langley and two farms in Marden, where on one occasion 'nearly a thousand persons were present'. At Staplehurst, a crowd marched on the rectory 'with a load of hop-poles' and a coffin labelled 'Extraordinary Tithes, died nineteenth century, after long suffering agitation'.[54] The conflict spread to the Hampshire–Surrey border, where a Farnham branch of the Anti-Extraordinary Tithe Association had been established. At a distraint auction of 41,000 hop poles on a big farm at Crondall (Hampshire), a journalist saw 'several rotten apples' thrown at an unfortunate auctioneer, 'some of them having the desired effect'.[55] By now, auctioneers were often going out of their way to assure farmers that they 'were opposed to the extraordinary tithe as much as anyone'. At Boyton Court Farm, East Sutton (Kent), where the dean and chapter of Rochester Cathedral had ordered an auction of 34,200 hop-poles, a journalist reported how, 'notwithstanding that a strong north-east wind was blowing and snow was falling [...] farmers and labourers, estimated at about 1500, attended to witness the carrying out of the sale'. The auctioneer told the crowd he had 'come on a mistaken errand' and took his departure 'amid great cheering'.[56]

The focal point of the conflict during these months was an affair arising from a distraint sale in Biddenden (Kent). In mid-January, bailiffs acting on the orders of the rector of Biddenden, Rev. William Peterson, impounded forty-seven sheep and a cow on Wagstaff Farm. Determined to ensure that 'no serious wrong [...] would be done to the property of the Church', Peterson had employed the services of his son, Edward

[52] 'Distraint for Extraordinary Tithe', *SEG*, 20 Aug. 1881.
[53] Granville Leveson Gower, 'Tithes: A Paper read at the Rochester Diocesan Conference', 31 May 1883.
[54] 'Tithe Distress Sales in Kent', *SEG*, 29 Mar. 1886; 'The Extraordinary Tithe Agitation', *SEG*, 5 Apr. 1886.
[55] 'Crondall', *Hampshire Chronicle*, 10 Apr. 1886.
[56] 'Distress for Extraordinary Tithe at East Sutton', *SEG*, 20 Mar. 1886.

Whit'tred Iltyd Peterson, a qualified solicitor, to serve distraint orders on several local farmers.[57] It would be the start of the younger Peterson's fifty-year involvement in the tithe controversy. 'About a thousand' people turned up to the auction at Wagstaff Farm. Chairing the protest meeting, Albert Bath told the crowd that 'passive resistance' was 'the only way to get public sympathy'.[58] Press reports of the event record a peaceful affair but, during a fracas, six local farmers were arrested and charged with assault and unlawful assembly. The auctioneer told Cranbrook magistrates that he had been pelted with 'cabbage stumps and disgusting refuse and found himself being rushed in the wagon towards a pond', while 'from above the womenfolk in the house emptied jugs of water over him out of a window'. After finding the farmers guilty, the magistrates denounced 'a most dastardly and disgraceful assault [...], a cowardly one, unprovoked, unreasonable and wrongful [for which] an example had to be made'. They sentenced George Cooper, a farmer from the village of Smarden, to one month's imprisonment with hard labour.[59]

Cooper quickly became known as 'the Smarden martyr'. Protest meetings demanding his release took place at Kentish markets and a petition of signatures reached fourteen feet in length. An intervention from the home secretary reduced the sentence by one week and Cooper's release from Maidstone Prison was the signal for 'exultant joy' and 'remarkable scenes'.[60] A journalist reported how a procession led by the freed prisoner wound its way through Wealden villages:

> The first vehicle, in which Mr Cooper was placed, contained banners with the words 'Welcome to our martyred friend' and 'the result of vindictive Toryism', while the traps which followed carried banners on which were prescribed 'Down with Tory tyranny' and 'Liberty and Justice to All'. All along the road the unique spectacle enlisted the attention of numbers of people who shouted their sympathy by cheering and remarks of approval [...] At Langley, a number of sturdy housewives greeted the procession with waving of aprons and clapping of hands, while at Sutton Valence the Smarden Brass Band put in an appearance [...] Arrived at Headcorn, farmers from Cranbrook and Frittenden greeted Mr Cooper and the village was for a time the scene of great animation. Refreshment was partaken of at the different inns in the village, and the greatest good humour prevailed amongst the crowd, while the band played 'See the Conquering Hero Comes'.[61]

---

[57] Peterson to Archbishop of Canterbury, 18 Apr. 1888, LPL, Benson 171/196.
[58] 'Distress Sale for Extraordinary Tithe', *SEG*, 23 Jan. 1886.
[59] *London Standard*, 26 Feb. 1886; *KE*, 27 Feb. 1886 and 6 Mar. 1886.
[60] 'Release of Mr Cooper. Lively Demonstration', *KE*, 20 Mar. 1886; 'The Anti-Extraordinary Tithe Agitation', *SEG*, 27 Mar. 1886.
[61] 'The Tithe Assault Case', *KE*, 20 Mar. 1886.

FIGURE 2. 'A Modern Eden': cartoon published by the Liberation Society, c.1886 (Lambeth Palace Library). A clergyman with a serpent's tail, emblazoned with 'Established Church' and, in the background, an auctioneer standing in front of a tree ravaged by a plague of locusts. Adam (Labour) and Eve (Agriculture) stand in defence of the tree of life.

Hops, Pantomime and Martyrs, 1881–86

A compromise 'as fair as could be expected'

The affair of the 'Smarden martyr' unfolded against the background of parliamentary debate over legislation to reform extraordinary tithe. In February 1884, the home secretary, William Harcourt, had pledged the Gladstone government's support for a new bill introduced by Frederick Inderwick. As with his 1881 bill, Inderwick proposed to end liability for extraordinary tithe on newly cultivated fruit and hop orchards. The additional provision was that existing extraordinary tithe would be transformed into a fixed 'substituted charge' of 4 per cent of the tithe's capital value. Assessed by the tithe commissioners, capital value would be calculated from average tithe receipts during the seven years 1878–1884, with a 25 per cent deduction for rates, taxes and other outgoings. The charge would be paid by the landowner, not the tenant farmer.[62] Inderwick's aim was 'to remove all liability to extraordinary tithe' from land and to 'make reasonable compensation to the present tithe owners'. Critics of the bill pointed out that the substituted charge meant not only that extraordinary tithe would continue, albeit under another name, but also that payments would remain even if the farmer ceased to grow hops or fruit.[63] Nevertheless, many on both sides of the conflict viewed Inderwick's bill as the basis of a settlement. Bolton said that, though it was 'not altogether satisfactory', the proposals were a 'reasonable attempt to compromise'.[64] Despite the promise of government support, the bill did not secure parliamentary time and its fate was settled when Inderwick lost his seat at the 1885 general election.

The new parliament, however, quickly saw the introduction of three private member's bills on extraordinary tithe, two of which were considered particularly opportune. The first was from Robert Norton, Conservative member for Tunbridge, who said he was speaking on behalf of Kentish Conservative MPs. It reflected a significant shift in the position of his party. While they continued to condemn 'unfair attacks on the Church and the clergy' and bemoaned the fact that they were discussing legislation 'based on agitation', most Conservatives recognised that 'the state of feeling' in Kent and East Sussex meant 'the time had arrived' to seek a cross-party consensus to resolve the conflict.[65] The second bill was presented by the newly elected MP Thomas Bolton, president of the Anti-Extraordinary Tithe Association. Bolton had been nominated by the local branch of the Farmers' Alliance as a Liberal candidate in West

---

[62] HC Deb., *Hansard*, 28 Feb. 1884; 'Extraordinary Tithe', *The Times*, 14 Mar. 1884.
[63] Lord Brabourne, HL Deb., *Hansard*, 23 May 1887.
[64] 'The Anti-Extraordinary Tithe Movement', *SEG*, 21 Apr. 1884.
[65] Herbert Knatchbull-Hugessen, John Talbot, Robert Norton, HC Deb., *Hansard*, 24 Mar. 1886; Lord Harris, HL Deb., *Hansard*, 21 June 1886.

Kent, but the whiggish leadership of the local association had vetoed his candidature. He was subsequently selected to stand in North St Pancras, a seat he won after a fierce contest with Lord Salisbury's assistant private secretary.[66]

The bills presented by Norton and Bolton were both similar to Inderwick's proposed 1884 legislation. They stipulated the prohibition of extraordinary tithe from newly cultivated land, the transformation of existing extraordinary tithe into a fixed charge (4 per cent of capital value) and the transfer of liability for payment to landowners, who would be encouraged to pay a lump sum 'to redeem' the tithe. The essential difference between them was over how capital value should be calculated. Bolton wanted to link it to 'the fair market value' of extraordinary tithe, while Norton proposed to give power to determine the level to the Land Commissioners (who had taken over the role of the tithe commissioners). For Bolton, this would give titheowners 'much more substantial compensation [...] than they were entitled to expect'.[67] Nevertheless, the president of the Anti-Extraordinary Tithe Association was prepared to compromise. A select committee was established to resolve the differences and drafted a bill that – with a few minor amendments – was close to Norton's proposal.[68] When Bolton, as chairman of the committee, steered the compromise through parliament, Conservative MPs praised his efforts, noting that his 'moderate language [...] was scarcely in accordance with his former utterances'.[69]

The debate around the Extraordinary Tithe Redemption Bill reached a conclusion as the crisis over Irish Home Rule consumed the Gladstone government. Yet ministers were determined to facilitate a solution to what the home secretary, Hugh Childers, described as an 'internecine war' between titheowners and farmers.[70] The bill was rushed through both houses of parliament and received the royal assent during the government's final days.

The biggest controversy provoked by the legislation occurred within the Church. Bishops in the House of Lords reluctantly supported the bill. The archbishop of Canterbury, Edward Benson, described it 'as fair a compromise as could be expected under the circumstances': the 'disgraceful scenes of disorder' had 'greatly hindered [...] the spiritual work of the Church' and the 'sore' would 'continue open, unless the compromise were agreed'.[71] But some prominent lay figures, along with

---

66 'The Farmers' Alliance and the Representation of West Kent', *SEG*, 19 May 1884.
67 HC Deb., *Hansard*, 24 Mar. 1886.
68 Committee (On Re-Commitment), *Hansard*, 17 June 1886.
69 Akers-Douglas, HC Deb., *Hansard*, 24 Mar. 1886.
70 Committee (On Re-Commitment), *Hansard*, 17 June 1886.
71 HL Deb., *Hansard*, 21 June 1886.

a significant section of tithe-collecting clergy, criticised the hierarchy's position. The Church Defence Institution organised a petition against the bill. In the House of Commons, the Conservative MP Stanley Leighton, a Church Defence Institution leader, read out complaints from clergy that their 'property was being taken away […] with indecent haste'.[72] Officials of Queen Anne's Bounty, an institution responsible for managing Church property and investments, urged Benson to 'resist the bill [which] would ruin a great number of clergymen' in the hop-growing counties.[73] A group of Kentish clergy told the archbishop to do 'his duty' and halt the 'public plunder' contained in 'Mr Bolton's bill'. Describing it as a 'partial disendowment bill', the rector of Southfleet criticised Benson for being conciliatory to agitators 'in whose minds there is no peace, so long as any hope of plundering the Church remains'.[74] The archbishop defended his position in a letter widely circulated amongst rural clergy. He argued that, given 'there was not the slightest chance of getting the bill thrown out […], the only thing to be done was to make the most out of it'.[75] Yet he was stung by the criticism. Over the next five years, Benson would show more resilience in facing down demands to reform tithe, particularly those emanating from the 'tithe war' that had just broken out in Wales.

The 1886 Act had the desired effect of calming the conflict around extraordinary tithe. Skirmishes over arrears continued in some localities. In 1888, bailiffs seized thirty-five bags of sheep-hoof manure from a gooseberry plantation in St Mary Cray. The same year, a vicar's agent attempted to recover a debt in Crockenhill: 'snowballs were thrown' and the bailiff retired having lost his hat.[76] A rather strange incident occurred in Yalding, where tensions were high between local hop-growers and the vicar, Rev. David Lamplugh, a spokesperson for tithe-owning clergy.[77] Complaining that he was being short-changed by his parishioners, Lamplugh withheld £84 in poor rates that he owed on his tithe to the parish. In December 1887, he received a distress warrant for non-payment and 'the churchwardens and overseers entered the vicarage and took possession of the pictures and furniture in the rev. gentleman's library, and after seizing them gave notice that they would retain them […] and

---

[72] Stanley Leighton, Committee (On Re-Commitment), *Hansard*, 17 June 1886.
[73] Telegram Aster to Benson, LPL, Benson 38/412; Leighton to Benson, 18 June 1886, LPL, Benson 38/373.
[74] Philip Horte, rector of Farnham, Surrey, 14 June 1886; rector of Staplehurst, 23 June 1886; G. F. Goddard, rector of Southfleet, 22 June 1886, LPL, Benson 38/370, 38/397 and 38/405.
[75] Archbishop Benson to rural deans, 10 Sept. 1886, LPL, Benson 38/433.
[76] *SEG*, 16 Apr. 1888; *Bicester Herald*, 23 Mar. 1888; Pittman, 'John Wood & Family', 34–5.
[77] Provisional Committee representing Owners of Extraordinary Tithe Rentcharge, LPL, Benson, 38/417.

would then sell'.[78] A drawn-out legal wrangle ensued, until – fifteen months later – the Court of Appeal found in Lamplugh's favour.[79]

These were isolated incidents. Predictions about the legislation's negative impact on the clergy proved to be greatly exaggerated. While income from extraordinary tithe was generally reduced, most clergy recognised the benefit of receiving a fixed sum and – because the charge was no longer the responsibility of tenant farmers – more reliable payments. Yet the 'open sore' did not heal. Extraordinary tithe remained as a 'perpetual' charge, permanent unless a landowner paid the fixed capital value to secure its redemption. Over the next fifty years, only 20 per cent of extraordinary tithe would be redeemed. Not only did the potential for renewed conflict remain, but the memory of the battle over extraordinary tithe had filtered into the consciousness of Kentish rural communities.[80]

[78] 'Distraint for Tithes: Important Point', *The Globe*, 7 Jan. 1888.
[79] 'The Yalding Distraint for Poor Rate on Tithes', *SEG*, 2 Mar. 1889; 'Lamplugh vs North', *Maidstone Journal*, 2 Apr. 1889.
[80] Royal Comm, 63.

3

Wales and Southern England, 1886–91

As the agitation around extraordinary tithe receded, the campaign for radical reform of ordinary tithe gathered momentum. July–August 1886 marks a new stage in the conflict. First, it saw the outbreak of what the press immediately dubbed 'the Tithe War in Wales'.[1] Beginning in Llanarmon-yn-Iâl, a village in the Denbighshire Hills, a tithe non-payment campaign spread throughout Denbighshire, Flintshire and Montgomeryshire, and then into counties on the western side of the Welsh nation.[2] The movement's dynamic was vigorous, its breadth extensive and its character overtly political. The Anti-Tithe League's manifesto (September 1886) declared that 'the refusal of the clergy to listen to the appeals made to them by the farmers for reductions in the tithe' has led to 'a louder demand […] for the disestablishment and disendowment of the Church of England'.[3] Secondly and simultaneously, tithepayers' organisations launched a coordinated and sustained campaign in the Home Counties and other parts of southern England. Well-publicised demonstrations at distraint auctions took place in Essex, Berkshire, Hampshire, Devon and elsewhere. The English tithepayers' movement lobbied for reform of tithe, as well as reductions to the charge to take account of the agricultural depression.

The third change was the political context. After the split in the Liberal Party over Irish Home Rule, an alliance of Conservatives and Liberal Unionists won a big majority at the general election (July 1886). As

[1] See the 'Tithe War Album' compiled by Charles Stevens, agent to the Ecclesiastical Commissioners, for photos and press cuttings relating to disturbances in Denbighshire, Flintshire, Montgomeryshire and Cardiganshire, North East Wales Archives, DD/DM/845 (available online). The 'Welsh Tithe War' still awaits a book-length scholarly study. See J. P. D. Dunbabin, *Rural Discontent in Nineteenth Century Britain* (New York: Holmes & Meier, 1973), 211–31; Donald Richter, 'The Welsh Police, the Home Office, and the Welsh Tithe War of 1886–91', *Welsh History Review*, 12, 1 (1984), 50–75; Pamela Horn, *The Tithe War in Pembrokeshire* (Fishguard: Preseli, 1982).

[2] See map of 'The Welsh Tithe War' in Charlesworth, *An Atlas of Rural Protest*, 178.

[3] 'Manifesto of the Anti-Tithe League', cited in Dunbabin, *Rural Discontent*, 282–3.

conflict grew in Wales, the prime minister, Lord Salisbury, announced he would introduce changes in law to thwart the tithepayers' movement and facilitate the recovery of tithe. Yet his government struggled to pass legislation through parliament. Between 1887 and 1890, five different tithe bills were introduced, only to be withdrawn. It was not until March 1891 that an 'Act to make better provision for the Recovery of Tithe Rentcharge in England and Wales' received the royal assent.

Tithe War in Wales

The Welsh tithe war was conditioned by the nature of Welsh rural society, described by a Royal Commission as 'the prevalence of a large number of small, separate farms of [...] the peasant and family type'.[4] Linked to broader demands for land reform, the movement was fuelled by nationalist sentiments and widespread antagonisms within nonconformist communities towards the Anglican Church. The founding conference of the Anti-Tithe League in Solva (Pembrokeshire) pledged 'righteous opposition to an unholy tax which has been imposed and maintained for the purpose of ecclesiastical tyranny, as well as the oppression of the people'.[5]

In Pembrokeshire, Cardiganshire and Caernarvonshire the conflict contained echoes of the Rebecca riots of 1839–43. The main targets of this earlier explosion of rural anger had been the Turnpike Trusts, who – against a background of poor harvests and falling agricultural prices – extended the number of tollgates on country roads. Describing themselves as 'Rebecca's faithful followers', large well-organised groups from farming communities destroyed the hated gates, often playing 'a cat and mouse game' with troops dispatched to quell the movement. Other grievances that spurred the Rebecca revolt included the poor law, high rents charged by absentee English landlords and resentment against the privileges of the Anglican Church, including its rights to tithe.[6] By the second half of the nineteenth century, Wales was marked by 'the clash of two societies'. In opposition to an anglicised landowning and gentry class, a 'people's culture' had emerged amongst small-scale tenant

---

[4] Royal Commission on Land in Wales and Monmouthshire (1896), cited in Kenneth O. Morgan, *Wales in British Politics, 1868–1922* (Cardiff: University of Wales Press, 1980), 9.

[5] 'The Tithe War in Wales', *St James's Gazette*, 9 Sept. 1886.

[6] Russell Davies, *Secret Sins: Sex, Violence and Society in Carmarthenshire, 1870–1920* (Cardiff: University of Wales Press, 2012), 136–8; the classic account of the Rebecca revolt (originally published in 1955) is David Williams, *The Rebecca Riots: A Study in Agrarian Discontent* (Cardiff: University of Wales Press, 1986).

farmers, agricultural labourers and communities of miners, lime-burners and slate-quarriers.[7]

The tithepayers' campaign began with demands from farmers in Denbighshire for a reduction in tithes to compensate for a collapse in livestock prices. When the rector of Llanarmon refused to negotiate, farmers pledged collectively to stop paying the charge. In August 1886, bailiffs served distraint orders at forty-five holdings and, hoping to persuade tithepayers that non-payment was futile, the rector announced the auction of cattle belonging to two prominent members of the campaign. A large protest disrupted the sales and, a few weeks later, the Farmers' Tithe Defence League was formed in a Llanarmon school room. It linked up with similar campaigns in other districts to form the Anti-Tithe League.[8]

Observers commented on the community nature of the movement. Neighbourhoods were alerted and mobilised against tithe agents through the raising of flags, lighting of bonfires, discharging of firearms and the blowing of 'tithe horns', a long tin instrument that came to symbolise the conflict.[9] Effigies became another characteristic. When a contingent of tithe collectors arrived in Anglesey in early 1888, they encountered 'effigies of the local clergy who were distraining [...] stuck about on haystacks and other prominent positions'.[10] In Pwllheli (Caernarvonshire), tithe distrainers entered a farmyard to be confronted by 'a big horse astride of which was an effigy of a parson in full surplice, waring huge sea-boots, and under his left arm a bottle of spirits'.[11] Reports emphasised the participation of young people and women. At Pontfaen (Pembrokeshire), 'lasses and youngsters' were amongst the large crowd that kept up a 'discord of sound [...] to the accompaniment of indescribable blasts on [...] tithe horns', while 'a number of lasses mounted guard in front of the door' [of the farmhouse] to prevent the tithe agent 'placing the distraint note underneath'.[12] Other commentators noted the mobilisation of workers. At an auction in Denbighshire, a crowd cheered the arrival of 'a procession' of quarrymen 'brandishing staves', which prompted the bailiffs to 'put [their] horse to a gallop' chased by forty men.[13] In

---

[7] Kenneth O. Morgan, *Rebirth of a Nation: Wales, 1880–1980* (Oxford: Oxford University Press, 1982), 10, 13–15.
[8] 'The Tithe War in Wales', *Daily News*, 23 and 28 Aug. 1886.
[9] Reports of the Chief Constable of Denbighshire, 27 May 1887 and 17 June 1887. TNA, HO 144/199/A57143C.
[10] 'The Tithe War', *Cardiff Times*, 3 Mar. 1888.
[11] Tithe Sales in Lleyn', *Caernarvon & Denbigh Herald*, 21 Dec. 1888.
[12] 'The Tithe Agitation Campaign in North Pembrokeshire', *South Wales Daily News*, 29 Jan. 1891.
[13] 'The Tithe War in North Wales', *Daily News*, 24 Aug. 1886.

FIGURE 3. The Welsh Tithe War: troops of the 9th Lancers, together with police and bailiffs, in Llanfair Talhaiarn (Denbighshire), late May 1888 (North East Wales Archives, Ruthin). The photo is part of a scrapbook compiled by Charles Stevens, agent for the Ecclesiastical Commissioners, who is most probably the man standing front-left next to the wall. After parading through the village, the troops set up camp 'in regular military fashion' in a nearby field. They began a 'campaign' in support of Stevens, who had distrained on several farms in the neighbourhood.

Flintshire, the authorities were particularly fearful of the activities of lead miners, who they believed possessed 'decidedly bellicose tendencies'.[14]

A series of well-publicised confrontations took place between demonstrators and the forces of law and order. Towards the end of May 1887, thirty-one people were arrested at Llangwm (Denbighshire). According to the Chief Constable, 'a mob [had] frustrated any attempt to remove the cattle', after which 'the Police [and] bailiffs [were] taken prisoners and marched to Corwen by several hundred excited Welshmen'. Ten days later, the War Office agreed a request from magistrates to send 'a troop of cavalry' to support police operations.[15] The military was deployed in several regions between 1887 and 1890. One of the most serious incidents took place on 16 June 1887 near Mochdre, where five farmers had refused to pay tithe to the Ecclesiastical Commissioners. Seventy-five police officers and seventy soldiers arrived by 'special train'. After a magistrate had read the Riot Act, the chief constable ordered his men to 'forcibly remove [...] a mob of several hundred [who had] become unruly, stoning and hustling the Police'. His actions 'effectually broke the mob who ultimately ran', though there were 'serious injuries' on both sides.[16] After questions in parliament, the government appointed a London magistrate to conduct an inquiry. His report condemned 'violence and lawlessness' and put the blame for 'the serious evils' on those urging farmers not to pay their tithe.[17]

The tithepayers' movement received active support from nonconformist ministers and a group of young Liberal Party activists, including David Lloyd George, who became secretary of the South Caernarvonshire Anti-Tithe League. In 1887, the Anti-Tithe League reconstituted itself as the Welsh Land, Commercial and Labour League, which widened the movement's demands to include tenants' rights, Welsh control of royalties from mining, reform of Game and Fishery laws and the disestablishment and disendowment of the Anglican Church. Animating the Land League were two radical Liberals, who were also popular Calvinistic Methodist preachers: John Parry, one of the first to face distraint at Llanarmon, became president, and Thomas Gee, an influential Denbighshire campaigning journalist, acted as treasurer.[18] In parliament, Welsh Liberal MPs championed the movement. In July 1888, Liberal MPs led a demonstration of the 'Welsh community' to Battersea Park for a

[14] 'The Tithe Agitation in Wales', *North Wales Chronicle*, 21 Jan. 1888.
[15] Chief Constable of Denbighshire, 27 May 1887; War Office, 6 June 1887; TNA, HO 144/199/A47143C.
[16] Chief Constable of Denbighshire, 17 June 1887, TNA, HO 144/199/A47143C.
[17] *Report of an Inquiry as to Disturbances connected with the Levying of Tithe Rentcharge in Wales* (1887).
[18] 'Mr John Parry, Llanarmon, at Glyndyfrdwy' and 'The Late Mr. John Parry of Llanarmon', *Llangollen Advertiser*, 23 Nov. 1888 and 11 June 1897.

rally, at which a resolution expressing solidarity with the 'Welsh toilers of the soil' was passed.[19] Some amongst an older, more cautious, generation of Liberals stayed more aloof from the agitation, fearing that it could lead to accusations that the movement was linked with militant activity for land reform in Ireland.

In fact, the Welsh campaign gained sustenance from events across the Irish Sea. Its leaders pointed out that the case for disestablishment in Wales was essentially the same as that underpinning the Irish Church Act of 1869: the unviability of an established church holding only the adherence of a minority of the population. Yet they also criticised the extent to which the Irish settlement had financially benefited the British state and big landowners. Liberal leaders of the Welsh movement proposed that tithe – as 'national property' – should be redistributed to fund Welsh cultural life, particularly education. This was a live issue, as the Aberdare Report of 1881 had recommended major reforms, including the extension and democratisation of Welsh intermediate schools and Higher Education.[20] But some in the movement argued that redirecting tithe 'to the County Councils or some other secular body for the purposes of education [would] withdraw attention from the real issue'. Tithe was, they argued, an 'unfair burden' and 'alteration of the hand to receive the tithe [would] not make a heavy tithe a light one'.[21]

Welsh tithe was collected by local clergy, the Ecclesiastical Commissioners, Winchester Cathedral and lay titheowners, including Christ Church, Oxford. The commissioners hired a London agent, Charles Stevens, who spent a fair part of three years touring the Welsh countryside issuing distraint orders. Christ Church also employed an agent who spent considerable time in Meiford (Montgomeryshire). In May 1887, he distrained cattle on six farms and sold them to a butcher in Welshpool. Bailiffs were hired to seize the animals, but a crowd of 800 people forced the agent to rethink plans for fear of 'a running fight for the eight miles to Welshpool'.[22] Bailiffs drafted in from London often faced such 'experiences of a very rough character', as a correspondent of the *Daily Telegraph* put it.[23] Local shopkeepers refused to serve them with food or provisions and farmers denied them lodgings. Ten London bailiffs working on behalf of the Ecclesiastical Commissioners in the region around Whitford (Flintshire) during deepest winter 'had to content

---

[19] 'Anti-Tithe Demonstration', *The Cambrian*, 3 Aug. 1888.
[20] Morgan, *Wales in British Politics*, 84–6, 29, 46–9 and 68–70.
[21] John Parry, a leader of the movement in Llanarmon, would join 'The Tithe Question Association', which argued this position. 'The Tithe Question Association', LPL, Benson 171/292 and 298.
[22] Dunbabin, *Rural Discontent*, 215.
[23] 'Adventures of Ten London Bailiffs', *Daily Telegraph*, 17 Dec. 1886. 'Whitford: The Tithe Agitation', *Flintshire Observer*, 16 December 1886.

themselves with sheltering in a dreary and draughty stone-floored barn, with no protection but their every-day clothing from the prevailing cold'. To make matters worse, 'during the storm, the bailiffs were snowballed remorselessly by the workmen at Mr Williams's farm'.

While the commissioners and Christ Church were, from the outset, determined to press for every penny, many local clergy were initially prepared to offer concessions to tithepayers. As the archdeacon of Cardigan explained to the archbishop of Canterbury, the clergy 'are poor [but] abstain from enforcing their rights'.[24] Yet attitudes quickly hardened. The anti-tithe movement's declared aim of disestablishment and disendowment led both clergy and lay members of the Church to perceive the conflict as a struggle for the Church's very existence in Wales.

In October 1886, a conference in Chester launched the Clergy Defence Association. Its purpose was to resist 'organised opposition to the payment of tithe' and to offer clergy 'such support as would enable them to withstand the pressure of the agitators'. Attending the conference were clergy from the four Welsh dioceses, prominent lay members of the Church and politicians associated with the Church Defence Institution, most notably Stanley Leighton MP and Lord Egerton de Tatton (Wilbraham Egerton). The Clergy Defence Association appointed agents to organise every aspect of tithe collection, including distraint of goods and their sale at auctions, and, in so doing, stiffened the resolve of the Welsh clergy to refuse the demands of the tithepayers' movement. The Association also sought to engage the help of landlords by asking them to collect tithe directly from their tenants. Some big landowners – including the duke of Westminster and Lord Windsor – became benefactors.[25] But the tithe war was putting a strain on the traditional solidarity between the Church and anglicised landlords, many of whom attempted to stay apart from the fray. In frustration, the Clergy Defence Association issued a public statement in January 1888 criticising landlords for 'the lack of assistance given them in their endeavours'.[26]

The Church Defence Institution also attempted to stiffen the resolve of the Welsh Church. In October 1887, the earl of Selborne, Roundell Palmer, addressed bishops and clergy together with 'eminent representatives' of the laity and students of St David's College in Lampeter Town Hall. The event began with a procession through the town and a message of support from the archbishop of Canterbury. After breaking with the Liberal Party in 1885, Selborne, who had been lord chancellor in two Gladstone administrations, would spend much of his remaining

---

[24] William North, archdeacon of Cardigan, 23 July 1887, LPL, Benson 171/115.
[25] 'The Tithe Crisis', *Cheshire Observer*, 30 Oct. 1886; 'The Clergy Defence Association's Manifesto', *Wrexham Advertiser*, 25 Feb. 1888.
[26] 'Progress of the Tithe War in Wales', *Cheshire Observer*, 21 Jan. 1888.

life as a 'church militant'.[27] 'Bear yourself like men,' he urged those assembled at Lampeter, in order to oppose the 'immorality', 'robbery' and 'persecution' posed by the 'tithe war'.[28] Selborne's son, William Palmer, Viscount Wolmer, elected in 1886 as a Liberal Unionist MP, also became a prominent advocate of Church defence, speaking out against any 'frightful degradation' of the role of tithe in the 'service of religion'.[29] Son-in-law of Lord Salisbury, he would later become a leading church strategist during the 'tithe war' of the 1930s.

Another man who became a link between the conflict of the 1880s and that of the 1930s was E. W. I. Peterson, whom we met during the extraordinary tithe war (Chapter 2). In early 1887, Peterson's activities in Biddenden – where he 'collected nearly all the outstanding tithes for his father' – prompted a Liberal MP to ask a question in parliament about the 'active assistance' provided to him by the police.[30] Later that year, Peterson was appointed agent for the Clergy Defence Association and began a series of forays into Wales, often teaming up with Charles Stevens, agent for the Ecclesiastical Commissioners. Peterson's modus operandi was to arrive in a district accompanied by a horse-drawn trap carrying eight 'emergency men'. Labelled 'bum bailiffs' by the anti-tithe movement, many emergency men were veterans of landlords' resistance to the campaign for land reform and tenant rights waged by the National Land League in Ireland. In parliament, Tom Ellis, the radical Liberal MP for Merionethshire, denounced their heavy-handed methods, including their use of 'staves unmercifully upon women, boys, and old men'.[31]

During December 1887 and January 1888, Peterson toured the region surrounding Hollywell (Flintshire) accompanied by a 'large force of police' and 'a detachment of Hussars', sometimes also with a magistrate in tow to read the Riot Act if necessary. In February, he made attempts to serve distraint orders on farmers in Anglesey. Confronted by 'a large crowd of men armed with heavy cudgels', he was 'compelled to abandon his work', but returned along with thirty-five police officers, including the chief constable. In March and April, he was back in the Vale of Clwyd, visiting farms around Llanynys, Llandyrnog and Llangwyfan. There was embarrassment when the driver of the trap carrying emergency men lost control of his horse when confronting a demonstration near Ruthin. A court heard that he had been 'very drunk'. Peterson moved on to

[27] David Steele, 'Palmer, Roundell, first earl of Selborne (1812–1895)', *ODNB* (2004).
[28] 'Lord Selborne on the Church in Wales', *The Times*, 29 Oct. 1887.
[29] 'House of Commons', *Evening Standard*, 1 May 1894.
[30] HC Deb., *Hansard*, 18 Feb. 1887.
[31] HC Deb., *Hansard*, 7 June 1888.

Montgomeryshire, including Meifod and Manafon, and concluded his activities in January 1891 in North Pembrokeshire.[32]

In 1890, Peterson took a break from his Welsh campaign to launch the Tithe Rent-Charge Owners' Union, which held its first conference in London in October. Other founding members included Henry Miers (chairman), a landowner from Clydach (Glamorgan), Rev. Henry Hayman (honorary secretary), who was a former headmaster of Rugby School, and several clergymen from Wales, Kent and Essex. The union's announced aim was 'to protect the interests of tithe rent-charge owners, to form a centre where information […] can be readily obtained […], to watch all attempts at legislation [and] to assist in cases where owing to agitation, or other reasons, payment of tithe rent-charge is refused.' It would create 'a powerful machinery that would come down on [the agitators] with the force of a Nasmyth hammer'. Five hundred members were recruited in the first few weeks and groups were established in Oxfordshire, Hampshire, Kent, Hertfordshire, Cumberland, Norfolk and Sussex.[33] The founding meeting of a group in Monkton (Pembrokeshire) was attended by about a dozen clergy. One participant (Rev. T. Walters) reported that he had received no tithes in Llangollen parish for four and a half years and now 'hoped that someone like Mr Peterson would come forward and help the clergy'.[34] Peterson remained the organisation's main animator for over fifty years. In 1932, he would write to the archbishop of Canterbury, promising to 'do all in [his] power […] to counter the activities of the tithepayers' organisations'.[35]

The Fair Tithe Association

Though it recruited members in Wales, the Tithe Rent-Charge Owners' Union was primarily a response to the activities of the tithepayers' movement in England. After the 1886 general election, tithepayers in

---

[32] 'The Tithe War in Flintshire', *Wrexham Advertiser*, 14 Jan. 1888; 'Progress of the Tithe in Wales', *Cheshire Observer*, 21 Jan. 1888; 'The Tithe War', *Cardiff Times*, 3 Mar. 1888; 'The Tithe Dispute', *Wrexham Advertiser*, 17 Mar. 1888; 'The Anti-Tithe Agitation', *Wrexham Advertiser*, 19 May 1888; 'The Tithe Agitation Campaign in North Pembrokeshire', *South Wales Daily News*, 29 Jan. 1891.

[33] Tithe Rent-Charge Owners' Union, 'Report of the Council and List of Members, 1890–91', LPL, Benson 101/282; W. H. Squire and E. W. I. Peterson, *Tithe Rentcharge Recovery Bill, 1890, with notes and criticisms* (London: Chant & Griffith, 1891).

[34] Rev. W. Thomas Whitland, *The Anti-Tithe Movement in Wales: Its Justice, Morality, and Legality* (Llanelly: South Wales Press, 1891), 84.

[35] The union changed its name, firstly, to the Church Property Defence Association and Tithe Owners' Union and, later, to the Churchmen's Defence Union. E. W. I. Peterson to archbishop of Canterbury, 1 Apr. 1932, LPL, Lang 71.

Essex were amongst the first to organise. In a now familiar scenario, a group of farmers pledged to withhold payment of tithe unless substantial reductions were offered. Titheowners refused to make concessions and, in January 1887, the rector of High Laver ordered the distraint of a haystack belonging to one of his parishioners. A few weeks later, bailiffs acting for a lay titheowner, Guy's Hospital, distrained and auctioned three bullocks on a farm at Great Bardfield. The sales acted as a catalyst for the launch of the Essex Tithe Reform Association.[36] Further distraint auctions would take place during 1888 and 1889, including another at High Laver, at Toppesfield and on Canvey Island, where three animals were sold 'to a stranger from London'. In all cases, the rectors refused farmers' demands for a 10 per cent reduction in tithe.[37]

The Essex campaign linked up with the Fair Tithe Association, which was also founded in 1887. The association acted as an umbrella for several campaigns. One branch, covering Bedfordshire and Buckinghamshire, was based at Leighton Buzzard, scene of two distraint sales in 1887.[38] Another was organised from Reading, calling itself the Berks, Oxon, Wilts and Surrey Fair Tithe Association. In March, it organised 'a great demonstration of tithepayers' in Reading Town Hall, after which farmers from eight counties travelled to London to lobby the government.[39] The Fair Tithe Association also coordinated a well-publicised campaign in the region surrounding Andover (Hampshire), where a significant proportion of the tithe was collected by Winchester College.

In parliament, Lord Salisbury drew a link between the activities of the Welsh and English tithepayers' campaigns, viewing both as a challenge to the Church and property rights.[40] Yet, while parallels can be drawn, the characteristics of the two campaigns were markedly different. In Wales, nationalist sentiments and demands for tenants' rights energised the movement, which remained associated with Liberalism and the demand that tithe should become 'a national property'. While a radical element existed, the tithepayers' movement in England was driven primarily by demands from farmers and a section of landowners to alleviate 'the burden on Agriculture', against the background of falling prices and rents. Politically, the English movement was more heterogeneous. Whereas during the early years of the 1880s campaigns for tithe reform

---

[36] 'The Tithe Question', *ChCh*, 14 Jan. 1887; 'The Tithe Agitation in Essex', *ChCh*, 11 Feb. 1887; 'Tithe Reform Meeting at Saffron Walden', *ChCh*, 4 Nov. 1887; Patricia Lynch, *The Liberal Party in Rural England: Radicalism and Community* (Oxford: Oxford University Press, 2003), 144.

[37] 'Another Distraint Sale at High Laver', *ChCh*, 8 June 1888; 'Tithe Distraint at Toppersfield', *ChCh*, 25 Jan. 1889; 'Tithe Distraint on Canvey Island', *Essex Newsman*, 29 Oct. 1889.

[38] 'Hockcliffe: Tithe Distraint Sale', *Leighton Buzzard Observer*, 20 Dec. 1887.

[39] 'The Tithe Movement Vindicated', *Newbury Weekly News*, 17 Mar. 1887.

[40] HL Deb., *Hansard*, 25 Mar. 1887.

had been linked with Liberalism, in the second half of the decade they received support from a coalition made up of Liberals, political nonconformists and radicals, but also a considerable number of Liberal Unionists and Conservatives.

The politics of the tithepayers' movement tended to reflect the varying social structure of English rural societies. In the highly tithed arable farming regions of East Anglia and other parts of southern England, a 'complex web' of 'authority relationships' produced a hierarchy of farmers, in which the most affluent acted as tribunes for the wider farming community. This paternalistic system could also encourage agricultural labourers to identify with the demands of their employers.[41] It would – during the tithe war of the 1930s – provide the basis for the agrarian colouration of the movement (discussed in Chapter 7). The big farmers, often Conservatives and Liberal Unionists, at the head of tithepayers' campaigns emphasised the need for legislation to 'revise' the way tithe was calculated, for tithe to become more 'equitable' and less of a 'discouragement to agricultural improvement'.[42]

In some parts of rural England, the movement retained a more radical identity. In Devon, farming was dominated by small- and medium-sized holdings, without a distinct class of large-scale capitalist farmers. Rather than paternalism, communities were bound by kinship ties, local identities and a collectivist anti-establishment tradition, which was reflected through support for Liberalism and nonconformism.[43] This helped to condition the make-up of the tithepayers' movement. At a distraint sale in Hemyock, near Tiverton (Devon), farmers described the local campaign as an alliance against 'a cold-blooded haughty priest'.[44] Radicalism also maintained a hold on the tithepayers' campaign in the open villages on the Kent and Sussex Weald. Campaigners spoke at market-day meetings to advocate that tithes – as national property – should 'go to maintain the sick and the poor and to keep up the public roads', rather than to the Church.[45] In Kent, Albert Bath remained the campaign's recognised leader. He also became an omnipresent figure at distraint sales and tithepayers' meetings throughout southern England, sometimes inspiring scenes reminiscent of events on his Halstead farm several years earlier. In July 1890, he led '100 anti-tithe men' at an auction on the Royal Arsenal Cooperative Society's farm in Abbey Wood, during

---

[41] Howard Newby, Colin Bell, David Rose, Peter Saunders, *Property, Paternalism and Power: Class and Control in Rural England* (London: Hutchinson, 1978).
[42] TQA, 'Extent of Re-Adjustment Required' (1890), LPL, Benson 171/299.
[43] Flynn et al., 'The Political Power of Farmers', 25–6.
[44] 'Distraint for Tithes at Hemyock', *WMN*, 19 Oct. 1887.
[45] 'The Tithe Agitation', *SEG*, 17 Jan. 1887.

which 'the auctioneer's hat was knocked off several times by potatoes being hurled at him'.[46]

The political diversity of the movement can be illustrated through a brief examination of the most prominent tithepayers' associations. The patron of the Essex Tithe Reform Association was Herbert Gardner, Liberal MP for Saffron Walden. During the 1885 general election campaign his Conservative opponent, Charles Strutt, had vigorously defended tithe as 'the property of the clergy', prompting heckling and shouts of 'take the tithe off' at his meetings. In contrast, Gardner's audiences erupted in 'loud cheers' and 'waving of hats' on hearing his promises of support for tithe reform and disestablishment of the Church.[47] Despite Gardner's patronage, the Tithe Reform Association distanced itself from such radicalism, stressing it 'did not want to pull down the Church' and pledging to work for tithe reform in 'a constitutional and legal manner'.[48] The association's leadership were large-scale farmers – the most prominent of them Liberal Unionists, one having recently left the Conservative Party. Soon the association secured the support of the two Conservative MPs representing Essex constituencies, Charles Gray (Maldon) and Frederic Carne Rasch (South-East Essex). In the county, tithe reform went from being an issue that helped to define Liberal and Conservative identities to becoming one that unified local representatives across the political spectrum.

As its name implies, the Fair Tithe Association did not object to tithe on principle, but sought legislation to reduce the charge to a 'just' level.[49] The association's main animator was George Baylis, a man who became celebrated in the late nineteenth century for making use of advanced agricultural techniques and fertilisers to buck the agricultural depression and managing to expand his business throughout Berkshire and Hampshire. A committed Conservative, chairman of his local association in Boxford (Berkshire), he later became known as 'one of the largest farmers in England'.[50]

In May 1887, Baylis coordinated a riposte to the distraint and auction of three ricks of hay on the land of a prominent member of the Fair Tithe Association in Shinfield (Berkshire), near Reading. Ordered by the dean and chapter of Hereford Cathedral, the sale took place at extremely short notice and while most local farmers were attending the cattle market. Baylis engaged in a public spat with Hereford Cathedral over the legality of the process. As if highlighting the problem posed by tithe for the

[46] 'Tithe Distraint at Woolwich', *Leominster News*, 25 July 1890.
[47] Lynch, *The Liberal Party*, 40–1.
[48] 'The Essex Tithe Reform Association', *Essex County Chronicle*, 22 Apr. 1887.
[49] 'The Tithe Question', *Leighton Buzzard Observer*, 12 Apr. 1887.
[50] Roy Brigden, 'George Baylis (1846–1936)', *ODNB* (2014); 'Boxford', *Berkshire Chronicle*, 31 Aug. 1886.

Church and Conservatives, the tithepayer in question was Rev. Bernard Body, a Church of England clergyman – and certainly no radical parson. Born into a prominent landowning family, Body was a regular attendee at functions organised by the Conservative Party and active in the Primrose League, the ostensibly independent organisation which acted as a bridge for the Tories into rural communities.[51]

The two wings of the tithepayers' movement – the conservative and radical – were both present during activities organised by the Fair Tithe Association in the Andover region. The campaign began when 200 farmers signed a pledge not to pay 'any more tithes, except on the condition that 25 per cent be deducted from the same' – a demand promptly rejected by Winchester College. In May 1887, the school carried out a distraint of cattle and crops on a farm operated by the campaign's most prominent figure, Alfred Butterworth. A Liberal Unionist, Butterworth was not only a large-scale farmer, operating four farms in Hampshire, but also a major Lancashire cotton manufacturer.[52] The auction in Hatherden attracted 'hundreds of men and women', many of whom were local agricultural labourers. They chanted 'tirades against the system of tithe' and sang 'snatches of political songs'. On the platform, alongside Butterworth, were George Baylis and the ubiquitous Albert Bath. Butterworth urged the crowd to 'obey the law and allow the sale to go on', an appeal which, according to a local journalist, prompted 'loud cries of no and uproar'. The auctioneer's efforts were 'of no avail, for the beating of broken tins by women, kettledrums by men, and the shouts of hundreds made up a din in which it was impossible for anyone to make himself heard'. Twenty men surrounded the wagon and 'pushed it off at a considerable speed down the field, amidst the shouts and groans of the crowd, the auctioneer being pelted with rotten eggs'.[53] Eventually, the sale was abandoned.

In the summer of 1889, a similar event took place thirty miles away in Warnford (Hampshire). Here, anti-tithe agitation was led by William Woods, a 'gentleman farmer' who had inherited his family's extensive estates, as well textile factories and coal mines in Wigan (Lancashire), where his father had been mayor and Liberal MP. Woods was adept at political opportunism. In 1889 he described himself as 'a democratic conservative' – though, soon after Conservative councillors appointed him mayor of Wigan in 1890, he joined the Liberal Party, speaking out in support of an eight-hour day for mine workers. In July 1889, a distraint sale of cattle on Woods' estate attracted 'parishioners and sympathisers from farms, villages and hamlets far and near', including Albert Bath,

[51] HC Deb., *Hansard*, 16 May 1887; 'Reading Primrose League Choir', *Reading Mercury*, 22 May 1897; 'Tithe Distraint Sale near Reading', *Reading Observer*, 7 May 1887.
[52] 'Tithe Agitation in Hampshire', *Salisbury and Winchester Journal*, 12 May 1887.
[53] Ibid., 21 May 1887.

who took 'an active part in the ceremony'. Though farm labourers had made two 'not over handsome effigies' of the rector and his wife, which were duly burnt, the whole event was 'very orderly', with 'bread, cheese and beer freely served to all comers'.[54]

In December 1889, the Fair Tithe Associations merged into a new body, the Tithe Question Association. It appointed representatives in ten counties (Bedfordshire, Berkshire, Buckinghamshire, Devon, Denbighshire, Essex, Herefordshire, Oxfordshire, Shropshire, Surrey) and gained supporters in several others, including Kent, Wiltshire, Lancashire and Sussex.[55] As well as unifying the English tithepayers' movement, the Tithe Question Association provided a link between the campaigns in England and Wales. Influential at the founding conference were George Baylis, who became honorary treasurer, Thomas Bolton, the former Anti-Extraordinary Tithe Association president who had (temporarily) lost his parliamentary seat in 1886, and Albert Bath. Three MPs also played an important role in the association: Robert Jasper More, the Liberal Unionist representing Ludlow (Shropshire), and the two Essex Conservatives Gray and Carne Rasch.[56] The more radical wing of the tithepayers' movement was represented by John Parry, a pioneering figure in the Welsh anti-tithe movement and president of the Welsh Land, Commercial and Labour League, and John Lloyd, who became the Tithe Question Association's chairman and honorary secretary. Son of the radical Brecon landowner of the same name, Lloyd had moved to London to pursue a legal career but soon became a well-known figure in the capital's politics. A member of the London County Council, he led the London Municipal Reform League, a coalition of Liberals, 'progressives' and Fabian socialists, which advocated municipal control of gas and water, improvements in working-class housing and reforms in health provision, poor relief and pensions. Lloyd gained a particular reputation as campaigner against the rapacious behaviour of the capital's landlords and utility companies. He was drawn to the tithepayers' movement by a deep antipathy for big landlords, combined with a rural radicalism internalised during his youth.[57]

The involvement of individuals such as Parry and Lloyd in the Tithe Question Association led some commentators to draw a link between the tithepayers' movement and socialistic arguments for fundamental changes in property relations. An article in *Political Science Quarterly* associated the 'prominence of the tithe question in England and Wales' with the 'general upheaval in relations between the comfortable and hard-pressed classes in society ... [a] social unrest that expresses itself

54 'The Tithe War Carried into Hampshire', *Hampshire Telegraph*, 27 July 1889.
55 Brochures and leaflets issued by the TQA are found in LPL, Benson 171/292–9.
56 'The Tithe Question', *London Daily News*, 12 Dec. 1889.
57 John Davis, 'John Lloyd (1883–1915)', *ODNB* (2006).

in denial of the right of private property'.[58] Yet the keynote speech at the Tithe Question Association's conference in March 1890 was delivered not by a radical but by Lord Brabourne.[59] Previously Liberal MP for Sandwich (Kent), Brabourne (E. H. Knatchbull-Hugessen) had drifted away from Liberalism – mainly on account of its advocacy of mild measures of state intervention and its association with political nonconformism – before taking a seat in 1880 on the Conservative benches in the House of Lords. A landowner with significant investments in the railways, he was an important figure in the Liberty and Property Defence League, a coalition of 'disgruntled Whigs, ultra-Tories and old-fashioned radicals, landlords and [...] commercial and industrial trade groups', all united by hostility to socialism and trade unionism.[60]

The Tithe Question Association's programme reflected the input of those politically close to Brabourne, rather than the influence of Parry or Lloyd. It emphasised that proponents of tithe reform should refute any 'spirit of confiscation of well-founded rights'.[61] It did not argue for tithe to become 'national property' but for a 'readjustment' to take account of the growth of its value in relation to the value of agricultural land. Proposed also was a major scheme of tithe redemption, with government loans at low rates of interest, to allow tithepayers to buy out titheowners. The association's principal aim was to influence government legislation on tithe, which it considered was being 'framed exclusively in interests of tithe-owners and wholly ignoring those of tithepayers'.[62]

Lord Salisbury's 'greatest misfortune'

At the time of the launch of the Tithe Question Association, Lord Salisbury's Conservative government was preparing its fifth attempt to steer a tithe bill through parliament. Shortly after winning the 1886 general election, Salisbury (Robert Gascoyne-Cecil) promised the Church hierarchy that he would introduce changes in law to facilitate the recovery of tithe.[63] He had fought election campaigns in 1885 and 1886 around the slogan 'Church in Danger' and was determined to address the tithe problem 'not only in Wales, but in the East of England [where]

---

58   Robert Brown, Jr. 'Tithes in England and Wales', *Political Science Quarterly*, 7, 2 (1892), 244.
59   'Lord Brabourne on the Tithes Bill', *St James's Gazette*, 27 Mar. 1890.
60   Edward Bristow, 'The Liberty and Property Defence League and Individualism', *The Historical Journal*, 18, 4 (1975), 761.
61   TQA, 'The Tithe-Owner's Position Examined' (n.d. 1890), LPL, Benson 171/293.
62   TQA, 'Extent of Re-Adjustment Required' (1890), LPL, Benson 171/299; 'The Tithe Question', *Morning Post*, 13 Mar. 1890.
63   Andrew Roberts, *Salisbury: Victorian Titan* (London: Faber & Faber, 2012).

sufferings have been endured by the clergy through their inability to obtain that which is their undoubted due'.[64]

Yet tithe became a major headache for Salisbury and his ministers. The first bill, introduced on 25 March 1887, was withdrawn in August after concessions to the Church fuelled opposition from landowners and farmers, including the agricultural lobby on the government benches in the House of Commons. In 1888, two new bills ran into similar difficulties. The withdrawal of a fourth bill in the summer of 1889 prompted accusations of government 'blundering' and 'cowardice'. The fifth bill was, as senior ministers privately admitted, particularly ill-thought out and was withdrawn in July 1890.[65]

The challenge posed by tithe for Salisbury's government was underpinned by deep-rooted processes. The Conservative Party was, during the 1880s and 1890s, a party in transition. Demographic shifts in population from country to town, the growing social and political weight of the urban elites and corresponding decline in that of the aristocracy, the need to secure an electoral base in the towns, particularly amongst the urban middle classes and the challenge posed by the rise of the labour movement and 'collectivist ideologies' all drove changes in the party's identity. Conservatives sought to appeal to a propertyless mass electorate by 'seizing the language of patriotism and Empire', a strategy deployed with considerable success in 1886 in relation to Irish Home Rule. Traditionally the political voice of the landlord class, the Conservative Party redefined itself as 'less the party of the land and more the party of property in general'.[66]

This transition in identity placed the farmer, rather than landlord, at the centre of Conservative rural policy. Salisbury and other leaders still viewed the aristocracy's role as essential for political and social stability, lauding its 'sensitivities' without which the Conservative Party would 'speedily fall to pieces'.[67] Yet mainstream Conservatism now also embraced the aim of creating a numerous class of owner-occupying farmers.[68] The policy was encouraged by the parliamentary alliance with the Liberal Unionists, whose MPs included Joseph Chamberlain and Jesse Collings (see pp. 33–4). Yet most Conservative leaders required little convincing. Politically, an extension of land ownership could help to resecure the party's rural base – the fragility of which had been illustrated by Liberal successes in 1880 and 1885. More fundamentally, it would, as Salisbury put it, 'constitute the strongest bulwark against revolutionary change and [afford] the strongest support for the Conservative feeling

[64] HL Deb., *Hansard*, 25 Mar. 1887.
[65] Note to Cabinet by Hicks Beach, 9 Aug. 1890, TNA, CAB 37/28/45.
[66] Green, *Crisis of Conservatism*, 78–199.
[67] Steele, *Lord Salisbury*, 209.
[68] Readman, *Land and Nation*, 161–80.

and institutions of the country'.[69] Economically, more owner-occupying farmers would revitalise agriculture, make Britain more self-sufficient in food production and halt the rural exodus. The outlook was also influenced by eugenicist ideology: strengthening rural property ownership would reverse 'the deterioration of the race', protect 'racial health' and strengthen the nation's 'moral fibre', combatting 'decadence' and 'decay' stemming from urban society. For Conservatives, the attributes of the 'sturdy yeoman' – the owner-occupier of high status – became the epitome of Englishness.[70]

Yet, as Ewen Green outlines, the Conservatives' transition to become the party of 'property in general' was not without difficulties. Finding a balance between the interests of industry, commerce, farming and land ownership meant that 'the relationship between Conservativism and Britain's various propertied elites was in a constant state of negotiation'.[71] Tensions opened on several fronts. Representatives of the landlord class complained that the party had abandoned defence of its interests and status, which they imagined to be under siege. During the 1880s, a significant number of landowners – faced with falling rents – sold off sections of their estates, strengthening in consequence the class of 'yeoman farmers'.[72] Many tenant farmers returned to the Conservative fold in 1886 (with a resulting decline of the Farmers' Alliance), but their relationship with the party was an uncomfortable one. Conservative parliamentarians in the party's 'Agricultural Committee' often reflected the pressure of this more 'militant and independent' constituency.[73] Representatives of the urban elites resented the hold by aristocratic grandees on the party's upper echelons, a problem accentuated by Salisbury's leadership from the House of Lords and his reluctance to promote bourgeois Tories sitting in the Commons. The party's ties with the Church of England also raised questions. A man for whom religion was 'a sheet anchor of his personality', Salisbury's link with the Church Defence Institution acted to reassure traditional Conservatives.[74] Yet many in the party pointed to the obstacles created by a close identification with Anglicanism when engaging with a mass electorate increasingly influenced by secular practices and ideas.[75] Some senior clerics also expressed concern. The archbishop of Canterbury saw risks for the Church's influence if it were to remain too associated politically with the Conservatives, commenting

---

[69] Salisbury in *The Times*, 3 Feb 1892, cited in Readman, *Land and Nation*, 52.
[70] Readman, *Land and Nation*, 161–80.
[71] Green, *Crisis of Conservatism*, 117.
[72] Newby et al., *Property, Paternalism and Power*, 35.
[73] Green, *Crisis of Conservatism*, 89–95 and 95–101.
[74] Paul Smith, 'Robert Arthur Talbot Gascoyne-Cecil, third marquess of Salisbury', *ODNB* (2011).
[75] Green, *Crisis of Conservatism*, 14–16.

that 'it is rather of bad augury that Lord Salisbury has made political Church defence a watchword'.[76]

Tithe brought these tensions to the surface. Henry Farquharson, Conservative MP for West Dorset and owner of a large country estate, described tithe as 'the greatest misfortune that has befallen Lord Salisbury's administration'. Given the other issues on the government's agenda – including the ongoing challenge posed by Irish nationalism and the increasingly complex, and potentially hazardous, diplomatic relations with other European powers – the statement may appear an exaggeration. Yet it possesses a kernel of truth. The government was, explained Farquharson, 'confronted [...] by two important but opposing sections of its own followers, the one [the Church] crying out for greater facilities for collecting the tithe, the other [farmers and landowners] demanding that some relief shall be given to agriculture from the intolerable burden of the tithe'.[77] The defence of what Salisbury called a 'very peculiar property' was not in question, but balancing the interests of the differing groups impacted by tithe proved immensely problematic.[78]

The government's allies – the Liberal Unionists – faced identical pressures. Though the new party included those 'scourges of aristocracy' Chamberlain and Collings, most of its MPs had been part of the 'moderate' Whig section of the Liberal Party. For them, 'unionism' was intrinsically linked to the defence of the property and wealth of the Anglo-Irish landlord class.[79] Some, such as those around the earl of Selborne, were zealous defenders of the vested interests of the Church of England. Chamberlain and his closest supporters absented themselves from the tithe debate, privately expressing the fear that the anti-tithe movement in Wales could follow the same 'perilous' path pursued by land reform campaigners in Ireland.[80] Yet a section of Liberal Unionists was sensitive to arguments from their social base amongst landlords and gentlemen farmers and prepared to voice opposition to measures that would weaken the agricultural interest for the benefit of the titheowners.

Tensions also existed within the Liberal Party. Liberals opposed all of the Salisbury government's tithe bills, arguing that each was designed to serve the interests of the Church and big landowners. It was a position consistent with the view that tithe should be treated as 'national property' rather than the 'sacred property of the church'. Yet while William Harcourt, effectively the deputy leader, associated the party with the demands of the Welsh anti-tithe campaigners, Gladstone had

[76] Benson's diary, 27 Nov. 1885, cited in Norman, *Church and Society*, 188.
[77] Henry R. Farquharson, 'The Case for the Tithe-Payer', *The National Review*, 15, 18 (1890), 545.
[78] Tithe Rentcharge Bill, HL Deb., *Hansard*, 23 Mar. 1888.
[79] Green, *Crisis of Conservatism*, 79–88.
[80] Morgan, *Wales in British Politics*, 87.

more 'ambivalent emotions'. His conspicuous silence during the entire controversy arose from a fear that the anti-tithe movement threatened to 'menace the structure of society'.[81] The argument that tithe should be classified as 'national property' led some in the party to oppose concessions to tithepayers. Reductions in tithe, it was argued, would undermine the value of a resource that should be redeployed 'to secular purposes' in the interests of the wider community. More mainstream Liberals argued that 'a national right' does not justify 'an individual wrong', pointing out that 'during bad times' Crown lands (another type of national property) offered rent reductions to tenants.[82]

Political impasse

The parliamentary impasse over tithe during these years is reminiscent of the pattern of events in the period leading up to the Tithe Commutation Act of 1836. Each of the Salisbury government's five unsuccessful bills had the same essential aim: to 'modernise' methods of tithe collection, thus relieving the Church of the unpleasant duty of having to collect the charge directly from farmers. The first bill had two main components. It sought to fix liability for tithe on to landowners by closing a loophole in the 1836 Act that allowed landlords to write responsibility for tithe payments into tenancy agreements. Under the new legislation, landlords would have to collect tithe from tenants as part of the rent and, in the event of non-payment, recover it as any other 'simple debt'. Secondly, the bill stipulated that the recovery of tithe arrears should be pursued through the county courts. This would replace the 'painful machinery' of distraint, which had, in Salisbury's words, created 'an almost impassable barrier between the pastor and many of his flock' and also encouraged 'the romantism of revolt'.[83] Landowners were offered three sweeteners in compensation. They would receive a 5 per cent discount in tithe, in recognition of the 'risk' and extra expense associated with collecting the charge from tenants. Secondly, they could apply to the county court to have the amount of tithe 'readjusted', if it were higher than the total value of rent collected on the land. Finally, they would be offered more favourable terms for 'tithe redemption', reducing the amount to be paid to the titheowner from twenty-five years of par value to twenty years – a 'fair-rate', argued Salisbury, given the prevailing economic conditions.[84]

The bill's proponents were initially confident of success. It received support from the benches on both sides in the House of Lords, where it was introduced, and had a relatively painless passage through its

---

[81] *The Times*, 29 Mar. 1890, 11; Morgan, *Wales in British Politics*, 88.
[82] F. S. Stevenson, HC Deb., *Hansard*, 5 June 1890.
[83] HL Deb., *Hansard*, 25 Mar. 1887.
[84] Ibid.

early stages.[85] Yet, trouble soon reared its head. Perhaps surprisingly, the first complaints arose from within the Church. The hierarchy and its political 'friends' applauded the government's approach: 'every effort must be made to pass [the bill] without delay', urged the Church Defence Institution.[86] Yet, simultaneously, senior Church figures lobbied Salisbury to drop the three concessions to landowners. The archbishop of Canterbury told the prime minister of the 'constant letters' that arrived from clergy, protesting that a 5 per cent reduction in tithe would lead to an 'unmanageable' fall in incomes. A group of lay leaders weighed in to claim that granting county courts powers to readjust the level of tithe was an infringement of titheowners' 'inalienable rights'. Summarising the Church's arguments, an anonymous 'Ecclesiastical Official' wrote to *The Times* to claim the bill was 'destroying about a million and a half [pounds] of income to the Church'.[87] The sustained pressure convinced the prime minister to withdraw the offending sweeteners.[88]

The concessions to the Church now galvanised opposition to the bill. The aristocracy represented in the House of Lords had been prepared to accept its provisions, partly because many of their class were titheowners as well as landowners. But many more modest landlords felt betrayed by their traditional party. Some remonstrated that the legislation would turn them into unpaid tithe agents, acquiring a share of the odium associated with the charge. A 'Conservative small landowner' from Berkshire wrote: 'If Lord Salisbury presses this question, it will probably break up his majority, and certainly weaken the party throughout the country, for many small landlords, who are good Conservatives, could not stand having the tithes put upon them.'[89]

Owner-occupying farmers were particularly hostile. Those framing the bill had largely overlooked their situation, despite the increased status of the yeoman farmer within the Conservative discourse. By making tithe a personal debt, rather than a charge linked to a piece of land, owner-occupiers with tithe arrears faced more severe enforcement measures, including the possibility of imprisonment. Tenant farmers in heavily tithed regions were also outspoken. The government had hoped to win their support on account of the bill's proposal to transfer liability from tenants to landlords – a policy advocated by the Farmers' Alliance, as well as by the Liberal Party in England. Yet tenant farmers in the tithepayers' movement argued that changing 'the hand that received the tithe'

---

[85] Contribution by Earl of Kimberley, HL Deb., *Hansard*, 7 July 1887.
[86] 'Report of meeting of EC of CDI, 26 Apr. (1887)', LPL, Benson 171/75.
[87] Benson to Lord Salisbury, 21 Apr. 1887, LPL, Benson 171/44; 'Committee of Titheowners held at Westminster', 21 Apr. 1887, LPL, Benson 171/43; 'The Tithe Bill', *The Times*, 8 Apr. 1887.
[88] HL Deb., *Hansard*, 23 May 1887.
[89] 'A Conservative Landowner on Tithes', *Newbury Weekly News*, 16 Dec. 1886.

without any 'readjustment' of the charge was an 'inadequate' concession. In Wales, the Anti-Tithe League stressed that 'transferring the burden from one shoulder to another' would mean Welsh farmers still enriching the funds of the Anglican Church.[90]

The bill faced cross-party opposition in the Commons. The Liberal Herbert Gardner described it as a 'titheowners' bill [...] a useless, mischievous and irritating' piece of legislation'.[91] Sir Thomas Grove, Liberal Unionist MP for South Wiltshire and a large-scale 'yeoman farmer', chaired a meeting of 200 tithepayers from eight southern counties at which a resolution 'expressing regret' that ministers had drafted 'a measure which does not recognise the half-ruined state of our agriculture' was unanimously agreed.[92] Members of the Conservative Party's agricultural committee, though tending to be cautious in public statements, expressed concern. The most developed critique from a Conservative was articulated in the House of Lords by Lord Brabourne. The bill would, he argued, not only allow tithe to 'cripple the resources of the greatest industry of the country' but also, by targeting 'the class of small owners' along with tenant farmers, 'would weaken and antagonise the very classes that provided the surest bulwark against collectivist doctrines'. The bill would also be counterproductive in relation to the Church: it would 'aggravate existing evils, alienate some of the best friends of the present Government, and bring us one step nearer to disestablishment'.[93] Yet many Conservatives were furious when the government, blaming a tight parliamentary timetable, withdrew the bill. A group of MPs associated with the Church Defence Institution spoke of the forces of law and order being routed by 'Welsh mobs': without legislation 'a repetition of such disturbances' would take place not only in Wales but also 'nearer home'.[94] The Conservative MP George Kenyon attacked a 'weak-kneed Government, which [had] bowed its knees to a few hon. and right hon. Tory fossils'.[95]

Salisbury returned to the House of Lords on 23 March 1888 to present two new tithe bills, with the promise of a third. By dividing the legislation into three sections, he hoped, according to *The Times*, to salvage some part

---

[90] 'The Essex Tithe Reform Association', *Bury & Norwich Post*, 14 June 1887; 'The Tithe War', *Wrexham Advertiser*, 28 May 1887.
[91] Herbert Gardner, 'The Tithes Question', *The People*, 10 Apr. 1887.
[92] 'Sir Thomas Grove and the Tithe Question', *Salisbury Times & South Wilts Gazette*, 9 Apr. 1887.
[93] HL Deb., *Hansard*, 23 May, 10 June and 7 July 1887; Brabourne, 'The Tithe Rent-Charge Bill', *The Times*, 3 Aug. 1887.
[94] See letter from four MPs, Thomas Salt, John G. Talbot, George T. Kenyon, Stanley Leighton, *The Guardian*, 29 July 1887.
[95] 'Lord Salisbury's Tithe Bill', *Chichester Observer*, 12 Oct. 1887.

of the 'shipwreck of last year'.[96] He attempted to reassure landowners that the revised legislation had been drafted to 'neither injure nor frighten' them. The first bill outlawed the signing of contracts that stipulated tenants would be liable to pay tithe, though existing contracts between landlords and tenants would remain in force until they expired. The second bill abolished the law of distraint and, as with the unsuccessful 1887 legislation, granted powers to county courts to enforce tithe collection. There was, however, an important difference: courts would chase occupiers, rather than landlords, for the debt. Injunctions could be issued to force tenant farmers to pay tithe before settling other demands, including rents. If tithe were not paid, farmers could be pursued by the 'ordinary process of law'. The bill also proposed to change the way in which tithe was calculated from a seven-year to a three-year average of the price of corn, a measure viewed as a concession to tithepayers.[97] The third bill never appeared. Its intention would have been 'to sweeten the draught' by offering more favourable terms for tithe redemption.[98]

The proposed legislation soon hit problems. From the Church, there were objections that linking tithe to the triennial average of corn would 'make a present to the tithepayer'.[99] Owner-occupiers pointed out that county courts would be able to appoint receivers to take possession of and farm their land until tithe debts were discharged. This, they said, made a mockery of the claim that the bill posed 'no practical harm' to landowners. A meeting of the Conservative-dominated Central Chamber of Agriculture concluded that the bill was 'not an adequate settlement of the tithe question'.[100] In early August, the government once again announced a halt to parliamentary debate on tithe.

The chaos surrounding tithe legislation deepened after a fourth bill was presented in June 1889. The aim this time was explicitly to bolster the laws on tithe recovery in order more effectively to resist the movement in Wales. The bill followed sustained lobbying from senior figures within the Church, who complained that the failure of previous bills had 'increased rather than diminished [...] the determination to refuse payment' of tithe.[101] It put wider controversies – limitations to the level of tithe, redemption schemes, liability of landowners to pay and so on – on the back burner. Titheowners would receive increased powers,

[96] 'Parliamentary Intelligence: The Government Tithe Bill', *The Times*, 24 Mar. 1888.
[97] HL Deb., *Hansard*, 23 Mar. 1888.
[98] 'Parliamentary Intelligence', *The Times*, 24 Mar. 1888.
[99] 'The Tithe Amendment Bill', *Norfolk Chronicle*, 19 May 1888.
[100] 'The Tithe Rent-Charge', *Norwich Mercury*, 5 May 1888.
[101] Alfred de Bock, Secretary Ecclesiastical Commissioners, to archbishop of Canterbury, 14 Jan. 1889, LPL, Benson 171/216.

which were targeted specifically on the occupiers (rather than owners) of tithable land. They would be able to sue for arrears in the county court, which could appoint bailiffs to execute recovery against not only agricultural produce but all personal property. If sufficient goods were unavailable, titheowners could be granted temporary possession of the land. The measures were to be 'without prejudice to any other remedy'; in other words, titheowners would retain their existing rights to distrain produce.[102] With some justification, Liberals dubbed the legislation a 'Clergy Relief Bill' and 'a bill to harass tenant farmers'.[103] The government presented the bill as an 'immediate' and 'simple measure [...] in the interests of the public peace and order', hoping that fear of breakdown of the 'proper execution of the law' would secure support from Conservative and Liberal Unionist sceptics.[104]

This was another miscalculation. Opposition from amongst the government's own supporters grew stronger than ever. While often disassociating themselves from the Welsh tithepayers' non-payment campaign, Conservative and Liberal Unionists attacked the bill for ignoring the plight of farmers and addressing only 'the fringe' of the tithe question. Some noted that the measures could also be used against English farmers.[105] Observing the debate, the National Secretary of the Church Defence Institution, Rev. H. G. Dickson, bemoaned the 'considerable hostility' to the bill 'exhibited by members *on both sides* of the House of Commons'.[106] On one vote (an amendment moved by Conservative MP Charles Gray), the government's majority was reduced to four.

With parliamentary time running out, and in an attempt to appease the bill's critics, Richard Webster, the attorney general and a prominent 'churchman', announced a series of government-sponsored amendments designed to provide 'safeguards' for farmers and landowners. Most notably, tithepayers would be granted remission if tithe amounted to more than the net profit derivable from tithable land over a twelve-month period. *The Times* spoke of a 'government surrender [...] made in deference to the pressure brought to bear upon them by Conservative and Liberal Unionist members for constituencies in which the tenant-farmer element was powerful'.[107] Yet, once again, the government's plan unravelled. In a moment of parliamentary drama, the speaker of the House of Commons ruled that the attorney general's amendments were out of order, on the grounds they amounted to legislation at odds with

---

[102] 'The Tithe Bill', *The Times*, 22 June 1889.
[103] HC Deb., *Hansard*, 18 July 1889.
[104] Michael Hicks Beach, President of the Board of Trade, HC Deb., *Hansard*, 18 July 1889.
[105] HC Deb., *Hansard*, 18 July 1889.
[106] H. G. Dickson, 7 Aug. 1889, LPL, Benson 78; his emphasis.
[107] *The Times*, 15 Aug. 1889.

the principles behind the original bill. Ministers had no alternative than to drop another tithe bill.

Conservative and Church opinion chastised the government. The agricultural expert and establishment figure Rowland Prothero (later Lord Ernle) chided ministers' 'half-hearted response' to the 'breakdown of existing law'.[108] During a round of diocesan conferences, nineteen different bishops referred to the tithe conflict and 'in nearly every instance' resolutions were passed 'more or less condemnatory of the dilatory conduct of the Government'.[109] A Central Lay Committee was established by Selborne and other Church Defence Institution personalities to mobilise 'all faithful Church People' and 'lovers of order' to pressure the government to resolve a question that was 'becoming more dangerous the longer it is delayed'.[110]

Yet cracks had opened within the camp of titheowners. The Church hierarchy and most of its 'friends' reluctantly were drawing the conclusion that – while continuing to resist demands from 'Welsh Liberationists' – they should support concessions to 'hard-pressed' farmers and particularly the agricultural lobby in southern and eastern England. The bishop of St Asaph drew a distinction between 'farmers finding it very difficult to pay the tithe' and the 'band of agitators [...] who had seized upon the depression as an opportunity for [...] agitation against the Church and the land'.[111] In an attempt to break the impasse, Selborne's Lay Committee, along with leading clerics, announced that they thought a bill based on the attorney general's amendments would be 'a good basis for legislation'.[112]

Others – including those who would shortly form the Tithe Rent-Charge Owners' Union – were determined to resist such a 'surrender'. Acting as their principal spokesman was the third Earl Grey, Henry George Grey, who was, as he put it, 'the last survivor of those who took an active part in framing the [1836 Tithe] Act'. In an extraordinary twenty-three-page essay, Grey attacked ministers for not using the 'whole civil and military force of the kingdom' against the 'unchristian' activities of Welsh 'agitators' who were endeavouring 'by combination and violence to prevent the execution of legal process for the recovery of money due from them' – vocabulary recalling that utilised to justify the 'pacification' of indigenous peoples during Grey's days as colonial secretary. Grey

[108] R. E. Prothero, *The Anti-Tithe Agitation in Wales* (London: The Guardian, 1889).
[109] 'The Government and the Welsh Church', *Pall Mall Gazette*, 6 Nov. 1889.
[110] John G. Talbot, 'The Lessons from the Loss of the Tithe Rent-Charge Bill', *The National Church*, Sept. 1889.
[111] 'The Bishop of St Asaph and the Tithes Question', *London Daily News*, 19 Sept. 1889.
[112] Selborne et al., 'The Present Position of the Tithe Question', *The Times*, 4 Dec. 1889.

said that the attorney general's amendments, particularly the clause granting some remission of tithe, would lead to 'incalculable evil'. They represented the same 'disregard for justice and the rights of property' as Gladstone's concessions to Irish nationalism, particularly the land bills, which had 'deprived [landlords] of a large part of the value of their estate'. Grey was shocked by the statement urging a compromise issued by Lord Selborne's committee of lay churchmen, whose signatures included Viscount Cranborne, the prime minister's eldest son and 'confidante on party and government business'.[113]

The government's fifth tithe bill was introduced at the end of February 1890 by Sir Michael Hicks Beach, president of the Board of Trade. Given that it was based on the unsuccessful amendments and, given the spirit of compromise emanating from within the Church, many observers expressed optimism over its chances of success.[114] A petition in support of the bill was signed by over 1,400 clergy, thirty-six bishops, ninety 'cathedral dignitaries' and 120 members of the Universities of Oxford and Cambridge, as well as 'many' parliamentarians and a 'large number of justices of the peace'.[115] Salisbury gave several private and, through his son, public assurances that the legislation would pass.[116] Yet the bill again quickly ran into difficulties. Proposals for the remission of tithe above the 'special rateable value' of land and for a redemption scheme under which tithepayers would make annuity payments over fifty years did not stand up to scrutiny. The bill's provisions for tithe recovery were also poorly conceived. The legislation would make landowners responsible for tithe payments but allow them to recover tithe 'as rent' from tenants. In practice, this meant that landlords would have stronger powers to enforce tithe collection from tenant farmers than those previously possessed by titheowners.[117] Highlighting these issues, a conference of the Tithe Question Association, with a significant group of Welsh Liberal MPs in attendance, pledged to oppose 'a bill of pains and penalties'.[118] In the House of Commons, a motion from Francis Stevenson, Liberal MP for Eye (Suffolk), calling for 'an equitable revision of tithes in accordance with the altered condition of agriculture', was defeated by only forty-three votes, after a section of Conservative and Liberal Unionist MPs failed to support

---

[113] Grey, 'The Government and the Tithes', originally published in *The Nineteenth Century*, Jan. 1890, LPL, Benson 171/239–48; Philip Williamson, 'Cecil, James Edward – fourth marquess of Salisbury 1861–1947', *ODNB* (2014).
[114] Church Defence Institution, 'The New Tithe Bill: A Short Summary of its Provisions with the Text of the Bill' (1890), LPL, Benson 171/223–37.
[115] 'The Tithes Bill', *The Times*, 18 Mar. 1890.
[116] 'The Tithe Bill will be Passed', *Western Mail*, 4 June 1890; 'The Tithe Bill', *The Times*, 8 July 1890.
[117] Note to Cabinet by Hicks Beach, 9 Aug. 1890, TNA, CAB 37/28/45.
[118] 'The Tithes Bill', *The Times*, 27 Mar. 1890.

the government.[119] On 14 July, the government withdrew the bill to cheers from the Liberal benches.[120] Hicks Beach told the Cabinet that the vote on Stevenson's motion had shown 'the strength of the desire that some relief should be given to the tithepayer among our supporters in the House of Commons'. He was 'convinced that, without some substantial concession to it, no Tithe Recovery Bill c[ould] become law'.[121]

The 1891 Tithe Act

Before presenting the eventually successful sixth tithe bill in November 1890, Hicks Beach met with potential critics on the Conservative benches and engaged in 'close communication' with Church leaders, including the archbishop of Canterbury.[122] By now, both the government and Church hierarchy were united on the need for some accommodation with the farming lobby in order to see the back of the tithe controversy. Government business managers were instructed to allocate adequate parliamentary time to ensure the legislation's passage.

The bill had three main sections. The first placed liability for tithe on landowners but – in a concession to tenant farmers – did not include the powers in the previous bill for landlords to recover tithe as rent. The second placed the county court at the centre of the recovery system. After three months of arrears, a titheowner could apply for an order against a tithepayer and, to recover the tithe, the court would execute the order using powers of distraint provided by the 1836 Act. In other words, tithe would remain a charge linked to a piece of land, rather than a personal debt. Though the titheowners' lobby secured an amendment allowing the court to take temporary possession of the land when sufficient distrainable goods could not be found, commentators noted that Salisbury and the Church had failed in their declared aim of abolishing the distraint system. This 'painful machinery' would continue, though now managed by bailiffs and auctioneers appointed by the county court rather than by the agents of titheowners.

The third section (Clause 8) was perhaps the most significant. Recognising hardship 'due to the temporary depression of agriculture', it allowed tithepayers to apply to the county court for remission if tithe exceeded two-thirds of the net annual value of the land (as assessed for income tax purposes). Hicks Beach told the cabinet that this was a 'much simpler' measure than his previous 'special rateable value' proposal. He reassured ministers that the reduction 'would only apply

---

[119] HC Deb., *Hansard*, 5 June 1890.
[120] *Morning Post*, 15 July 1890, 2.
[121] Note to Cabinet by Hicks Beach, 9 Aug. 1890, TNA, CAB 37/28/45.
[122] Benson to Grey, 26 Dec. 1890, LPL, Benson 171/270.

in comparatively few cases', which certainly proved to be the case.[123] The clause's significance, however, was not its effectiveness but its recognition that there were circumstances in which tithe was 'excessive'. In other words, it implied that the right of titheowners to the 'full fruits' of their property was not absolute. The government made a further proposal in order to soften potential opposition. After a formal request by forty-seven Conservative MPs, along with some Liberal Unionists and Liberals, ministers agreed to establish a Royal Commission to examine issues relating to tithe redemption.[124] They also signalled that, in the near future, the government might be prepared to subsidise a redemption scheme.[125] The concessions were sufficient to appease the agricultural lobby on the government benches. An erstwhile Conservative critic, Charles Gray, praised the bill's 'spirit of compromise'. He was speaking against an amendment drafted by the Tithe Question Association – moved by Herbert Gardner – which would have postponed legislation until after an inquiry into the workings of the 1836 Act. Other Conservatives from southern and eastern England stressed that, while they 'did not care very much for some parts of the bill', they hoped it would 'effect a necessary settlement'.[126]

Much of the opposition from the Liberal benches was lukewarm. William Harcourt, the party's main spokesperson, intervened on numerous occasions, but 'his manner was subdued and unprovocative', and, according to his biographer, he 'must have been relieved when the bill finally reached the Statute Book'.[127] Gladstone, who stayed out of the debate, had offered ministers drafting the bill a 'friendly hint' about how to make improvements in the recovery system.[128] Most Welsh Liberals remained hostile, pointing to the bill's failure to address the Welsh people's objection to 'a tax' that funded the Anglican Church. David Randell, MP for Gower, complained that the Welsh had been 'deserted […] by the leaders of the Liberal Party'.[129] Yet Samuel Evans, MP for Mid-Glamorganshire, mused privately that 'the bill is a good one and will suit us admirably'.[130]

Some Liberals criticised the bill on the basis that the proposals for tithe remission threatened to 'whittle away' the value of 'national property'. The former champion of extraordinary tithepayers, Thomas Bolton,

[123] Note to Cabinet by Hicks Beach, 9 Aug. 1890, TNA, CAB 37/28/45.
[124] Hicks Beach, HC Deb., *Hansard*, 1 Dec. 1890.
[125] Note to Cabinet by Hicks Beach, 9 Aug. 1890, TNA, CAB 37/28/45.
[126] HC Deb., *Hansard*, 1 Dec. 1890. See speeches by Charles Gray, Walter Barttelot (West Sussex), W. J. Beadel (Chelmsford, Essex).
[127] Patrick Jackson, *Harcourt and Son: A Political Biography of Sir William Harcourt, 1827–1904* (Madison, NJ: Fairleigh Dickinson University Press, 2004), 198.
[128] Note to Cabinet by Hicks Beach, 9 Aug. 1890, TNA, CAB 37/28/45.
[129] HC Deb., *Hansard*, 1 Dec. 1890.
[130] Samuel Evans, cited in Morgan, *Wales in British Politics*, 89.

moved an amendment to allow titheowners to pursue all tithepayers in a parish collectively in a single application to the county court, arguing that this would ensure less 'uncollected' tithe being 'frittered away'. Fellow Liberals ridiculed him. Harcourt likened Bolton to 'the Roman Emperor who expressed a wish that his people had only one neck in order that he might cut off all their heads with one blow'.[131] Another Liberal to speak against the bill's remission clause was James Picton, a nonconformist minister and MP for Leicester, who viewed the tithe conflict as a 'landlords' quarrel'. Picton argued that reductions in tithe would be 'putting money into the landlord's pocket' and amount to 'a surrender of the nation's rights'. If landowners claimed that land could not 'bear the burden' of tithe, then their land should, he said, 'be surrendered' to the nation.[132] But, unlike Picton, other Liberals drew a distinction between big landowners and owner-occupying farmers. Herbert Gardner pointed out that in Kent 382 landowners possessed more than 500 acres, while 7,000 farmers owned between 100 and 500 acres. Nationally, 92,000 owner-occupiers farmed an average of thirty-one acres. Gardner warned supporters of the bill, with some prescience, that, while its provisions may have 'relieved the tenant farmers', they had increased 'the burden' on 'small yeoman farmers', who were 'the men you are going to make responsible for payment of tithe'.[133]

Outside parliament, the militant wing of titheowners railed against the bill. In a pamphlet issued by the Tithe Rent-Charge Owners' Union, Peterson described it as a retreat in the face of 'the methods of the agitator, aided by the cupidity of the small landowners and tenant farmers'.[134] A widely circulated article by the rector of North Benfleet (Essex) described clause 3 as 'an insidious piece of piecemeal disendowment'.[135] Lord Grey stepped up his crusade. Lobbying the archbishop of Canterbury, he called on the Church to demand a change in the government's 'course of action' and, in the absence of that occurring, to appeal directly to the head of state. 'Friends of the Church' should, he suggested, move an 'Address to the Crown' in the House of Lords. It should point to 'the great danger to the security of all property and to the peace of the country' caused by the 'systematic resistance' to tithes and 'pray' the queen 'to give orders to her servant [the government] to use all legal means available [...] to enforce strict obedience to the law'.[136] The archbishop's reply indicates his deep frustration with the tithe debate. 'This tithe bill has been to me a matter

[131] HC Deb., *Hansard*, 5 Feb. 1891.
[132] HC Deb., *Hansard*, 1 Dec. 1890.
[133] Ibid.; 'Tithe Question Association', *Saffron Walden Weekly News*, 13 Mar. 1891.
[134] Squire and Peterson, *Tithe Rentcharge Recovery Bill*, 7.
[135] D. J. Davies, Rector of North Benfleet Rectory, 'The 3rd Clause of the Tithe Bill', *Guardian*, 28 Jan. 1891, LPL, Benson 38/191.
[136] Grey to Benson, 'The Tithes Bill (November 1890)', LPL, Benson 171/253.

of great anxiety and constant consideration [and] I am bound to concur generally in the views you express,' he told Grey, barely concealing a sense of betrayal:

> Though the direction you mark out for action would have probably availed much at first, […] the supineness of the Government in the earlier stages of the agitation in Wales, where we trusted the 'friends of the Church', and the failures of the successive attempts at Legislations make [us] feel that it is too late to initiate the action suggested.[137]

For the archbishop and others in the Church hierarchy, the bill possessed serious flaws, but it was the only deal now possible.

The bill received a big parliamentary majority and was granted the Royal Assent on 26 March 1891. The more radical wing of the tithepayers' movement viewed its passing as a serious setback. 'We have been beaten clear,' announced John Lloyd of the Tithe Question Association, with 'several difficulties' contibuting to the defeat. The first was the differences between the movement in Wales – where tithe 'was regarded as one of principle in relation to religion' – and in England, where it was approached 'from a pounds, shillings and pence point of view'. Another was the regional nature of the tithe problem in England, where grievances were largely confined to the southern counties. Thirdly, Lloyd pointed to the lack of political fight from English Liberals, which was in marked contrast to the stance taken by Liberals in Wales. He singled out for particular criticism those Liberals, some of whom – such as Bolton – were associated with the Tithe Question Association, who argued against reductions in tithe for fear of diminishing the value of a national property. Their position had, said Lloyd, exposed the tithepayers' movement to 'cross fires'. While supporters of the Church were 'determined to keep the tithe up to the highest pitch', a considerable section of the Liberal Party was 'equally resolved to prevent any lessening of the tithe' as their 'object was to maintain [it] intact for the nation'.[138] Lloyd concluded that the Tithe Question Association should reconsider its strategy. The association had put its case 'in a plain, intelligible manner' and its action had been of a 'moderate and reasonable character', but 'the majority of both Houses of Parliament [had] simply ridden roughshod over the tithepayers of England and Wales'. Now, Lloyd argued, only 'more aggressive work' could 'obtain a hearing for our claims to justice and fair treatment'.[139]

Titheowners were also considering how to prepare for the next phase in the conflict. Prominent lay members of the Church established a new

---

[137] Benson to Grey, 26 Dec. 1890, LPL, Benson 171/270.
[138] 'The Tithe Question: Interview with Mr John Lloyd J.P.', *South Wales Daily News*, 10 Apr. 1891.
[139] John Lloyd to supporters of TQA, 6 Apr. 1891, LPL, Benson 101. 'The Tithe Question', *South Wales Daily News*, 10 Apr. 1891.

body, the Central Tithe Committee, to 'watch over the working of the new Tithe Act' and 'give advice in cases of special difficulty'. With Selborne as president and Cranborne in the chair, its three dozen members were divided equally between clergy – including six bishops and a former vice-chancellor of the University of Cambridge, Rev. George Philips – and prominent lay representatives, including MPs and peers. Plans were laid to form committees in each diocese to coordinate activity. 'We need hardly say,' the organisers assured the archbishop of Canterbury, 'that we are endeavouring to carry out what is proposed with as little publicity as possible.'[140]

Simultaneously, the Tithe Rent-Charge Owners' Union drew up its own, more belligerent, plans. In May, Peterson told its annual conference, an event attended almost exclusively by clergy, that the passing of the Act would 'encourage people who thought they had some kind of grievance to join their forces and generally harass the titheowners'. But, he urged, if the Union 'kept their enemies all separate, they could deal with them in the way in which the proverbial bundle of sticks was dealt with, viz. – break them up one after the other'.[141] Peterson's strategy to 'break' the tithepayers' movement involved establishing a limited liability company to act on behalf of titheowners. The idea had originally come from Lord Grey, who tried unsuccessfully to convince the archbishop of Canterbury of its worth. The company would, explained Grey, 'resolutely use all the means of enforcing claims', including 'the ordinary legal process for compelling debtors to pay their creditors, or by the criminal law against conspiracy'. It would become 'too powerful to be resisted [by] illegal combinations' of tithepayers. The company would charge a fee for its services and could be expected to make a profit but, suggested Grey, its shareholders would 'probably consider [donating] what they might receive as money [to] Church purposes'.[142] After 1891, the plans for a tithe-collecting company remained on the drawing board. They would be resurrected forty years later, when Church institutions and lay titheowners formulated the proposal to launch General Dealers Ltd.

1891 marks the receding of a decade-long tithe agitation. In Wales some 'disorderly scenes' at distraint sales continued, particularly in Cardiganshire, and journalists wrote occasionally of the 'revival of the Tithe War'. Yet by 1895 the movement had petered out. Its legacy, however, was profound. The movement gave a decisive impetus to the campaign for disestablishment of the Church in Wales – pressure that

[140] 'Central Tithe Committee', 26 May 1891, LPL, Benson 101/276; Granville Dickson & G. H. F. Nye to Benson, 2 July 1891, LPL, Benson 101/279.
[141] Tithe Rent-Charge Owners' Union, 'Report of the Council and List of Members, 1890–91', 9, LPL, Benson 101/286.
[142] Grey to Benson, 'The Tithes Bill (Nov. 1890)', LPL, Benson 171/253.

led eventually to the Welsh Church Act of 1914.[143] Protests over tithe also fizzled out in southern and eastern England. Rather than launching a 'more aggressive' campaign, the Tithe Question Association was wound up, a casualty of the waning movement and internal division. Some commentators put the movement's decline down to the 1891 Tithe Act 'working well'.[144] Certainly, the fact that tenant farmers would no longer be pursued directly for tithe removed much heat from the situation. Yet equally important was the dramatic drop in the level of the charge. Its link to a seven-year average of corn prices meant the value of tithe fell from £107 in 1881 to £76 in 1891, and further to £66 10s in 1901 – an overall decline of 38 per cent.[145]

In the two decades or so before the Great War, tithe made only fleeting appearances on the political agenda. The Royal Commission on Tithe Redemption reported in March 1892. After taking evidence from protagonists on both sides of the 1880s 'tithe war', including George Baylis, Alfred Butterworth and E. W. I. Peterson, it recommended a scheme to encourage tithepayers to buy-out titheowners, including unspecified 'advances of public money'. But the plans remained on the table after the defeat of Lord Salisbury's government in the summer of the same year.[146]

Controversy arose briefly in the summer of 1899, when Salisbury's new administration rushed the Tithe Rent-Charge (Rates) Bill through parliament. The legislation, which followed a campaign over 'clerical poverty' from within the Church, reduced rates paid by clergy on income from tithe by 50 per cent, a concession in line with a rebate on rates on agricultural land introduced by the Agricultural Rates Act of 1896. Some familiar protagonists crossed swords. Peterson lobbied on behalf of clergy, who complained of the impact of falling tithe revenue on their living standards. John Lloyd maintained that titheowners had already been compensated for higher rates when the par value of tithe was calculated at the time of the 1836 Act. In parliament, the Liberal leadership opposed the bill as an attempt to 're-endow the Church of England out of taxpayers' pockets'.[147]

The agitation of the 1880s can be viewed as the first stage of a half-century long tithe war. The 1891 Act, along with significant changes

---

[143] 'The Tithe Agitation in Cardiganshire', *South Wales Daily News*, 15 June 1891; 'Revival of the Tithe War in Wales', *St James's Gazette*, 21 Apr. 1892.
[144] *York Herald*, 9 Apr. 1892.
[145] Lee, 'The Tithe Rentcharge', 312.
[146] *Royal Commission on Redemption of Tithe Rentcharge in England and Wales, Minutes of Evidence* (1892); 'Political Notes', *The Times*, 8 and 9 Mar. 1892, 6 Feb. 1893.
[147] 'The Rating of Tithe Owners', *Morning Post*, 3 Jan. 1899; 'The Clerical Tithes Bill', *Morning Post*, 14 July 1899; HC Deb., *Hansard*, 22 and 27 June 1899.

in agricultural land ownership, would alter the characteristics of the conflict. Owner-occupying farmers would now be in the front line – and they would face not only titheowners but the machinery of the court recovery system. Most significantly, the memory of events would live on in many farming communities. The formation of tithepayers' associations and the idea of 'passive resistance' – non-payment of tithe and mobilisations to disrupt auctions and seizures of distrained goods – all became defining features when the 'war' re-emerged in the inter-war years. The 1891 Act had failed to resolve the fundamental problem: the persistence of a medieval tax that had during the preceding century been abolished in most other European countries.

4

Tithe after the Great War

Canterbury Cathedral's tithe agent

The ceremony in the chapter house at Canterbury Cathedral on 2 December 1911 was conducted according to long-established tradition. Frank Richard Allen appeared before the cathedral's clergy and made, in Latin, a declaration of obedience to the dean. It was a requirement of his promotion to become *Registrarius Sive Clericus Computi* (cathedral registrar), a post bestowing upon him a place in the cathedral's foundation (historic community) and a statutory emolument, along with his usual salary. Born in 1877 into a modest family in Walthamstow – his father was a warehouse worker in the shoe trade and later a commercial clerk – Allen had become the cathedral chapter's head clerk in 1902, previously working as a supervisor in the works department of London County Council.[1] His influence at the cathedral grew steadily. Soon after his promotion in 1911, the illness of the seneschal (the senior lay official) led Allen to take on an extensive portfolio of responsibilities: management of property, collection of rents, maintenance of the precincts, supervision and negotiation of wages and conditions of employees, administration of the chapter's meetings, finances and correspondence. He also collected tithes and, in 1918, became officially the cathedral's tithe agent.

Fast forward to the Great Eastern Hotel in London on 6 January 1925: the same Frank Allen can be found sitting at the top table during the inaugural meeting of the National Tithepayers' Association. Chairing the meeting was Sir Henry Rew, the distinguished agricultural statistician and economist, whose civil service career had included responsibility for coordinating food supplies during the Great War. The meeting appointed Allen as secretary of the new association, an obvious choice given his role in organising the event and drafting the rules and constitution.

Allen would remain at the helm of the NTA throughout the tithe war of the 1930s, developing strategy, coordinating activities, giving legal and practical advice, writing bulletins and articles, speaking on

---

[1] National Census, 1881, 1891, 1901.

public platforms and in debates and negotiating with ministers and titheowners. In her account of the conflict, Doreen Wallace wrote: 'Allen has a legal mind, and is invaluable in directing policy; to the tithepayers, he is almost a legend – allowing the barest minimum of time for food and sleep, he works night and day.'[2] Rev. Roderick Kedward, NTA president, remarked on several occasions that 'every shot I've fired on the [public] platform has been forged by Allen'.[3] Given his background as Canterbury Cathedral's tithe collector, the role of Frank Allen – or, as he was invariably known, F. R. Allen – is one of the more remarkable stories of the tithe war: a classic case of gamekeeper turned poacher.

As the cathedral's tithe agent, Allen collected monies from farmers and other landowners and paid stipends to clergy and income tax and poor rates to the appropriate authorities. His professionalism and efficiency were recognised by his employer. At a special meeting of the chapter in November 1919, the dean, the Very Reverend Henry Wace, expressed the 'high appreciation of the service which Mr Allen had rendered during the year in conducting the work of the Agency'. On New Year's Day 1920, Allen was rewarded with a 25 per cent increase in salary.[4]

At times, the cathedral's tithe agent went to extraordinary lengths to pursue outstanding payments. Facing problems of collection in Minster (Kent), he toured the area to note 'portions of fields [that] appear[ed] to have been cultivated'. He wrote to local farmers asking them 'to kindly let me know the name and address of the owner', warning that 'if I cannot find who he is for certain [...] I shall have to apply to the County Court for notice to be served through you.'[5] Elsewhere, he pursued farmers for arrears owed by previous owners of land even if they had no responsibility for, or knowledge of, the debt. Demanding tithe from a farmer in Tenterden, he wrote that 'the former owner [...] when he sold the land to you [...] knew that the tithe was owing [...] I think you should have enquired at the time whether it had been paid.'[6] Allen's attitude towards farmers in financial difficulty was often curt and unsympathetic. He wrote to one: 'I am sorry your wife is ill [...] But I must say your actions are not such as entitle you to much consideration at the hands of the Dean and Chapter. They allowed you £13 [...] and you rewarded their kindness by refusing to pay anything.'[7] In November 1921, a Hampshire

---

2   Wallace, *The Tithe War*, 89.
3   George Gill to Marjory Allen, Sept. 1933, Modern Records Centre, University of Warwick, LAH, MSS.121/F/3/3/6.
4   Special Meeting of the Chapter, 15 Nov. 1919, Minutes of Meeting, 1 Jan. 1920, CCA, CCA- DCc-CA17.
5   Allen to Mr Dewberry, 28 May 1924, CCA, CCA-DC-LB/53.
6   Allen to Capt. E. Lloyd Hardcastle, 19 Dec. 1923, CCA, CCA- DC-LB/51.
7   Allen to G. Hollands, 25 Jan. 1919, CCA, CCA-DC-LB/41.

farmer wrote to *The Times* complaining of the 'heavy toll of tithe and rates', particularly as many farmers had been 'practically forced to buy their farms [and] thus became liable for tithe'.[8] Allen replied that tithe was set at such a 'low altitude' that it was the titheowner, rather than the tithepayer, who was being 'robbed'.[9]

Yet, whilst carrying out his responsibilities as collector in an assiduous manner, Allen also raised concerns about the functioning of the tithe system. As early as 1911 he wrote to the archbishop of Canterbury, Randall Davidson, warning that the Church's continuing dependence on compulsory tithe would potentially create 'grave injury' to the institution. The archbishop thanked him for expressing his argument 'with singular freshness and force'.[10] On a later occasion, in March 1919, Allen's warnings – delivered in a talk to the Canterbury Farmers' Club – contained a fair dose of prescience:

> I look forward to the year 1929 and thereabouts with some misgiving. […] Should the provisions of this Tithe Act with regard to redemption prove to be not so effective as is expected, and should it happen that in 1928 or 1929 tithe rises above its present level, and should there be at the same time, as may be the case, a depression in agriculture, then there may be serious trouble.[11]

Despite his anxieties about the tithe system, it is unlikely that Allen would have left employment at the cathedral at the end of 1924 without the appointment earlier that year of Rev. Dr George Bell as dean. Relations between the two men were frosty from the outset. An energetic and innovative personality, Bell felt that the scale of Allen's responsibilities was hindering plans to modernise the running of the cathedral. He proposed to divide Allen's post into two: a new appointment would take over the duties relating to the chapter, precincts and cathedral; Allen would remain tithe agent, dealing solely with the administration and collection of tithes, for which he would be rewarded on a commission basis. Allen was not prepared to accept the terms. After twenty-two years of loyal service, and with a young family, he was being asked to relinquish a permanent post for one without a guaranteed income and which could be terminated at short notice. The row became personalised and acrimonious and, though Bell hoped to reach 'a friendly conclusion', Allen accused him of attempting to 'discredit', 'spoil' and 'depreciate the value' of his work. Bell told Allen that the chapter was taking such

---

[8] 'The Farmer's Dilemma', *The Times*, 7 Nov. 1921.
[9] *The Times*, 14 Nov. 1921, 6.
[10] 'Recollections', *Tithe*, Mar. 1934.
[11] Mr F. R. Allen, 'The Tithe Act of 1918, The Substance of a Paper read before the Canterbury Farmers Club and Chamber of Agriculture, 15 Mar. 1919', LPL.

comments as a refusal of the offer of tithe agent and, at the end of July, a new agent was appointed in his place.[12]

On 29 November 1924, Allen was summoned to appear in front of the cathedral's clergy in the chapter house. As with the ceremony in 1911, the meeting followed well-established procedure. This time, however, Allen faced charges under the auspices of ecclesiastical law. He was found guilty of 'repudiating obedience and reverence' and the nature of the offence was deemed to be 'of a grave kind'. The chapter decreed that Allen 'should be expelled by the Dean and Chapter and utterly amoved from the said Cathedral Church [and] the advantageous privileges and emoluments thereof'.[13]

The termination of Allen's employment by the cathedral coincided, therefore, with his activity to launch the NTA. But, despite his criticisms of the functioning of the tithe system, Allen was at this stage far from being opposed to the principle of tithe. Alongside his work with the NTA, he attempted to establish a business as an independent tithe agent, renting a small office at 19 Saint Margaret's Street, a stone's throw from the cathedral's main gates. For over two decades, the office would serve as the contact address for the NTA.

For several years, Allen had no compunction in collecting tithe for some wealthy clients who paid good commission, such as the Surrenden-Dering Estate in Pluckley, for whom he collected tithe until 1929. He even worked for sections of the Church – for example, collecting clerical tithe in Barham until 1926.[14] Increasingly, however, Allen began to hire his services primarily to tithepayers who were being pursued by the Church for payments, or who wanted to sort out 'apportionments' (responsibilities of different landowners for tithe after plots of land exchanged hands). He also increasingly devoted time to coordinating the work of the NTA. To his new role, Allen transferred the loyalty, efficiency and hard work he had offered to the Church for over two decades. Moreover, his long career as the cathedral's tithe collector meant that he had accrued expertise in tithe regulation and law. Soon, the cathedral chapter viewed him as a nuisance. Meetings of the chapter heard complaints from the new tithe agent about the advice Allen was offering to tithepayers being pursued for payment in the courts.[15] His activities got under the dean's skin so much that a meeting of the chapter decided that any letters arriving

[12] Rev. G. K. A. Bell, Monthly Meeting of the Chapter, 31 May 1924; F. R. Allen, 5 June 1924; G. K. A. Bell, 16 June 1924; F. R. Allen, 21 June 1924; Special Meeting of the Chapter, 5 July 1924, CCA, CCA- DCc-CA17.

[13] Order of Expulsion of Frank Richard Allen, 20 Dec. 1924, CCA, CCA-DCc-MB/4/15.

[14] 'Statement of Evidence submitted by Mr F. R. Allen, Canterbury', Royal Commission on Tithe Rentcharge, 6 December 1934, 170.

[15] Minutes of Meeting of the Chapter, 27 June 1925, CCA, CCA-DCc-CA/18.

for Allen at the cathedral should be 'returned to sender' rather than forwarded to his office.[16]

Longstanding doubts about the functioning of the tithe system together with a sense of injustice arising from treatment by his employer acted as catalysts for Allen's transformation from tithe collector to tithe campaigner. But catalysts speed up already existing processes. Over the previous six or so years Allen's doubts about the functioning of the tithe system had matured significantly. The Great War had put tithe back on to the political agenda. Its impact led to three pieces of legislation – in 1918, 1920 and 1925 – and shaped much of the debate about tithe throughout the 1920s.

Watershed moment

The Great War was a watershed moment for tithe for several reasons. First, government intervention in agriculture, designed to increase output and safeguard food supplies, led to substantial increases in the level of the charge. In 1915, War Agriculture Executive Committees were established to coordinate and increase production and, in 1917, the Corn Production Act guaranteed minimum prices for wheat and oats; the Act also established wage boards to set minimum wages for agricultural workers, a measure demanded by the labour movement but designed also to stabilise the rural labour force. The outcome of government policy was that between 1914 and 1918 the price of a quarter of wheat rose from 35s to 73s, oats from 21s to 49s and barley – despite its exclusion from the pricing measures – from 27s to 59s. This meant that the annual value of tithe steadily increased. Between 1910 and 1915, tithe rose from £70 to £77, increasing further to £92 in 1917 and £109 3s 11d in 1918 – representing a wartime increase of 44 per cent. Moreover, the linkage of tithe to the average septennial price of grain meant further big rises were in the pipeline. Forecasts were that tithe would reach £180 in 1922 or 1923.[17]

Landowning interests led the protests. The 1891 Tithe Act had stipulated the responsibility of landlords to pay tithe, outlawing previous practices of writing the charge into tenancy agreements. By the beginning of 1918, landowners were complaining that, while their tenant farmers had experienced prosperity, they were receiving demands for an 'abnormal increase' in tithe.[18] They also pointed out that opportunities to raise pre-war rents, which had been at a relatively low level, were restricted not only by existing leasing and tenancy agreements but also by restraints imposed in the Corn Production Act. A landowner from Devon wrote to *The Times*:

---

[16] Minutes of Meeting of the Chapter, 28 February 1925, CCA, CCA-DCc-CA/18.
[17] 'Tithe Rent-Charge: Another Large Increase for 1918', *The Times*, 2 Jan. 1918.
[18] 'Tithe and Settlement', *The Times*, 6 Apr. 1918.

> I have just returned home, after three years soldiering, to find, amongst other evils, an enormous increase in the tithe. I have some twenty tenants, small farmers mostly. How am I going to pass on the increase to them? [...] It is a popular delusion that the landlord can 'take it out on the tenant'.[19]

Complaints from owner-occupying farmers were more muted. For the moment, handsome profits – particularly for cereal producers in southern England – more than compensated for the increases in tithe. Some argued, however, that the increases would still negatively impact agricultural production as well as the incomes of all working on the land, including tenant farmers and agricultural workers.[20]

A second watershed moment linked to the war was the major change in the composition of tithepayers brought about by a sharp rise in the number of owner-occupying farmers. A tendency for landowners to sell parts of their estates to tenants had begun in the final decades of the nineteenth century. In 1919 land sales became 'a deluge'. The scale of the transfer is often likened to that following the dissolution of the monasteries in the sixteenth century, though some suggest it had not been seen 'since the Norman Conquest'.[21] By the mid-1920s, 37 per cent of farmland was in the hands of owner-occupiers, compared with 13 per cent in 1908. This 'diaspora' from the land symbolises the decline in power and prestige of the English aristocracy and leading layers of the gentry, though of course they continued to own the majority of the nation's land and to maintain significant influence in politics and the state. Their unsuccessful battle against Lloyd George's Land Value Tax policy (1909–10) had been more of a political than a financial blow, but it induced the rural elite to find ways to convert income from land into broader portfolios of property and investments. Heavy war casualties – with resulting implications for death duties – also influenced decisions to sell land.[22]

Many farmers had little choice other than to purchase their holdings in order to remain in business and retain their homes. But, often, tenants were willing buyers, in some cases taking the opportunity to increase the size of their farms. In addition, a significant number of middle-class ex-servicemen bought land to take up farming; some took advantage of the Land Settlement (Facilities) Act (1919), which encouraged provision of

---

[19] Hugh Money-Coutts, *The Times*, 12 Apr. 1918, 9.
[20] 'Farmers and Tithe', *ChCh*, 22 Mar. 1918; 'Tithe and Agriculture', *DiEx*, 8 Feb. 1918.
[21] Newby et al., *Property, Paternalism and Power*, 37; Eric Hobsbawm, *Industry and Empire* (London: Penguin, 1999), 179.
[22] Alun Howkins, *The Death of Rural England: A Social History of the Countryside Since 1900* (London: Routledge, 2003), 37–8; David Cannadine, *The Decline and Fall of the British Aristocracy* (London: Yale University Press, 1990).

Tithe after the Great War

holdings to war veterans without background or training in agriculture.[23] Prices for land tended to be high and new owners took out mortgages or bank overdrafts at high rates of interest. Yet, in the heady optimism of the post-war years, there seemed to be little serious risk. Following the recommendation of the majority report from the Royal Commission on Agriculture (1919), parliament passed the Agriculture Act (1920), which extended minimum prices for wheat and oats for an indefinite period and stipulated four years' notice if the guarantees were to be abolished. The revolution in land ownership was, as Eric Hobsbawm noted, 'hardly noticed' at the time – a fact that, as will be seen, influenced the debate over tithe.[24] It meant that the class of owner-occupying farmers grew from around 55,000 to almost 150,000, and began to assert itself as a 'separate and distinct political and social force'.[25]

A third change linked to the Great War relates to the relationship between the Church and wider society. Though concerns over social issues were well established before 1914, the Church's experience during wartime pushed social justice high up its agenda. Reports from 3000 chaplains working with the army, many of whom expressed shock at the lack of 'Christian knowledge' amongst those living and dying in the trenches, illustrated the Church's failure to establish roots in urban communities where the values of the labour movement had made rapid headway. Views about how to meet the challenge varied but, as Edward Norman notes in a classic study, 'there were very few Church leaders who did not adopt attitudes critical of existing industrial organisation and social order'.[26] In 1918, a report on 'Christianity and Industrial Problems', commissioned by the archbishops of Canterbury and York, argued for cooperation between the social classes, but also for restrictions on profits, a progressive taxation system, measures against unemployment and a 'living wage' for workers. More radical was the position taken by the future archbishop of Canterbury, William Temple, who built links with trade unionists and, in 1918, announced his membership of the Labour Party. The Church's radicalism had its limits: the upper echelons of the clergy, as well as the most prominent representatives of the laity, were drawn from privileged layers of society and the Church's conservative wing remained powerful. One of its representatives, Hugh Cecil, the youngest child of Lord Salisbury, described the social conscience displayed by many clergy as 'the great evil of priestcraft'.[27] Yet, despite still being firmly tied to the ruling elites, the Church of England was attempting to

---

[23] Cooper, *British Agricultural Policy*, 46.
[24] Hobsbawm, *Industry*, 179.
[25] Howkins, *Death of Rural England*, 36–42 and 63.
[26] Norman, *Church and Society*, 222.
[27] Ibid., 243–4, 255 and 259.

shed its image of the 'Conservative Party at prayer' and become – in terms of its politics – a 'broad church'.

Concerns about social justice conditioned the Church's discussion about tithe. In the autumn of 1917, senior clergy and lay officials began to express fears that projected increases in tithe would leave the Church open to charges of wartime profiteering. Some warned of an 'unusual situation' in which landowners – a group not accustomed to currying favour with the wider population – would be able to gain a 'popular following [...] by turning the complaint [about tithe] into a cry against titheowners profiting by the war'.[28] Others reported that some clergy were pledging to donate their extra tithe to the Red Cross.[29] The archbishop of Canterbury began a consultation on whether it was 'desirable that concessions [on tithe] should be made in order to prevent the hindrance that may arise to the power of good to the Church, if it is thought by the public that the Church is making a profit out of the war'.[30] Stanford Downing, a senior official at the Ecclesiastical Commission, wrote two lengthy articles in an attempt to prompt wider debate.[31] In February 1918, a fourteen-person committee of clergy was established to prepare a report on tithe for the Lower House (representatives of clergy) of the Convocation of Canterbury.[32]

The Church's discussion was also conditioned by the experience of the disestablishment of the Church in Wales. Whatever their differences on social issues, Church leaders had been virtually unanimous in their opposition to the Welsh Church Bill, introduced in 1912 by the Liberal government. Despite a vigorous campaign by the Conservative Party and obstruction by the House of Lords, the legislation was passed in 1914, though the outbreak of war delayed it being put into operation. The Act stipulated that ecclesiastical tithe collected in Wales would provide funds for secular institutions, including Welsh county councils and the University of Wales, although, in the winter of 1917–18, parliament had still to finalise how the Church should be compensated for the loss of its endowments.

At that time many senior figures in the Church feared that – after the failure to halt the Welsh Church Act – disestablishment and disendowment of the Church of England could re-emerge as a major issue after the

[28] 'Observations by Mr Downing on Mr Le Fanu's Memorandum', 27 Oct. 1917, CERC, ECE/SEC/TITHE/P1.
[29] Bishop of Norwich, HL Deb., *Hansard*, 25 Apr. 1918.
[30] Memorandum from W. R. Le Fanu (on request of the archbishop of Canterbury), 'Increase in the Value of Tithe Rentcharge', 20 Oct. 1917, CERC, ECE/SEC/TITHE/P1.
[31] 'Tithe Rent-Charge', *The Guardian* (a newspaper linked to the Church, not to be confused with the *Manchester Guardian*) 25 Oct. and 1 Nov. 1917.
[32] 'Report of the Committee on Tithe Rent Charge', Convocation of Canterbury, Lower House, 8 Apr. 1918, MERL, P2890. Box 1/07.

war. In the event, the view was mistaken. The war served to speed the decline of political nonconformism and demands for disestablishment, ushering in more cordial relations between Anglicans and particularly the Methodists. In 1919, the relationship between Church and state would be redefined by the 'Enabling Act', which divested some of the powers of parliament to the Church Assembly, a body with separate 'houses' for bishops, clergy and laity. Nevertheless, in 1917–18 the threat of disestablishment was perceived to be real, and many feared that, as in Wales, grievances over tithe could fuel support for the demand.[33]

The archbishop's consultation on tithe reached a general consensus. It was accepted that, given that a significant portion of the increase in tithe was linked to the Corn Production Act, most landowners did indeed have cause for complaint, though some did not, as the Act had swelled the profits of owner-occupying farmers. But, most importantly, the Church needed to recognise the public mood. 'The Clergy [...] are men of sensitive conscience,' reported the tithe committee of clergy to the Convocation of Canterbury, '[they] would hate to expose themselves to a charge of profiteering, one of the most odious offenses of which any man can be guilty during a time of war.'[34] The Church would be acting fairly and wisely if it were to support legislation, the initiative for which should come from the Church itself, rather than appearing 'to be a measure forced [...] by the government'.[35] As the tithe committee explained, 'the clergy are anxious to avoid even the appearance of evil [...] and if some concession should be made, they would prefer to make it of their own free will.'[36]

There was less agreement about the content of the legislation. One of the Church's most prominent experts on tithe, Rev. George Brocklehurst, argued for measures to spread the tithe burden to tenant farmers, whose wartime profits had increased 'beyond their wildest dreams'.[37] More controversial were the proposals from Frank Allen. In an eight-page paper, Canterbury Cathedral's tithe agent argued for a progressive tax on 'excess tithe' to be paid by both clerical and lay titheowners; the richest titheowners, including the ecclesiastical corporations and well-off clergy, paying the lion's share, while the poorest clergy would be exempt. Stanford Downing brusquely dismissed Allen's ideas as 'impractical'

---

[33] Le Fanu, 20 Oct. 1917, CERC, ECE/SEC/TITHE/P1.
[34] Report to Convocation of Canterbury, 8 Apr. 1918.
[35] Le Fanu, 20 Oct. 1917, CERC, ECE/SEC/TITHE/P1.
[36] Report to Convocation of Canterbury, 8 Apr. 1918.
[37] George Brocklehurst, 'The Case for Redemption', *The Times*, 11 Apr. 1918. Several years earlier, Brocklehurst had published a book entitled *Tithes and Tithe Rentcharge* (New Romney: Bale & Co, 1911).

and a 'gross interference' with the 'contract' between tithepayers and titheowners.[38]

The paper eventually forwarded by the archbishop of Canterbury to the home secretary 'for consideration of Government action' was drawn up by Sir Lewis Dibdin, the dean of the Arches (a judge in the provisional court of the archbishop of Canterbury).[39] It contained two elements. First, tithe should be frozen at its par value – in other words, £100 – for so long as the Corn Production Act remained in operation, after which it would revert to a septennial average. Secondly, an extensive programme of tithe redemption should be encouraged by offering more favourable and flexible terms to tithepayers.

Tithe redemption had emerged as a major theme during the archbishop's consultation. Existing legislation required the tithepayer and titheowner to make a joint application and stipulated also, for most clerical tithe, the consent of the appropriate bishop. The payment had to be at least twenty-five years of tithe at its par value – in other words, £2,500 for each £100 of tithe. That few tithepayers found either the procedure or the terms attractive was indicated by the miniscule number of applications over the decades. The paper sent to the home secretary proposed to do away with the minimum twenty-five years' purchase price as well as the need for consent from bishops, giving instead an oversight role to the Board of Agriculture (soon to become Ministry of Agriculture).[40] Previously, the Church had opposed proposals for more attractive and flexible tithe redemption terms. But all now agreed – archbishops and bishops, officials of Queen Anne's Bounty and Ecclesiastical Commissioners, the tithe committee of clergy, Rev. Brocklehurst and Frank Allen – that encouraging redemption would be the most effective way to do away with 'a troublesome form of property'.[41]

Some argued that the threat of disestablishment made the issue of tithe redemption even more urgent. In a paper prepared for the archbishop of Canterbury, William Le Fanu, the senior official at Queen Anne's Bounty, argued that though it 'may be too late to save the disendowment of the Church of England', a successful policy of tithe redemption 'would largely diminish the practical power behind the disendowers'. In other words, if disendowment were to happen, it would be easier for the Church to keep possession of the capital gained from tithe redemption than to argue that it should maintain a share in tithe, which would, in the event of disendowment, be collected by the state. Tithe redemption

---

[38] Frank Allen, Memorandum on Tithe Rent Charge, Jan. 1918; Stanford Downing, 'Observations on Mr Allen's Memorandum', 11 Feb. 1918, CERC, ECE/SEC/TITHE/P1.
[39] Memorandum by Sir Lewis Dibdin, 2 Nov. 1917, CERC, ECE/SEC/TITHE/P1.
[40] Ibid.
[41] Report to Convocation of Canterbury, 8 Apr. 1918.

would, explained Le Fanu, 'be a very great advantage to the Church [...] even at a considerable sacrifice'.[42]

Three pieces of legislation, 1918–20

By the spring of 1918, the sentiments of landowners and Church leaders had convinced ministers that legislation on tithe was necessary. Describing 'a minor but urgent problem', an editorial in *The Times* urged the government to show 'determination [...] to see whether the solution of an ancient problem cannot be made to square with the new requirements of the national life'.[43] Yet the bill presented to the House of Commons on 24 July avoided any serious reappraisal of the tithe problem. It was described as 'a temporary expedient' by its mover, the president of the Board of Agriculture, Rowland Prothero, who had in 1889 chastised the 'illegal' Welsh tithepayers' movement for wanting to 'starve out the clergy'.[44] The Act reached the statute book in November, the first of three pieces of legislation concerning tithe to be passed by parliament in consecutive years. All were guided by expediency – and each would deepen rather than resolve the ancient problem.

The 1918 Tithe Act was based on the proposals submitted by the archbishop of Canterbury, except its terms were more favourable to titheowners. The Church had suggested fixing tithe at its par value (£100), recognising that any 'increase above 100 [would] be entirely due to war conditions'.[45] But the Act set the charge at its 1918 value of £109 3s 11d, which would be frozen for seven years. After January 1926, tithe would revert to a variable value, though calculated by a fifteen-year average of the price of grain (instead of a septennial average). Another concession to the Church, this change aimed to prevent sharp variations in tithe income for the clergy, but it meant also that titheowners would, for a few years at least, benefit from the high wartime price of grain.

The second part of the Act introduced new mechanisms for tithe redemption. Land with tithe above 20s – the limit imposed by the 1846 Act – was now eligible for redemption and applications from tithepayers would no longer require the consent of the titheowner or approval from the bishop. Payments could also be made in instalments. The Act permitted tithepayers and titheowners to negotiate an appropriate sum. If there were no agreement, the amount to be paid would be decided by the Ministry of Agriculture. Up until 1 January 1921, tithepayers could redeem at twenty-one years' purchase of commuted tithe, instead of the previous minimum twenty-five years (£2,100 instead of £2,500). The

---

[42] Le Fanu, 20 Oct. 1917, CERC, ECE/SEC/TITHE/P1.
[43] 'Tithe and Settlement', *The Times*, 6 Apr. 1918.
[44] HC Deb., *Hansard*, 24 July 1918; Prothero, *Anti-Tithe Agitation in Wales*, 21.
[45] Dibdin, 2 Nov. 1917, CERC, ECE/SEC/TITHE/P1.

rates and land tax paid by the tithe owner would also be deduced from the calculation, meaning that payments for most clerical tithe would be around eighteen and a half years of par value and for lay tithe around sixteen and a half years – the difference arising on account of parochial clergy paying half rates on tithe. After 1 January 1921, a committee of experts established by the Board (Ministry) of Agriculture would recommend what constituted 'fair compensation', a figure that would be binding in the event of titheowners and tithepayers failing to agree a settlement. The committee would attempt to calculate a sum that when invested in government stocks would produce an income equivalent to the gross annual income from tithe. Sir Charles Longmore, who had both a legal and a landowning background, was appointed chairman.[46] The two other committee members were William Le Fanu of Queen Anne's Bounty and Sir Henry Rew, who would, a few years later, help to form the NTA.

Given the habitual controversies surrounding tithe legislation, the most remarkable aspect about the 1918 Tithe Act was its painless passage through the House of Lords and House of Commons. During the committee stage, Llewellyn Williams, a Welsh Liberal, moved that the fixed rate of £109 3s 11d should apply equally to the price Welsh institutions were to pay to take possession of the Church's tithe in Wales. His proposal was rejected by a majority of forty-six, a decision that would have significant implications (see below).[47] Yet there were few other contentious issues. This can be explained, partly, by the conciliatory culture of war-time coalition politics and, partly, by the fact that politicians were focused on more epoch-making events: the bill's final debates took place against the background of the Armistice and its aftermath. But most MPs – including Liberal and Labour representatives – could see no reason to interfere with what seemed a sensible arrangement agreed between the Church hierarchy and landowners, one which would supposedly have minimal impact on either farming communities or the wider public.

In general, the parochial clergy accepted the compromise as inevitable and even desirable. The only dissent came from Peterson's Tithe Owners' Union, which described the fixing of tithe at £109 as a 'further injustice on the long-suffering clergy'.[48] One complaint, however, was widely expressed: the liability to pay rates on the charge. Clergy complained that while income from tithe had been frozen by the Act, rates were rising significantly, especially in rural areas. A vicar in Devon, Rev. Dr W. C. Tuting, became a 'passive resister' when he told his parish overseers that he would not be paying rates on tithe. Announcing that he was 'fighting the battle' on behalf of all incumbent clergy, he would 'decline to pay

[46] 'Sir Charles Longmore', *The Times*, 7 Feb. 1930.
[47] HC Deb., *Hansard*, 30 Oct. 1918.
[48] R. Bruce Dickson, 'Government Tithe Bill', *The Times*, 5 Oct. 1918.

Tithe after the Great War

[…] until such time as the monstrous injustice under which tithe-owning clergy suffer so cruelly has been duly and publicly exposed'.[49]

Arising from its status as property, the issue of rates on tithe had been a long-standing grievance within the Church. In 1899, a lobbying campaign led to the Tithe Rentcharge (Rates) Act, which granted rate relief to clergy of 50 per cent. Now the Church hierarchy sought further concessions. In December 1919, a 'large and representative deputation' from the Church Assembly's Central Board of Finance met the chancellor of the exchequer to demand that, given the decision to freeze tithe, the Church should be 'compensated' through rate relief of 75 per cent on all clerical tithe. The coalition government rejected the demand, proposing instead to introduce legislation to limit rates on tithe to their 1918–19 levels.[50] Nevertheless, the Church stepped up the pressure. In parliament, a private member's bill introduced by the Conservative Sir Samuel Hoare proposed the total exemption of clerical tithe from rates. When the bill received a majority of 116 at its second reading, the government announced it would seek a compromise. The Ecclesiastical Tithe Rentcharge (Rates) Act 1920 granted 100 per cent rate relief to the poorest clergy – those with incomes under £300 – and 75 per cent relief to those with annual incomes under £500. The measures were to continue until tithe reverted to a variable rate in January 1926.[51]

In parliament, there was, in the words of one MP, a 'general chorus of approval' for the legislation. One dissenting voice was the Coalition Labour MP, George Barnes, who warned that 'other ratepayers would have to put their hands in their pockets and pay out large sums […] in order to make up the deficiency.'[52] Barnes was proved correct in his prediction. Rates in some parishes, particularly in rural areas, rose significantly. Even some of the Act's most fervent supporters were later forced to admit that they 'doubted whether parliament [when voting for the legislation] fully realised the implications of its actions'.[53] In farming communities, the Act prompted considerable anger. Branches of the NFU recorded 'disapproval' and 'protest' about 'the parson being allowed his rates back' at a time 'when everybody's rates are very materially increased'.[54] At a meeting in Canterbury, a farmer announced that he was refusing to pay his tithe in protest. A resolution declared:

---

[49] 'Vicar as Passive Resister', *The Times*, 9 Feb. 1920.
[50] 'Memorandum by the Chancellor of the Exchequer', 4 Feb. 1920, TNA, CAB 24/97/74.
[51] 'Memorandum by the Minister of Agriculture and Fisheries', 19 Mar. 1920, TNA, CAB 24/100/84.
[52] HC Deb., *Hansard*, 21 Apr. 1920.
[53] Edward Wood, HC Deb., *Hansard*, 18 June 1925.
[54] 'Farmers' Union', *Western Chronicle*, 22 Oct. 1920; 'Camelford Farmers', *Cornish Guardian*, 15 Oct. 1920.

> That in the opinion of this meeting of East Kent farmers the levy of tithe upon men of all creeds for the upkeep of one religious denomination is an offence against the principles of English liberty, injurious to the Established Church itself, and harmful to the moral and religious well-being of the nation, and should be abolished.[55]

In effect, the legislation on rates fuelled generalised complaints about tithe from farmers, the first time such grievances were openly expressed in the post-war period.

A third piece of legislation would also help to shape the forthcoming tithe conflict, particularly in Wales. In 1919 parliament approved the Welsh Church (temporalities) Act, which finalised arrangements for the disendowment of the Church in Wales. The Church Act of 1914 had transferred ecclesiastical tithe to thirteen Welsh county councils, four county borough councils, the National Library of Wales and the University of Wales with its constituent colleges. By reclassifying tithe as national property, the Act represented the achievement of a long-standing aim of Liberals and political nonconformists. Yet it also stipulated significant compensation for the Church, including a sum to ensure clergy could continue to draw tithe while they remained in office. Under the provisions of the Act, the Welsh secular institutions had to pay the Church a 'capitalised sum' based on tithe's septennial average. To do so, they would have to take out substantial loans. A new entity was established to manage the whole process: the Commissioners for Church Temporalities in Wales, which would become known as the Welsh Church Commissioners. Welsh tithepayers would continue to pay tithe, but it would now be collected by the Commissioners, who would service the loan and pass remaining monies to the county councils and other institutions.

The implementation of the 1914 Act was delayed by the war and, by 1919, several developments had impacted the way in which it could be put into operation. The first was the changed political context: a coalition government in which Conservatives were playing an increasingly important role. Though a number of Conservatives led by Robert Cecil (another son of Lord Salisbury) were attempting to reverse the disestablishment process, most Tories had reviewed strategy and were seeking to secure the most favourable financial settlement for the Church. Fronting this campaign was the parliamentary secretary to the Board of Agriculture, Sir Arthur Griffith-Boscawen, an individual who would play a prominent role in the inter-war tithe conflict. Son of an anglicised Welsh landowner, Griffith-Boscawen was also chairman of the Church Committee for Defence and Instruction (formerly the Church Defence Institution). In 1919 he boasted to MPs that 'no one in this House ha[d]

---

[55] 'Tithes and the Rates', *DE*, 10 Aug. 1923.

opposed Disestablishment and Disendowment in Wales longer or more vigorously' than he.[56] In 1920, Griffith-Boscawen was appointed minister of agriculture.

The second development was the big increase in the septennial average of tithe. If the war had not intervened, the Welsh institutions would have compensated the Church at the rate of £77 for each £100 of tithe. The wartime explosion in the price of cereals meant that the compensation was, instead, based on £140 12s – an increase of 82 per cent. As noted above, when debating the 1918 Tithe Act, parliament rejected a proposal to set the Welsh 'commutation rate' at the same level as other tithe (£109). By 1919, the charge of 'war profiteering' had lost much of its resonance. The result was, as Sir Arthur Griffith-Boscawen later admitted, in somewhat of an understatement: 'the Church got good terms'.[57] A third change was the significant increase in interest rates. In order to fund the compensation, the Welsh Church Commissioners received a payment of £1,000,000 from the government but still had to take out a loan of £2,350,000 from the National Debt Commission. The interest was set at 5.5 per cent – the pre-war rate had been 3.5 per cent.

Two major implications flowed from all this. First, though tithe in Wales was now 'national property', around 70 per cent of tithe collected by the Welsh Church Commissioners would be used to repay and service the loan taken out to compensate the Church, rather than be available for use by the county councils or the University of Wales. Moreover, the payments were due to continue until 1954.[58] Secondly, a new tithe collecting entity had been established. Despite its name, the Welsh Church Commission was a secular body, and the tithe it had responsibility for collecting was designated as lay tithe. But it was intrinsically linked to the state and imbued with an ethos of duty towards the established Church. That culture would be further reinforced in 1923, when Griffith-Boscawen was appointed chairman of the Welsh Church Commissioners.[59]

Negotiating a 'new bargain'

The provisions in the 1918 Tithe Act and 1920 Rates Act were linked to the assumption that the price of cereals would remain relatively stable. The same expectation encouraged many farmers to buy their holdings,

---

[56] R. J. Q. Adams, 'Boscawen, Sir Arthur Sackville Trevor Griffith (1865–1946)', *ODNB* (2008); HC Deb., *Hansard*, 6 Aug. 1919.
[57] *Royal Commission on Tithe Rentcharge, Minutes of Evidence*, 21 Feb. 1935 (London: HMSO), 469.
[58] The par value of tithe in Wales was £223,500. The annual debt repayment (capital and interest) was £160,814. *Royal Commission on Tithe Rentcharge, Minutes of Evidence*, 21 Feb. 1935, 457–80.
[59] 'Ecclesiastical News', *The Times*, 30 June 1923.

leading to the rapid expansion in the number of owner-occupying farmers. Yet the optimism of the immediate post-war years quickly evaporated. In August 1921, faced with a fall in cereal prices on the international market, the government – ignoring its undertaking to give four years' notice of any change – repealed the price guarantees on wheat and oats provided by the Corn Production Act (1917) and the Agriculture Act (1920). The price of a quarter of wheat collapsed from 89s 3d in June 1921 to 45s 8d in December.[60] Behind the scenes, the minister of agriculture, Griffith-Boscawen, managed to appease farmers' leaders by abolishing the minimum wage for agricultural workers and offering subsidies for the 1921 harvest. Yet, as prices continued to fall, the government's behaviour became known in farming communities as 'the Great Betrayal'.[61]

Against this background, policy makers in government and the Church realised that 'a difficult situation' would arise in 1926 when tithe reverted to a variable charge and the concessions on rates expired. While the prices of agricultural produce were spiralling downwards, the value of tithe was likely to increase from £109 to around £130 and continue to rise for several more years. Church officials realised that tithe at £130 would, after rates had been paid, bring in hardly more income than tithe at £109 – that is, if it could be collected. Writing in *The Times*, Rowland Prothero stressed the urgency of resolving the situation: 'experience warns us that an anti-tithe agitation may be expected. There are not wanting signs that it has already begun.'[62] A widely circulated speech by Canon Allen Bell delivered at the Convocation of Canterbury (House of Clergy) expressed the concerns of many parochial clergy. Reviewing the history of tithe since 1836, Bell concluded that 'no legislation had been really satisfactory' and it would be 'foolish to propose any further alteration of tithe by an Act of Parliament'. He also admitted that the Rates Act of 1920 had 'brought new troubles' as 'many Clergy felt they would rather bear anything than endure the calumnies of those who said the parsons were putting their rates on the poor.' The 'only solution', Bell argued, was 'one which would relieve them of tithes altogether and provide them with an annual income free from rates, and from all the unpleasantness which the ownership of tithes had involved.'[63]

Immediately after the Conservative Party's victory at the general election in October 1922, Stanford Downing of the Ecclesiastical Commissioners approached officials at the Ministry of Agriculture to request assistance in opening discussions with tithepayers' representatives. He had drawn up

[60] Cooper, *British Agricultural Policy*, 54.
[61] Howkins, *Death of Rural England*, 45–6.
[62] Lord Ernle, 'Tithe Rent-Charge: The Problem of Redemption', *The Times*, 5 Feb. 1923.
[63] Lower House of Convocation, 16 Feb. 1923, CERC, ECE/SEC/TITHE/NEG/1.

a draft policy for 'universal redemption' of tithe, which could, he hoped, become the basis of 'a new bargain' between titheowners and tithepayers.[64] Under the plan, tithe would become a fixed charge, continuing for a period of fifty or so years. Tithepayers would make an additional payments into a 'sinking fund', which would accumulate over the same period into capital, on which the interest would eventually replace income from tithe. The problem of rates would be resolved by reclassifying tithe payments as annuities, thus removing tithe immediately from the category of rateable properties. Following Downing's approach, the minister, Sir Robert Sanders, sounded out Lord Clinton and Ernest Pretyman, representatives respectively of the Central Landowners' Association (CLA) and the Land Union. Despite expressing important reservations, including the fear that landowners would be forced to pick up the shortfall in rates, they indicated that the landowners' associations were prepared to enter talks.[65]

Preparations to begin formal negotiations continued throughout 1923. The Church's starting position was agreed in June at a special conference convened by the Central Board of Finance and attended by representatives of diocesan bishops and Diocesan Boards of Finance.[66] The CLA volunteered itself as the main representative of tithepayers, on the basis that it was 'concerned with this question more than any other body'. Both sides – the Church and the landowners' associations – agreed on the need to 'settle the tithe question once and for all'.[67]

The negotiations began on 26 February 1924, one month after the formation of Ramsay MacDonald's minority Labour government. Though Noel Buxton, the minister of agriculture, considered the reintroduction of Wages Boards to regulate the working conditions of agricultural labourers a greater priority, he recognised the importance of resolving the tithe issue. A senior official at the ministry briefed him that without legislation the value of tithe would 'rise considerably' and 'such a position in 1926 would be calculated to encourage opposition to the payment of Tithe'.[68] Buxton hoped that negotiations between titheowners and tithepayers would reach agreement on the essential elements of legislation, but made it clear that, whatever the outcome of the talks, a bill would be introduced

---

[64] S. E. Downing to F. A Jones, 30 Oct. 1922, CERC, ECE/SEC/TITHE/NEG/1.
[65] Letters between S. E. Downing and F. A. Jones, Oct. 1922–Jan. 1923, CERC, ECE/SEC/TITHE/NEG/1.
[66] Conference on Tithe Rent Charge, 8 June 1923, CERC, ECE/SEC/TITHE/NEG/1; 'Ecclesiastical News', *The Times*, 9 June 1923.
[67] R. Strachan Gardiner, 27 June 1923, CERC, ECE/SEC/TITHE/NEG/1. The words are those of Lord Clinton (26 Feb. 1924).
[68] 'Memorandum by the Legal Advisor' (Frank A. Jones), 12 June 1924, CERC, ECE/SEC/TITHE/NEG/1.

in 1925 'to avoid the trouble' that would arise when the provisions of the 1918 and 1920 Acts expired.[69]

The titheowners' negotiating team of twelve people had been elected at the Church's June 1923 tithe conference. It included representatives of the clergy (from the Tithe Committees of the Canterbury and York Convocations) and senior lay officials. As well as Stanford Downing, prominent roles were played by Sir Frederick Radcliffe and Canon Frank Partridge, the Church Assembly's financial secretary, who acted as secretary for the negotiating committee. Representatives of lay titheowners were not invited to the conference table. The Church's conference had considered inviting the Oxford and Cambridge colleges but resolved that 'it was unnecessary', the assumption being that they and other lay titheowners would support an agreement that was acceptable to the Church.[70] A representative of lay titheowners was, however, nominated by the Church Assembly to preside over the talks: Griffith-Boscawen, chairman of the Welsh Church Commissioners. Griffith-Boscawen was by no stretch of the imagination an impartial chair – in fact, the Church had originally selected him as part of its negotiating team[71] – and played a major role in the negotiations. As a former minister of agriculture, he provided a back-channel to officials at the ministry and held several meetings with Buxton 'with a view to ascertaining how far the government would support suggestions made, and to what extent it would be prepared to assist'.[72]

The tithepayers' negotiating team, also twelve people, was drawn from three organisations: the CLA, the Land Union and the NFU. 'Born with a silver spoon in its mouth' in 1907,[73] the CLA had around 2,600 members, among whom earls, barons and viscounts were well represented.[74] Its principal representative at the negotiations was Lord Clinton (Charles Hepburn-Stuart-Forbes-Trefusis), owner of extensive estates in Devon and Scotland. Clinton had steered the 1918 Tithe Bill through the House of Lords while serving as parliamentary secretary to the Board of Agriculture. Though claiming to be representative of tithepayers' interests, the CLA had divided loyalties, as its membership included a significant number of lay

[69] Griffith-Boscawen to Downing, 16 June 1924; Griffith-Boscawen, 23 June 1924, CERC, ECE/SEC/TITHE/NEG/1.
[70] Conference on Tithe Rent Charge, 8 June 1923; Stanford Downing, Memorandum (n.d. July 1924), CERC, ECE/SEC/TITHE/NEG/1.
[71] 'Joint Session of Canterbury Convocation Tithe Committee, York Convocation Tithe Committee and Legal Committee of the Central Board of Finance', 5 July 1923, CERC, ECE/SEC/TITHE/NEG/1.
[72] Memorandum by Sir Arthur Griffith-Boscawen, n.d., CERC, ECE/SEC/TITHE/NEG/1.
[73] Simon Moore, 'The Agrarian Conservative Party in Parliament, 1920–1929', *Parliamentary History*, 10, 2 (1991), 354.
[74] The figure was given at the CLA's annual meeting in March 1921.

titheowners.[75] The Land Union was also an organisation of big landowners. Established in 1910 to organise 'active self-defence' against Lloyd George's Land Tax policy, it pledged to 'safeguard the rights of property [...] against the attacks of land nationalisers, or socialists subsidised by foreign coin'.[76] It was represented at the negotiations by the former long-serving Conservative MP Ernest Pretyman, a man described by contemporary journalists as 'a typical country squire'.[77]

The Church had not envisaged that the NFU would have a place at the negotiating table. During the discussions that led to the 1918 Tithe Act, Church authorities had consulted the CLA, but had not considered talking to the NFU. Similarly, in 1923 Downing and his team expected that the 'new bargain' would be arranged through agreement with the landowners' associations. Like many others, they had failed to notice the rapid growth in the number of occupying farmers or recognise its significance in regard to the tithe problem. It was the CLA that advised the Church that the NFU's representation of 'farmer-owners [meant] they would have to be reckoned with'.[78]

In the years following its formation in 1908, the NFU had viewed itself primarily as an organisation of tenant farmers, though spurning the radicalism associated with its predecessor, the Farmers' Alliance. Its role was to assert farmers' interests in relation to government policy and the functioning of the agricultural market and against the demands of agricultural workers' trade unionism. In short, the NFU was an organisation representing the interests of agricultural employers.[79] Drawn into cooperation with government to manage food supplies during the war, the NFU emerged from the conflict with enhanced authority. It established a network of officials and branches, offered a range of services (including insurance and legal advice) and grew steadily, including amongst the new owner-occupying farmers. It reached 99,000 members in 1923 and 106,000 in 1927. The repeal of the Agricultural Act in 1921 marked a temporary end to its partnership with government and the union reverted to an incongruous position: aversion to state 'interference'

[75] In a memorandum, Downing suggested that lay titheowners were 'represented [at the negotiations] by the Landowners' Societies who [...] would be concerned with their interests as much as with the interests of landowners'. Downing, Memorandum (n.d. July 1924), CERC, ECE/SEC/TITHE/NEG/1.
[76] LU leaflet, cited in Readman, *Land and Nation*, 56.
[77] 'Mr E. G. Pretyman', *Hartlepool Northern Daily Mail*, 26 Nov. 1931.
[78] R. Strachan Gardiner to Rev. Canon Partridge, 27 June 1923, CERC, ECE/SEC/TITHE/NEG/1.
[79] On the NFU, see Graham Cox, Philip Lowe and Michael Winter, 'The Origins and Early Development of the National Farmers' Union', *AgHR*, 39, 1 (1991), 30–47; Jonathan Brown, 'Agricultural Policy and the National Farmers' Union, 1908–1939', in J. R. Wordie (ed.), *Agriculture and Politics in England, 1815–1939* (Basingstoke: Macmillan, 2000), 178–98.

in the agricultural market, while simultaneously demanding subsidies, tax concessions and protectionist measures. Its proclaimed 'non-political' stance was equally contradictory. The decline of the Liberal Party and the Labour Party's association with the interests of agricultural workers and its policy of land nationalisation propelled the NFU into an 'unofficial alliance' with the Conservative Party. Yet, despite the fact that its four sponsored MPs all sat as Conservatives, the NFU's relationship with the party was far from harmonious.[80]

The NFU's team at the negotiations was led by Thomas Ryland, its president in 1923–24. Also taking part was Rowland Robbins, a towering figure in the union during the 1920s, who became president in February 1925, his second term in office.[81] Both men had a fraught public relationship with Stanley Baldwin, the prime minister and Conservative leader from 1923. Despite championing the 'spiritual independence' of the English farmer, Baldwin's dewy-eyed ruralism often grated with NFU leaders, who were more interested in the impact of government policy on their industry's short-term profit and loss accounts. Typically, at the start of the negotiations, Ryland was unwilling to discuss proposals for a long-term settlement of the tithe problem. The NFU had come along 'not to consider the question of redemption', he told the Church representatives, it simply 'wanted to know […] what the farmers would pay in 1926'.[82]

The starting point for the negotiations was the position agreed at the Church's tithe conference (June 1923), a modified version of the proposals made by Downing in his initial approach to the Ministry of Agriculture. Three issues were particularly contentious: rates on tithe, whether redemption should be compulsory, and the amount to be paid by tithepayers. To reach an agreement, Griffith-Boscawen convened a 'negotiating committee' of three delegates from each side (Clinton, Pretyman and Ryland for the tithepayers; Downing and representatives from the Canterbury and York Tithe Committees for the Church).[83] In regard to rates, the tithepayers' representatives refused to countenance their removal from tithe without a guarantee that other ratepayers would not have to pick up the bill. The issue was resolved when Buxton signalled that legislation would ensure such an arrangement. The question of compulsory redemption was also settled with relative ease. At the first negotiating meeting, Ryland had described the idea as 'absurd', arguing that it was a basic principle of the market that no-one should be forced to

---

80 Moore, 'The Agrarian Conservative Party in Parliament'.
81 Guy Smith, *From Campbell to Kendall: A History of the NFU* (Wellington: Halsgrove, 2008), 37–40, 49–52.
82 'Abridged Report of a conference between titheowners and tithepayers', 26 Feb. 1924, CERC, ECE/SEC/TITHE/NEG/1.
83 Rev. J. V. Bullard from the York Tithe Committee and Canon Robinson from the Canterbury Convention Tithe Committee.

buy something that they did not want.[84] But, after Clinton and Pretyman made clear their support for the measure, and without any alternative policy of his own, Ryland fell in line. He later told NFU activists that 'he had found the Church people [...] wonderful good business people [and] had come to realise [their] position'.[85] The principles of a compulsory redemption scheme were ratified by all twenty-four negotiators and a conference of NFU county branches (25 July 1924) approved it as 'the only solution of the tithe question'.[86]

The unresolved issue was the figure at which tithe should be set. The two sides were not far apart. They both agreed that tithe should continue at a fixed rate for another sixty years, along with an additional payment to a 'sinking fund'. Church representatives had proposed fixing tithe at £104 16s, the value set that year as the basis for tithe redemption by the Ministry of Agriculture's panel of experts. They argued that the 'very large concessions' made under the 1918 Act meant the Church 'ought to meet with generous treatment now'.[87] But, privately, Church negotiators had decided that they 'would probably be prepared to accept £100 [...] provided the scheme was in other respects satisfactory'. The CLA and Land Union had both, at the outset, indicated that they were prepared to agree tithe at £100. The NFU offered a lower figure of £97 6s, the average value of tithe since the 1836 Act, but withdrew the proposal when it was rejected by the other parties.[88] At the NFU annual meeting, Rowland Robbins warned of potential 'chaos resulting' from a failure to reach an agreement and urged members to 'make an honest attempt to look at the question from the other fellow's point of view'.[89] In February 1925, the joint negotiating committee (NFU, CLA and Land Union) issued a report recommending compulsory redemption of clerical tithe, a sinking fund of 4 per cent and tithe to be fixed at £100. There were clear signs that the tithepayers' representatives were close to agreeing a deal with the Church.[90]

Launch of the National Tithepayers' Association

At this point, the emergence of a new voice disrupted the negotiations. On 3 December 1924, around twenty tithepayers attended a meeting in London convened by Sir Henry Rew and Frank Allen. The attendees

[84] 'Conference between titheowners and tithepayers', 26 Feb. 1924.
[85] *NFU Record*, Feb. 1925, 111.
[86] Sir Arthur Griffith-Boscawen, 'Tithe Rent-Charge Negotiations' (1 Jan. 1925), Church Assembly, 1925, CERC, PB.221; NFU General Purposes Committee, 18 Feb. 1925, MERL, SR NFU, AD1/7; NFU Land Tenure Committee, 21 Oct. 1924, MERL, SR NFU, AD1/6.
[87] 'Conference between titheowners and tithepayers', 26 Feb. 1924.
[88] Downing, Memorandum (n.d. July 1924), CERC, ECE/SEC/TITHE/NEG/1.
[89] NFU Annual General Meeting (21 Jan. 1925), *NFU Record*, Feb. 1925, 111.
[90] NFU General Purposes Committee, 18 Feb. 1925, MERL, SR NFU, AD1/7.

appointed a 'provisional committee' to draft the rules and constitution for a National Tithepayers' Association. One month later (6 January 1925), another meeting, better attended, launched the association. Fifteen people, mainly owner-occupying farmers, were elected to a National Council and plans were laid to organise public meetings in important agricultural regions. Over the next few months, the NTA developed a small network with members in Kent, Berkshire, Gloucestershire, Essex, Hampshire and Hertfordshire.

The association's aim was to provide tithepayers with independent representation at the negotiating table. Tithepayers, it said, should 'not be party to, or in any way committed to' a settlement agreed by organisations that were only 'purporting to represent tithepayers'.[91] The CLA and Land Union were made up 'mainly of large landowners, some of whom [were] tithe owners' and the NFU was equally unable to speak for tithepayers because 'the majority of their members were tenant farmers who [had] no interest in tithe'.[92] Acting as a distinct organisation, the NTA would represent 'the interests of tithepayers and of ratepayers in districts where the rates are affected by the tithe rent-charge', demand 'equitable treatment' in future legislation, give 'assistance and advice to members' and 'organise and educate public opinion' on the issue of tithe.[93] Regarding the ongoing negotiations, it would oppose any deal that made terms for tithe redemption less favourable than those stipulated in the 1918 Act, demand that tithe should continue to be assessed for rates and call for immediate legislation to remove all legal measures that were 'unfair to tithepayers'.[94]

The launch of the NTA took place against the background of anti-communist fervour stirred by the Zinoviev Letter. Published in the *Daily Mail*, this forged document, supposedly written by the head of the Communist International, revealed that the re-election of a Labour government would lead to revolution in Britain and throughout the empire. Some zealous defenders of tithe accused those seeking tithe reform of 'bolshevism, pure and simple'. The 'tithepayer owning land,' wrote one, 'lives in a glass house, and in the face of the Socialist and Communist, should take warning and not set the example by Church robbery. His turn would come.'[95] In response to such arguments, Henry Rew stressed that 'in forming the association [they] were not attacking the

[91] 'Tithepayers and the Government', *The Times*, 28 Feb. 1925.
[92] 'Report of the Council of the National Tithepayers' Association', 11 May 1925, LSE Special Collections.
[93] 'Tithepayers: National Association Formed', *The Times*, 4 Dec. 1924; 'Protection of Tithe Payers', *F&S*, 12 Jan. 1925; 'Protection of Tithepayers', *The Times*, 7 Jan. 1925.
[94] 'Tithepayers' Policy on Redemption, *The Times*, 17 Mar. 1925.
[95] 'Tithes and the Harvest', *WMN*, 13 Oct. 1924.

titheowners in any sense, nor were they challenging the tithe rent-charge as a form of property'.[96] The Tithepayers' Association did not propose the abolition of tithe, or that farmers should withhold payments. It proposed a programme to reform the tithe system, including measures to reduce 'excessive' tithe and to make the system more transparent. It argued for tithe to be fixed at £90 and for the 1891 Act to be amended to grant remission if tithe reached more than 50 per cent of the value of the land (instead of two-thirds).[97]

The two men who took the initiative to establish the NTA had first met in 1921. After retiring from a glittering Civil Service career shortly after the war, Henry Rew stood twice, unsuccessfully, as a parliamentary candidate for the Liberal Party (in 1922 and 1923).[98] He was drawn into the tithe controversy after his appointment in 1921 to the Ministry of Agriculture's committee of experts on tithe redemption. Allen met him while giving evidence to the committee in his capacity as tithe agent at Canterbury Cathedral. The fact that the two men lived less than twenty miles apart helped to cement their relationship.

Rew and Allen had been hopeful that the more attractive and flexible redemption provisions of the 1918 Act would provide the beginnings of a solution to the tithe problem. Initially, the measures encouraged a significant increase in redemption applications: between 1836 and 1918, tithe valued at £73,000 had been redeemed; in the three years between 1918 and 1920, the figure leapt to £340,000. If this rate of redemption were to continue, noted Rew, then the 'whole of tithe rentcharge payable in this country' would be 'extinguished' in around ten years.[99] For his part, Allen campaigned to persuade farmers to take advantage of the more favourable redemption opportunities, organising meetings of farmers to prepare applications and warning of serious difficulties if the scheme were to be unsuccessful.[100] But Rew and Allen were dismayed when the number of redemption applications collapsed after the passing of the Rates Act in 1920.

The concessions on rates to tithe-owning clergy impacted on redemption in two ways. First, rates paid by tithepayers increased to mitigate monies previously collected from the local parson, which meant less funds were available for payments to redeem tithe. Secondly, the removal and reduction of rates led to an increase in redemption charges, on account

---

[96] 'Tithepayers', *The Times*, 4 Dec. 1924.
[97] 'Report of the Council of the National Tithepayers' Association', 11 May 1925, LSE Special Collections.
[98] Sir R. Henry Rew, *Journal of the Royal Statistical Society*, 92, 2 (1929), 297–9.
[99] Henry Rew, 'Tithe Redemption', *The Times*, 2 June 1925.
[100] Mr F. R. Allen, 'The Tithe Act of 1918, The Substance of a Paper read before the Canterbury Farmers Club and Chamber of Agriculture, 15 Mar. 1919', LPL.

of the 1918 Act stipulating that titheowners' rates should be deducted when calculating a settlement. Rew described the legislation as having 'dammed the flow of applications', which fell from 11,159 in 1920 to 1,792 in 1923.[101] Speaking in August 1923 at a meeting in Canterbury organised by the National Union of Farmers, Allen described the 1920 Act as 'one of the greatest blunders committed by the Church in recent times'.[102] By now, the cathedral's tithe agent had become a regular guest at meetings of the Club and Chamber, becoming accustomed to farmers' grievances about tithe and beginning to empathise with their arguments. One of his talks prompted a 'long discussion [...] in which several members spoke of the inability of farmers to pay the present tithe charge'.[103] Allen also began to make contact with critics of the tithe system in other parts of the country.

One of these was Alfred Blomfield. Well known amongst farmers in East Anglia, Blomfield helped to build support for the NTA's launch and was elected its treasurer at the inaugural meeting. Before the war, he had for three decades been manager of the Gosfield Hall estate (Essex). In 1919, Blomfield purchased his own rather less grand country estate at Little Maplestead, from which he combined a successful arable and dairy farming business with a prominent role in local political and civic life. He once told the Sudbury branch of the NFU that he was 'a larger titheowner than tithepayer'.[104] A member of the Liberal Party and a Congregationalist, sometimes describing himself as a 'cantankerous deacon', Blomfield formed part of the nonconformist strand in the tithepayers' movement, later to be represented by Rev. Roderick Kedward.

The launch of the NTA was widely reported in the agricultural press and, during December and January, the tithe issue dominated the letters pages of *The Farmer & Stockbreeder*, then an unofficial mouthpiece of the NFU. Owner-occupying farmers wrote to complain of demands from titheowners. A purchaser of a small farm of twenty acres in Crundale (Kent) explained how he had received bills from both his local clergyman and 'the earl of Winchelsea [sic] and Nottingham': 'Now, Sir, can you tell me how this thing started and why it should continue? [...] it seems to me like robbery', he asked with a mixture of anger and incredulity. Correspondents expressed support for the NTA, but often demanded more far-reaching solutions than those proposed by the association. Tithe should be 'commuted by the state,' wrote one. It should be 'abolished at once to keep pace with the times,' added another. One farmer (L. W. S. Long) summed up the frustration of many:

[101] Henry Rew, 'Tithe Redemption', *The Times*, 2 June 1925.
[102] 'Tithes and the Rates', *DE*, 10 Aug. 1923.
[103] Canterbury Farmers' Club, *DE*, 25 May 1923.
[104] 'The Tithe Bill', *Suffolk and Essex Free Press*, 18 June 1925; 'Essex Congregational Union', *ChCh*, 24 Apr. 1925.

I bought this farm in 1920 with my eyes equally wide open to the two facts – namely, that there was a tithe on the land and also that there was an assurance given by the British government that wheat should not fall below a given price for a given period. [...] I think it was reasonable to presume that the Government guarantee would be as stable as the Government's imposition of tithe.[105]

The NTA's launch and propaganda had an immediate impact within the NFU. Branches and individual activists criticised the leadership's willingness to sign up to a compulsory redemption scheme on unfavourable terms. The annual meeting of the Devon county branch took Ryland to task for 'doing nothing' to resolve the tithe problem. The Norfolk executive rejected the proposals of the joint negotiating team and suggested fixing tithe at £90, with a 3.5 per cent payment to the sinking fund, rather than 4 per cent.[106] In a consultation, twenty-eight county branches approved the position of the negotiators, but eleven expressed serious doubts – and these included branches covering the most heavily tithed regions. After a lengthy debate, the NFU council on 19 February approved the 'general principles' of the negotiators' report but rejected much of the detail. It instructed 'the representatives of the Union to press to the utmost extent possible for concessions in respect to the details of the scheme on the basis of the representations [...] received from the county branches'.[107] In effect, a rebellion from the membership had ensured that NFU negotiators could not sign up to an agreement with the Church. The rancour generated by the episode would define the relationship between the NFU and NTA for the next decade. Ryland and Robbins could neither forgive nor forget the 'mischievous activities of the Tithepayers' Association', which had, they claimed, 'cut clean across the work' of the CLA, Land Union and NFU with 'deplorable results'.[108]

The 1925 Tithe Bill

By now, a Conservative government was back in office with a landslide parliamentary majority and a commitment to continue the work of the previous administration in 'dealing with the readjustment and redemption of Tithe Rentcharge'.[109] The minister of agriculture, Edward Wood (later Lord Halifax), received briefings from Griffith-Boscawen, representatives of the landowners' associations and the Church. On 27 February, he met a delegation from the NTA, the first official recognition

---

[105] *F&S*, 12 and 19 Jan. 1925.
[106] *F&S*, 2 Feb. and 2 Mar. 1925.
[107] NFU General Purposes Committee, 18 Feb. 1925, MERL, SR NFU, AD1/7; 'Meeting of the Council of the Union', *NFU Record*, Mar. 1925, 129–30.
[108] 'The Tithe Question', *NFU Record*, June 1931, 212.
[109] King's Speech, 9 Dec. 1924, TNA, CAB 24/169/16.

of the new organisation.[110] Wood concluded that, despite the failure of the negotiations, the fact that the parties had been close to agreement meant that the government could draft a bill that would be received as an acceptable compromise by titheowners and tithepayers, perhaps with the exception of a minority represented by the NTA. A high-powered cabinet committee was appointed to draw up the legislation. Along with Wood, its members included William Joynson-Hicks (home secretary), Winston Churchill (chancellor of the exchequer), Neville Chamberlain (minister of health) and Laming Worthington-Evans (secretary of state for war).[111] Amongst those to advise on the level of tithe was the bursar of King's College Cambridge, the economist John Maynard Keynes.[112]

The tithe bill was published at the end of May.[113] It fixed ecclesiastical tithe at £105, with an additional payment of £4 10s for the 'sinking fund'; payments would continue for eighty-five years (eighty-one and a half years for ecclesiastical corporations). Lay tithe would also be fixed at £105 'in perpetuity', without a sinking fund or compulsion on tithepayers to redeem it. Tithe due to incumbent clergy would in future be collected by Queen Anne's Bounty. This followed a request from senior clergy, who had come to believe that post-war changes in land ownership had increased potential sources of friction between tithe-collecting clergy and their parishioners.[114] Rates would no longer be collected directly from clergy, but Queen Anne's Bounty would pay £5 out of each £105 of tithe to the Inland Revenue in lieu of rates. Ecclesiastical corporations (cathedral chapters, etc.) would see no change to their rates, continuing to pay around 16 per cent of collected tithe. Overall, the Church's total contribution to rates would be reduced from £375,000 to £95,000, the shortfall financed from the public purse, rather than directly by other ratepayers.

Although Church leaders and officials spoke of a 'settlement that fell short of real justice', they found it hard to hide their opinion that they had gained a good deal. Two participants in the negotiations, Canon Partridge and Griffith-Boscawen, described the bill as 'statesmanlike' and 'exceedingly fair'.[115] In contrast, the NTA described the bill as 'unjust'. It pointed out that tithepayers would end up paying around 50 per cent more to redeem tithe in a compulsory scheme than they could have paid in the voluntary scheme established by the 1918 Act. Not a single living farmer, nor most of their children, would live to see the day when

[110] 'Tithepayers and the Government', *The Times*, 28 Feb. 1925.
[111] Cabinet, 'Tithe Rentcharge. Report of Committee', 8 May 1925, TNA, CAB/24/173.
[112] Memorandum by the Secretary of State for War, 1 Dec. 1925, TNA, CAB/24/176.
[113] 'Tithe and Rates', *The Times*, 28 May 1925.
[114] HC Deb., *Hansard*, 18 June 1925.
[115] 'The Tithe Bill', *The Times*, 10 and 18 June 1925.

tithe ceased to exist. Moreover, even after the 85-year period, lay tithe would continue to survive. The association warned that the legislation raised 'grave questions' about the constitutional position of the Church, complained that the views of tithepayers had been ignored and declared that the bill could not be accepted 'as a final or satisfactory settlement'. It demanded a Royal Commission 'to consider the tithe question in all its bearing'.[116] Writing to *The Times*, Henry Rew touched a raw nerve within the Church by maintaining that fixing tithe at £109 10s for eighty-five years could 'only be defended by arguing that clerical tithe-owners are entitled to make a permanent profit out of the war'.[117]

The landowners' associations (CLA, Land Union) gave reluctant support to the bill. Its provisions were inferior to those that had been on the table during the talks. Tithe would be set 5 per cent above the figure the Church had been prepared to accept. Similarly, the contribution to the sinking fund (4.5 per cent) was higher than the 4 per cent previously proposed. Clerical tithe would be fixed at £109 10s – 13 per cent above its average value since 1836 – and continue at this level for eighty-five years, rather than the sixty agreed during the talks.[118] The CLA highlighted such points, but was not prepared to oppose the bill. Clinton explained that the negotiations had come 'to actual agreement upon many of the most important points' and these 'definite agreements are very largely the foundation' of the bill. He warned that failure to pass legislation with the 'effect of tithe rising to a high figure next year […] will increase the unwillingness to pay among a very large number of people [and] create a condition in many agricultural parishes of social unrest'.[119]

The NFU expressed opposition to the bill. An editorial in the *NFU Record* echoed the points made by Henry Rew: the Church would gain 'every farthing of benefit' from the war and 'escape all the difficulties that would attend the collection of tithe at unprecedently high values'; its 'loss' through its 'voluntary self-denial' in 1918 was now 'being repaid with interest'.[120] The proposed legislation could not, declared the union, lead to 'an equitable and permanent settlement' and if it 'should become law', the NFU would seek to amend it 'at the earliest opportunity'.[121]

The tithe bill served to deepen the already strained relations between the NFU and the Conservative government. Baldwin had fought the 1924

[116] 'The Tithe Problem', *Sussex Agricultural Express*, 6 Nov. 1925; 'Statement from Council of the NTA', *Exeter and Plymouth Gazette*, 2 Nov. 1925.
[117] Downing wrote a rather tetchy riposte. Henry Rew, 'Tithe Redemption', *The Times*, 2 June 1925; S. E. Downing, 'Tithe Redemption', *The Times*, 3 June 1925.
[118] 'Injustice of the Tithe Bill', *F&S*, 22 June 1925.
[119] HL. Deb., *Hansard*, 3 Dec. 1925.
[120] 'The Tithe Bill', *NFU Record*, July 1925, 225–6.
[121] NFU, General Purposes Committee, 15 Apr. 1925; NFU Parliamentary, Press & Publicity Committee, 16 June 1925; NFU Parliamentary, Press & Publicity Committee, 20 Oct. 1925, MERL, SR NFU, AD1/7.

general election with a pledge to reject duties on food imports, a policy that contributed to electoral success but antagonised farmers' leaders seeking measures to protect agriculture from deepening depression. The days when Conservatives could consider agriculture as the 'greatest of all trades and industries'[122] were no more. It was an industry like any other, in need of modernisation and integration into the needs of the wider economy. Moreover, while the Conservative heartland remained rural, the number of parliamentarians from an agrarian background had continued to decline – in 1924, only 12.5 per cent of Conservative MPs were landowners, and only two were classed as 'professional farmers'.[123] The NFU accused the government of pursuing policies that put the interests of manufacturing industries and the urban population ahead of agriculture. It opposed the Rating and Valuation Bill (1925), which it claimed would increase rates on farm buildings. It also claimed that the cost of the government's limited welfare programme – national insurance, extension of pensions to widows, unemployment relief – would fall disproportionately on agriculture compared with other industries, claiming 'there was no need' for such measures in agriculture.[124]

The NFU's opposition to the tithe bill led members of the cabinet to fume against the actions of the 'truculent Farmers' Union'.[125] The relationship deteriorated further when, in November 1925, Walter Guinness was appointed minister of agriculture. Under the electoral law of the day, an MP taking a paid public post over nine months after a general election was required to stand for re-election and, consequently, a by-election was triggered in Bury St Edmunds.[126] In an unsuccessful attempt to unseat Guinness, the NFU openly supported the Liberal candidate, George Nicholls, a nonconformist minister and advocate for the interests of agricultural workers and smallholders.[127] The by-election campaign would, announced NFU headquarters, 'serve to focus the opposition to the [tithe] bill that prevails in Suffolk'.[128]

A settlement to 'keep the sore open'

Despite the government's majority of 209, the tithe bill's passage through parliament was more reminiscent of the controversies of the 1880s than the smooth ride given to the legislation of 1918. Most

[122] The words of Unionist, Joseph Chamberlain, cited in Green, *Crisis of Conservatism*, 207.
[123] Moore, 'The Agrarian Conservative Party', 348–9.
[124] 'The Government and Agriculture', *The Times*, 17 July 1925.
[125] Memorandum by the Secretary of State for War, 1 Dec. 1925, TNA, CAB/24/176.
[126] 'Liberal Candidate Selected', *Framlingham Weekly News*, 14 Nov. 1925; 'Farmers and Tithe Rent Charge', *The Times*, 4 Jan. 1926.
[127] *BuFP*, 14 Nov. 1925; 'Farmers and Tithe Rent Charge'. *The Times*, 4 Jan. 1926.
[128] NFU Newsheet, 9 Nov. 1925, MERL, SR NFU P4/A5.

Conservatives, particularly those with a background in industry and commerce, considered the bill to be a sensible compromise that would protect the interests of the Church and mitigate against social tensions in the countryside. But some Conservatives, those with links to the farming community or representing the Oxford and Cambridge colleges, expressed disquiet, a number abstaining or voting with the Labour and Liberal opposition.

The NFU-sponsored MPs, most prominently Joseph Lamb and Ernest Shepperson, led one strand of dissent. Stressing that the 'bulk of payers' were not 'large landowners but men in small circumstances, many of whom have had to buy their farm', they proposed to fix tithe at £100 and to reduce the redemption period to sixty-five years.[129] They won support from influential figures in the Conservative Party's parliamentary agricultural committee, including Sir Henry Cautley and Sir Granville Wheler, MP for Faversham (Kent). 'Speaking as a churchman,' Wheler told the House, 'I deprecate very strongly the attempt of the Government to drive through any bill containing the figures proposed.' It would 'create a feeling of bitterness between the parson and [...] some of his best supporters in the parish'. Another aristocratic Tory representing a heavily tithed region, William Vanneck (Lord Huntingfield), MP for Eye (Suffolk), added that farmers could 'ill afford to pay it at this time when farming is at such a low ebb'. When Lamb and Shepperson's amendment was not selected by the speaker, they backed a 'compromise' moved by Cautley, which sought to fix tithe at £102 10s. This amendment was defeated by 117 votes.[130]

An amendment moved by MPs representing university constituencies gathered more support. As already noted, lay titheowners, including the Oxford and Cambridge colleges, had not been represented at the negotiations. They were aggrieved that the settlement was far less favourable for them than for the Church. Reducing the fixed level of tithe from £109 to £105, without 'any compensating measures' (a reduction in rates), would, they argued, mean 'heavy losses'. They argued that a higher rate of tithe was justified because global cereal prices were, in the immediate decade or so, more likely to rise than to fall, referencing what would prove an incredibly awry forecast by John Maynard Keynes.[131] John Rawlinson, a Conservative representing Cambridge University, and Herbert (H. A .L.) Fisher, a Liberal representing Combined English Universities, proposed an amendment to revert the calculation of tithe due to universities, public schools and other charitable institutions – such as almshouses and hospitals – to the septennial average of cereals that existed before the war. In short, they were demanding higher

---

[129] HC Deb., *Hansard*, 18 June 1925.
[130] HC Deb., *Hansard*, 19 Nov. 1925.
[131] HC Deb., *Hansard*, 18 June 1925.

tithes. Support for the Oxford and Cambridge titheowners arrived from some die-hard Conservatives, such as Lord Hugh Cecil, who spoke of 'robbery' and 'confiscation' by a 'government which purports to be here to defend the rights of property'. It also came from the Labour Party, whose front-bench spokesperson, Josiah Wedgwood, declared that, in choosing between 'the rival claims' of landlords and educational institutions, his party would 'put money on education every time'.[132] The amendment received 147 votes, as against 186 – in the context, a narrow defeat.

A descendent of the famous potter, Wedgwood was one of a number of former Liberals who influenced Labour agricultural policy during the first half of the 1920s. Before the war, he had led the League of Taxation of Land Values, which campaigned for the policies announced in Lloyd George's 'people's budget' (1909).[133] Influenced by the ideas of the political economist Henry George, he viewed taxation as the means of 'freeing the land' from the landlord class, reducing the burden of taxation for the wider population and providing finances for measures of social reform.

Wedgwood viewed the tithe bill through this optic. The government's increased subsidy of rates was, he argued, an attempt 'to shift the hereditary burden carried by the land on to the body of the general taxpayers'. Differences between tithepayers and titheowners were essentially a conflict over 'the division of the spoil of [...] two sets of robbers'. Yet it was necessary to protect the interests of deserving sections of society whose livelihoods and activities were dependent on tithe. The bill was, argued Wedgwood, a 'new breach of contract introduced by the Government in order to deprive the clerical incumbents and the charitable institutions of this country of the rights that they had enjoyed since 1836'. It should be opposed 'on the grounds of honesty, tradition and sanctity of contract'.[134] Under Wedgwood's direction, the Labour Party proposed to fix tithe at a higher level of £110, rather than £105. It opposed the amendment to reduce tithe to £102 10s and supported the proposal to relink tithe paid to universities and public schools to the septennial average. Wedgwood also proposed that payments of ecclesiastical tithe should be extended beyond eighty-five years if the sinking fund had not built sufficient capital to pay clergy an appropriate income. Paradoxically, Wedgwood's antagonism to landlordism had led him to defend the interests of titheowners and the principle of tithe, a 'peculiar form of property' rooted in medieval times.

Wedgwood's position is an indication of the extent to which the Labour leadership had, like the Church a few years earlier, failed to recognise

---

[132] HC Deb., *Hansard*, 19 Nov. 1925.
[133] Griffiths, *Labour and the Countryside*, 226–7.
[134] HC Deb., *Hansard*, 19 Nov. 1925.

the post-war transformation in farm ownership. His understanding of rural social relations remained posited in a nineteenth-century template of landlords, tenant farmers and labourers. Throughout the debate, Wedgwood described tithepayers as 'landlords'. If the bill were defeated and tithe reached £131, it would be 'only the landlord' that would be 'injured', he told MPs.[135] Opposing the amendment supported by NFU-sponsored MPs to reduce tithe to £102 10s, he complained: 'We hear about the lamentable condition of the farmers. But honourable members opposite know perfectly well that the man who pays [the tithe] is the landlord, and this does not affect the farmer in the least.'[136] Quite simply, Wedgwood could not grasp that many farmers were now also landowners, and therefore liable for tithe.

Some on Labour's front bench were even more resolute in their defence of the rights of titheowners. Sir Henry Slesser had been solicitor-general in the previous Labour government. A prominent Anglo-Catholic, he was a member of the League of the Kingdom of God, an association that in 1924 became part of the Christian Order in Politics Economics and Citizenship (COPEC), a movement described as 'Christian socialism in its latest phase'.[137] Slesser argued that the 1836 Act had enshrined the clergy's 'absolute right to tithe'. It had been wrong in 1918 to force the Church to 'make a sacrifice' by fixing tithe at a level far below the septennial average of cereals. The new bill should be opposed because it would take away about a third of the amount to which the clergy were entitled. The Labour Party opposed the bill, he explained, because under its provisions 'the general doctrine of property is mutilated and distorted'.[138]

Some backbench Labour MPs spoke against the bill from an entirely different perspective and opposed the basic principle of tithe. In decline as a force, political nonconformism was no longer a preserve of the Liberal Party, but still had a significant presence on the Labour benches. For Cecil Wilson, tithe was 'distasteful' because many people, including nonconformist Christians, had 'to contribute something in which [they did] not believe'. Similarly, James Barr opposed a 'new entrenchment of the establishment', a measure against 'civil justice and spiritual freedom and religious equality'.[139] Some on the Labour benches, such as George Lansbury, took 'a plague on both your houses' position: 'if we have time to waste on a bill of this kind, then we ought to have time to deal with

---

[135] HC Deb., *Hansard*, 18 June 1925.
[136] HC Deb., *Hansard*, 19 Nov. 1925.
[137] Conference on Christian Politics, Economics and Citizenship; Norman, *Church and Society*, 286–7.
[138] HC Deb., *Hansard*, 18 June 1925.
[139] Ibid.

the condition of the people, millions of whom literally are unable to get a decent standard of living.'[140]

Nursing its wounds after the bruising electoral defeat of 1924, the Liberal Party remained remarkably quiet during the debate. Some MPs maintained the party's traditional critique of the charge tithe, attempting to rekindle the party's role as the political voice of nonconformism. Beddoe Rees, a prominent member of the National Free Church, asked 'what would happen' if the nonconformist Churches asked the state to 'pay the rates and taxes on the house in which their ministers live?'[141] But others around David Lloyd George tended to dismiss the owner-occupying farmers as 'three-quarters Conservative' and were prioritising policies to rebuild Liberal support amongst agricultural labourers and smaller tenant farmers. The party became embroiled in controversy over Lloyd George's 'cultivating tenure' policy, effectively a form of land nationalisation (though the word was not used). The scheme aimed to appeal to agricultural labourers by encouraging the extension of smallholdings as well as increased provision of allotments and larger gardens. Farmers would be given security of tenure and no longer face obstacles preventing investment, such as large mortgages or increased rents from landlords. Conservatives attacked the policy as 'socialist in all but name' and the NFU gave it short shift. This came as no surprise to Lloyd George, whose main objective was to regalvanise Liberal support amongst the rural poor – increasingly attracted to Labour – without losing the support of those smallholding farmers who traditionally voted Liberal. But 'cultivating tenure' prompted controversy within the party and some considerable opposition. The result was that, as the tithe issue came to the fore, Liberals were engaged in heated discussion over rural policy and tended to avoid the tithe controversy for fear of further complicating matters.[142]

One of those to speak out on both issues was the peer Edward Strachey (Lord Strachie), who was an early – though temporary – adherent to the NTA. A west-country landowner who had served as parliamentary secretary to the Board of Agriculture in the 1906 Asquith government, Strachey argued that 'cultivating tenure' did not reflect the needs of rural communities and would antagonise farmers whose support was needed by the party.[143] He led opposition to the tithe bill in the House of Lords, arguing that the legislation would keep 'open the sore [of tithe] for the next eighty years'.[144]

[140] HC Deb., *Hansard*, 19 Nov. 1925.
[141] HC Deb., *Hansard*, 18 June 1925.
[142] Dawson, 'Liberal Land Policy', 273.
[143] C.S. Orwin, revised by H. C. G. Matthew, 'Strachey, Edward (1858–1936)', *ODNB* (2004).
[144] HL Deb., *Hansard*, 3 Dec. 1925.

The bill had a majority of 139 at its Third Reading and received the Royal Assent on 22 December 1925. Back in June, when proposing the legislation, Edward Wood had sought 'to frame a permanent and final settlement' to the tithe problem.[145] The Church hierarchy heralded the bill as 'a new bargain' that would lead to the winding up of tithe in a gradual and painless way. It was, said the archbishop of Canterbury, a bill that would 'confer a real benefit on the Church and the country'.[146] In reality, two years of negotiations and political debate had failed to produce a consensus. Even after the Third Reading, the Cabinet was forced to consider a request from the lord chancellor George Cave for a 'postponement' of the bill's provisions for two or three years whilst a 'further committee' examined objections from lay titheowners. The government's dilemma was summed up by Sir Laming Worthington-Evans, who told the Cabinet that 'there was no solution which will reconcile all views'.[147]

The debate around the 1925 Tithe Act had, indeed, opened many sores. Those close to the farming community knew that farmers' resentment at the 'settlement' was deep. In the House of Commons, the NFU-sponsored MP Joseph Lamb had the last word in the debate. Just before the vote on the Third Reading, he warned that 'those who hope this will be a permanent settlement are going to be painfully disillusioned in the future'.[148] But many titheowners also felt short-changed. Resentment amongst lay titheowners would encourage them to try to extract every last drop of their entitlement to tithe. Within the Church, despite the position of the hierarchy, a significant section of clergy felt aggrieved. In 1918, the clergy had supported the freezing of tithe, recognising that its high value was a direct result of the war. Seven years later, many felt that another 'sacrifice' was unjustified and unnecessary. As if to signal their discontent, 1,800 parish clergy took advantage of a clause allowing them to opt out of the Queen Anne Bounty's new tithe-collecting machinery. Predictably, the Tithe Owners' Union, organised by Edward Peterson, denounced the bill as 'confiscation [and] interference with the status of the clergy'.[149] Peterson even approached the NFU asking it to cooperate in a campaign to force a postponement of the bill.[150]

---

[145] HC Deb., *Hansard*, 18 June 1925.
[146] HL Deb., *Hansard*, 3 Dec. 1925.
[147] 'Tithe Bill', Memorandum by the Secretary of State for War, 1 Dec. 1925, TNA, CAB/24/176.
[148] HC Deb., *Hansard*, 26 Nov. 1925.
[149] Letter from Alfred Batchelor, Harry Beck and E. W. I. Peterson, *The Times*, 7 Dec. 1925.
[150] NFU, Parliamentary, Press and Publicity Committee, 17 Nov. 1925, MERL, SR NFU, AD1/7.

The new and, for many, unexpected feature of the debate around the 1925 Act was the emergence of the voice of owner-occupying farmers – reflected through the launch of the NTA and activity within the NFU. The word 'tithepayer' was no longer synonymous with 'landlord'. Difficulties concerning tithe could not be resolved through cosy discussions between the Church and landowning associations. Moreover, the owner-occupiers had stayed the hand of the NFU leaders, who had been ready and willing to sign up to a deal. In important ways, their intervention had redefined the character of the tithe problem.

5

The Settlement Unravels, 1927–31

Calm before the storm

There was a brief hiatus in the tithe controversy during the four years after the Tithe Act reached the statute book. Despite the lack of consensus in the debate over the legislation, many institutions with a stake in tithe began to believe that the controversy had been resolved, at least for the foreseeable future. The transfer of the collection process to Queen Anne's Bounty required considerable preparation and, in consequence, the implementation of the Act was postponed until 31 March 1927. After that, all appeared to be working reasonably well. The Queen Anne's Bounty governors reported that, between April 1927 and December 1928, collections were 'proceeding satisfactory, and [...] have been organised [...] with an efficiency which is having increasingly good results'.[1] The Church hierarchy and senior officials became increasingly confident that – once inevitable teething troubles were ironed out – the 'settlement' would indeed become 'permanent and final'. The prevailing mood amongst leaders of the landowning associations and the NFU was a sense of relief that the Act had averted the 20 per cent hike in tithe due in 1926. Officially, the NFU was committed to try to amend the legislation at the 'earliest opportunity'. Yet, having signed up to its essential elements, its leaders were unable and unwilling to explain what aspects should be changed. In reality, the NFU was happy to live with the Tithe Act.[2]

The major political parties also considered the tithe problem settled. Tithe did not feature in the Conservative Party's agricultural programme drawn up for the 1929 general election, which promised to provide farmers with cheaper credit, help to find markets and improvements in rural amenities.[3] The same was true for the programmes of the Liberal and Labour parties. Having abandoned the idea of 'cultivating tenure'

---

[1] Governors of Queen Anne's Bounty, 20 Feb. 1929, CERC QAB/2/1/46.
[2] *NFU Record*, Feb. 1930, 106.
[3] 'Party Agricultural Policies', *NFU Record*, June 1929, 216.

and fighting the election primarily on the theme of unemployment, the Liberals proposed the 'revival of the countryside' through the creation of rural industries and public works, including better drainage, upgrades for rural roads and a plan for electrification in rural areas.[4] Some candidates raised the tithe issue on the stump. In Chelmsford (Essex), the unsuccessful Sydney Robinson promised 'a reduction [of] this very heavy burden on agriculture'.[5] Tithe also featured in the campaign in Eye (Suffolk). Arthur Soames, the Conservative candidate, accused Edgar Granville, standing for the Liberals, of attempting 'to attract the agriculturist vote by suggesting that the Liberal Party would abolish tithe'. He claimed that farmers with grievances over tithe were 'desiring to avoid their obligations'.[6] Granville won the seat on a 15 per cent swing from the Conservatives, a result almost certainly influenced by the exchange over tithe.

The novelty in Labour's agricultural policy was that it was no longer aimed exclusively at agricultural labourers. Admitting that it was no longer defensible to leave agriculture as 'the last item on the agenda', the party attempted to appeal to farmers by promising a system of organised marketing, price stability for agricultural produce and easier access to credit. It also continued to advocate 'public control' of land, which would be administered by county councils and leased to farmers. The policy was designed to reverse the 'deterioration' of conditions relating to soil, buildings and drainage, which arose from the 'hampering restrictions' of private ownership of the landed estates. But, despite its promise of security of tenure, the policy did not win many friends amongst those owner-occupying farmers who had recently purchased their holdings.[7] Despite an increased awareness of issues relating to agriculture, tithe did not feature in Labour's programme. Some candidates in highly tithed regions raised the issue of their own volition. In Bury St Edmunds (Suffolk), Percy Astins, who stood against Walter Guinness, the outgoing minister of agriculture, declared that 'tithe was unjust' and that 'the Labour Party stood very definitely for its abolition'.[8] But such a position was immediately refuted by Noel Buxton, who was to become minister of agriculture in the Labour government.[9]

---

4   'Liberal Policy', *The Times*, 2 Mar. 1929; Liberal Party, *We Can Conquer Unemployment: Mr Lloyd George's Pledge* (London: Cassell, 1929).
5   'The Liberal Campaign', *ChCh*, 10 May 1929.
6   'The Eye Division', *DiEx*, 24 May 1929.
7   G. T. Garratt, *Agriculture and the Labour Party* (London: Fabian Society, 1929); 'Party Agricultural Policies', *NFU Record*, June 1929, 216.
8   'NFU and Bury Candidates', *BuFP*, 18 May 1929.
9   HC Deb., *Hansard*, 22 July 1929.

The Settlement Unravels, 1927–31

Optimism about the effects of the Tithe Act in the years 1926–29 was based on the belief that the worst of the agricultural depression was over. Between 1920 and 1922, the price of wheat had spiralled downwards. It plateaued during the following two years and, for the next half a decade, displayed 'a slight decreasing trend', though still remaining above pre-war levels.[10] Farmers in the highly tithed eastern counties – especially those operating on a large scale – found ways to compensate for the fall in cereal prices. Many diversified their output, particularly by introducing more dairy production. Some moved into sugar beet cultivation, benefiting from the subsidies provided in the British Sugar (Subsidy) Act of 1925. Road improvements reduced distribution costs and opened urban markets for dairy products, as well as fruit and vegetables. Following the failure of the 'great strike' by agricultural labourers in Norfolk in 1923, farmers reduced costs further by driving down wages to 'levels which must have involved acute deprivation'.[11] Perhaps most significantly, the 1925 Tithe Act had stabilised tithe payments for farmers. At £109 10s, the new rate of ecclesiastical tithe was only slightly higher than the £109 3s 11d set in 1918. Lay tithe was reduced to £105. During the years 1926–29, few leading people in the Church, government or farming industry anticipated that tithe would very soon re-emerge as a major political and social problem.

Early years of the National Tithepayers' Association

Yet grievances about tithe bubbled beneath the surface. One indication is the sharp increase in the number of distraint orders for non-payment issued in the county courts. In 1913, there had been 540 such orders. In 1927, there were 1,968 and in the following year the number had risen to 2,558 – nearly 500 per cent more than the pre-war figure.[12] Most of the cases involved owner-occupiers and, in the vast majority of instances, the charge was paid before a distraint was carried out. The figures suggest that a significant number of farmers were prepared to stretch legal proceedings to the limit as a form of individual protest. Some of those doing so would later play a significant role in the tithe war of the 1930s. Amongst farmers from Elham summoned to appear at Hythe county court (Kent) on 18 March 1927 was Kingsley Dykes. Serious injury while serving during the war had prevented the Cambridge-educated Dykes

---

[10] Gema Aparicio & Vicente Pinilla, 'The Dynamics of International Trade in Cereals, 1900–1938', *Sociedad Española de Historia Agraria*, 1504 (2015), 15–16.

[11] Edith H. Whetham, *The Agrarian History of England and Wales, Vol. VIII, 1914–1939* (Cambridge: Cambridge University Press, 1978), 142–71.

[12] 'Statement of Evidence submitted by the Lord Chancellor's Office', Royal Comm, Minutes of Evidence, 627.

from pursuing a career in medicine and, in 1921, after pursuing studies in agriculture, he bought Ottinge Court Farm, the most prestigious farm in the district.[13] With his status in the community enhanced by the award of an OBE and Military Cross for wartime endeavours, Dykes became secretary of the Elham NFU branch, a senior officer in the Conservative Party's Canterbury Division and, when the tithe war began, the chairman of Elham Tithepayers' Association. In 1934, he faced charges of 'conspiring to promote an unlawful assembly' for his part in the 'Battle of the Ducks'. A few months later, on 28 October 1927, some close neighbours of Dykes, the Gammon brothers, were also summoned to Hythe county court.[14] Owners of Stonebridge Farm, the Gammons would be mentioned in police reports of disturbances at an auction in Stelling Minnis in September 1931 and would, in late 1932, be prominent in the well-publicised confrontation in Elham between local farmers and representatives of New College, Oxford (see pp. 179–82).[15]

In Essex and Suffolk, farmers organised a more direct challenge to titheowners. In 1927, they began forming 'occupying owners' associations' to deal with 'questions of common interest', of which the 'unfair treatment' by titheowners was high on the list. In October, around forty farmers in villages around Halstead and Sudbury challenged Queen Anne's Bounty's demands for tithe in the county court. One of those participating was Joshua Owen Steed (brother of Henry Wickham Steed, editor of *The Times* between 1919 and 1922), who, as well as farming pigs in Long Melford (Suffolk), ran a firm of solicitors in Sudbury. Advised by Steed, the associations sought to trigger the provision in the 1891 Tithe Act that allowed remission if tithe exceeded two-thirds of the value of land. Lawyers for Queen Anne's Bounty put up a vigorous defence against what they described as 'an organised campaign to get out of paying tithes'. Faced with mounting costs, thirty farmers felt pressurised to drop the case and Queen Anne's Bounty pursued the remaining eleven for both tithes and legal costs. In its annual report, the Bounty boasted that it had successfully 'resisted a movement' by farmers for tithe remission.[16]

During these years, the NTA remained a small pressure group, lacking resources and without local branches. It held an annual meeting each January and somewhat irregular meetings of its national council. The

---

[13] 'Mr Dykes, the farmer with many interests', *Folkestone Herald*, 11 Sept. 1965.
[14] Proceedings under Tithe Act, County Court at Hythe, 1927–1934, KHLC, HC-C/HY 7–2.
[15] Superintendent Golding, 'Tithe Sale at Selling', 2 Oct. 1931, TNA, HO 144/19199.
[16] 'Owner-Occupiers' Association', *Suffolk & Essex Free Press*, 27 Oct. 1927; 'Payment of Tithe', *Suffolk & Essex Free Press*, 8 Dec. 1927; 'Report by the Governors of Queen Anne' Bounty', 20 Feb. 1929', CERC, QAB/2/1/46.

The Settlement Unravels, 1927–31

association suffered an early blow when Henry Rew became seriously ill and stood down as chairman in January 1926, two years before his death. This left Frank Allen to direct most of the work single-handed. He drafted and dispatched information sheets combining propaganda with practical advice about the intricacies of tithe legislation, wrote letters to newspapers and kept up correspondence with supporters and sympathetic politicians. His Canterbury office became a port-of-call for farmers with queries about tithe or seeking to contest the amount they were being charged by titheowners. Allen was also invited to share his expertise at public events. Speaking in July 1927 in Chelmsford (Essex) at a meeting organised by the NFU county executive, he declared that, given the Tithe Act had 'added to the troubles of the tithepayer', it was 'now or never' if farmers wanted to get some movement on the issue.[17]

Alongside Allen, three other men played a significant role in these early NTA activities. The first, Alfred Burrows, replaced Henry Rew as the association's chairman in January 1926. Well known in the farming world, Burrows had for some years run the fortnightly livestock auction at Ashford (Kent) and, more recently, organised the competition for best-managed farm at the annual cattle show. He was a partner in Messrs Knight, Frank and Rutley, a prestigious land valuer and estate agency whose clients included the duke of Westminster and Winston Churchill. The firm's plush Mayfair offices became the venue for NTA meetings. Burrows was also a past president of the Auctioneers' and Estate Agents' Institute, at which he lectured on matters relating to agriculture, including tithe. Conditioned by his business interests, his arguments on tithe were reminiscent of those put forward by agricultural lobbies in the early nineteenth century: tithe distorted the market for land and was, generally, an obstacle to the profitability of agriculture.[18]

The second, Michael Christopher McCreagh, was a colourful character. Born into a Derbyshire landowning family (McCreagh-Thornhill) and educated at Eton and Oxford before qualifying as a barrister, he inherited the family estate, Stanton Hall, at Matlock, at the age of twenty-five. A further inheritance was a large tract of land – made up of six farms and other holdings – in and around the village of Barton Stacey (Hampshire). In 1921, bailiffs and police turned up at one of the Barton Stacey farms to execute a distress warrant for non-payment of rates. It seems likely that McCreagh was protesting against rate increases to cover concessions to clergy in the 1920 Ecclesiastical Tithe Rentcharge (Rates) Act. Seized items included horses and a wagon, with the effect that the corn harvest was delayed and subsequently ruined by bad weather. A sense of

[17] 'Tithe Problems', *ChCh*, 15 July 1927.
[18] Alfred J. Burrows, 'The Injustice of Tithe', *Estates Gazette*, 4 Oct. 1931; Alfred J. Burrows, 'Tithe, A Paper', The Auctioneers' and Estate Agents' Institute of the United Kingdom, 1 Nov. 1934, CERC, ECE/SEC/TITHE/P7.

injustice arising from the affair informed McCreagh's activism on tithe and, during the late 1920s and early 1930s, his legal expertise was 'much appreciated' by activists within the tithepayers' movement.[19] While maintaining activities within the NTA, in December 1930 McCreagh set up the Tithe League, an organisation which claimed 150 members. He also began publishing a quarterly bulletin called *The Tithepayer*, writing in its first issue that tithepayers should only 'rely on themselves and no longer put their trust in party politicians and non-tithepayers'.[20] In Barton Stacey, he earned a reputation as 'a poor man's friend'. By the end of the 1930s, he had allowed the estate to fall into disrepair with, according to one report, tenants 'who pay no rent' and 'the 40-roomed manor house resound[ing] each night to the snores of tramps sleeping on the floors'.[21]

Albert G. Mobbs was a third influential but very different personality. A spokesperson for dairy farmers around Lowestoft, Mobbs was chairman of the NFU's Beccles branch and a member of its Suffolk county committee.[22] After contacting Allen in January 1929, he quickly became the NTA's main voice within the NFU. In May, the NFU national council considered a resolution, originally proposed by Mobbs at the Suffolk committee, which argued 'that agriculture can no longer support the burden of tithe, and that if it were to continue it should be borne by the State as a whole and not by one industry alone'. The council rejected Mobbs' resolution on two grounds: first, that it was 'not an opportune time' to agitate on tithe and, secondly, that the NFU could not accept the 'confiscation' of a form of property by the state.[23] The Suffolk NFU committee was not satisfied. It demanded that the resolution be circulated to NFU branches and called on the union headquarters to convene a special conference to formulate policy on tithe. Mobbs also submitted his resolution to the NTA for consideration at its annual meeting to take place at the end of January 1930. At the NFU's annual meeting, held earlier that month, Mobbs criticised the lack of action on tithe by union headquarters. He received a sympathetic hearing from delegates but an angry response from Rowland Robbins. 'No man in the whole country [had done] more than he to fight the unfair and iniquitous 1925 Act,' thundered Robbins. But having

---

[19] Suffolk TPA, Minutes of Executive Committee, 10 Mar. 1931, SuRO, GC32/1.
[20] Evidence submitted by The Tithe League to the Royal Commission, 24 Jan. 1935, 356; *The Tithepayer*, Oct. 1931, 1. McCreagh published the bulletin until July 1938.
[21] 'A Distraint Case', *Hampshire Advertiser*, 17 Feb. 1923; 'Queer, Quaint, and Questionable', *Derby Daily Telegraph*, 9 May 1940.
[22] Allen to Mobbs, 18 Jan. 1929, Mobbs Papers; Twinch, *Tithe War*, 32–3, 45 and 53–4.
[23] *NFU Record*, June 1929, 210–11; Oct. 1929, 11.

'fought and lost', delegates had 'to ask themselves whether this was an opportune time to raise the [tithe] question'. In Robbins' view it was not.[24]

Agricultural prices

It is perhaps surprising that Robbins and other NFU leaders were unaware of how the new collapse in agricultural prices that began in the winter of 1929–30 was reigniting the tithe controversy. World markets had already become saturated before the shock waves of the Wall Street Crash depressed them further. British farmers faced sharpened competition, not only from traditional sources but also from 'dumping', described by Labour MP George Dallas as 'bounty-fed cereals from Germany, bounty-fed flour from France and convict-produced potatoes from Algeria'.[25] Cereal prices dropped below their pre-war level, the index of wheat falling from 100 in 1929 to 80 in 1930 and 56 in 1931, the year of a weather-blighted harvest. Prices of other produce (including sugar beet and milk) also fell, though not so sharply.[26] The highly tithed cereal-growing regions in eastern and southern England were particularly hard hit. Only the largest farms, capable of producing high yields at relatively low cost, avoided 'disastrous losses' in the years immediately after 1929. Farmers who had bought their farms in the aftermath of war, often still saddled with debt and with limited access to credit, faced the biggest difficulties. Tracts of land were taken out of cultivation. Many labourers and some small farmers found themselves in a destitute state, forced to rely on relief from the Poor Law, as the government had in 1925–26 excluded agriculture from its unemployment insurance scheme.[27] Farmers could not help noticing that, while cereal prices were in free fall, tithe payments remained fixed, an ever-increasing percentage of their overheads.

Two newly elected Conservatives on the protectionist and agrarian wing of the party were the first to raise the tithe issue in parliament after the general election. The MP for Basingstoke, Gerard Wallop, styled Viscount Lymington (later becoming the ninth earl of Portsmouth), supported by Michael Beaumont, MP for Aylesbury, asked the minister of agriculture, Noel Buxton, whether the Labour government would establish a Royal Commission to examine tithe's 'unequal incidence'. Lymington reminded Buxton that many Labour and Liberal candidates had campaigned for tithe reform during the general election. Replying,

---

[24] *NFU Record*, Feb. 1930, 106.
[25] 'The Call of Agriculture', *Wiltshire Times and Trowbridge Advertiser*, 12 Apr. 1930.
[26] Ministry of Agriculture figures, quoted in Cooper, *British Agricultural Policy*, 174.
[27] Whetham, *Agrarian History*, 232–3 and 235–6.

Buxton ruled out either a Royal Commission or legislation, claiming that 'the present arrangement' was 'satisfactory' and presented 'no serious difficulties'.[28] Lymington was consciously attempting to build his reputation as a champion of farming communities. But he was also a crusader against 'racial degeneration' and 'moral decadence', an obsession that would, in the words of one biographer, take his career into the 'muck, mysticism, and the more esoteric reaches of British fascism'.[29] 'It would be better to have a Mussolini organising the agriculture of this country than to see it go to ruin, as it is doing today,' he told the House of Commons.[30]

Two Liberal MPs also became vocal on tithe: Edgar Granville, who had campaigned against the charge during the general election, and Rev. Roderick Kedward, a surprise victor in Ashford (Kent). Both challenged Buxton on whether he was 'aware of the very great dissatisfaction' on tithe 'among the agricultural community'. Buxton replied that the matter 'had not been brought to [his] notice'.[31] Kedward was in many respects the archetypal social liberal. Born in Kent on a farm rented by his parents from the Westwell estate, owned by Lord Hothfield, he developed his oratorical skills early in life as a Methodist preacher. At the age of 17, he was prosecuted for contravening a byelaw by 'shouting in the street' with 'a loud and strident voice' while conducting an open-air service in the Cotswold village of Chipping Campden. Refusing to pay the fine, he was taken to Worcester gaol, though released after several days when the penalty was anonymously paid. The case was raised in the House of Commons by the Liberal MP Robert Perks.[32] Kedward became closely associated with Liberal Party politics after his appointment in 1908 to a Wesleyan ministry in Hull. Campaigns on social welfare – including conditions facing tenants and those living in workhouses – earned him the epithet 'the fighting parson'. After serving as a padre in Egypt and on the Western Front, he stood unsuccessfully in Hull Central at the 1918 general election before moving to London to become superintendent of the South London Methodist Mission. At the 1923 general election, Kedward won Bermondsey West from the sitting Labour MP, Alfred Salter, but lost the seat in 1924.[33] His radicalism had its limits. As an MP in 1924, he led thirteen Liberal rebels in voting with the Conservatives

28   HC Deb., *Hansard*, 22 July 1929.
29   Malcolm Chase, 'Wallop, Gerard Vernon, ninth earl of Portsmouth (1898–1984)', *ODNB* (2009).
30   HC Deb., *Hansard*, 26 May 1930.
31   HC Deb., *Hansard*, 4 Nov. and 11 Dec. 1929.
32   'Chipping Campden', *Gloucestershire Echo*, 20 July 1899; 'An Evangelist Goes to Prison', *Blackburn Standard*, 22 July 1899; HC Deb., *Hansard*, 11 July 1899.
33   Jaime Reynolds, 'The Fighting Parson', *Journal of Liberal History*, 48 (2005), 33; Carol Twinch, 'Roderick Morris Kedward, 1881–1937', *Bygone Kent*, 24, 7 (2003), 645.

against the Labour government's cancellation of the 'Poplar Order', sanctions imposed on the Poplar board of governors for paying 'illegal' levels of unemployment relief.[34]

At the 1929 general election, he waged a dynamic campaign in Ashford, with mass meetings at the market and 'community singing' at rallies. He won enthusiastic support from farming communities on the Kentish Weald, a region with significant nonconformist traditions, and where the anti-extraordinary tithe campaign of the 1880s and particularly the imprisonment of George Cooper – the 'Smarden Martyr' – remained strong in the collective memory.[35] Shortly after winning his seat, Kedward himself became a tithepayer when, in July 1929, Lord Hothfield sold part of his Kentish estate and Kedward was one of nine tenants to purchase their farms. Around the same time, he began to cooperate with the NTA and was in regular contact with Allen to discuss policy in advance of the association's annual meeting in January 1930.

The Tithe Remission Bill

The annual meeting on 27 January marked the beginning of the NTA's transformation from a pressure group to the coordinator of a significant movement of farmers. It was the association's largest meeting since its launch, and also the most representative, with many attendees influential within their local NFU branches. The main debate revolved around the resolution submitted by Mobbs (advocating that tithe should be 'borne by the state'). In the weeks before the annual meeting, the resolution had divided members of the association's national council. Most gave it a cool reception, not considering the demand for tithe abolition 'practical politics'. Burrows was amongst those who 'were not enamoured of the resolution'. McCreagh also 'doubted the wisdom' of adopting it. Allen was more sympathetic but tried to persuade Mobbs that, while a good 'ultimate objective', it was 'hopeless' to expect the government would consider taking over the payment of tithe. 'Something smaller must therefore be attempted first, although there is no reason why [abolition] should not be put forward as an ultimate objective,' he argued.[36]

At the annual meeting, Kedward moved an amendment to Mobbs' resolution. He argued that a campaign to abolish tithe would be unable to win broad public support – 'we would have three parts of the country against us' – but a campaign to limit tithe to a reasonable level would be more successful. It could also, he suggested, provide the basis for a successful private member's bill in parliament. Kedward proposed that remission should be extended to cover 'excessive tithe', which he

[34] HC Deb., *Hansard*, 26 Feb. 1924; 'The Poplar Division', *The Times*, 28 Feb. 1924.
[35] See pp. 42–3.
[36] Allen to Mobbs, 15 Jan. 1930, Mobbs Papers.

characterised as tithe in excess of three shillings in the pound of the annual value of land; in other words, above 15 per cent of land value. Delegates at the annual meeting supported his proposal unanimously.[37]

Drafted in consultation with Allen,[38] Kedward's Tithe Remission Bill was presented to the House of Commons on 26 March 1930. The first of three clauses covered the proposal on 'excessive tithe'. Essentially, it amended the provision (clause 8) in the 1891 Act that allowed farmers facing proceedings for recovery to apply for remission on tithe above two-thirds of the value of tithable land. Applications could now be made to remit tithe of more than 15 per cent of land value. The second clause removed tithe on land washed away by the sea, or otherwise destroyed. The third changed the practice whereby a landowner could be made liable for tithe when another person was owner of part of the land. Along with Kedward, eight Liberal MPs put their name to the bill, including Edgar Granville, William Lygon (Viscount Elmley), MP for East Norfolk, and James de Rothschild, MP for the Isle of Ely. The bill was also sponsored by the Labour MP George Dallas.[39] Some Conservatives offered support, including Oswald Lewis, who represented the heavily tithed region around Colchester (Essex).[40] After a few weeks of delay, Lymington pledged support and began cooperating with the NTA. In July, he accepted an invitation to become the association's president. Shortly afterwards, William Lygon agreed to act as vice-president.[41]

The National Tithepayers' Association launched a publicity campaign around the Remission Bill. Allen drafted press releases and produced leaflets outlining its proposals, which were distributed in highly tithed regions. Kedward's statements received extensive coverage in the agricultural press. Within the National Farmers' Union, supporters of the NTA argued that the union should lend its support. Some NFU county committees called for a special national conference on tithe; others demanded immediate action to secure the repeal of the 1925 Act. County branches in Suffolk, Hertfordshire, Shropshire, Northamptonshire, Essex, Somerset, Berkshire and elsewhere gave explicit support to the bill.[42] Yet Kedward's optimism that his proposed legislation would win wide political support had been misplaced. The minister of agriculture, Buxton, rejected it out of hand. At the time of its first reading, he was preoccupied with the 'agricultural conference', an attempt to tackle the agricultural crisis by bringing together representatives of landowners, farmers and

[37] 'Protests against Tithe', *F&S*, 3 Feb. 1930.
[38] Allen to Mobbs, 1 and 25 Feb. 1930, Mobbs Papers.
[39] HC Deb., *Hansard*, 26 Mar. 1930.
[40] 'Tithepayers' Protest at Colchester', *Essex Chronicle*, 8 May 1931.
[41] Allen to Mobbs, 12 Aug. 1930, Mobbs Papers.
[42] *NFU Record*, Mar. 1930, 135; *F&S*, 3 Mar. 1930; 'Meeting of the Council of the Union', *NFU Record*, June 1930, 206.

workers. Ten meetings during the first five months of 1930 concluded, as *The Times* noted, with 'no suspicion of a policy'.[43] Buxton's failings drew criticisms from within the Labour Party: 'useful little schemes here and there [...] are no use in a crisis,' the MP Ellen Wilkinson told him.[44] Shortly after this censure, Buxton withdrew as minister for health reasons. His replacement, Christopher Addison, displayed more freshness of thought. His Agricultural Marketing Bill (1931) sought to bring stability to markets by establishing a number of commodity-based 'boards', which would buy produce from farmers and fix the selling price. Yet, in relation to tithe, Addison was not prepared to countenance any change of policy. Edgar Granville, one of the sponsors of the Remission Bill, asked if he was 'aware of the growing dissatisfaction with the position of tithe payment in relation to agriculture; and if he [was] prepared to receive a representative deputation on this problem'. Addison replied that he was 'unaware of any ground for relieving such owners of their legal obligation and [did] not think that a deputation would serve any useful purpose'.[45]

The National Farmers' Union also refused to support the bill. The union's initial position was a fudge: it claimed that whether or not to endorse the bill was a hypothetical question as it could not progress due to the congestion of parliamentary business.[46] But as support for the bill grew amongst NFU members, national leaders realised that refusing to engage with the tithe issue was no longer an option. Some began to fear that the union could be outflanked by the NTA, despite the association's relatively small size. On 7 November 1930, NFU headquarters convened a 'Tithe Conference', which was attended by delegates from twenty-four counties. Dominating proceedings, Robbins stressed again that he 'did not consider the time favourable for action' on tithe. The conference concluded by adopting an ambiguously worded resolution that the NFU 'would press for a drastic revision of the 1925 settlement [at the] first favourable opportunity'.[47] But when, soon afterwards, it became clear that NFU leaders were interpreting the resolution as meaning there would be no change in tithe policy, considerable anger arose in the union's ranks. Another round of resolutions from county branches demanded that the NFU take 'immediate action' on tithe.[48] Robbins was now forced to acknowledge the 'feeling that existed on the matter' and agreed to request a meeting with Addison. Despite previously ruling out such a meeting,

---

[43] 'Mr Buxton on Agriculture' and 'Agricultural Needs', *The Times*, 13 May 1930.
[44] *DHe*, 19 May 1930 (quoted in the *NFU Record*, June 1930, 211).
[45] HC Deb., *Hansard*, 31 July 1930.
[46] 'Meeting of the Council of the Union', *NFU Record*, June 1930, 206.
[47] 'The Tithe Problem', *NFU Record*, Dec. 1930, 58.
[48] Resolutions arrived from Berkshire, Essex, Hertfordshire, Lincolnshire, Shropshire and East Sussex. NFU Parliamentary, Press & Publicity Committee, 17 Feb. 1931, MERL, SR NFU, AD1/13.

Addison met an NFU delegation on 26 February 1931. As well as national officials, the delegation included eight tithepaying farmers, including two NTA activists, Mobbs and Vernon Drewitt, from Berkshire.[49] Addison stressed there was 'no prospect of my asking the Government to reopen the tithe question', claiming that the 1918 and 1925 Acts had 'stabilised the position'. He argued that the tithe problem was intrinsically linked to the agricultural depression and would be resolved once it was again possible 'to make agriculture pay'. In the meantime, farmers 'could not repudiate [their] obligations'.[50]

The NFU finally took a position in June 1931. Rejecting a resolution from the Essex committee urging support for the bill 'until such time as tithe could be made a national charge or abolished' and another from Monmouthshire calling for tithe to be reduced by 50 per cent, the national council approved a statement that defended the legitimacy of tithe:

> That this meeting is unable to support the Tithe Remission Bill [...] since the principal Clause of that measure proposed to confiscate property in tithe without compensating the owner thereof wherever such tithe exceeds three shillings in the pound of the annual value of the land charged therewith. Such a proposal [...] cannot be accepted by any who would be concerned to resist the appropriation without compensation of other forms of property.[51]

Despite its failure to win support from the political parties and the NFU, the NTA saw its authority enormously enhanced by its agitation around the Tithe Remission Bill. It gained credibility through its advocacy of a practical measure and through its association with a small group of MPs. Two further developments were critical in the NTA's transformation: its identification with the idea of collective non-payment of tithe and the launch of local tithepayers' associations.

Passive resistance

Many farmers had (as noted above) for several years been making individual protests against tithe by withholding payment until the recovery process was underway. Such was the stance taken by Ebenezer Haffenden, who farmed seventy-three acres in Pluckley, a village on the Kentish Weald and part of Kedward's parliamentary constituency. A nonconformist and long-standing member of the Liberal Party, Haffenden had engaged in 'passive resistance' in 1907 when refusing to pay the education portion of the local poor rate in protest at public

---

[49] 'Meeting of the Council of the Union', *NFU Record*, Mar. 1931, 134.
[50] 'The Tithe Question', *NFU Record*, Apr. 1931, 163–4.
[51] *NFU Record*, July 1931, 231.

funding of schools run by the Anglican Church.[52] When, in June 1930, bailiffs from the county court arrived at his holding with a distraint order, Haffenden refused to pay his tithe or cooperate with them in any way. The bailiffs seized furniture and personal effects and, on 20 June, court officials organised an auction at his farm. A large number of local people turned up to express solidarity with Haffenden. So too did Frank Allen, who at a hastily organised protest meeting said that everyone 'owed a great debt to Haffenden, and hoped farmers would not let him down'. Though the goods were auctioned to 'an outsider [...] specially imported for the purpose', the NTA secretary had for the first time, by identifying with Haffenden's action, sanctioned the non-payment of tithe.[53]

Even more significant were the decisions taken at a meeting held in the Guildhall in Sandwich (Kent) on 17 December 1930. Between 100 and 120 people were present, a number exceeding the expectations of the chairperson George Christopher Solley, who had convened the meeting at the request of a local farmer, Arthur Woodhams. In attendance were prominent members of the NTA, including Frank Allen and Michael McCreagh. Tithe was particularly high on land surrounding Sandwich. Whereas, nationally, average tithe was 3s 6d an acre, farmers close to the village of Ash were paying around 14s an acre and some as much as £1 an acre. The meeting was called to 'consider whether the time had not arrived when more active measures should be taken to penetrate governmental indifference'.[54]

The meeting debated whether to pursue a tactic of 'non-payment' of tithe. For some, such as Arthur Woodhams, 'anything short of a refusal to pay' would be ineffective. He was supported by Michael McCreagh, who moved a resolution that 'until a Tithes Remission Bill [...] had been passed into law, all present should join in a general refusal to pay'. This was too much for some of the 'leading agriculturists of Kent' who were present. Edward D. Rice, great-grandson of the Whig MP, who had spoken in favour of tithe commutation on Barham Downs in 1834, urged a more moderate stance. He proposed that a committee be appointed to 'consider methods of bringing pressure to bear on the legislature and on the tithe owners to obtain relief from the excessive burden of tithe on agriculture and [...] report to a future meeting'.[55] In the end, a compromise was reached. It was agreed 'to suggest' to tithepayers 'who consider that the present law is unjust' that they should 'support their protest by the perfectly legal method of refraining from paying the demands *before* an

[52] 'Passive Resistance', *Sussex Agricultural Express*, 12 Oct. 1907.
[53] 'A tithepayer's protest', *KE*, 27 June 1930.
[54] 'Non-Payment. A Statement by Alderman G. C. Solley, of Sandwich', *Tithe*, Jan. 1934.
[55] 'The Heavy Tithe Charges', *DE*, 19 Dec. 1930.

order for recovery is made [emphasis in original].'[56] It was also agreed to establish the East Kent Tithepayers' Association to represent the interests of local tithepayers. A committee was elected, and membership cards issued. Solley became chair and Frank Allen was appointed secretary.[57]

Born in 1869 into what he described as a family that had farmed as both 'Yeomen and Tenant Farmers since 1490 AD', Solley had been a founding member of the NTA. His relationship with Allen went back to the early 1920s, when he was chairman of the Canterbury Farmers' Club and Allen was tithe agent at Canterbury Cathedral. Solley's interests extended well beyond farming. He ran a prestigious estate and land agency and was a budding entrepreneur, attempting to promote schemes for the industrial development of the Wantsum Valley and River Stour. He was also a justice of the peace, magistrate of the cinque ports and an alderman, and, in the years following the war, had been mayor of Sandwich. Such was his influence in local economic, political and cultural life that he became known by the sobriquet 'Solley of Sandwich'. Politically, Solley was a long-standing member of the Conservative Party. One of the ironies of the anti-tithe movement is that in 1930 he volunteered services to the Conservative candidate in Ashford, Michael Knatchbull (the fifth Lord Brabourne), offering him help and advice to defeat the sitting MP, Roderick Kedward.[58] The following year, Solley and Kedward were working together as leaders of protests at tithe auctions.[59] In fact, by 1930, Solley had become so disillusioned with the Conservatives that he joined Lord Beaverbrook's 'Empire Crusade', attracted by its pledges to protect the livelihood of farmers, as well as its xenophobic language.[60] This was the first stage in a rightward political journey that would lead Solley to join Oswald Mosley's British Union of Fascists in August 1934.

The decision taken at the Sandwich meeting was ambiguous on several levels. It 'suggested' tithe non-payment but did not commit the new tithepayers' association to the tactic. It was unclear about whether to advise farmers who refused to pay their tithe to continue or to end their protest once the distraint process had begun. It did not stipulate how the association would practically support farmers facing distraint, or even whether it would actually do so. It stressed that withholding payment was 'legal' – because tithe was linked to land ownership and not

---

56 'The Tithe Question. Memorandum by the Committee of the East Kent Tithepayers' Association', 28 May 1934, DWPap.
57 'Objects of the Association' (1931), KHLC, EK/U1276/B4/105.
58 Solley Papers, KHLC, EK/U1507/Z3.
59 Superintendent, W. J. Robertson, 2 Oct. 1931, TNA, HO 144/19199.
60 'The Empire Crusade and Agriculture', F&S, 13 Jan. 1930. 'The Empire Crusade', 19 Feb. 1930, Solley Papers, KHLC EK/U1507/Z3.

a personal liability – but did not address the fact that non-payment could mean defying orders issued in a court of law.

Despite these ambiguities, many Kentish farmers interpreted the Sandwich decision as a green light to begin a campaign of tithe non-payment. Over the next two months, 332 farmers in the county took a pledge not to pay the charge.[61] A large batch of non-payers, including Arthur Woodhams, was summoned to appear at Deal county court on 6 February. The same week, Roderick Kedward successfully contested an order for tithe non-payment taken out by the Ecclesiastical Commissioners at Ashford county court. After the judge ruled that the notice had been incorrectly issued and awarded him costs, Kedward told a 'large crowd' outside the court that 'he was not going to pay another single penny'. When facing a new court order in May, he declared that 'his action ha[d] been like putting a match to a prairie fire [...] Farmers everywhere are refusing to pay.'[62]

The Sandwich strategy polarised opinion within the NTA. At its annual meeting on 22 January 1931, a row erupted after Solley reported that farmers in his area 'were steadfastly resolved to abstain from paying the tithe [and] were convinced that no Parliamentary measure would be successful until their action was followed up throughout the country'. He called on everyone present to organise meetings to establish local tithepayers' associations and to adopt a non-payment policy similar to the one agreed in Sandwich. Burrows and Lymington made their opposition clear. Burrows said that the NTA was 'unable to associate themselves officially with any campaign for refusing to pay the tithe. They did not pledge themselves to support or countenance any proceeding of that kind.'[63] Lymington issued statements stressing that tithe should be fought by 'constitutional means' and 'that nothing could be done without legislation'.[64]

Local tithepayers' associations

During the first half of 1931, meetings of tithepayers were convened in, amongst other places, Ashford and Sittingbourne (Kent), Rye (Sussex), Ipswich, Stowmarket, Framlingham, Sudbury, Bury St Edmunds, Eye, Saxmundham and Halesworth (Suffolk), Colchester, Chelmsford, Saffron

---

61 The figure was reported by Roderick Kedward, 'Suffolk Objects to Tithe', *F&S*, 23 Feb. 1931.
62 'Farmers sued for Tithe', *The Times*, 7 Feb. 1931; 'Tithe Act of 1925', *The Times*, 18 Feb. 1931; MP and Tithe', *Daily Telegraph*, 3 Feb. 1931; MP's Tithe Protest Spreading', *Daily Telegraph*, 9 May 1931.
63 'Tithepayers' Protest', *The Times*, 23 Jan. 1931.
64 'Tithe denounced as "slavery"', *F&S*, 26 Jan. 1931; *Hampshire Advertiser*, 2 Aug. 1930, Wallop, Earls of Portsmouth Archives, HRO, 15M84 F132.

Walden, Romford, Braintree, Canvey Island and Epping (Essex), Norwich and Fakenham (Norfolk), Wallingford (Berkshire) and Cambridge (Cambridgeshire).[65] Local associations were constituted, members recruited, committees elected, and finances gathered.

The East Kent association established a number of local groups, including a vibrant one in Elham. Amongst those at its inaugural meeting was George Gill, who had bought his farm of fifty-five acres in 1924. Its condition was 'terribly neglected [and] practically waterless' and 'no profit and but little produce came [...] for several years'. Gill later wrote:

> I went [to the meeting and] found the Schoolroom crowded, mainly by owner-occupiers of small farms in the district. I knew most of them [...] they were by no means an aggressive lot. They had a tolerant respect for the Church, even if they did not frequent it. They had asked their Member of Parliament to preside at the meeting. He frankly told them, 'You haven't a dog's chance to get rid of the tithe', an opinion from which they audibly dissented.[66]

One of the largest and best organised of the new county-wide associations was the Suffolk Tithepayers' Association, established in Ipswich on 24 February. It is possible to trace its evolution through a minute book and list of membership subscriptions held in the county archives. General meetings were attended by around 200 farmers and the due-paying membership rose to 406, peaking at 554 in 1934. An executive committee chaired by Mobbs met fortnightly to coordinate activities. Local 'protest meetings' were organised in market towns and outside farms; posters and leaflets produced; a 'propaganda tent' set up at the county agricultural show. Financial support was offered to farmers facing distraint and members mobilised to obstruct the activities of bailiffs.[67] Founding members of the Suffolk Tithepayers' Association included two women whose names became associated with the conflict. Evelyn Balfour was a niece of former prime minister Arthur Balfour. Farming at Haughley, Lady Eve, as she was known, was from 'a profoundly aristocratic background' but also someone 'who embraced modernity and lived a decidedly bohemian life style', becoming, after the Second World War, well known as a pioneer of the organic farming movement.[68] She began her activities in the

---

[65] NTA, 'Excessive Tithe Rentcharge', 20 Apr. 1931, Essex Record Office, D/Q23/16/8.
[66] George J. Gill, *A Fight against the Tithes* (Haslemere, 1952), 9 and 36.
[67] Suffolk Tithepayers' Association, SuRO, GC32/2 and GC32/1.
[68] Matthew Reed, *Rebels for the Soil: The Rise of the Global Organic Food and Farming Movement* (London: Earthscan, 2010), 47; Erin Gill, 'Lady Eve Balfour and the British Organic Food and Farming Movement' (unpublished PhD thesis, Aberystwyth University, 2010).

tithepayers' movement by writing a short pamphlet outlining the history of tithe and the case against it.[69] Doreen Wallace had moved to the region after studying at Somerville College to take up a teaching post. She met and married Rowland Rash, an archetypal representative of the 'established, educated local farming class'. The couple lived well, employing domestic servants, taking foreign holidays and educating their children privately. They both also joined the Conservative Party. Rash's desire to show off his status led in 1930 to the purchase of Wortham Manor, a twenty-roomed house with forty acres of parkland, a purchase achieved through a substantial mortgage and sizeable bank loans. It provided a suitable environment for Wallace to develop her career as a writer.[70] After joining the tithepayers' association, she made tithe a theme in her novel *The Portion of the Levites*, the story of a farmer and his wife whose fragile relationship undergoes additional stress because of demands from a titheowner.[71]

Elsewhere in East Anglia, the Norfolk Tithepayers' Association was launched on 18 April at a meeting attended by 'several hundred farmers' in Norwich. Organised by Stanley Kidner, part of a 'well-known Norfolk family of agriculturists', the meeting was addressed by three Liberal MPs (Granville, Elmley and Kedward), as well as by Mobbs. Over the next few months, the association's due-paying membership grew to 320.[72] In Essex, public meetings to form associations took place in a number of localities. On 9 May, a meeting in Wickford established the Essex Tithepayers' Association as a federation of groups with a claimed membership of 1,400 farmers.[73]

The organisation to cover the region between the Chiltern and Cotswold hills was launched at a meeting in Wallingford on 12 June organised by Vernon Drewitt, a member of Berkshire NFU. Those present agreed to set up the Wallingford and District Tithepayers' Association. Like other associations, it declared itself 'non-political' and 'un-sectarian'. The Wallingford group produced a weekly bulletin and, over the next few months, organised meetings and built support amongst farmers in Chipping Norton, Witney, Maidenhead, Oxford, Reading, Abingdon, Newbury, Didcot and Faringdon. In early 1932, it was reconstituted as the

---

[69] Lady Eve Balfour, *What is all this about Tithe?* (Stationers' Hall, 1933).
[70] June Shepherd, *Doreen Wallace, 1897–1989, Writer and Social Campaigner* (New York: Edwin Mellen Press, 2000), 37–9, 51–2 and 60.
[71] Doreen Wallace, *The Portion of the Levites* (London: Ernest Benn, 1933).
[72] 'Tithe Payers meet at Norwich', *DiEx*, 24 Apr. 1931; *Royal Commission on Tithe Rentcharge, Minutes of Evidence*, 11 Jan. 1935, 311–12 and 316–22.
[73] 'Tithe "Revolt"', *ChCh*, 17 Apr. 1931; 'Tithepayers Combine', *ChCh*, 24 Apr. 1931; 'Tithepayers' Protest at Colchester', *ChCh*, 8 May 1931; 'Tithe Protest at Wickford', *Essex Newsman*, 16 May 1931; 'Romford Tithe Meeting', *ChCh*, 29 May 1931; Tithe Protest at Epping', *ChCh*, 26 June 1931; *Royal Commission on Tithe Rentcharge, Minutes of Evidence*, 21 Dec. 1934, 231.

Berks, Bucks & Oxon Tithepayers' Association, with its committee meeting held each month in Oxford. A separate association was established in July 1931 to cover South Wiltshire, based around Winterslow and other villages close to Salisbury.[74]

The growth of county tithepayers' associations posed the question of regional and national coordination. On 14 May, an East Anglian conference took place, with delegates from tithepayers' associations in Suffolk, Norfolk, Essex and Cambridgeshire. On 3 June, an 'inter-county' conference in London was convened jointly by Frank Allen and Mobbs. It agreed to establish a 'Central Council' made up of two representatives from each existing county association and to begin plans to establish a national federation.

In general, the new associations tended to adopt a more radical policy than that previously advocated by the NTA. Most agreed to campaign for the Tithe Remission Bill and supported attempts 'to secure any measure of relief from the burden of tithe'. Some also made explicit their opposition to the principle of tithe. At the founding conference of the Essex federation, tithe was described as 'a crying evil [that] at all costs must be put down'.[75] The Chelmsford Tithepayers' Association condemned it as 'legalised robbery'.[76] In Suffolk, the tithepayers' association's first bulletin described opposition to tithe as a 'great principle of common justice', for which 'many are prepared to suffer, if necessary, in support of that principle.'[77] Statements by local leaders challenged the concept that tithe was legitimate property. Increasingly, tithepayers' associations began to describe tithe as 'a medieval tax'. The 10 per cent had been, historically, a voluntary and then a legally enforceable tax on produce, rather than possessing the quality of private property. This allowed tithepayers' leaders to refute the accusation – voiced by both the Church and the NFU leadership – that the tithepayers' movement wanted 'to confiscate' private property. At a members' meeting in Ipswich, Mobbs argued that 'the sole object of their movement was to prevent confiscation,' he said, 'the whole

[74] *Berks & Oxon Advertiser*, 19 June 1931, 26 June 1931, 23 Oct. 1931; Berks, Bucks & Oxon Tithepayers' Association, n.d. (probably Sept. 1932), Berkshire Record Office, D/Ex 2547/4/6/5; *Taunton Courier and Western Advertiser*, 10 July 1931.
[75] 'Tithe Protest at Wickford', *Essex Newsman*, 16 May 1931.
[76] 'Tithe "revolt"', *ChCh*, 17 Apr. 1931.
[77] Suffolk Tithepayers' Association, bulletin (n.d.), Essex Record Office, D/Q 23/16/8.

history of tithe was one long tale of confiscation [...] of another man's skills and energy.'[78]

The Suffolk association was one of a number of tithepayers' associations that hesitated over whether to adopt a general tactic of tithe non-payment. In early April, after a long discussion, the association concluded that the movement 'was not yet in a position to recommend its members to a general refusal to pay'. Instead, it agreed to select a number of 'test cases': farmers who would refuse to pay to gain publicity 'in a way calculated to expose as fully as possible the intolerable burden of tithe'. The association's secretary, Philip J. Butler, volunteered to act as one of the test cases. A Quaker, Butler and his wife ran Kennel Farm in the village of Barking. Out of the proceeds, they hoped to fund an orphanage and they also offered work to orphan children on leaving school. Butler believed that the tithe system was 'inconsistent [...] with the teaching of the New Testament'. On 1 May 1931, Butler was one of fifteen tithe defaulters to appear before Stowmarket county court and later the same year a pony and harness was distrained on Kennel Farm and sold by tender to satisfy the tithe claim.[79]

The tactic of non-payment quickly gained ground. In Essex, the Colchester district tithepayers' association called on its members to make a 'general refusal to pay their April tithe'. This prompted the Suffolk executive committee to reconsider policy and on 5 May it resolved to advise members not to pay their tithe.[80] The following week, the East Anglian conference of tithepayers reached 'general agreement with regard to refusing to pay the tithe due in April [...] and the hope [...] that members generally would be willing ultimately to face distraint'.[81] At a meeting in Fakenham (Norfolk), Mobbs defended the use of 'unconstitutional methods'. Tithepayers were, he said, 'in a minority and their only method of fighting the injustice was by passive resistance'.[82]

Protests begin

The first skirmish took place in Essex. Under the headline 'Tithe War on Canvey Island', the *Daily Telegraph* reported an 'extraordinary battle' involving, rather than farmers, occupants of bungalows that had been

---

[78] 'Good Progress of the Tithe Protest Movement', Suffolk TPA Bulletin no. 3, 6 Oct. 1931, SuRO, GC32/1.
[79] 'Tithe Court Protest', *BuFP*, 2 May 1931; Suffolk TPA, Executive Committee, 15 Dec. 1931.
[80] Suffolk TPA, Minutes of General Meeting of Members, 7 Apr. 1931; Suffolk TPA, Executive Committee, 5 May 1931, SuRO, GC32/1.
[81] Minutes of Joint Conference of Suffolk, Essex, Norfolk & Cambridgeshire tithepayers, 14 May 1931, SuRO, GC32/1.
[82] 'NFU and Tithe', *F&S*, 18 May 1931.

built on pasture land with liability for tithe. In May 1931, bailiffs executed a distraint order for Queen Anne's Bounty and seized six cartloads of furniture from the home of a 70-year-old former Post Office worker, Arthur Groves. They demanded he pay all the tithe due in the vicinity and then recover the monies from his neighbours. 'The only income I have got is my Post Office pension,' Groves told the paper, 'there are dozens of other bungalows on the 100 acres for which I am being charged.' A Queen Anne's Bounty official explained: 'You've no idea how difficult it is to collect tithes in Canvey Island. It is an extremely awkward place in which to travel about, and as soon as they hear that the bailiffs are coming the bungalow owners bar their doors. [...] Such people have only themselves to blame for not having [the tithe] properly apportioned when they buy the property.' Embarrassed by the publicity, Queen Anne's Bounty instructed the court to withdraw the furniture from the auction on receipt of £6 costs from Groves. 'A grave injustice has been averted', announced the *Telegraph*.[83]

The first big protest by farmers took place on 8 June at three farms owned by James Jones in Stoke-by-Clare (Suffolk). Jones had purchased the land in 1929 when it was in a 'practically derelict' condition, but his plans to establish a successful business were thwarted by the collapse in the price of wheat. Jones paid his first six-monthly tithe instalment, which was due to a private titheowner living in the West Country, but said he possessed insufficient funds to meet the second. The titheowner turned down Jones' proposal to pay tithe only on the land that had been put into cultivation and also his offer of some of the remaining land in lieu of tithe. After a court case, bailiffs distrained almost everything of value on the farms: four lorries, two tractors, two binders, carts, drills, six cart horses, a cow and calf, even a pair of ladders. The Suffolk and Essex tithepayers' associations called a protest meeting to coincide with the auction. The first advertised date had to be postponed after local auctioneers refused to officiate. When the auction was rescheduled, between 400 and 500 people turned up. A local journalist reported:

> Groups of people were more or less picketing all approaches to the farm. Everyone who was in sympathy with the protests [...] was asked to wear a white carnation, and it appeared as if there were none but sympathisers present. [...] On the barn wall at the back was placarded: 'Surrender never', and 'Britons never will be slaves'.

During the auction, a 'chorus of no more' went up after the first bid for each lot. Most of the lots were knocked down for nominal amounts to either Albert Mobbs or W. H. Harvey, secretary of the Essex

---

[83] 'Tithe War on Canvey Island', 'Canvey Island Tithe War', 'Tithe Injustice Averted', *Daily Telegraph* 18, 19 and 20 May 1931.

Tithepayers' Association. In total, the sale realised less than £6. The journalist concluded:

> What was intended to impress resisting tithe payers as to the pains and penalties which they would incur by the non-payment of the dues required of them by law, was turned into a comedy in which the law of the land was made to look ridiculous.[84]

Although a judge at Sudbury County Court (21 July) ruled the auction abortive and decreed the titheowner had the right to distrain again, the protest, which received widespread publicity in the national and regional press, gave a big fillip to the tithepayers' movement.[85]

Three weeks later, on 26 June, similar scenes took place at an auction in Icklesham (East Sussex). The tithepayer, William Crump, a prominent figure in the East Sussex farming community and member of the county council, had failed to pay a charge of £7 11s 9d, for which bailiffs had seized all the furniture and personal effects within his farmhouse, excluding bedding and clothing. In total, Crump owed ecclesiastical tithe totalling £130 in nine different parishes and five other warrants were outstanding. He said he had 'been a lifelong member of the Church of England and that his wife was a Church worker' and member of the choir. A local journalist reported:

> Crowds of farmers from all over south-eastern England reduced the sale to a ludicrous farce. There were only two bidders, Mr G. Butcher, chairman of the newly-formed East Sussex Tithepayers' Association, and Mr J. H. Cooke, treasurer of the association, of which Mr Crump is himself vice-chairman, and between them they bought almost the entire contents of the house for £1 10s. 6d. No single article fetched more than 1s. 6d. [...] The sale was over in less than ten minutes, and ended with cheers for Mr and Mrs Crump.

Amongst those to address the crowd was Roderick Kedward, who said 'all should honour the man who took steps to resist the payment of excessive tithe charges'.[86]

The growth of the tithepayers' movement and, particularly, the publicity surrounding the auctions prompted an intervention by Addison, the minister of agriculture. Despite previously stating that the situation had been 'stabilised', Addison sought to establish negotiations to find ways to mitigate some of the grievances behind the 'anti-tithe agitation'. On 25 June, representatives of titheowners – Queen Anne's

---

[84] 'Extraordinary Stoke-by-Clare Scene', *BuFP*, 13 June 1931.
[85] Suffolk TPA, Executive Committee, 28 July 1931, SuRO, GC32/1; 'Stock Seized for Tithe', *The Times*, 9 June 1931.
[86] 'Sold up for 30s', *Hastings & Saint Leonards Observer*, 27 June 1931; 'Farmers and Tithe Payments', *The Times*, 27 June 1931.

Bounty, Ecclesiastical Commissioners, Welsh Commissioners and Oxford and Cambridge colleges – attended talks at the ministry. Reports described the discussions as 'informal and friendly'.[87] Two weeks later, on 7 July, Addison met organisations representing the interests of tithepayers. Three MPs were present, one from each major party (Kedward, Lymington and Dallas). The NTA sent a five-member delegation, and eight county tithepayers' associations were also represented. Two representatives attended from the NFU, the Chambers of Agriculture, the CLA, the Land Agents' Society, the Auctioneers' and Estate Agents' Institute and the Royal Institution of Chartered Surveyors.[88] Relations between the different parties were, according to reports, rather fraught. After Kedward outlined the position of the tithepayers' associations, contributions from representatives of the landowners, surveyors and auctioneers argued 'a different point of view' and were 'received [by the tithepayers' delegates] with derision'.[89] Then, on 29 July, the Ministry of Agriculture convened a 'joint conference' of titheowners and tithepayers. Kedward, Allen and Lymington attended on behalf of the NTA.[90] Addison's aim was, as one newspaper put it, 'to try to smooth matters over and possibly re-arrange the system of payment to avoid hardships'.[91] He sought 'understanding' on both sides: recognition from tithepayers of the 'rights' of titheowners and a more flexible approach from titheowners towards farmers facing financial difficulties. According to the official communiqué, all parties agreed to reconvene at the ministry to 'further examine' a series of issues.[92]

The negotiations came, however, to an abrupt halt. Addison's intervention in the tithe conflict coincided with the crisis that engulfed and then split apart the Labour government. Addison refused to follow Ramsay Macdonald into a National Government – essentially a coalition with the Conservative Party – and was on 25 August replaced as minister of agriculture by Sir John Gilmour, a Conservative. The new minister promptly cancelled any further talks.

September 1931

Almost immediately, a new series of auctions reignited the conflict. The first six took place on farms on the Kentish Weald, close to Ashford. Distrained stacks of hay were auctioned on 15 September at Ruckinge,

[87] F. G. Hughes, 'Report of Conference on 25 June between the Minister of Agriculture and Fisheries and Tithe Owners', CERC, QAB/2/1/48.
[88] Suffolk TPA, Executive Committee, 14 July 1931, SuRO, GC32/1.
[89] *The Tithepayer*, No. 1, Oct. 1931.
[90] Suffolk TPA, Executive Committee, 28 July 1931, SuRO, GC32/1.
[91] 'Tithe', *The Courier*, 29 July 1931.
[92] 'Conference at Ministry of Agriculture', *The Times*, 30 July 1931.

The Settlement Unravels, 1927–31

Hamstreet, Shadoxhurst and Kingsnorth; and, the following day, at Westwell and Little Chart. On 24 September, an auction was held at a smallholding at Stelling Minnis, near Canterbury, and another sale took place in Icklesham (East Sussex). For the first time, reports spoke of violence and 'disorder'.

Events at the sales on 15 and 16 September followed a familiar script. First, Kedward addressed the crowd, saying that farmers 'had tried every constitutional way of protest against tithe and it only remained for them to refuse to pay until the injustice was remedied by Act of Parliament'.[93] When the auctioneer opened the bidding, members of the tithepayers' association made derisory offers. On 15 September, all the stacks of hay were sold for a few shillings to Ebenezer Haffenden, who since the distraint of his possessions the previous summer had become a leading figure in the local tithepayers' association. The following day at Westwell the county court bailiff refused a bid of 5s from Kedward, declaring a 'no sale'. At Little Chart, all the produce was purchased for a nominal sum by George Christopher Solley, chairman of East Kent Tithepayers' Association.

A variation on the general scenario took place at Ruckinge, where a member of the Churchmen's Defence Union, the new guise of E. W. I. Peterson's Tithe Owners' Union, attempted to participate in the sale. After Kedward opened the bidding – offering 5s for hay that had been valued at £25 – the Churchmen's Defence Union member shouted 'nine guineas'. According to the police observer 'Mr Kedward then bid £500. The rest of the farmers became very hostile towards the person bidding nine guineas. [...] The man was escorted to his motor car by Police, and he left the Farm. The sale began again and the stack was sold to Mr Haffenden for 10s.'[94] The incident at Ruckinge infuriated Church authorities. The secretary of Queen Anne's Bounty, Frederick Hughes, complained to the Home Office that, despite requests for 'adequate police protection', only one police constable had been deployed at the auction. The bidder sent by the Churchmen's Defence Union had been 'pelted with manure and bricks and only escaped with difficulty in a motor car of which the wind-screen was broken and the tyres slashed with knives. The driver was hit in the ribs by two bricks and very severely bruised.' Recognising the seriousness of the situation, the letter continued:

> A time has now come when it will probably be necessary for [Queen Anne's Bounty] to ask the County Courts to proceed to distrain in a large number of cases [...] There can be no doubt that if the agitators

---

[93] *The Times, Evening Standard, Morning Post*, 16 Sept. 1931. TNA, HO 144/19199.
[94] Superintendent W. J. Robertson, 'Re Tithe Sales, Ashford Division', 2 Oct. 1931, TNA, HO 144/19199.

were able to render the sales ineffective, the agitation will spread very widely [...] It seems a matter of national importance that this should be prevented.[95]

Ruckinge also marked the beginning of participation in the 'tithe war' by Lord Selborne (William Palmer) and his son, Lord Wolmer (Roundell Cecil Palmer). During the conflicts of the 1880s, Selborne had vociferously defended the Church from attempts 'to rob' it of tithe. He now rekindled his campaign as Chairman of the House of Laity in the Church Assembly.[96] Lord Wolmer held similar sentiments and, on the day after the Ruckinge events, wrote to Sir Thomas Inskip, the Solicitor General:

> There is a carefully organised conspiracy (of which Kedward is one of the heads) to frustrate the collection of tithe in certain areas. As you know, the Church is very anxious not to move in the matter, and in this question ecclesiastical titheowners are in no different position to lay titheowners. I do feel, and I am sure you will agree, that both are entitled to the protection of the Crown in the enjoyment of their property. May I therefore respectfully suggest to you that the Law Officers should consider the advisability of instituting a prosecution against the ringleaders for conspiracy.[97]

Demands from titheowners for more police protection and for legal proceedings to be taken against the 'agitators' and 'ringleaders' prompted the Home Office to start monitoring the tithepayers' movement. Files relating to the tithe disturbances in Wales during the 1880s were re-examined for lessons on how best to deploy the forces of law and order. A Home Office minute expressed the fear that 'under existing economic conditions the farmers [...] may allow themselves to be led into very bitter opposition to the payment of tithes, which they are inclined to regard as the last straw on the already severely burdened back of agriculture.' It also warned that 'any unduly precipitate action might only lead to additional trouble or even to events such as happened in the 80s and 90s in Wales.'[98] In relation to the incidents at Ruckinge and other sales on the Kentish Weald, enquiries indicated that reports of serious violence had been 'exaggerated': 'there had been no serious disturbances of the Peace at any of them' and 'no damage to any person or property', wrote the senior police officer on duty.[99] The chief constable of Kent admitted,

---

[95] F. G. Hughes to Sir John Anderson, 23 Sept. 1931, TNA, HO 144/19199.
[96] D. George Boyce, 'Palmer William Waldegrave, second earl of Selborne (1859–1942)', *ODNB* (2008).
[97] Viscount Wolmer to Sir Thomas Inskip, 16 Sept. 1931, TNA, HO 144/19199.
[98] Home Office Minute, 23 Sept. 1931, TNA, HO 144/19199.
[99] Superintendent Robertson, 2 Oct. 1931, TNA, HO 144/19199.

Figure 4. 'Lively Tithe Sales in Kent': front page of *Daily Mirror*, 25 September 1931 (© Mirrorpix Daily Mirror). The article reports 'remarkable scenes' at tithe sales at Stelling Minnis and Icklesham. At Stelling Minnis, 'the sale was conducted amid a rain of missiles, including clods of mud and a wet sack knocked off the hat of the Chief Constable of Kent and smothered his waistcoat with dirt'. At Icklesham, 'bullocks were stampeded […] and scattered bidders, police and the auctioneer'.

nevertheless, 'that there had been mistakes made [...] which he was determined would not occur again'.[100]

Consequently, the authorities and the Church viewed the next auction, which was due to take place at Stelling Minnis (Kent) on 24 September, as a serious test. The chief constable attended in person, together with a considerable force of officers. A host of journalists from the national and local press also travelled to observe proceedings. From the point of view of the tithepayers' movement, the circumstances of the farmer, who owed tithe to Queen Anne's Bounty, could not have provided better opportunities for propaganda. A police report outlined events:

> Little Prim farm [...] is occupied by Thomas Clarke, who resides there with his wife and three children. Mr Clarke is, without doubt, in poor circumstances. The farm consists of about eighteen acres only, and Mr Clarke deals in wood to assist him in obtaining a livelihood. Mrs Clarke also works in the fields. The amount owing in respect of tithe was £19 2s. 0d. which was for a period of three years. The various lots to be sold included one horse, one waggon, 2 small stacks of hay and a quantity of wood. [...] At 3 pm the auctioneer endeavoured to commence the sale, and the crowd then commenced shouting and drowned his voice. There was not one genuine bid made, neither did I hear of any single person present who had the intention of making a genuine bid. The whole affair appeared to be a farce, and was simply a good advertisement for the Tithe Payers' Association.[101]

The same day, a sale at Icklesham (East Sussex) was also disrupted. The chief constable of East Sussex reported:

> There were about fifty farmers present, chiefly local, and two persons from a place around thirty miles away who came to bid for the animals. The methods adopted by the farmers present were to bid two or three together, and the auctioneer in consequence was unable to decide who made the bid. This method was adopted for about five times and suddenly a shout arose 'they're sold', and the animals were rushed into an adjoining field. All the gateways were left open, and before they could be headed the animals were five fields away. Before the Police could arrange to get the animals back the auctioneer said 'I have decided to make it a no-sale'.[102]

The Stelling Minnis and Icklesham sales brought the tithe war to the front pages of the national press. 'Lively Tithe Sales in Kent: Bullocks Stampeded. Auctioneers Pelted with Mud', headlined the *Daily Mirror*. 'Police Injured in Tithe Sale, 200 farmers try to "lynch" auctioneer',

---

[100] J. H. Burrell, 'Note of Interview', 18 Sept. 1931, TNA, HO 144/19199.
[101] Superintendent F. H. Golding, 2 Oct. 1931, TNA, HO 144/19199.
[102] Chief Constable of East Sussex, 7 Oct. 1931, TNA, HO 144/19199.

announced the *Daily Herald*. 'Hand-to-hand fights between police and famers. Police Cordons broken again and again. The auctioneer knocked down, trampled on and finally escorted to a motor-car by 20 police through an infuriated crowd,' began the article. A similar, though more sober, report of the Stelling Minnis auction appeared in *The Times*:

> The sale proceeded amid derisive cheers and a rain of missiles, one of which, a wet sack, removed the hat of the Chief Constable of Kent and smothered his waistcoat with mud. [...] Although protected by police, [the auctioneer] was borne to the ground and many constables were seen struggling on the ground with the demonstrators.[103]

In the aftermath of the auction, the registrar of Hythe county court, who was responsible for carrying out the distraint order, wrote to the home secretary complaining of violence and intimidation. He claimed that the 'possession man' put in place by the bailiff had been 'threatened with an axe' by the farmer's wife, leading him to withdraw from the premises, and that the windows of the auctioneer's office had been 'broken' in the early hours of the morning.[104]

The National Government viewed the tithe conflict as essentially a matter of defending property rights against unlawful activity and announced a firm stance towards the tithepayers' movement. In parliament, Will Lawther, a Labour MP, asked the minister of agriculture whether he would be 'prepared to meet the Tithepayers' Association with a view to discussing their problems and coming to an agreement on the subject'. Gilmour replied that he was 'quite satisfied that no useful purpose would be served by such a meeting'.[105] On the same day, Gilmour met leaders of the NFU and told them that there could be no review of the tithe issue 'in the face of the unconstitutional action which was being taken by certain tithepayers in different parts of the country'.[106] Answering questions on 30 November, the minister ruled out any legislation on tithe and confirmed he was cancelling the talks between government, titheowners and tithepayers arranged by his predecessor.[107]

Simultaneously, the Home Office conducted a review of the tactics to be deployed by police. Chief constables covering what were considered agitation hotspots – Kent, East Sussex, Oxfordshire, Buckinghamshire, Berkshire, Essex, Norfolk and east and west Suffolk – were asked for

---

[103] *Daily Mirror*, 25 Sept. 1931; *DHe*, 25 Sept. 1931; 'Chief Constable's Hat Knocked Off', *The Times*, 25 Sept. 1931.
[104] Dallas Brett & Son to Home Secretary, 26 Sept. 1931, TNA, HO 144/19199.
[105] HC Deb., *Hansard*, 24 Sept. 1931.
[106] NFU, Parliamentary, Press & Publicity Committee, 13 Oct. 1931, MERL, SR NFU, AD1/13.
[107] HC Deb., *Hansard*, 30 Nov. 1931.

details of the situation. A summary of their reports concluded that 'farmers, even those who are in a position to pay their tithes, appear to be adopting a determined attitude and the agitators behind the movement are doing their best to foment trouble and opposition.' The Home Office circulated chief constables a legal opinion from 1892, which suggested that police should 'use necessary force to disperse [demonstrations] and in this way indirectly assist the entry of the bailiff'.[108] The lord chancellor's office advised that any assembly by tithepayers, whether on private or public land, that had 'the purpose of intimidating or preventing by force the execution of lawful process' was unlawful and those involved in 'creating the disturbance' should be prosecuted.[109]

The National Government was returned with a landslide majority at the general election on 27 October. Roderick Kedward lost his Ashford seat, depriving the tithepayers' movement of its most prominent parliamentary champion. Although Kedward had stood as a 'national liberal' in support of the government, local Conservatives put up a 'national conservative' candidate. The tithe conflict was a major factor in their decision. 'A law maker of England' should not 'associate himself with law breaking in his constituency as Mr Kedward had done,' explained a local Tory representative. By 'adopting those methods', Kedward could not 'be considered worthy of representing a great constituency in parliament'.[110]

NTA–NFU relations

The growth of the tithepayers' movement led to further tensions between the NTA and NFU headquarters. Under pressure from their membership, NFU senior officers stepped up attempts to show they were taking the tithe issue seriously. In July 1931, they asked county executives for views 'as to the precise nature of the amendments to the 1925 Act the union should seek'. The union also began to lobby ministers for an inquiry to establish 'the best means of bringing the Tithe Act of 1925 into line with existing conditions'.[111] The demand for an inquiry became one of 'six points' of policy highlighted on NFU leaflets and recruitment material. But the NFU's announcement in June 1931 that it would not support the Tithe Remission Bill was treated with dismay by many members in heavily tithed regions. Berkshire was just one region to pass a resolution

---

[108] 'Tithe Sales – Disturbances', 3 Oct. 1931, TNA, HO 144/19199.
[109] 'Tithe Distress Sales', Draft from Lord Chancellor's Office on Advice to County Court Officers on Recovery, 31 Nov. 1931, TNA, HO 144/19199.
[110] 'Fight between "National" Candidates', *Sevenoaks Chronicle and Kentish Advertiser*, 23 Oct. 1931.
[111] NFU, Parliamentary, Press & Publicity Committee, 15 Sept. 1931, MERL, SR NFU, AD1/13.

'greatly regretting' the decision.[112] The agricultural press carried letters critical of the NFU. In the absence of activity from a 'moribund' NFU, 'it remains for tithepayers themselves to unite and refrain from paying tithe', wrote a farmer from Tackley, Oxfordshire. 'Tithepayers have made far more progress in six months towards getting redress than the NFU council has in six years,' suggested another from Essex.[113]

The debate within the NFU was polarised. Some regions offered support to the national leadership's position. The executive in Lancashire, a lightly tithed county, argued that tithe was 'a legitimate investment' and should not therefore be abolished: those farmers protesting against it had known full well that they would be liable for tithe when they bought their land, and had accordingly paid a lower price.[114] Even some committees in heavily tithed regions joined the criticisms of the NTA. In Kent – one of the NTA's heartlands – the NFU officers wrote to the archbishop of Canterbury warning him of the 'gravity' of a situation 'causing a cleavage between the Church and those engaged in the Agricultural industry which is both deplorable and undesirable'. They assured him of their opposition to the Tithe Remission Bill, which would 'confiscate property without compensating the owner', and stressed they had 'never countenanced or given support to any of the unconstitutional methods which have been adopted by some farmers in the county in resisting the payment and recovery of tithe'.[115] In Kent, as elsewhere, the county NFU leadership was dominated by 'gentleman farmers' who sought to promote a 'respectable' image and disassociate themselves from 'the agitators'.

Tensions between the NFU and NTA were particularly sharp in Norfolk, where the county branch also came out in opposition to the Tithe Remission Bill. The Norfolk NFU secretary, Jimmy Wright, was a devout member of the Church of England and also a representative of the laity on Queen Anne's Bounty's area tithe collection committee. Leaders of the tithepayers' association accused him of having a conflict of interest. A tithe auction on 9 November in the village of Shelfanger brought matters to a head. Tithepayers' associations throughout the eastern counties mobilised for the sale, at which sheep and cattle valued at around £170 were knocked down for £1 9s 6d. Speaking at the rally after the auction, Mobbs described Wright as a 'wolf in sheep's clothing'. In response, the

---

[112] 'Tithe and Confiscation' *F&S*, 20 July 1931.
[113] *F&S*, 9 Feb. and 27 July 1931.
[114] 'Fair Play for Tithe Owners', *F&S*, 20 July 1931; NFU, Parliamentary, Press & Publicity Committee, 17 Nov. 1931, MERL, SR NFU, AD1/13.
[115] J. Hillier French, NFU Kent branch to Cosmo Lang, 18 June 1932, CERC, ECE/SEC/TITHE/P7.

Norfolk NFU said that Mobbs' language would be 'deprecated by every fair thinking famer in the country'.[116]

Mobbs increasingly made public criticisms of NFU policy and claimed that many farmers were leaving the union because of its failure to campaign on tithe.[117] Simultaneously, NFU leaders attacked the 'unconstitutional action' by tithepayers' associations at auctions.[118] According to Robbins, this 'had prejudiced the union's chance of getting anything done in the matter'.[119] Robbins even tried to blame the NTA for the 1925 Tithe Act. 'If those who were affected [by tithe] had spoken with one voice at the time [...] instead of breaking away and joining another Association, things might not have been so difficult as they are today,' he told the National Council.[120] In June 1931, the *NFU Record* devoted an entire page to criticising the NTA, 'who seem to be more concerned to place difficulties in the way of the achievement of the union's policy than to serve the real interests of tithepayers'.[121] The NFU's position won plaudits from leaders of the Churchmen's Defence Union. E. W. R. Peterson, son of its founding member and himself a Churchmen's Defence Union activist, wrote of the 'honourable policy' of the NFU, which has not had 'anything to do with the agitation'.[122]

A major row between the NFU leadership and supporters of the tithepayers' movement erupted at the NFU annual meeting in January 1932. Mobbs pointed out that the growth of tithepayers' associations was a direct result of the union's mistaken belief that 'the time was not opportune' to reopen the tithe question. A farmer from East Sussex, who had been present at tithe auctions, said he would not apologise for his 'unconstitutional action': 'considering the results, he thought the ends justified the methods employed. [...] If headquarters had taken the matter up, he did not think they would have been forced to adopt the methods which had been used.'[123] In response, Robbins demanded that tithepaying farmers should show loyalty to the NFU. 'For heaven's sake if you believe that the Tithepayers' Association can do better for you than the Union can, go to the association. But if you do, you have no right to come to us as well.' The implication that farmers had to choose between membership of the tithepayers' associations and the NFU prompted gasps of astonishment and protests from the conference floor.[124]

---

[116] 'Farmers Make Tithe Sale a Farce', *DHe*, 10 Nov. 1931; 'A Tithe Distraint Sale at Shelfanger' *DiEx*, 13 Nov. 1931; '32 Sheep for Half a Crown', *F&S*, 16 Nov. 1931, 'The Norfolk NFU and Headquarters', *DiEx*, 27 Nov. 1931.
[117] 'Tithe "revolt"', *ChCh*, 17 Apr. 1931; *F&S*, 18 May 1931.
[118] *NFU Record*, Nov. 1931, 33.
[119] *NFU Record*, Dec. 1931, 82.
[120] *NFU Record*, Mar. 1931, 134.
[121] 'The Tithe Question', *NFU Record*, June 1931, 212–13.
[122] E. W. R. Peterson, 'Tithe Rent-Charge', *SEG*, 22 Mar. 1932.
[123] *NFU Record*, Feb. 1932, 107.
[124] 'A Troublesome Question: Tithe', *F&S*, 25 Feb. 1932; *NFU Record*, Feb. 1932, 108.

The Settlement Unravels, 1927–31

The non-payment campaign and reports of violence at auctions also fuelled tensions within the NTA. Lymington and Albert Burrows continued to oppose 'non-constitutional' action at national meetings and arguments broke out in some local associations. At the October meeting of the Colchester Tithepayers' Association, the chairman, G. J. Mitchell, told those 'playing about with these distraint sales' that 'if you get yourselves locked up, I won't come and bail you out. You have just about gone as far as you can with the judges.' Another prominent Essex member, Ralph Blewitt, demanded a halt to 'rowdyism' at sales 'before we meet our match in a strong police force and suffer defeat, which we shall undoubtedly do'. After buying his farm in 1922, Blewitt had built a substantial business, employing around twenty-five farm labourers and other casual workers. He stressed that farmers were 'a law-abiding people' who could not be tarnished by the type of protests more associated with protests by the unemployed workers' movement. In response, a farmer, Arthur Goddard, blamed provocations by the titheowners and county courts, who 'issued summonses in an indiscriminate way, independent of whether a man was able to pay or whatever his position, and feeling ran so high in some cases that it was impossible, however much the tithepayers' officials might try, to stop rowdyism.'[125]

On 30 December 1931, a national conference of tithepayers' associations took place in London. Representatives attended from established associations in the eastern and southern counties and also from recently formed groups, including those in Hampshire, Wiltshire, Devon and parts of Wales. The conference agreed to establish a 'united tithepayers' association', effectively a merger of the original NTA with the local associations. A further conference on 3 February 1932 launched the new organisation, which retained the name NTA. It elected a central council and sub-committees to deal with policy, legal matters and representation. It also announced its willingness to negotiate with Queen Anne's Bounty on behalf of tithepayers and offered to come to a 'working agreement' with the NFU around a common policy.[126] The conference unanimously elected Kedward as chairman and Allen as secretary of the reconstituted association.[127]

The relaunch of the NTA was the signal for a section of members opposed to the non-payment strategy to leave the tithepayers' movement. In the weeks before the conference, Lymington and Burrows resigned

---

[125] East Anglian Film Archive, Boxted Hall Farm Scenes, 1925: http://www.eafa.org.uk/catalogue/709; 'Tithe Distraint Defiance', *Ipswich Evening Star*, 19 Oct. 1931.
[126] 'Farmers Unite in the Tithe War', *DHe*, 31 Dec. 1931, 'Tithepayers Form National Body', *F&S*, 8 Feb. 1932.
[127] Allen to Mobbs, 8 and 22 Jan., 3 Feb. 1932, Mobbs Papers.

from the NTA and other defections took place at local level. Yet the NTA began 1932 in confident mood. Politicians and the agricultural press had been forced to take its arguments seriously. It seemed to be making headway in the debate within the NFU. Local associations were recruiting members and branches were being formed in new areas. Moreover, mobilisations at auctions had managed to disrupt every attempt at tithe distraint. NTA leaders, however, were anticipating a concerted riposte from titheowners and the authorities.

6

The Bounty and General Dealers

The Bounty's tithe committee

The centralisation of ecclesiastical tithe collection through Queen Anne's Bounty had not been suggested during the negotiations of 1924–25. But, as civil servants drafted the tithe bill, senior clergy argued that the opportunity should be taken to relieve parish clergy from the 'unwelcome' duties associated with tithe collection, and the government was happy to oblige. The archbishop of Canterbury, Randall Davidson, told the House of Lords that the measure would 'make the relationships between parson and people, between titheowner and tithepayer as smooth and as free from friction as possible'.[1] No-one seemed to anticipate the consequences of establishing a centralised tithe-collecting machinery that was remote from communities and administered by agents with limited knowledge of local circumstances.

Established in 1704, The Bounty of Queen Anne for the Augmentation of the Maintenance of the Poor Clergy – to give it its full name – has been described as one of the Church's two 'Temporal Pillars', the other being the Ecclesiastical Commission. Both 'pillars' were administrative departments, responsible for the management of property, revenues, investments, payments to clergy and a range of associated matters.[2] The Bounty's affairs were overseen by a general court of governors appointed by the monarch. Normally chaired by the archbishop of Canterbury, who was sometimes described as 'President of the Bounty', the general court met annually and included bishops and deans of cathedral chapters. But the position of governorship was also conferred on

---

[1] 'Tithe Rentcharge: Report of Committee', 8 May 1925, TNA, CAB/24/173/30; archbishop of Canterbury, HL Debate, *Hansard*, 3 Dec. 1925; 'Tithe Bill', *The Times*, 4 Dec. 1925.
[2] G. F. A. Best, *Temporal Pillars: Queen Anne's Bounty, The Ecclesiastical Commissioners and The Church of England* (Cambridge: Cambridge University Press, 1964).

the Speaker of the House of Commons, the Master of the Rolls, the Privy Councillors, the Lieutenants of the Counties of England and Wales, the Deans of Cathedral Churches, the Judges of the Courts of Queen's Bench and Common Pleas, the Barons of the Court of Exchequer, the Sergeants-at-law, the Attorney and Solicitor General, the Advocate General, the Chancellors and Vice-Chancellors of Oxford and Cambridge Universities, the Major and Alderman of the City of London, the Mayors of York and English Cities, the officers of the Board of Green Cloth,[3] the Queen's Counsel, and the Clerks in Ordinary of the Privy Council.

There were also 'lay governors' – mostly Church benefactors, peers and officers of state.[4] Before the 1925 Act, the Bounty's responsibilities for tithe had exclusively concerned tithe redemption. It collected redemption payments from tithepayers, invested them and distributed monies to those clergy whose tithe had been bought out. Although such tasks increased substantially after the passing of the 1918 Act, from an administrative point of view they remained relatively uncomplicated.

The 1925 Act transformed Queen Anne's Bounty into a sizeable bureaucracy with a range of responsibilities. It had the task of collecting and managing tithe on behalf of around 7,200 benefices and forty-one ecclesiastical corporations. It also collected the vestiges of other forms of tithe: 520 cases of corn rent (charges on land agreed in lieu of tithe before the 1836 commutation act), 427 charges awarded under the Extraordinary Tithe Act (1886), certain 'house tithe' in urban areas, and tithe in kind still collected on fish.[5] One remaining anomaly was the Act's failure to cover tithes collected by parishes within the City of London. Queen Anne's Bounty made payments to clergy, calculated and paid monies due to the Inland Revenue in lieu of rates, liaised with the Inland Revenue over Land Tax, dealt with disputes about entitlements, wrote off 'permanently unrecoverable tithe', dealt with sequestrators and at times made cash advances to needy clergy.

The Bounty's tithe responsibilities were directed by men with a conservative mind-set, who viewed their duties as primarily administrative: acting as servants of Church and state, helping to provide financial security to the clergy and implementing decisions of parliament. Tasks were carried out by a team of around thirty people based in an office in Dean's Yard, Westminster. Managing the staff was the legally trained Frederick Hughes, who replaced William Le Fanu as QAB's secretary and treasurer in 1925. He was assisted by William

[3] Officials of the Royal Household.
[4] William R. Le Fanu, *Queen Anne's Bounty: A Short Account of its History and Work* (London: Macmillan, 1921), 10–11.
[5] 'Report by the Tithe Committee of the Governors of the Queen Anne's Bounty', 22 Apr. 1936, 16, CERC, QAB/2/1/53.

Hannah, who had worked for the Bounty since leaving school in 1883 and, after being encouraged by his employer to study law, became QAB's official solicitor, acquiring a 'widely respected' expertise on ecclesiastical law.[6]

Fifteen area committees were established to organise the practical tasks of collection. These were made up of archdeacons from the dioceses covered, representatives of tithe-owning clergy and representatives of the laity. In most cases, a local solicitor was appointed as committee secretary/convenor. Tithe collectors were employed on a commission basis: 762 people in 1928, though the number had been reduced to 420 by 1931.[7]

Queen Anne's Bounty's tithe committee decided policy, gave direction to the staff at Dean's Yard and kept a tight rein on the work of the area collection committees, appointing officers, approving membership, vetting expenses and insisting on regular reports. It instructed the area committees to take a firm line in the event of arrears, making clear to tithepayers that 'after the expiration of three months' grace [...] proceedings would be taken without further notice'.[8] Two lay officials played a pivotal role on the QAB tithe committee. In 1927, the 66-year-old Sir Frederick Radcliffe was appointed chairman. A trained solicitor, Radcliffe had displayed impressive administrative skills as chairman of the Liverpool Cathedral Committee and, later, as chairman of the legal board of the Church of England. He worked closely with Sir Stanford Downing, who had been influential in the negotiations leading up to the 1925 Tithe Act. As well as sitting on the tithe committee, Downing continued to serve as secretary and financial advisor to the Ecclesiastical Commissioners, overseeing much of the Church's business affairs until his death in 1933.[9]

Clerical representation on the tithe committee was led by two bishops, both officiating in dioceses in which tithe formed a significant proportion of Church income. Bertram Pollock, the bishop of Norwich, had a long-standing interest in tithe, at times speaking on the matter in the House of Lords.[10] A former master of Wellington College, an institution with a 'tradition of Protestant militaristic patriotism', he earned a reputation as a 'zealous defen[der] of national religion', most notably during the controversy around the revision of the Book of Common Prayer (1927–28).[11] His brother, Lord Hanworth (Ernest

---

[6] 'Mr W. G. Hannah', *The Times*, 29 Nov. 1945.
[7] QAB, Tithe Committee, 20 Aug. 1931, CERC, QAB/2/1/48.
[8] Governors of Queen Anne's Bounty, 20 Feb. 1929, CERC QAB/2/1/46.
[9] 'Church Assembly', *The Times*, 13 June 1933.
[10] HL Deb., *Hansard*, 25 Apr. 1918.
[11] John G. Maiden, 'English Evangelicals, Protestant National Identity, and Anglican Prayer Book Revision, 1927–1928', *Journal of Religious History*, 34, 4

Pollock) had for many years been a Conservative MP before, in 1923, being appointed master of the rolls. Walter Whittingham, bishop of St Edmundsbury and Ipswich, brought business acumen to the tithe committee. Holding similar political views to Pollock, he was not averse to offering spiritual guidance to the task of tithe collection.[12] Asked whether or not 'it is a Christian act to insist on payment of tithe' when agriculture had fallen on hard times, he contemplated:

> When I try to weigh as a matter of Christian principle the ownership of tithe on the one hand with the proceedings taken by the Tithepayers' Association on the other, there does not seem to me much question where the Christian principle is most effectively deployed. It is certainly not by the Tithepayers' Association.[13]

The Bounty's tithe collection machinery faced teething problems. Often agents had difficulty in ascertaining who exactly was legally liable for tithe. A QAB report noted that 'tithe collection lists in use were seriously defective' and 'in many parishes entirely new lists had to be prepared involving local surveys of the lands'.[14] Sometimes, collection committees had to decide how best to pursue payments when land had been sold and divided between different owners. Under tithe legislation, titheowners could demand one landowner pay the charge for tithable land and then recoup the money from other landowners, effectively forcing them to act as an unpaid tithe collector. This was, as at Canvey Island, a source of grievance for tithepayers and the Bounty's staff spent considerable time picking over complaints. One weighty batch of correspondence concerned a case in the diocese of Winchester, where a tithe demand had been sent to a farmer, Mr F. J. Penny, even though he owned only eighty of the 511 acres on which it was due.[15]

The collection of tithe on fish posed another problem. In the village of Cockerham (Lancashire), the vicar's rights to a proportion of the local salmon had long been a source of conflict. In 1904, the Lancashire Fishery Board had prosecuted a fisherman working on behalf of the vicar for catching the fish without a licence. The court dismissed the case after it was argued that the vicar had the right to tithe under a charter granted by King John and could by custom claim the salmon on two days each month.[16] Although collection of the fish was now the responsibility of Queen Anne's Bounty, it was agreed, after considerable

---

(2010), 439; Matthew Grimley, 'Bertram Pollock (1863–1934)', *ODNB* (2014).
12 'Dr. W. G. Whittingham', *The Times*, 19 June 1941.
13 'Trouble over Tithe', *The Times*, 3 Feb. 1932.
14 'Governors of Queen Anne's Bounty', 20 Feb. 1929, CERC QAB/2/1/46.
15 QAB, Tithe Committee, 9 Apr. 1930, CERC, QAB/2/1/47.
16 'Salmon as Vicar's Tithe', *Lancaster Standard & County Advertiser*, 19 Aug. 1904.

discussion, 'that in the special circumstance of the case' the vicar should be permitted to continue taking the fish 'as at present'.[17]

A wider difficulty arose from the decision by 1,800 members of the parochial clergy to continue collecting their tithe directly, though legally they now did so as 'agents of Queen Anne's Bounty'. When an incumbent died or left the parish, responsibility for tithe collection would automatically transfer to the relevant collection committee. But, in the meantime, Queen Anne's Bounty was sometimes required to step in to settle problems encountered by their 'agents', including disputes with tithepayers. Quite often they had to chase clergy who were slow to hand over their 5 per cent contribution to the rates.[18]

The biggest difficulty faced by the Bounty was how to ensure a regular income to parochial clergy. Those drafting the legislation had overlooked the fact that, even if there were no problems in collecting the tithe, a delay would occur before it reached Queen Anne's Bounty central coffers on account of the time needed for collection committees to carry out administrative tasks. Moreover, the amounts arriving were bound to fluctuate because farmers settled their accounts at varying times of the year. Letters began to appear in *The Times* describing the 'parlous' position experienced by poor tithe-owning clergy facing 'the double burden of a big decrease in income and a lengthened interval before it is paid'.[19] The Queen Anne's Bounty admitted 'serious difficulties', explaining that 'not a few incumbents were feeling the stress of the cumulative effect of the Tithe Act'. After an intervention by senior clergy, the Church Assembly in 1928 adopted 'The Tithe (Administration of Trusts) Measure'. This allowed the Ecclesiastical Commission to advance funds (approximately £700,000 a year) to the Queen Anne's Bounty in order to ensure quarterly payments to clergy 'irrespective of the amounts actually collected'.[20] The decision would have repercussions for the tithe conflict in that it encouraged clergy to believe they would receive regular payments underwritten by the Commissioners, regardless of collection difficulties.

Confronting 'agitation'

Leaving aside teething problems, Queen Anne's Bounty faced few serious obstacles in collecting tithe during the first three years in which it implemented the provisions of the 1925 Act. The first recognition of difficulties came in the tithe committee's annual report issued in February

---

[17] QAB Tithe Committee, 17 July 1935, CERC QAB/2/1/52.
[18] Governors of Queen Anne' Bounty, 20 Feb. 1929, CERC QAB/2/1/46.
[19] Letter from George B. Charles, 'The Tithe Act', *The Times*, 8 July 1927.
[20] 'Report by the Governors of Queen Anne' Bounty', 20 Feb. 1929, CERC QAB/2/1/46.

1931. It acknowledged a 'serious decline' in tithe collection in areas affected by agricultural depression, particularly 'East Anglia and a few districts of Kent and some other Southern counties'. Nevertheless, the report concluded, with an air of complacency, that the collection remained generally 'satisfactory'.[21]

Yet, just over two months later, the mood had changed dramatically. Opening a meeting of convenors and chairmen of area collection committees on 8 May, Radcliffe spoke of the 'storm' that had arisen 'owing to the agitation in some districts on the part of tithepayers'. The bishop of Norwich added his concern: 'the arguments advanced by the agitators might seem weak, but these arguments were not being answered.'[22] The meeting discussed a draft document, which would be circulated under the title 'Tithe and the Agricultural Depression'. The text was, in essence, the Church's response to the emergence of local tithepayers' associations and, particularly, to the arguments behind Kedward's Tithe Remission Bill. While expressing 'sympathy' for farmers facing a difficult economic situation, the stance of document was uncompromising. The 1925 Act had been 'a permanent and final settlement'. Machinery already existed in the 1891 Act to reduce tithe at a time of agricultural crisis, and there could be 'no further indulgence'. The only concession Queen Anne's Bounty was prepared to offer was 'a reasonable extension of time for payment' in cases of severe hardship. The document finished with a warning: titheowners had the right to take court proceeding to recover tithe 'from all or any part of the land' to which it relates and 'in certain cases from other land in the parish'. As a last resort, they could even obtain 'possession of the land'.[23]

The mobilisation of farmers at the auctions at Stoke-by-Clare and Icklesham in June taught the Bounty's officers that pursuing such a policy would not be without difficulties. On 30 June, a sub-committee of the tithe committee – including Radcliffe, Downing and the bishop of Norwich – met to consider 'the lawlessness' at the two auctions. They also expressed concern at the outcome of another sale at Hundon (Suffolk), where two fields of crops had been sold for a 'derisory' £1 11s. They recognised that the auctions had acted as a fillip to the tithepayers' movement and agreed on the 'very great importance that no further sales under distraint should take place if the results are likely to be such as they were'. County court registrars should be asked 'to suspend for the time being any further attempts to sell goods, crops, etc., which have been distrained upon, until a definite

[21] 'Report by the Governors of Queen Anne's Bounty' 26 Feb. 1931, CERC, QAB/2/1/48.
[22] QAB, 'Report of Proceedings at Conveners' Meeting, 8 May 1931', CERC, QAB/2/1/48.
[23] QAB, 'Tithe and the Agricultural Depression', 15 July 1931, CERC, QAB/2/1/48.

line of action has been decided upon, with a view to preventing any similar failures occurring'.[24] In effect, by mobilising at the auctions, the tithepayers' movement had forced Queen Anne's Bounty to suspend its tithe recovery operations.

Over the next few weeks, Bounty officials drew up a strategy to counter the activities of the tithe 'agitators'. Radcliffe met Canon Partridge, financial secretary of the Church Assembly, to ask him for funds to ensure 'the possibility of supporters of the Church organising steps for bidding at sales for the recovery of ecclesiastical tithe'. Partridge found a way to allocate the money without seeking approval from the Church Assembly. Next, Radcliffe discussed tactics with Edward Peterson, who enthusiastically offered the services of the Churchmen's Defence Union. Peterson agreed to organise a team of CDU members, who would be dispatched to tithe auctions to bid for and purchase distrained goods.[25]

On 14 July, the plans were outlined by Frederick Hughes at a specially convened meeting of representatives from the six collection committees facing the most serious non-payment agitation (those covering Norfolk, Suffolk, Essex, Kent, Oxfordshire and Hampshire/Sussex). Each area was told to select carefully at least one 'good case' for a distraint sale. The amount to be recovered should not be large; the goods to be sold should be easily transportable and 'the owner should be a person of some means who could pay if he liked; and preferably a leader, or at any rate a member, of the local Tithepayers' Association'. If a friendly court registrar would cooperate, several sales could be arranged at different places on the same day, which might, it was suggested, stretch the resources of the tithepayers' associations. Attention should also be given to obtaining adequate police protection but, stressed Hughes, it was essential that 'the whole matter should be kept as secret as possible'. The area representatives were told to go back to make preparations, but not to put them into operation 'without further instruction from the Bounty Office'. The plans remained on hold while Addison, the minister of agriculture, attempted to organise talks between titheowners and tithepayers. It was 'desirable not to create [...] any atmosphere that would be prejudicial to a settlement,' stressed senior Bounty officials.[26]

---

[24] QAB, Sub-Committee of Tithe Committee, 30 June 1931, CERC, QAB/2/1/48; W. G. Hannah, 'Memorandum. Vindication of Powers of Recovery – Unexecuted Orders', 31 May 1932, CERC, QAB 2/1/49; W. G. Hannah, 'Memorandum', 20 July 1932, CERC, QAB 2/1/49.

[25] QAB, Tithe Committee, 13 Oct. 1931, CERC, QAB/2/1/48.

[26] QAB, 'Conference of Representatives of Area Collection Committees affected by prevailing agitation against payment of tithe rentcharge', 14 July 1931, CERC, QAB/2/1/48.

On 6 August, as prospects of an agreement brokered by Addison appeared to be stalling, a special meeting of the tithe committee gave the green light to the plans. The minutes record:

> In view of the approach of harvest it would be dangerous to continue any longer a general suspension of distress orders particularly in view of the arrangements which have been made for countering concerted opposition to distraint sales [...] The execution of distress orders in a few selected cases along the lines indicated [...] might also facilitate recovery of tithe in other cases. [...] Having regard to the large number of outstanding distress orders [...] with the substantial arrears outstanding in some districts in East Anglia, Kent and East Sussex, it was urgently necessary that Area Committees should, with proper discrimination, proceed to the recovery of the arrears.[27]

A letter sent to collection convenors stressed that any delay might encourage farmers to 'think that the [Queen Anne's Bounty] Governors have a weak case or that something is likely to happen whereunder they may get a remission, and an impression may spread among tithepayers that it would be desirable for them not to pay tithe at present'.[28]

Yet the demonstrations at the auctions on the Kentish Weald on 15–16 September and those on 24 September at Stelling Minnis and Icklesham put a halt to Queen Anne's Bounty's offensive. Not only were the sales disrupted, but the Bounty also lost the propaganda battle. Publicity in the media about the desperate economic circumstances of the farmer and his family at Stelling Minnis contradicted claims that farmers facing tithe distress were men 'of some means who could pay if [they] liked'. As an attempt at damage limitation, a Church official wrote to *The Times*: 'Before the sale the poverty of the tithe-payer was not generally known to Churchpeople. When it was ascertained that the tenant was a poor man the articles sold were returned to the debtor as a gift from Churchpeople, the claims of justice having been satisfied.'[29] As in June, the Bounty had failed to inflict a blow on the tithepayers' movement and it was again forced to reconsider its strategy.

Balancing the books

First, however, Queen Anne's Bounty had to tackle the financial difficulties created by tithe non-payment. The tithepayers' associations had recommended that their members withhold payments from 1 April 1931. In December, the tithe committee received an assessment of the boycott's impact. Arrears in the six 'difficult areas' totalled 20.8 per

---

[27] QAB, Tithe Committee, Special Meeting, 6 Aug. 1931, CERC, QAB/2/1/48.
[28] W. G. Hannah, 'Anti-Tithe Agitation', 31 July 1931, CERC, QAB/2/1/48.
[29] 'Stelling Minnis Tithe Sale', *The Times*, 26 Sept. 1931.

cent. In Suffolk, they were almost 40 per cent; in Essex, 22 per cent; in Norfolk 19.4 per cent, in Kent 18 per cent. Given the large amounts of tithe still collected from the landlord class, these were significant figures, indicating widespread nonpayment by owner-occupying farmers. Faced with a shortfall of income, the tithe committee proposed a schedule of cuts in the tithe stipends paid to incumbent clergy to start on 1 January 1932.[30]

The announcement of cuts prompted a wave of protests from affected clergy and, as a result, the tithe problem landed as an unwelcome problem on the desk of Cosmo Lang, archbishop of Canterbury. Writing to Lang about the hardship in his diocese, the bishop of St Edmundsbury and Ipswich said that clergy were demanding a moratorium on payments for church repairs and mortgages, in order to make up the shortfall in tithe collection and guarantee their wages. They also wanted a discussion on the implications of tithe non-payment at the approaching Lower House of Convocation. It would be 'unfortunate that this should be raised,' cautioned the bishop, concerned that publicity about the Church's difficulties would further encourage the tithepayers' campaign.[31]

A few days before Christmas, Rev. John Macmillan, bishop of Dover, and the archdeacon of Canterbury wrote to Cosmo Lang. They warned of 'actual hardship involved to men whom we know' creating the danger of 'a widespread sense of grievance and criticism of central Church authority':

> [The deductions] will be in many cases a severe shock to the men concerned, for which we do not think they have sufficient warning [...] We are not only concerned over individuals in our own diocese, but we fear the appearance of complaints and criticisms when the Church Assembly meets at the beginning of February.

The two men asked the archbishop to request that the Ecclesiastical Commissioners make a new loan to Queen Anne's Bounty. 'We do not,' they emphasised, 'suggest a gift by the Commissioners, because we can see the unwisdom in face of the anti-tithe agitation of any announcement to this effect.' But a loan would allow the Bounty to spread deductions over a longer period and 'lighten the shock'.[32] Cosmo Lang acted immediately. Sir Stanford Downing was summoned to Canterbury on 23 December and an announcement that the reductions to clergy would be scaled back followed.[33] All parties agreed that the arrangement by which the Ecclesiastical Commission would further underwrite Queen

[30] QAB, Tithe Committee, 1 Dec. 1931, CERC, QAB/2/1/48.
[31] Bishop of St Edmundsbury and Ipswich to archbishop of Canterbury, 1 Jan. 1932, CERC, ECE/SEC/TITHE/P7.
[32] Bishop of Dover to archbishop of Canterbury, 21 Dec. 1931, LPL, Lang 71.
[33] Archbishop of Canterbury to Downing, 21 Dec. 1931; Cosmo Lang, 'Memorandum', 23 Dec. 1931, LPL, Lang 71.

Anne's Bounty should receive minimal publicity. 'If suggestions are made,' warned a policy document, 'that any loss of tithe throughout England should be borne by some Central Fund of the Church, this would probably lead to a slackening of payment by many who now pay tithe.'[34] The document also warned of the dangers that any discussion of tithe at the forthcoming meeting of the Church Assembly 'would involve some risk of giving an extended and exaggerated importance to the agitation'. A resolution had been tabled by Canon Brocklehurst, the renowned authority on tithe matters, calling for a committee to review the Church's position. With some of the heat removed, the archbishop, assisted by the bishops of Dover and St Edmundsbury and Ipswich, persuaded Brocklehurst to withdraw his resolution, thus avoiding an 'inconvenient and undesirable' debate.[35]

Having secured its financial position, Queen Anne's Bounty reconsidered its policy to deal with the tithepayers' movement. First, the tithe committee reappraised the strategy outlined the previous summer in 'Tithe and the Agricultural Depression'. Notables in rural society and voices within the Church had begun to urge a more flexible attitude towards farmers. Amongst those to lobby the archbishop of Canterbury was Lord Cornwallis, a landowner in Kent well connected to the regional leaders of the NFU. 'Many farmers in the county entirely dissociate themselves from Mr Kedward [and his] friends' activities at auction sales but they do feel very strongly that tithe is too heavy and an unfair burden on them at the present time,' he told the archbishop.[36] During a sermon to Essex clergy in Chelmsford Cathedral, the archdeacon of Southend said that conditions for tithepayers were 'difficult' and that 'whatever could be done to help the farmer should be done. [...] If there were cases in which the land simply could not carry the burden of tithe, let those cases be carefully considered and justice done.'[37]

Queen Anne's Bounty began to devise a concession policy. It divided tithe non-payers into two categories: farmers facing genuine hardship, but who were prepared to pay tithe if they could, and those who were taking advantage of the agricultural crisis to foment opposition to the principle of tithe. Tithepayers in the first category were described as 'hard cases'. For these, the Bounty would be willing 'to consider the desirability of granting some special concession' in order 'to rehabilitate' the farmer, securing 'a payment within his capacity and a reasonable

[34] 'Policy of Queen Anne's Bounty as to Recovery of Tithe Arrears in Areas of Special Agricultural Depression', 19 Jan. 1932, LPL, Lang 71.
[35] Correspondence between archbishop of Canterbury, bishop of St Edmundsbury and Ipswich and Rev. A. C. Don, 22, 23, 26 Jan. 1932, LPL, Lang 71; 'Church Assembly', *The Times*, 4 Feb. 1932.
[36] Lord Cornwallis to archbishop of Canterbury, 21 Dec. 1931, LPL, Lang 71.
[37] 'Essex Tithepayers', *The Times*, 16 May 1931.

prospect of regularity in future'. It issued a leaflet explaining how farmers could 'apply for special consideration'. To do so, they would have to provide an investigator appointed by Queen Anne's Bounty with particulars of every aspect of their finances. A decision would then be taken on possible concessions, each case evaluated on its merits.[38]

The other prong in the new strategy was to find more effective ways 'to frustrate the efforts' of the second category – 'the anti-tithe agitators' – and thereby 'vindicate the rights' of titheowners. This would require, in the words of the Bounty's secretary, 'a considerable amount of organisation and possibly substantial funds'.[39] The first step was to make a series of applications in the county courts for items seized for tithe to be sold by tender, rather than at auctions. After Stelling Minnis, farmers had continued to thwart distraint sales at Shelfanger (Norfolk) on 9 November, at Stradishall (Suffolk) on 23 November and at three farms in Boughton Aluph (Kent) in late January 1932. According to Frank Allen, the Boughton Aluph auction, at which there was not a single bid, had been 'one of our most successful jobs […] the titheowners were flabbergasted'.[40]

Queen Anne's Bounty believed that the sale of distrained goods by tender would restrict opportunities for the tithepayers' associations to obstruct the recovery process. It would also resolve the problem that an increasing number of auction houses, particularly those with business relating to agriculture, were refusing to undertake tithe sales.[41] Starting in Kent, judges agreed to sales by tender if there existed a significant risk that auctions would be disrupted. The Ashford county court annulled the disrupted auctions of September 15 and 16 and ordered that the distressed goods should be resold by tender, awarding costs against the tithepayers' movement. In Wiltshire, the judge at Salisbury county court granted the Bounty's application after hearing that 'one and all' auctioneers in the area had 'declined to undertake the job'. Courts in Suffolk also ordered sales by tender, including impounded stock and possessions of prominent members of the tithepayers' association. A drawn-out case began on 25 January 1932 at Ipswich county court, when the judge asked Charles Westren, a farmer from Elmsett, whether he was a member of the Suffolk Tithepayers' Association. When Westren

---

[38] 'Policy of Queen Anne's Bounty' 19 Jan. 1932, LPL, Lang 71; F. G. Hughes, 'Tithe Arrears in Areas of Special Agricultural Depression', Jan. 1932, CERC, QAB/2/1/49.

[39] W. G. Hannah, 'Vindication of Powers of Recovery. Memorandum', Tithe Committee, 20 July 1932, CERC, QAB/2/1/49.

[40] 'Farmers Make Tithe Sale a Farce', *DHe*, 10 Nov. 1931; 'Farmers in Revolt', *BuFP*, 28 Nov. 1931; 'No Bids at Tithe-Rent Sale', *Warwick and Warwickshire Advertiser*, 23 Jan. 1932; Allen to Mobbs, 24 Mar. 1932, Mobbs Papers.

[41] 'Auctioneers and Tithes', *Taunton Courier & Western Advertiser*, 11 May 1932.

replied in the affirmative, the judge ordered sale by tender in order to 'prevent a mock auction'.[42] Elsewhere, judges approved 'special conditions' at auctions, setting reserve prices and enabling bids to be made by absent bidders.[43]

The Bounty's second step was to secure sufficient financial resources for the campaign around tithe recovery. The Churchmen's Defence Union had proved its impotence at the auctions, greatly overstating its capabilities and failing to mobilise more than a handful of individuals. Even more worrying was a message from Canon Partridge that he could no longer offer financial support without official approval from the Church Assembly – and, as already noted, the prospect of such a public discussion was viewed as likely to encourage the tithepayers' movement. A number of options were explored. Radcliffe suggested an appeal to establish a group of churchgoers prepared to provide funds for purchasers and underwrite costs in the event of litigation.[44] He volunteered a donation of £200 to set the ball rolling. Others argued that the scale of the challenge required the guarantee of more substantial funding. The Ecclesiastical Commissioners again agreed to step in. They pledged to organise and finance bids for tendered stock in a selected number of cases 'through special agents'.[45]

So, the main duties of Queen Anne's Bounty – the payment of clergy and the collection of tithe – had become increasingly reliant on resources drawn from the Ecclesiastical Commissioners. In 1928, the commissioners had agreed to contribute financially to guarantee prompt payments of stipends to clergy; at the end of 1931, they agreed to provide funds to prevent losses to the clergy arising from tithe non-payment. Now, at the beginning of 1932, they offered money and organisational support to combat the tithepayers' movement. The plans were circulated to senior clergy, including the archbishop of Canterbury. No doubts were raised about the desirability of 'vindicating' the right to tithe through using one church institution (Ecclesiastical Commissioners) to purchase goods seized for debt due to another (Queen Anne's Bounty). Nor was consideration given to the problem that, while the Ecclesiastical Commissioners might have little difficulty in submitting tendered bids, they would still have to organise the removal of the seized goods from the farms, and potentially face demonstrations by the tithepayers' associations.

[42] Hughes to J. C. MacIver, 11 Nov. 1931, TNA, HO 144/19199; 'Kent Tithe Development', *F&S*, 16 Nov. 1931; 'A Wiltshire Sale', *F&S*, 29 Feb. 1932; 'Tithe Distraint', *F&S*, 1 Feb. 1932.
[43] W. G. Hannah, Memorandum, QAB, Tithe Committee, 20 July 1932, CERC, QAB/2/1/49.
[44] QAB Tithe Committee, Special Meeting, 13 Oct. 1931, CERC, QAB/2/1/48.
[45] W. G. Hannah, QAB, Tithe Committee 20 July 1932, CERC, QAB/2/1/49.

'Hard cases'

Farmers were slow to apply for concessions under the Bounty's 'hard case' scheme. Even those not associating themselves with the tithepayers' movement tended to baulk at the idea of opening their accounts to 'investigators' appointed by the Church. By the end of May 1932, only thirty-nine investigations (in Kent, Essex, Suffolk and Norfolk) had led to settlements, through agreements to pay reduced tithe or through instalments. Eleven investigations had failed to reach any settlement and eighty-eight cases were still pending.[46] Yet, over the summer, Bounty officers grew more optimistic about the scheme's potential. This was because, after a series of meetings, they secured support for its application from the Central Chamber of Agriculture and, more significantly, from the NFU.

Talks with the Chamber and NFU began after Charles Waley Cohen, of the Central Chamber of Agriculture, wrote to the Ecclesiastical Commissioners offering to provide 'arbitrators' to evaluate whether tithepayers should be entitled to concessions.[47] He argued that farmers would be more likely to open their accounts if they had confidence in the impartiality of those making decisions on their ability to pay. He proposed that, before legal action was taken, Queen Anne's Bounty should give tithepayers an opportunity to appear before an 'investigating committee' made up of an appointee of the Bounty, a representative of tithepayers (provided by the Chamber of Agriculture) and an independent chairman.[48]

With a membership of around 15,000, the Central Chamber of Agriculture had seen its aspirations to act as a representative voice of the farming industry supplanted by the growth of the NFU. Waley Cohen's intervention was partly an attempt to reassert its status. It was also a symptom of the growing fears created by the tithe conflict amongst rural notables. A big farmer from West Sussex and former parliamentary candidate for the Liberal Party, Waley Cohen was amongst those warning that the Church needed to show more understanding of the position facing farmers or risk driving many into the hands of 'extremists'. He told Queen Anne's Bounty that the tithe situation was 'dangerous, difficult and alarming' and, while firmly opposing any action that was 'unconstitutional or contrary to law', urged it 'not to push the law too far'.[49]

---

[46] W. G. Hannah, 'Memorandum: Investigation of cases of hardship in Areas of Agricultural Depression', 31 May 1932, CERC, QAB/2/1/49.

[47] C. Waley Cohen to George Middleton, 26 Apr. 1932, CERC, ECE/SEC/TITHE/CAS/3.

[48] Memorandum, 30 May 1932, CERC, ECE/SEC/TITHE/CAS/3.

[49] 'Condensed shorthand note of informal conversations between a deputation nominated by the Central and Associated Chambers of Agriculture and

An 'informal conference' to discuss Waley Cohen's proposal was established between members of the Bounty's Tithe Committee, including Radcliffe, Downing and the bishop of Norwich, and a delegation nominated by the Central Chamber. For the first meeting on 30 May 1932, Waley Cohen brought with him a representative of the Surveyors' Institution and also Frank Allen, as representative of the tithepayers. The Bounty's representatives were, initially, extremely sceptical about Waley Cohen's scheme. Sir Stanford Downing asked: 'What sort of assurance have we that if this procedure were adopted, it would result in people paying their tithe?' [...] Should we for instance receive any sort of undertaking from the Tithepayers' Association that their activities in the way of urging people not to pay their tithe would cease?'[50]

Allen's participation in the conference prompted criticisms from within the National Tithepayers' Association. His invitation was recognition of the NTA's authority as leaders of the tithepayers' movement, but it was also an attempt to draw the association into some sort of compromise. As Waley Cohen admitted, his aim was to devise a scheme that could 'be dressed up' in such a way that 'Mr Allen's organisation' would agree to it.[51] At the NTA national council, McCreagh and Mobbs argued that the tithepayers' movement should have nothing to do with any 'hard cases' scheme as it substituted negotiations by individuals for collective activity by the tithepayers' movement.[52] Allen himself had previously made the point that 'tithepayers who are merely concerned with their personal inability to pay, and are prepared to pay the tithe as soon as they have money to do so without any regard to the principles of the issue can scarcely be reckoned satisfactory members of the Association'. Nevertheless, he welcomed the intervention of the Chamber of Agriculture and thought that there could be conditions under which the tithepayers' association would be prepared 'with caution' to participate in a remission scheme. Allen was motivated by the desire to maintain a tithepayers' movement that represented both those refusing to pay tithe on principle and those not paying – whether they were able to pay or not – because the tithe demand was 'excessive'.[53]

Allen said little at the 'informal conference'. 'I am supposed to represent those who are usually characterised as extremists,' he told the Bounty's representatives, before pointing out that most of his members had 'a long

---

    members of the Queen Anne's Bounty Tithe Committee', 30 May 1932, CERC, ECE/SEC/TITHE/CAS/3.
50 'Report by the Tithe Committee of the Governors of Queen Anne's Bounty', 6 Apr. 1933, CERC, QAB/2/1/50.
51 'Condensed shorthand note', 30 May 1932, CERC, ECE/SEC/TITHE/CAS/3.
52 Suffolk TPA, EC, 2 Aug., 20 Sept. 1932, SuRO, GC32/1.
53 Allen to Mobbs, 3 Mar. 1932, Mobbs Papers; 'Thanks from the NTA', *F&S*, 1 Aug. 1932.

history behind them of adherence to the Church and the State'. Allen challenged the premise behind QAB's promise to treat hard-pressed tithepayers in the way that 'a wise landlord would apply to a tenant in difficulty'. He argued that tithe arrears were unlike mortgages, rents and interest payments. Tithe Rentcharge was an impost on land created by an act of parliament, whereas other debts arose from a contractual obligation. A remission policy should not, therefore, relate to the personal circumstances or the financial reserves of a landowner. The question to be investigated was whether or not the land was producing sufficiently in order to pay the tithe attached to it. If not, the tithe was 'excessive' and remission should be granted. Allen's arguments were, in essence, those underpinning the Tithe Remission Bill and received short shrift from the Bounty's representatives.[54]

The National Tithepayers' Association was not invited to the second meeting of 'conference' on 15 June. This time, Waley Cohen brought along representatives of the National Farmers' Union and the Central Landowners' Association. After the first meeting, the NFU had signalled to Waley Cohen its support for the scheme and, almost certainly, insisted that the invitation to the NTA be rescinded. At the conference, its representatives pledged 'hearty cooperation' to anything that might lead to 'friendly settlements' between individual tithepayers and titheowners. They hoped, reciprocally, for 'an assurance' from Queen Anne's Bounty that it 'would raise no opposition' to the union's demand for an 'enquiry into the tithe situation with a view to the introduction of amending legislation'.[55]

The parties reached an agreement that adhered broadly to the principles of Waley Cohen's original proposal. In areas of severe agricultural depression, Queen Anne's Bounty would, before beginning legal proceedings, appoint an investigator to examine the circumstances of any tithepayer who 'pleaded hardship or there is reason to think that there may be hardship'. If a farmer failed to cooperate with an investigator's recommendations or wished to dispute them, a 'tithepayers' friend', appointed by either the NFU or Chamber of Agriculture, would attempt to find a settlement agreeable to both parties, though Queen Anne's Bounty would remain the 'final judge'. The Bounty had made some important concessions. Redefining its concept of 'hardship', it had recognised that an application for remission may be acceptable if the farmer could show that full payment of tithe meant eating into capital or would come from

---

[54] 'Condensed shorthand note', 30 May 1932, CERC, ECE/SEC/TITHE/CAS/3.
[55] W. Hill Forster, Central Chamber of Agriculture, 1 July 1932, CERC, QAB/2/1/49. NFU News Sheet, 22 Aug. 1932, MERL, SR NFU P4/A12; Letter from Cleveland Fyfe, General Secretary NFU, to QAB, 18 July 1932, published in *NFU Record*, Sept. 1932.

resources other than farming, or would lead to land being withdrawn from farming.[56]

Overall, however, Queen Anne's Bounty was highly satisfied with the outcome. It 'had not forgone any of its rights' but had recognised that a 'settlement with a moderate concession might in many cases be more profitable than recovery in full after delay, disturbances and expense'.[57] It had also flatly refused to give support to the NFU's demand for an inquiry into wider issues surrounding the 1925 settlement. Most importantly, it had managed to draw the Chambers of Agriculture and NFU into the process of tithe collection. Arguments that tithe was 'unjust' or 'excessive' could be countered by the fact that settlements had been sanctioned by a representative farming organisation. The Bounty's annual report claimed that the involvement of the Chambers of Agriculture and the NFU had helped to ensure 'that all tithepayers might have confidence in the fullness and fairness' of the investigations.[58]

Yet Bounty officials at Dean's Yard remained aware of the potential dangers of the scheme. First, the time needed to carry out investigations into a large number of cases risked slowing up the recovery process and, in the short term, increasing the amount of tithe arrears. Secondly, the scheme might provide farmers with opportunities to filibuster, or make facetious claims of hardship. Some in the tithepayers' movement certainly deployed this tactic. After a visit to Federland Farm at Worth (Kent), the Queen Anne's Bounty's investigator reported:

> Pragnell [the farmer] is a surly, obstinate fellow, and very hot Anti Tithe. He would listen to no arguments and would give no information. He could only grumble and say Tithe was unfair and unjust. Said he made an offer months ago to pay 1/3 of his Tithe and that was all he would do and wanted a receipt for full settlement. There were Anti Tithe Posters stuck up on the Trees.[59]

By far the biggest problem faced by the Bounty was that a sizeable number of farmers were simply not prepared to cooperate. Tithepayers' associations reminded their members that there would have been no concessions from titheowners 'if there had been no Tithepayers' Associations and if certain individual tithepayers [...] had not refused to pay'. Frank Allen warned that

---

[56] QAB, 'Scheme for Reorganisation of Work in Connection with Investigation of Hard Cases, 15 Aug. 1932; Conference with Representatives of the Dean and Chapter of Canterbury, 28 Sept. 1932, CERC, ECE/SEC/TITHE/CAS/1.
[57] Ibid.
[58] 'Report by the Tithe Committee of the Governors of Queen Anne's Bounty', 6 Apr. 1933, CERC, QAB/2/1/50.
[59] G. S. Rowell, 9 June 1932, CCA, CCA-DCc-TITH/37/33.

the main object [of the remissions policy] was not to make arrangements for payment based on any just principles, but to break up the Association; so that, if and when that is accomplished, Queen Anne's Bounty may resume the recovery of the tithe in full. They will offer concessions [...] because it is hoped to detach as many members as possible from the Association.

He appealed for tithepayers to remain loyal to each other and to the tithepayers' movement.[60] With the tithepayers' associations promising to obstruct the 'hard cases' policy, the other prong of QAB's strategy – that of thwarting attempts at 'passive resistance' and 'vindicating its powers of recovery'– remained crucial.

Gloom at Dean's Yard

At the start of 1932, Bounty officers were optimistic that the replacement of auctions with the tendering of distrained goods would ensure the enforcement of tithe recovery. They chose forty-seven 'test cases' for which distraint orders would be executed and, with the help of the Ecclesiastical Commissioners, the goods sold by tender. Many of the chosen cases involved activists within the tithepayers' movement. On 31 May, a report to a conference of chairmen and secretaries of area collection committees outlined the results. The Commissioners had convinced seventeen farmers to pay their tithe, or to make a satisfactory agreement to pay, by threatening that 'the order of Court was to be executed'. In five cases (three in Suffolk, two in Kent) the Commissioners had purchased distrained goods and managed to remove them from the farms.[61] In March, horses and fowl had been removed from the farm of Stanley Kidner, chair of the Norfolk Tithepayers' Association, who farmed at Shadingfield (Suffolk). The same month, a hundred pigs and three horses were taken from the Long Melford (Suffolk) holding of Joshua Owen Steed, who acted as legal representative of tithepayers in the region. In another five cases no attempt had been made to remove the goods and in twenty cases the sale had yet to be advertised. In short, out of forty-seven 'test cases', there had been twenty-two positive outcomes.

The mood at the conference in Dean's Yard was gloomy. While the report from the Bounty's assistant secretary William Hannah claimed 'a good deal of success', the results were by any reckoning miniscule in face of the magnitude of the task. Since 1 January, 1,926 distraint orders had been issued in county courts in the six 'areas of anti-tithe

---

[60] F. R. Allen, re Arrears of Tithe, 10 Sept. 1932, DWPap.
[61] W. G. Hannah, Memorandum. Vindication of Powers of Recovery – Unexecuted Orders, 31 May 1932, CERC, QAB/2/1/49.

agitation'. If orders issued in 1931 were included, a total of 2,715 orders were outstanding, 975 of them in Suffolk. In addition, the area committees had deferred taking a further 2,600 cases to the courts in the knowledge that there would be 'difficulties' in enforcing the distraint. A report to the conference indicated that the non-payment campaign was holding firm: arrears for tithe due on 1 October 1931 in the six 'difficult areas' totalled 21.4 per cent. Most worrying was the report that sales by tender had not halted opportunities for resistance. The tithepayers' associations had, reported Hannah, 'given their attention to a vigorous campaign of obstructing the removal of goods by the Commissioners' agents and [...] these efforts have proved temporarily successful'.[62]

Indeed, the tithepayers' movement had reconsidered tactics after the first cases of distrained goods sold by tender. Instead of mobilising for auctions, associations sought to disrupt purchasers' attempts to remove produce and possessions from farms and farmhouses. In Ipswich, a meeting on 8 March convened by the Suffolk Tithepayers' Association and attended by 200 farmers heard plans to put farms 'likely to have their goods seized and removed' into 'a state of defence'. An 'emergency committee' was established to coordinate the action.[63] The NTA issued advice to its affiliated groups:

> The Tithe Owners now press for sale by tender. [...] A single small advertisement in the local paper and they are able to tender for your goods and get them at their own price. [...] Very unfortunately for the tithe owners, however, things are not working like that. Your Committee will tell you what to do. Warn all your friends and neighbours to be ready [...] If you can get to the Church bells, these make a very good signal for arousing the neighbourhood; if not, a signal maroon can be obtained from the Committee which will arouse the country for miles around. Warn everyone that there must be no violence shown to anyone who may come for the goods. If lorries are sent, talk to the drivers. These men [...] have probably been engaged for the job in ignorance of what it was. [...] You owe it to yourself, your fellow Farmers, and to Justice, to make the best fight you can against Tithe. [...] If all tithepayers would resist, there would be an end of Tithe. [...] Even now the Tithe Owners are feeling the agitation severely, and will do so even more as it grows.[64]

In the first week of May, action by tithepayers' associations halted the removal of stock from farms in East Sussex and Suffolk. At Iden, near Rye, 130 sheep were moved into a field containing another 150 sheep, making

[62] Hannah, Memorandum, 31 May 1932; Hannah, Memorandum, Tithe Committee 20 July 1932, CERC, QAB/2/1/49.
[63] Suffolk TPA, General Meeting of Members, 8 Mar. 1932.
[64] NTA, 'Advice on Procedure', n.d. (early 1932), DWPap.

it impossible for the Ecclesiastical Commissioners' agent to identify the purchased animals. A journalist reported that when the agent arrived to collect the sheep,

> angry farmers summoned by tolling of the church bells punctured the tyres of his car and placed a dead sheep in the front seat. 'Take that to the parson and tell him it's all he'll get,' shouted the farmers. [...] Later, when the man had driven off on flat tyres, the dead sheep was buried on a green, and a wooden cross erected bearing the words, 'Queen Anne's Bounty. R.I.P.'[65]

Another mobilisation thwarted attempts to move eight haystacks from the farm of Charles Westren at Elmsett (Suffolk). For the Church authorities, recovering tithe from Westren had become something of a litmus test. On 1 March, Sir Herbert Trustram Eve had travelled to Ipswich to turn up unannounced at the executive committee of the Suffolk Tithepayers' Association. Well connected to Conservative politicians, the upper echelons of the civil service and – through the Farmers' Club – the farming and landowning elite, Trustram Eve had been involved in many of the post-war deliberations about tithe legislation. He was, as Frank Allen put it, 'one of the leading Lay members of the clique at Church headquarters at Westminster'.[66] Trustram Eve told the executive that the Ecclesiastical Commissioners would 'remove the stacks whatever the cost of so doing and however far it might be necessary to go'. They would take every penny that the produce raised. But he offered a deal: if the Commissioners were allowed 'to realise on the stacks where they stood', they would only take £140 (the amount they had bid for them) and return the rest of the money to Mr Westren. Trustram Eve promised there would be 'no publicity in the newspapers' if his deal were accepted. The Suffolk tithepayers agreed unanimously to 'disregard the offer'.[67] On 2 May Trustram Eve and other representatives of the Commissioners were back in Suffolk, this time seeking to remove the stacks. The front page of the *Daily Herald* reported:

> Police and haulage contractors [...] arrived at 6.30 am but the owner of the farm [...] sent telephone messages that brought sympathisers from miles away in Essex and Norfolk. [...] His wife, who was the widow of a clergyman, tolled the parish church bells as an alarm and car after car arrived. Farmers gave their men a holiday to swell the number of protesters, and by midday hundreds of people crowded the narrow private lane down which the hay-stacked lorries had to come. After three and a half hours' labour the contractors gave it up. Farm

---

[65] 'Farmers and Tithe Collection', *West Sussex Gazette*, 12 May 1932.
[66] Allen to Mobbs, 3 Mar. 1932, Mobbs Papers.
[67] Suffolk TPA, Minutes of Executive Committee, 1 Mar. 1932, SuRO, GC32/1.

vehicles and fowl houses were dragged into the lane and their wheels removed and for a last barricade farm hands were felling a great elm tree to crash across the lane, when the haulage attempt was given up. Cheers, speeches and a tithe-protest meeting greeted the departure of the contractors. [...] Women rang the church bells again, this time as a peal of triumph.[68]

The Suffolk Tithepayers' Association described the 'remarkable event' as 'a landmark'. The Ecclesiastical Commissioners had 'ignominiously failed, not withstanding a large force of police' and 'since then there has not been any attempt to carry out distraint in respect of tithe collected by Queen Anne's Bounty'.[69]

The conference of the Bounty's area collection committees recognised a crisis. Hannah's report concluded soberly:

> The problem [...] is how best to overcome or defeat the efforts which have, at any rate temporarily, prevented removal. [...] If the Ecclesiastical Commissioners cannot satisfactorily remove goods and effects and no other purchasers are prepared to assist, the anti-tithe boast that sales [ordered] by Court have been rendered ineffective, may be fulfilled. The present position is extremely serious, and the release of the execution of further orders is being temporarily postponed pending careful enquiry as to what can be done in the matter.[70]

For the third time, action by tithepayers' associations had forced Queen Anne's Bounty to halt its recovery programme and review its strategy. In fact, QAB was in a bind. Putting a hold on the execution of court orders risked giving further encouragement to the farmers' movement, but so did the failure to seize and remove stock distrained from tithe non-payers. Those in the front line of tithe collection began to express 'gravest apprehension' at the situation. The area collection committee covering Essex and Hertfordshire sent a resolution to the Queen Anne's Bounty governors:

> The impression has gone abroad that payment of tithe probably cannot be enforced. Month by month the number of people who can pay and do not is increasing. [...] The present policy of enforcing about six orders every two or three months against ring leaders is not sufficient, and in this Committee's opinion little or no progress can be made until machinery has been created powerful enough to execute with certainty

---

[68] 'Bells Peal Tocsin for Tithes Battle', *DHe*, 3 May 1932.
[69] Suffolk TPA, Second Annual Report, 28 Feb. 1933, SuRO, GC32/1.
[70] W. G. Hannah, Memorandum. Vindication of Powers of Recovery – Unexecuted Orders, 31 May 1932, CERC, QAB/2/1/49.

and despatch at least forty orders a month in this area as well as the necessary number in others.[71]

The mood within the Bounty darkened further when Sir Frederick Radcliffe announced his resignation as chairman of the tithe committee. In an exchange of letters with Cosmo Lang, Radcliffe said he was no longer able 'to do justice to the job' and proposed that George Middleton, the First Estates Commissioner, should replace him. The archbishop pleaded for Radcliffe to reconsider, or at least to delay his departure for six months, but without success.[72]

Two reasons motivated Radcliffe's decision to resign. First, he was frustrated by the inadequacy of the Church's response to the tithepayers' non-payment campaign. In October 1931, following the debacle at Stelling Minnis, Radcliffe had advocated launching an appeal to lay members to provide funds to purchase distrained goods (see above). In early June 1932, he wrote to Lord Selborne to urge that the leadership of the House of Laity should 'come to the assistance of the [Ecclesiastical] Commission' and 'get together a body of men who would, even on a modest scale, show that private buyers are not ashamed or afraid to buy by tender at Tithe sales, and that the burden is not solely on the semi-public funds of the Commission.' Bemoaning the 'difficulty in finding persons who have the courage to bid for the goods', he continued:

> While bids had to be made at a public auction, in the presence of a mob, this difficulty was understandable though not very creditable to the courage or public spirit of the church people of the diocese concerned. Now that the Courts are permitting the bids to be made by tender in writing, the continued absence of interest on the part of the well-disposed laity of the district is lamentable. [...] The position now presented to the public is [...] that goods offered for sale in respect of tithe are taboo – not a soul in England can be prevailed on to touch the unholy thing except an Ecclesiastical body using the ancient endowments of the Church itself. No one will bid even by tender! [...] I write to suggest to your Lordship that it is important to every Churchman, and indeed every Englishman, that the orders of the Court for sale of goods should not be rendered ineffective by agitators. What terrorism does in this respect today in the case of sales by the Court for Tithe, it may do tomorrow in respect of sales for any other debt.[73]

---

[71] 'Resolution from Area Committee no. 10.' QAB, Tithe Committee, 20 July 1932, CERC, QAB/2/1/49.
[72] Exchange of letters between Radcliffe and Cosmo Lang, 25, 31 May and 18 June 1932, LPL, Lang 113.
[73] Radcliffe to Selborne, 2 June 1932, CERC, ECE/SEC/TITHE/GD/1.

Selborne responded that Radcliffe's suggestions were 'not practical'. He argued that the problem was not one of 'finding laymen of good-will' but 'technical'. It was not simply a question of bidding for and purchasing seized stock, but the goods also had to be removed from farms, stored and sold. What was needed was 'an organisation with machinery'. Establishing such an organisation should, he argued, be considered by a conference of titheowners, including the Oxford and Cambridge colleges, the Welsh Commissioners and other private titheowners.[74] Undoubtedly, Selborne had in mind the plan drawn up by Lord Grey in 1890 to establish a limited liability company to 'resist illegal combinations of tithepayers' and 'enforce the claims of titheowners'.[75] His proposal was the first step in the process that would establish General Dealers, a company specifically created to deal in goods seized for tithe. Radcliffe had deep reservations about taking such a course. 'The position seems to me to lack moral support and to be very dangerous,' he warned.[76]

Radcliffe explained the second reason for his resignation in a remarkably frank letter to Cosmo Lang. Stressing again that 'the whole collection of tithe' could 'gradually fall into disorder' if payments were not 'rigidly and rapidly' enforced, Radcliffe argued that the church institution with the 'means and the will' to lead the response was the Ecclesiastical Commission. Given that 'any ultimate loss caused by failure to enforce tithe collection must [...] fall on them', they should 'actively participate in the control of policy to be pursued by the Bounty'. It would not only be fairer but also more effective if the chairman of the commissioners became also chair of QAB's tithe committee. In his view, George Middleton, the First Estates Commissioner, would be able to 'view the position as a whole' and, against the background of a 'really serious crisis', ensure that there was no 'division of responsibility or diversity of views [which] might have lasting consequences'.[77]

The 'tithe chief'

The archbishop of Canterbury's nomination of George Middleton as chairman of the tithe committee was approved by the Bounty's general court of governors on 28 July 1932. Middleton had begun working life as a Post Office sorting clerk before being promoted to telephonist. He became active in the Union of Post Office Workers and, possessing a quick wit and good command of language, rose through its ranks to become editor of the union newspaper. He served as Labour MP for

---

[74] Selborne to Radcliffe, 7 June 1932, CERC, ECE/SEC/TITHE/GD/1.
[75] See p. 78.
[76] Radcliffe to Selborne, 4 June 1932, CERC, ECE/SEC/TITHE/GD/1.
[77] Radcliffe to archbishop of Canterbury, 7 July 1932, LPL, Lang 113.

The Bounty and General Dealers

FIGURE 5. 'The Tithe Chief': Sir George Middleton, chair of Queen Anne's Bounty tithe committee and Church Estates Commissioner (© National Portrait Gallery). The photo is from 1924 when Middleton sat in the House of Commons as a Labour MP.

Carlisle between 1922 and 1924 and again between 1929 and 1931, speaking in parliament on social issues, including unemployment, equal pay for women and trade union rights. On Ramsey MacDonald's recommendation in 1924 and again in 1929, he was appointed Second Estates Commissioner, effectively the MP responsible for representing the established church in the House of Commons. Middleton identified with the Church's liberal wing, broadly associated with William Temple – those advocating social reform, a renewed sense of community to replace class conflict and active intervention to improve lives, not only spiritually but materially. As parliamentary Estates Commissioner, he was drawn into the Church bureaucracy. It was work in which 'he found a natural interest'.[78] In December 1930, MacDonald appointed him First Estates Commissioner, the Church's most senior lay official

---

[78] 'Sir G. Middleton, The Ecclesiastical Commission', *The Times*, 26 Oct. 1938.

with responsibility for managing the Church's property portfolio and other assets.

Middleton immediately put his mark on the work of Queen Anne's Bounty. Tithe committee meetings became better prepared, with more detailed reports, and new members possessing particular expertise were co-opted. Policy remained unchanged, but it was pursued with more clarity. Queen Anne's Bounty statements expressed more sympathy with the position faced by farmers. While stressing its role was to act as 'trustees for the clergy', Middleton argued that the Bounty also had a duty 'to relieve really hard pressed payers so as to help them to tide over the terribly difficult times'.[79] Nevertheless, he stridently opposed any amendment to the 'settlement of 1925'. A general reduction in tithe would, he argued, 'constitute a gift to thousands of tithepayers' in areas where tithe was relatively small but do little to solve the situation facing 'a man whose capital and credit were at vanishing point'.[80]

Middleton launched a propaganda campaign aimed at farming communities and the wider public. Members of the tithe committee had previously baulked at the idea of speaking directly to farmers, flatly turning down invitations from tithepayers' associations. When discussing how to answer the arguments of 'agitators', the bishop of Norwich said he 'prefer[ed] to speak in Parliament'.[81] In contrast, schooled by experience in the labour movement, Middleton felt comfortable on the public stage. Throughout 1933, he spoke at debates sponsored by the tithepayers' movement and at public meetings organised by Queen Anne's Bounty, presented a talk on the radio on the 'history of tithe' and gave interviews to popular newspapers, which began to describe him as the 'tithe chief'.[82] Middleton's first public debate was in April 1933 at a packed gathering in the Tithe Barn Theatre in Hinton St Mary (Dorset). He shared the platform with Frank Allen, Viscount Lymington and George Pitt-Rivers, animator of the 'Wessex and Southern Counties' Tithepayers Association.[83] A journalist noted that Middleton's 'calm and courageous defence of the Bounty in a hostile atmosphere was admired by the gathering'.[84] The following week, he spoke in Ipswich at a meeting organised by the area collection committee. In August, he addressed a 'mass meeting of farmers' at Saffron Walden (Essex),

[79] Appendix A, d) General Remarks as to dealing with the Situation, QAB Tithe Committee, 30 May 1933, CERC, QAB/2/1/50.
[80] QAB Tithe Committee, 30 May 1933, CERC, QAB/2/1/50.
[81] QAB, Report of proceedings at Convener's Meeting on 8 May 1931, QAB/2/1/48.
[82] 'Tithe Chief meets Farmers', *Gloucester Citizen*, 30 Aug. 1933. QAB, Tithe Committee, 18 Oct. 1933, CERC, QAB/2/1/50.
[83] See pp. 205–10.
[84] 'The Tithe Controversy', *WG*, 14 Apr. 1933.

which was also attended by 'most of the clergy in the district'.[85] In October, he debated with Frank Allen in Canterbury. According to the organiser, 'under the shadow of the Cathedral [...] an audience of 500 farmers, landlords, tenants and farm workers, and clergy' experienced 'huge excitement and a very fair set to'.[86] In March 1934, 'the tithe chief' spoke in Tiverton (Devon) and in April he was guest at a meeting 'full principally of farmers' hosted by Methodists in the Salisbury Free Church Council.[87] In September, he was greeted at Bude (Devon) with cries of 'robbery' and during a raucous debate with Albert Mobbs 'could hardly make himself heard'.[88] As well taking his own initiatives, Middleton retained the services of Edward Peterson of the Churchmen's Defence Union 'for propaganda work on suitable occasions arising and at appropriate fees'.[89]

When speaking in public, Middleton's script remained consistent. He began by stressing sympathy for the farmers' financial situation. The 'real trouble' was not tithe but the fact that farmers 'were fighting with their backs to the wall especially those who had bought their farms after the war at very high prices and often with borrowed money'. Given the 'hard times', Queen Anne's Bounty would show 'utmost consideration to hard pressed cases'. Secondly, Middleton explained and defended the role of the Bounty. As trustees for several thousand clergy, the institution was not motivated by self-interest but by a legal and moral duty to collect tithe. It had no choice but to pursue 'without mercy' those in a position to pay but who refused to do so. Finally, he introduced his main theme. Tithe was 'inherited property like other inherited property'; it was 'a property as inviolate as land itself'. Defenders of tithe had made this argument for several centuries. But now, within the context of the 1930s, Middleton raised the threat of a left-leaning Labour government. He told farmers that 'agitators who set out for confiscation without regard to the owners of tithe were forging a very ugly weapon which may be turned against themselves': 'If the time came when a Government which, in its reforming zeal, wanted to put an end to this or that form of injustice, did they suppose they were going to distinguish between the tithe owner and leave the landowner free?' Middleton's aim was to drive a

---

[85] 'A Public Meeting', *BuFP*, 15 Apr. 1933; 'Tithe Meeting at Saffron Walden', *Essex Newsman*, 2 Sept. 1933; 'Farmers Hear Tithes Defended', *DMa*, 30 Aug. 1933.

[86] George Gill to Marjory Allen, 16 Oct. 1933, Modern Records Centre, University of Warwick, MSS.121/F/3/3/8.

[87] '"Tithe Must be Paid"', *WG*, 20 Apr. 1934.

[88] '600 Farmers at Tithe Debate', *Farmers' Weekly*, 3 Oct. 1934; 'Organised Attempt to Influence Tithepayers', *Western Times (WT)*, 28 Sept. 1934.

[89] QAB Tithe Committee, 26 Apr. 1933 CERC, QAB/2/1/50.

wedge between a section of farmers who, though unhappy about tithe, held conservative values and had respect for the law, and the 'agitators' of the tithepayers' movement who by challenging property rights were 'playing a dangerous game'.[90]

As well as meetings and debates, Middleton kept up a dialogue with politicians and senior clergy. He sought to resist the growing pressure to reopen the 'settlement' of 1925, through either amendments to the Act or the establishment of a public inquiry. In July, he signed off a position paper for government ministers. It argued that the whole 'tithe trouble [was] largely factitious', stirred up by 'anti-tithe agitators', and suggested that as 'prices improve, the tithe trouble [would] probably subside'.[91] Middleton's public position was that there was a 'growing tendency [by farmers] to settle [tithe demands]' and the return of a 'hopeful spirit in agriculture'.[92] Yet information from tithe collectors and investigators in the regions painted a less optimistic picture. Summarising their reports, a document noted that – while there were variations between regions and types of farming – the impact of the depression remained severe.

> In Shropshire, the fall of prices has seriously impoverished the farmer and in Lancashire and Staffordshire the difficulties of tithe collection have increased. In Herefordshire, Worcestershire and Gloucestershire the depression has been felt for the last two years, but hop and fruit-growing have had an ameliorating effect.
>
> In the county of Somerset and in the agricultural districts around Bristol, the depression has increased during the last year. Prices for sheep, beasts, milk and cheese have been low though there are signs of improvement [...] The depression has been severe in the Wolds of Lincolnshire and it is extremely severe in the uplands of Cambridgeshire and Huntingdonshire. In these areas a very considerable and rapidly increasing acreage is going out of cultivation. [...] In the rich Fen lands of Cambridgeshire and Huntingdonshire the depression is severe, due to heavy losses on potatoes in recent years coupled with high prices at which the lands were bought. Mortgages in some cases are in excess of today's land values. The fruit-growing industry in the Cambridge and Wisbech areas has suffered severely.
>
> The pasture and dairying lands in Northamptonshire, Rutland and Leicestershire are not yet seriously affected but there are indications

---

[90] 'The Tithe Controversy', WG, 14 Apr. 1933; 'Tithe Again', DiEx, 5 May 1933; 'Tithe Meeting at Saffron Walden', Essex Newsman, 2 Sept. 1933.
[91] 'Tithe: The Views of Queen Anne's Bounty', 31 July 1933, CERC, ECE/SEC/TITHE/GD5.
[92] 'Report by the Tithe Committee of the Governors of Queen Anne's Bounty', CERC, QAB/2/1/51.

of the depression spreading, particularly in grazing. In these areas in the last two years there has been a loss of 50% in the value of sheep.

In Norfolk and Suffolk where the depression has long continued there is little or no improvement in the agricultural conditions. The farmers are deriving considerable benefit from the wheat payments but this has been to a considerable extent set off by poor prices for barley, and there can be but little doubt that a large part of the wheat deficiency payments has gone into the hands of bankers to reduce overdrafts.

In Essex, the convenor reports that there is an improvement and a hopeful attitude and possibly a slight <u>actual</u> improvement as distinguished from a <u>mere hope of improvement</u> [emphasis in original]. Similarly in Kent, speaking generally, the agricultural position has improved during 1932 as compared with the two or three preceding years. [...] Wheat, hops, fruit-growing and poultry-keeping have 'held the fort' while market gardening, dairying and graziers have had a bad year. [...]

In the counties of Berkshire and Oxfordshire the depression has continued and there has been a consequent tendency for the tithe to fall into arrear. In East Sussex, where the rearing and fattening of stock, both sheep and cattle, form the larger part of farming operations, the depression has been severe.

In West Sussex and Hampshire, farmers have been hit by the low prices ruling for general farm produce. Large growers of wheat have, however, benefited by the deficiency payments. In Dorset and Wiltshire the position of a large number of farmers is acute, and the Convenor considers it difficult to see have they can ever recover. He doubts whether a revival in agriculture will in itself be sufficient to reinstate a large number of farmers, their position being due not so much to the slump in prices of stock and produce, as to the fact that they purchased their farms at exorbitant figures, borrowing the bulk of the money.[93]

For Middleton, the report's findings highlighted the need to take a sympathetic approach to farmers' circumstances, though this should not imply relaxation of attempts to break the campaign of passive resistance. He was determined to establish a mechanism to enforce payment from 'the man who was quite able to pay but hoped that by combining with others he could escape the discharge of his obligations'.[94] In the regions, tithe collectors were demanding measures with more

---

[93] QAB, 'Report of joint meeting of Chairmen and Convenors of Area Collection Committees with members of the QAB Tithe Committee', 30 May 1933, Appendix A, a) Agricultural Depression, CERC, QAB/2/1/50.
[94] Ibid.

teeth. A resolution from the area collection committee covering Essex and Hertfordshire noted

> that the impression has got abroad that non-payment of tithe results in no hardship to the incumbent but falls upon a wealthy corporation. This is causing a hostile attitude and affecting the Church prejudicially. It should be emphatically repudiated [...]; that many [cases] have shown the Anti-Tithe Associations that by simply doing nothing a landowner can probably avoid payment of much, if not all, of his tithe; that the remissions so far granted after investigation have not to any considerable extent brought payment of arrears.

The resolution called for 'a really efficient organisation for effecting the purchase and removal of all goods seized by the courts to enforce payment of sums which it is decided after full investigation should be paid'. It warned: 'failure to provide this organisation is making tithe collection impossible and fostering an unhealthy lawlessness in the country.'[95]

General Dealers

On 11 October 1932, Middleton took centre stage at the major conference of titheowners that had been suggested by Lord Selborne at the time of Radcliffe's resignation. On the agenda was his proposal to establish 'a private limited liability company [...] to protect the legitimate interests of tithe owners'. As well as representatives of Queen Anne's Bounty and the Ecclesiastical Commission, the conference was attended by delegates from the Welsh Church Commission; public schools, including Eton College, Winchester College and Christ's Hospital (Bluecoat School); Oxford and Cambridge colleges, including Christ Church, Oxford, Trinity College, Cambridge and King's College, Cambridge – whose delegate was John Maynard Keynes; and other titheholding institutions, including Norwich Union Life Insurance Society and the Haberdashers Company. Some aristocratic titheowners were represented, including the Conservative MP, Edward Turnour, the earl Winterton. The Central Land Association was represented by the Conservative MP Howard Clifton Brown.[96]

Middleton's proposal was seconded by Griffith-Boscawen, chairman of the Welsh Church Commission. Sir Stanford Downing, who had carried out much of the preparatory work for the conference, explained that 'the company' would show 'that proceedings for recovery can be made effectual [and] would have its influence in damping down organised

---

[95] Resolution passed by Area Committee no. 10 (21 Sept. 1932), QAB Tithe Committee, 19 Oct. 1932, CERC, QAB/2/1/49.
[96] Conference of Lay Tithe Owners, Bounty Office 11 Oct. 1932, CERC, ECE/SEC/TITHE/GD/1.

The Bounty and General Dealers

opposition to the enforcement of the rights of the tithe owners'.[97] A briefing paper stressed the importance of secrecy:

> The advantages of the scheme would be: a) that so far as publicly available particulars with regard to the Company are concerned there would be nothing to show who are behind it, or the amount or source of its funds; b) as an entity quite separate from any individual titheowner it would not be hampered or embarrassed in the conduct of its business by considerations which might of necessity weigh with some at least of the titheowners.[98]

A committee to work out details of the launch was appointed. As well as Middleton and Downing (representing Queen Anne's Bounty and Ecclesiastical Commission respectively), it included Reginald Primrose, a solicitor attached to the Welsh Church Commissioners, Captain G. T. Hutchinson of Christ Church, representing the Oxford and Cambridge colleges, and Sir Hereward Wake of the CLA, as representative of lay titheowners.

The Central Land Association's participation at the conference and the appointment of Hereward Wake to the launch committee led to some embarrassment within the association. On several occasions – including negotiations during 1924, meetings with Addison in 1931 and talks with Queen Anne's Bounty about 'hard cases' in 1932 – the CLA had presented itself as representative of tithepayers. Yet it had signed up to secret plans by titheowners to break 'passive resistance' by the tithepayers' movement. Complaints from some of its tithepaying members led senior figures to have second thoughts. Hereward Wake told the conference committee that while 'he might in his private capacity of titheowner be ready to approve it', it would be 'inadvisable' to join its work as a representative of the CLA. The landowners' association president, Conservative MP Clifton Brown, scribbled a note to Downing saying that given 'the great majority of our members are tithe payers […] you will understand our difficulty in the matter'. But, he added, 'I have no doubt that some of our members who are tithe owners may individually support you.' Downing replied that he 'fully understood the position' and promised to strike the name of the Central Land Association and its participants from records of the conference proceedings.[99]

---

[97] Downing to Selborne, 7 Oct. 1932, CERC, ECE/SEC/TITHE/GD/1.
[98] Memorandum, non-dated (7 Oct. 1932).
[99] Correspondence between Downing and Clifton Brown, 22, 27 and 31 Oct. 1932, CERC, ECE/SEC/TITHE/GD/1. For some reason, Carol Twinch writes: 'the CLA, having a less complicated membership, was slightly more vocal in defence of the tithepayer than was the NFU and its hierarchy was to fight on the front line' (*Tithe War*, 31).

Arrangements to launch the company were carried out over the next two months. It was established with nominal capital – £100 in shares of £1 each – but only two shares were issued. These were in the name of two clerks in Deacon and Co., the firm of solicitors in which Primrose of the Welsh Church Commissioners was a partner.[100] Ernest Russell, an experienced clerk and accountant who had been employed on a temporary contract for the Ecclesiastical Commission, was appointed company secretary.[101] To hide the identity of those behind the company, the directors were not named in the articles of association.[102] They were initially Primrose and John H. Marriot, another partner in Deacon and Co. In April 1933, Primrose would be replaced by John Power, in a further attempt to camouflage connections between the company and titheowners. A suggestion to name the enterprise Realisation Ltd was rejected in favour of General Dealers Ltd.[103]

The day-to-day operations of 'the company' – the euphemism used consistently in Church documents – were placed in the hands of two managing directors, both appointed on the recommendation of Stanford Downing. Major Geoffrey Thornton Miller was based in London and had various business interests, including management of the First Avenue Hotel Restaurant in High Holborn. He proposed to employ some of General Dealers' staff at the hotel when they were not deployed on 'tithe-related activities'. Captain William Parlour was based in Darlington, where he owned land and ran a prestigious land and estates agency.[104] Questions were raised about how he could, given his location, fulfil his responsibilities to General Dealers. Major Miller explained, using language underlining the military culture that would pervade the organisation, that Captain Parlour would employ out of his salary 'a first rate assistant, who would be at the entire disposal of the company, but who would primarily act as Captain Parlour's lieutenant'.[105] The two managing directors were given a contract for a minimum of two and a half years with an annual fee of £1,500 (equivalent to over £100,000 in 2023), a generous remuneration when compared to the £208 annual salary offered to Russell, the experienced company secretary.[106]

---

[100] The clerks were Henry C. Blackborow and M. C. Powell. Memorandum and Articles of Association of General Dealers Limited, 13 Dec. 1932, CERC, ECE/SEC/TITHE/GD/2.

[101] Downing to Primrose, 12 Dec. 1932, CERC, ECE/SEC/TITHE/GD/1.

[102] Memorandum and Articles of Association of General Dealers Limited, 13 Dec. 1932, CERC, ECE/SEC/TITHE/GD/2.

[103] Memorandum, Primrose to 'tithe committee' (n.d.), CERC, ECE/SEC/TITHE/GD/1.

[104] Primrose to Middleton, 10 Nov. 1937, CERC, ECE/SEC/TITHE/GD/2.

[105] Miller to Downing, 2 Nov. 1932, CERC, ECE/SEC/TITHE/GD/1.

[106] Deacon & Co, Agreement between General Dealers Limited and Major G. T. Miller and Captain W. Parlour, 14 Dec. 1932, CERC, ECE/SEC/TITHE/GD/2.

Lay titheowners and the 'fiasco' of Elham

On Christmas Day 1932, John Maynard Keynes found time to write to Stanford Downing to ask for a progress report on 'the company'. He said that he had 'two or three cases where it would be of great advantage for me to be able to avail myself of such facilities'.[107] The renowned economist's interests in tithe were two-fold. On several occasions, civil servants and ministers had sought his professional advice, asking, for example, for forecasts of the price of wheat when deciding details of the 1925 Tithe Act. But Keynes also had plenty of practical experience. As bursar of King's since the early 1920s, he had 'sole charge' of tithe collection for his college.

Most Cambridge colleges, as well as the University itself, drew income from tithe. Particularly significant amounts were collected by Christ's, Clare, Gonville and Caius, Jesus, Magdalene, Pembroke and St John's. In the case of Trinity and King's, tithe formed, according to the Cambridge bursars, 'so large a proportion of their gross external revenue, 25 per cent and 14 per cent respectively, that any serious diminution in the annual value of tithe would imperil their capacity to maintain their present provision of Fellowships and Scholarships'. King's drew its tithe largely 'from districts of special difficulty' – including Essex, Suffolk, Norfolk, Wiltshire and Devon – and was 'probably more difficult to collect than that of any other Cambridge college'.[108]

Keynes was critical of the Church's concessions to tithepayers, which he considered too generous and liable to encourage the tithepayers' campaign. Queen Anne's Bounty was, he complained to Downing, 'inclined to make remissions where they are satisfied that farm losses have been made', whilst he was 'more disposed to require evidence of real inability on the part of the tithe payer to meet his liabilities'.[109] In his view, collection 'difficulties' could be 'attributed partly to the great growth in the number of owner-occupiers [and] partly to the agricultural distress' but were also 'due to a very small number of individuals, more often than not comparatively substantial, who, on grounds of principle or misunderstanding or an obstinate and litigious habit of mind, refuse to pay tithe except under compulsion and employ all the methods of obstruction, legal and otherwise'.[110] To confront such attitudes, Keynes was keen to deploy the 'facilities' offered by General Dealers Ltd.

---

[107] Keynes to Downing, 25 Dec. 1932, CERC, ECE/SEC/TITHE/GD/4.
[108] 'Statement of Evidence submitted by a Committee of Bursars of the Cambridge Colleges', *Royal Commission on Tithe Rentcharge, Minutes of Evidence*, 8 Mar. 1935, 556–7.
[109] Keynes to Downing, 4 Oct. 1932, CERC, ECE/SEC/TITHE/GD/1.
[110] 'Statement of Evidence submitted by Mr J. M. Keynes', *Royal Commission on Tithe Rentcharge, Minutes of Evidence*, 8 Mar. 1935, 574.

In general, non-clerical titheowners were less tolerant when dealing with the tithepayers' movement. Most remained aggrieved by the 1925 'settlement' and had little hesitation in insisting on the enforcement of court orders, even at the cost of unfavourable publicity. Sometimes they considered it a duty to take on 'the extremists'. One prominent lay titheowner, James Harris, the earl of Malmesbury, believed that 'a large part in these anti-tithe agitations [was] the work of the Socialist and Communist parties'. 'It is not because the Socialists and Communists in any way sympathise with the tithepayers,' explained the Conservative peer, but 'they saw in the agitation the thin end of the wedge against the payment of rent and the private ownership of property'.[111]

Some of the most publicised 'battles' in the tithe war involved non-clerical titheowners, including the first mobilisation by tithepayers against an auction in June 1931 at Stoke-by-Clare, Suffolk (see Chapter 5). During 1932, a number of other controversial cases offered good propaganda for the tithepayers' campaign. In late February, a private titheowner executed a court order and bailiffs entered the Woodbridge home of Miss Hester Whittome, a member of the executive committee of Suffolk Tithepayers' Association, who farmed at Hacheston (near Wickham Market). At the time, Miss Whittome was seriously ill in a nursing home and the bailiffs confronted her 86-year-old mother, impounding furniture and other household articles. A short time later, Hester Whittome died. Her goods were advertised for sale by tender on the same day as her funeral.[112]

Often lay titheowners had no connection with the areas from which they drew tithe. For local farming communities, they were not only outsiders, but also symbols of wealth and privilege. In Hooe (East Sussex), farmers paid tithe to Alexander Peregrine Fuller-Acland-Hood, the second Baron St Audries, whose estate was in Somerset. On 3 June, an auctioneer arrived in the village to sell stock distrained on two farms (a haystack on the first, six cows and two pigs on the second). The auction prompted the first case of effigy burning in the 1930s' tithe war. A local journalist reported how 'farmers from all parts of East Sussex, together with practically all the villagers, gathered to register their indignation in the liveliest possible fashion.' The demonstration led to the cancellation of the auctions and the day culminated in a 'siege by an angry crowd of the Red Lion Inn, in an upper room of which the auctioneer, Mr Frank F. Budd, of Eastbourne, was forced to take refuge':

[111] 'Statement of Evidence submitted by the Earl of Malmesbury', *Royal Commission on Tithe Rentcharge, Minutes of Evidence*, 8 Mar. 1935, 585–6.
[112] 'Tithe-Collecting "Frightfulness"', *DHe*, 9 Mar. 1932. Suffolk TPA Executive Committee, 1 Mar. 1932, Suffolk TPA, General Meeting of Members, 8 Mar. 1932, SuRO, GC32/1.

The Bounty and General Dealers

The crowd was in the region of 300. An effigy of Lord St. Audries, to whom the tithe of both farms is payable, was erected by village youths, near the haystack at Sadler's Farm, and beside it they placed a card bearing the words: 'Lord St. Audries, Approx £600 a year for nothing. The parson, £300 a year. Total £900 all out of about 20 farmers at Hooe. Is it fair?' The effigy and board were carried aloft along the road, and on arrival at the [second] farm they were placed in a prominent position on a mound in front of the auctioneers' stand. [...] When Budd reached the farm, derisive epithets were hurled at him, and as he proceeded to read the conditions of sale the paraffin-soaked effigy was ignited and a great cheer went up from the crowd as flames shot upwards and the straw stuffing crackled furiously. [...] An unprecedented scene followed. Headed by the auctioneer, under police escort, the farmers and villagers formed a procession and marched four abreast along the country road which leads to the Inn.[113]

Oxford colleges were even more dependent on tithe than their Cambridge counterparts and their bursars were especially bitter that the 1918 and 1925 Tithe Acts had forced them 'to suffer a large loss'.[114] Seventeen colleges collected tithe from 5,858 tithepayers: Christ Church was the largest titheowner, with tithe making up a quarter of its income; in second and third position were Merton and New College. In late 1932, these two colleges were involved in a confrontation with the farming community around the village of Elham (Kent). The conflict began in October when Merton, the owner of most of the tithe in Elham, successfully applied to the county court for distraint orders against ten farmers in the vicinity of the village. Animals and produce were put out to tender, including cows and calves, sheep, poultry, a horse, haystacks and a motor vehicle. The stock was purchased by Merton's neighbours, New College.

The Elham Tithepayers' Association had become one of the best-organised local groups in the country. Some of its activity can be traced through the scrapbook kept by its chairman, Kingsley Dykes, and in the correspondence of its secretary, George Gill (both of whom we met in Chapter 5).[115] Gill is an interesting personality. Son of a Congregationalist missionary and uncle of Eric Gill, the now controversial sculptor, he had turned to farming after a career as collector for the Metropolitan Water Board. One of his sons, Colin, became a talented artist; his daughter, Marjory, married the socialist

---

[113] 'Titheowner's Effigy Burnt. Extraordinary Scenes at Abortive Hooe Sale', *Bexhill-on-Sea Observer*, 4 June 1932.

[114] 'Evidence submitted by Bursars of Oxford Colleges', *Royal Commission on Tithe Rentcharge, Minutes of Evidence*, 7 Mar. 1935, 518–56.

[115] I thank Jeremy Wilson of Ottinge Court Farm for access to his grandfather's scrapbook, 'Elham Tithe War, 1932–1934'.

and pacifist Reginald Clifford Allen and, as Lady Allen of Hurtwood, became a leading campaigner for children's rights. One letter from Gill describes the situation facing farmers around Elham:

> There are few small farms which make any profit at all, costs are terrible, prices at their lowest but the tithe remains fixed at an average of 7/- to 10/- an acre and mounting in some cases round here to 18/- an acre. Take our case. [...] We make a loss each year on the production of the farm valued at current wholesale prices and with stabilised costs (wages etc.). Moreover this abnormal summer has bereft us of every drop of water on the farm and we are now carting water from Canterbury for over forty stock at a ruinous daily cost. But the College [...] are suing us [...] for the full tithe.[116]

On 7 November, a contractor hired by the bursar of New College dispatched three lorries acquired from Great Western Railways to pick up the distrained stock. They were accompanied by a representative of the college and ten bailiffs. The tithepayers' association had drawn up sophisticated plans to mobilise the local community and neighbouring supporters. They were put into effect when police and county court officials, who had arrived to assist in the operation, were spotted at the railway station. Pickets were posted outside the ten farms and 200 people assembled in the village square, along with vehicles and 'scouts' on motor cycles. When the lorries were spotted a few miles outside the village, they were 'surrounded' by a large group of farmers. The drivers were persuaded to leave the area and the lorries departed 'with motor cyclists and cars hanging on their tails'. The events were dramatised in the national press: 'Tithe men flee before farm army' was the headline in the *Daily Herald*.[117]

Undaunted, New College planned a second attempt to remove the stock. One problem for the college was news that, after his experience in Elham, the contractor 'was not going to accept the job again at any price'. A solution appeared on hand when, on 10 November, a visitor arrived at the bursar's office, a certain Mr Birks, who introduced himself as a haulage contractor. The bursar and Birks discussed arrangements, including the necessity of having 'more police' and maintaining secrecy. But details of the conversation were rapidly relayed back to Elham. Birks was, in fact, a private detective employed by the tithepayers' association

---

[116] George Gill to Marjory Allen, n.d. (Aug. 1933), Modern Records Centre, University of Warwick, LAH, MSS.121/F/3/3/16.

[117] 'Tithe Men Flee before Farm Army', *DHe*; 'Farmers' Tithe Defiance', *Morning Post*; Farmers' Army outwits Tithe "Raiders"', *DEx*; 'Bailiff flouted by Farmers' Flying Squad', *DMa*; 'Tithe SOS by Rockets', *Daily News*; '"Battle Line" of Farmers', *Daily Sketch*; 'Tithe Dispute in Kent', *The Times*, 8 Nov. 1932.

The Bounty and General Dealers

– part of what Gill describes in a letter as 'a wonderful tale of espionage, much of which can never be told on paper'.[118]

The college eventually renewed its operation on 21 December, but the tithepayers' movement was well informed of its plans. When four lorries liaised early in the morning in Canterbury, they were met by two young men from Elham, who informed the unsuspecting drivers that they had been hired for a 'tithe raid'. After contacting their employer, a contractor from Essex, the drivers took the lorries back to base. Another lorry, however, arrived in Elham accompanied by the New College solicitor, a bailiff of Hythe County Court and a very large contingent of police. Some of the officers were posted in the village and others at the farms; some were held in reserve in two large vans.

Difficulties quickly arose. The solicitor and bailiff went from farm to farm but could not identify the distrained stock, which had either been moved to neighbouring farms or hidden. They had some success at one farm, from which they managed to seize two leghorn chickens out of the twenty-five that they had been attempting to collect. A local journalist reported that 'the result of a six hours' tour of the farms was that a large lorry left for London with two hens, plus an egg which one of the birds laid in a vehicle'. The police operation also ended in farce. Their vans were not suited to the steep, narrow lanes surrounding Elham. The journalist reported: 'While one of the vehicles was descending a hill, the brake partially failed and the van ran on, bumped into another vanload of police at the bottom of the hill and finished up in a small ditch on the side of the road. Some of the police were shaken up.'[119] The affair made national headlines: '100 Policemen in Farm Tithe Raids Comedy', headlined the *Daily Express*; 'Police Panto Chorus', offered the *Daily Herald*; 'Vans laden with police collide' in a 'fowl hunt comedy', reported the *London Evening News*.[120] On Christmas Day, George Gill wrote to his daughter about the events. He described the 'loyalty of devotedness' demonstrated by the local community and the 'humour and uproarious fun with which it has been accomplished'. But he also expressed anger that 'on this week of all weeks', the 'Christian

---

[118] Letter from T. J. Birks to K. Dykes, 10 Nov. 1932, Kingsley Dykes Scrapbook; George Gill to Marjory Allen, 25 Dec. 1932, Modern Records Centre, University of Warwick, MSS.121/F/3/3/17.i.

[119] 'Tithe Raid Fiasco', *KG*, 23 Dec. 1932.

[120] 'Tithes Cause a Spot of Bother', *Evening News*; '50 Raiding Police in Smash', *The Star*, '50 Police in Collision on Way to Tithe Raid', *Evening Standard* (all 21 Dec. 1932); 'Tithe Raid Comedy', *Daily News*; '50 Policemen in Crash on Way to See Tithe Seizures', *Daily Mirror*; '50 Raiding Police in Crash', *The Star*; 'Police Panto Chorus', *DHe*; 100 Policemen in Farm Tithe Raids Comedy, *DEx* (all 22 Dec. 1932); 'Tithe Raid', *Daily Sketch*, 23 Dec.

Oxford Colleges [...] strove to provoke us with 200 police and brutal, insulting, domineering tactics'.[121]

The 'Company' in action

For the titheowners – both secular and ecclesiastical – the fiasco at Elham reinforced the urgency of launching General Dealers. By early January 1933, the technical preparations had been finalised. The company had purchased lorries and motor vehicles, along with harnesses, ropes and other sundry tools.[122] Twelve farms owned by the Ecclesiastical Commissioners had been selected to store goods and livestock after removal from tithepayers' farms. These included two in Yorkshire and three in Lincoln – well away from the contentious regions – and others in Norfolk, Cambridgeshire, Huntingdon, Berkshire and Kent, including the theatre for the 'battle of the ducks', West Court Farm in Shepherdswell.[123]

One remaining task was to brief the Home Office. On 18 January, Primrose met Sir Ernley Blackwell, legal advisor to the under-secretary of state, to outline the plans for General Dealers. He wanted to know how much police assistance would be available in the event of opposition from the tithepayers' movement. Blackwell admitted that there might be occasions when the senior officer felt that 'his force was insufficient to deal with the mob', but stressed that the company was 'entitled to employ its own servants who could use force to meet forceful opposition'. Primrose wanted a firmer commitment and asked whether – if police could not handle the situation – 'the assistance of the Military could be invoked'. Blackwell replied that he 'doubted whether the home secretary would be likely to approve [this] but made it clear that this is a question which could only be decided when it arises'. Nevertheless, he 'expressed willingness to help the Company in any way he could with regard to any particular difficulty which may arise'.[124]

General Dealers Ltd made its first public excursion on 24 March 1933, when its employees arrived in a lorry and, accompanied by a contingent of police, seized two horses, a wagon and other implements from Coldharbour Farm in Iden, near Rye (Sussex). By the time local farmers realised what was happening the two horses were drawing the seized

[121] George Gill to Marjory Allen, 25 Dec. 1932, Modern Records Centre, University of Warwick, MSS.121/F/3/3/17.i. Gill later wrote a colourful account of events in Gill, *A Fight Against Tithes*, 68–71.
[122] General Dealers Limited, Statement of Receipts and Expenditure, 14 Dec. 1932–30 Sept. 1933, CERC, ECE/SEC/TITHE/GD/2.
[123] Downing to Major Miller, 16 Jan. 1933, CERC, ECE/SEC/TITHE/GD/4.
[124] General Dealers Limited. Memorandum of interview with Sir E. Blackwell, 18 Jan. 1933, CERC, ECE/SEC/TITHE/GD/5.

goods to Rye Station, where, according to a journalist, 'one man lay down on the sleepers in an attempt to stop the property being wheeled into the train'. Members of the local tithepayers' association later 'admitted that they had been outwitted'.[125]

Throughout the summer, further seizures took place with a similar *modus operandi*. In the early hours of 27 June, a lorry arrived at the Trago Farm in St Pinnock (Cornwall), the venue of an aborted auction three weeks earlier. It was accompanied by another wagon 'filled with police'. A journalist observed that 'while the farmer and his family were still asleep, the stock originally advertised for sale was quickly loaded into the lorry', after which

> the bailiff of the County Court knocked up [the farmer] and served him with a formal notice that the animals had been taken possession by General Dealers, who had purchased them by private treaty. [...] The raid was carried out so swiftly and with such secrecy that no one in the vicinity was aware of the occurrence until everything was over.[126]

One of the 'most skilful and well-planned raids' was on 17 July at Hundon (Suffolk), where an auction had been disrupted in the summer of 1931. Twenty men, with a twenty-five-strong police accompaniment, arrived in three trucks to recover tithe owed to Jesus College, Cambridge. The farmer told the *Daily Herald* that 'he did not know that a raid had taken place until the raiders had disappeared and his 34 cattle had gone'.[127]

The 'company' soon began to receive unwelcome attention from investigative journalists. The *Daily Herald* named sites in Wallingford (Oxfordshire) and Catterick Bridge (Yorkshire) used as 'clearing stations' for seized sheep and cattle, from which animals were taken to northern markets. A 'village carrier' told how he had rejected a 'small fortune' from General Dealers to visit farms in southern England 'to take possession of animals distrained by tithe'.[128] Journalists failed, however, to uncover details of either how the company organised its operations or the exact nature of its relationship with titheowners. Representatives of the NTA often spoke of 'a very close association' between the company and the titheowners – but they would have been shocked at the scale of the subterfuge deployed to disguise the links.

General Dealers' activities were coordinated with the Home Office and local police chiefs. In September, the company seized furniture from Dean Park Farm at Tenbury Wells (Worcestershire), owned by

---

[125] 'Distraint in Farmer's Absence', *Kent & Sussex Courier*, 31 Mar. 1931.
[126] 'Sequel to Tithe Auction', *WMN*, 28 June 1933.
[127] 'Tithe Swoop on Farm Unseen', *DHe*, 18 July 1933. The farm was owned by F. H. Clark.
[128] 'Tithe Sheep Sent Across Country For Sale', *DHe*, 12 July 1933.

Thomas Howard, chairman of the tithepayers' association covering Worcestershire and the southern part of Shropshire and a prominent figure in the regional NFU. A Home Office official wrote to the chief constables of Shropshire and Worcestershire asking for 'all practical police measures' to be taken to ensure a court order was successfully applied against Howard, 'a leader of the tithe resisters and an extremely awkward man to deal with'.[129] When Major Jack Becke, chief constable of Shropshire, heard that the registrar of Tenbury county court intended to issue a distraint on Howard's cattle, Becke pointed out 'the inadvisability and difficulties of this suggestion and persuaded him to distrain on the furniture in the house'.[130] On 30 September, General Dealers arrived with 'a large force of men', a furniture van and two cattle trucks. Local farmers had barricaded the driveway with tree trunks and trucks filled with bracken but, with thirty-eight police officers deployed in support of the operation, the obstacles were easily taken down and the distrained furniture removed.[131] Becke wrote a detailed report to the home secretary: 'I am quite certain that over-powering numbers [of police] played the most important part in preventing a disturbance. [...] As the furniture was leaving, Mr Howard's friends began to mobilise but they were too late, and overawed by the number present.'[132] In reply, the Home Office sent Becke a 'semi-official letter of thanks and appreciation' of his efforts.[133]

The work of General Dealers was overseen by the Tithe Recovery Control Committee (sometimes known as the Controlling Committee). It consisted of Middleton, who chaired its meetings, Hughes and Hannah (representing Queen Anne's Bounty), Primrose (Welsh Church Commissioners) and Downing (Ecclesiastical Commissioners). After his death in 1933, Downing was replaced by Sidney Brister. The control committee's remit was to 'determine what cases the company should take up and generally to advise and direct on questions of policy'.[134] Meeting bi-monthly, its members perused lists of farmers to decide against whom recovery orders should be executed. For each case, a report outlined whether a concession had been offered, whether the farmer had 'an ability to pay', often with comments from the local parson about a

---

[129] G. D. Kirwan to Chief Constable of Shropshire, 1 Sept. 1933, TNA, HO 144/19199.
[130] Major Becke to Under Secretary of State, Home Office, 2 Oct. 1933, TNA, HO 144/19199.
[131] 'Tenbury Tithe Seizure', *Kington Times*, 7 Oct. 1933.
[132] Major Becke to Under Secretary of State, Home Office, 2 Oct. 1933, TNA, HO 144/19199.
[133] Home Office minute, 9 Oct. 1933, TNA, HO 144/19199.
[134] Memorandum of Agreement between the Governors of Queen Anne's Bounty, the Ecclesiastical Commissioners of England and the Welsh Commissioners, 13 Dec. 1932, CERC, ECE/SEC/TITHE/GD/2.

farmer's circumstances, and whether or not the farmer was a supporter of the tithepayers' movement. A typical report amongst the nineteen discussed on 13 April reads:

> A. W. Smith (Cholsey, Berkshire) [...] a prominent member of the local tithepayers association. Up till about 1921 he was a butcher in Reading, when he retired and took up farming. He informed the investigator that he had a large increasing overdraft and has lost £10,000 since 1921. He lives, however, in a very good house and the incumbent is of the opinion that he is able to pay.[135]

Another, concerning a farmer on the Romney Marsh, reads:

> Mr H. J. Blacklocks is a strong supporter of Messers. Kedward and Allen. The Investigator reported that Mr Blacklocks was a capable farmer whose activities have not been restricted by a lack of capital. [...] The incumbent of Lydd is of the opinion that Mr Blacklocks is in a better position to pay than any other farmer in the parish.[136]

Amongst the thirty-four farmers on the list on 13 June were: J. Lane (Ewyas Harold, Herefordshire), who 'has no intention of paying and seems a clear case of defiance'; F. Joy (Beaumont-cum-Mose, Essex), of whom 'the investigator reported [...] should be able to pay if he wished but he is under the influence of the tithepayers' association'; and C. B. Shepherd (Stourmouth, Kent), 'a member of the TPA' who stated 'he intended to withhold payment in sympathy with his neighbours'.[137]

After taking a decision to execute a recovery order, the control committee passed the case files to the directors of General Dealers. A Queen Anne's Bounty document explained the process:

> A representative [of the Company] goes down to the property and makes enquiries in the neighbourhood as to the chances of opposition, as to the means of access to the goods, as to the methods of removal and generally as to the general position, so as to ensure the successful carrying away of the goods.

Such 'painstaking work' was conducted at 125 different locations between February and September 1933.[138]

General Dealers had a small core staff and relied on casual workers for its operations. An account of the company's activities by one such worker

---

135 Control Committee, 22 Feb. 1933, CERC, ECE/SEC/TITHE/GD/5.
136 Ibid.
137 Control Committee, 13 Apr. 1933, CERC, ECE/SEC/TITHE/GD/5.
138 QAB, 'Appendix A. General remarks as to dealing with the situation', 30 May 1933, CERC, QAB/2/1/50; General Dealers Limited, 'Particulars of expenses incurred in the inspection of cases to 30 September 1933', CERC, ECE/SEC/TITHE/GD/2.

was carried in a publication of the British Union of Fascists. Describing himself as 'a member of a gang of six desperate men, glad to have work,' the man worked out of the hotel 'controlled by Captain Parlour' in which there were always in the yard two cattle lorries, 'fully equipped [...] with picks, shovels, wire cutters, crowbars, planks and ropes':

> Our destination was always kept secret. Only the driver of the leading lorry, who in his spare time acted as Major Miller's chauffer, ever knew where we were going. [...] Often, I have travelled hundred of miles in the pouring rain crouching with five other raiders in the back of these open lorries with only two blankets between us, to arrive before dawn at the farm where the cattle was to be claimed. [...] None of the men were experienced at handling animals, and I remember one raid when we had to take away three heifers and some pigs, which were all bleeding by the time we had finished.[139]

Soon, the reliance on recruiting men from the Labour Exchange led to what its directors called a 'problem of personal'. Captain Parlour explained to the control committee: 'We do not always get the same men and a lot of people get to know about our movements and naturally talk. The men are not always reliable and from a practical point of view, as far as handling stock is concerned, the majority of them have no experience.' It was necessary, he said, to find a 'better class of men':

> The men we select will be big men who understand handling cattle and horses, and have been in the army and are used to discipline, and they will help to leaven up the occasional men who it will still be necessary to employ in big cases [...] We must have some reliable men on our expeditions. Four trained men are much more use to us than 6 inexperienced chaps and when we encounter trouble we must have men we know can be relied upon.[140]

Shortly after writing this letter, Parlour paid a visit to find suitable recruits at the Army Vocational Training Centre, near Swindon, a camp dedicated to preparing regular soldiers for a return to civilian life.[141]

The financing of General Dealers was kept a closely guarded secret. General Dealers received a series of 'loans' of £2,000 – 'as and when necessary' – from the Queen Anne's Bounty, the Ecclesiastical Commissioners and the Welsh Commissioners. The three institutions agreed to share their commitment in proportion to the value of tithe they collected (so the Bounty paid 81 per cent, the Ecclesiastical

---

[139] 'Tithe-Raiding Gangsters', *FW*, 16 Mar. 1934.
[140] W. Parlour to R. Primrose, 12 June 1933, CERC, ECE/SEC/TITHE/GD/5.
[141] General Dealers Limited, 'Particulars of expenses incurred in the inspection of cases to 30 September 1933', CERC, ECE/SEC/TITHE/GD/2.

Commission 11 per cent and the Welsh Commission 8 per cent).[142] The funds were channelled to General Dealers through Deacon & Co. to ensure 'there [would] be no record on the Company's minutes of any connection between it and the three Bodies'.[143] Any 'direct expenditure' – costs arising from the seizing and disposing of distressed stock – would be financed by contributions from those titheowners 'making use of the services of the company'.[144] Although it was envisaged that 'the Company [...] ought to be able to operate without loss, or at any rate without any great loss',[145] demands for funds were incessant. Every three months Deacon & Co. reported to Middleton that the company's coffers were 'practically exhausted'.[146] On each occasion, another unsecured loan of £2,000 was forwarded. The monies recuperated from selling farm stock seized by General Dealers were tiny when compared to this outlay. The profit and loss account for the company for the year 1933 records £8,000 in unsecured loans and a net trading loss of £6,037 1s 6d. The following year's figures are similar: 'loans of £8,000 and a loss of £5,994 15s 6d.'[147]

Despite this considerable allocation of ecclesiastical money, those directing the work of General Dealers believed the investment both justifiable and fruitful. At times, Middleton acted to quell discontent amongst sections of the clergy embarrassed by the company's activities. In October 1933, a resolution to the Chelmsford Diocesan Conference expressed 'grave concern the injury to the cause of religion and the spiritual service of the Clergy' created by the tithe war and urged 'the bishops to formulate a constructive policy for solving the difficulties'. Middleton's arrival at the conference was, for many, 'unexpected'. In an uncompromising speech, he warned that the resolution and debates risked 'hampering the Bounty in its work' and refuted suggestions that the Church was directly involved with the work of General Dealers. The clergy had, he promised, 'nothing to be ashamed of [and] there was no need for the church to stand in a white sheet'. After Middleton's intervention, the

---

[142] Memorandum of Agreement, 13 Dec. 1932, CERC, ECE/SEC/TITHE/GD/2.
[143] Deacon & Co to Downing, 20 Dec. 1932, CERC, ECE/SEC/TITHE/GD/2.
[144] George Middleton, 'Report to the conference of the Committee appointed at the Meeting of the conference on the 11 Oct.'; S. E. Downing, Adjourned Meeting held at the Office of Queen Anne's Bounty, 28 Oct. 1932', CERC, ECE/SEC/TITHE/GD/1.
[145] Downing to Lord Selborne, 7 Oct. 1932, CERC, ECE/SEC/TITHE/GD/1.
[146] Deacon & Co to George Middleton, 5 Apr. 1933, CERC, ECE/SEC/TITHE/GD/2.
[147] General Dealers Ltd, Balance Sheets and Profit and Loss Accounts for 1933 and 1934, CERC, ECE/SEC/TITHE/GD/2.

bishop of Chelmsford managed 'to adjourn the discussion', prompting headlines that dissident clergy had been 'muzzled'.[148]

Throughout 1933, titheowners became more adept at securing unpaid tithe through distraint sales and, with Middleton at the helm of Queen Anne's Bounty, more confident at presenting their case in public. In addition, the authorities were more willing to act against obstruction of the recovery process, mobilising police resources in support of General Dealers. 'We are meeting the opposition a good half-way in these days,' Middleton told Lord Wolmer in a private note, 'I am glad to say that the position of the ecclesiastical tithe-owners is not so gloomy as it is portrayed.'[149] Yet at the end of the year the tithepayers' campaign of 'passive resistance' was holding firm. The number of unexecuted distraint orders continued to stack up. Even if at a technical level 'the company' had not 'failed', its activities had certainly raised the heat of the tithe war. A highly publicised intervention by the British Union of Fascists would increase the temperature a few degrees more.

---

[148] 'Tithe Muzzle on Clergy', *DHe*, 12 Oct. 1933; 'Ecclesiastical News', *The Times*, 12 Oct. 1933.
[149] Middleton to Lord Wolmer, 4 July 1933, CERC, ECE/SEC/TITHE/NC/3.

7

English Agrarianism and Fascism

Enter the Fascists

On 6 August 1933, uniformed members of the British Union of Fascists arrived at Woodlands Farm in Ringshall (Suffolk). Further contingents joined them over the following days, including a group from BUF headquarters in London. The Fascists set up tents and blockaded entrances with obstacles and farmyard waste. A loudspeaker van announced they were there 'to help resist tithe seizures, even by force'. Ringshall was the first organised intervention in the tithe war by Oswald Mosley's Blackshirts.[1]

The farm was owned by Hannah Waspe, a 70-year-old widow who worked it with her two sons; all three were members of the Suffolk Tithepayers' Association. Mrs Waspe had stopped paying tithe to King's College, Cambridge, in April 1931 and ignored 'repeated applications' for the overdue charge. Hers was one of the cases Keynes had in mind when he wrote to Stanford Downing on 25 December 1932 to request access to the facilities offered by General Dealers.[2] By June, the case was being followed closely in Whitehall. Frank Newsam, principal private secretary to the home secretary, wrote to George Staunton, chief constable of East Suffolk, asking him to take 'whatever steps may be thought necessary' to prevent the obstruction of the distraint order. Staunton replied that people who refused to pay tithe 'were in the same category as those who refuse to pay Rent, Income Tax or Rates, and I intend to use every lawful method to kill this movement in this county'.[3]

On 28 July, twenty police officers escorted the court registrar and a team of bailiffs to the farm. They executed distraint orders on two fields of growing crops and, for the next twelve days, three police officers and a possession man (a former policeman recommended by Staunton) camped on the farm. On the road outside, 'large crowds' mobilised by tithepayers' associations

---

[1] For a full account of the BUF intervention in East Anglia, see Mitchell, 'Fascism in East Anglia', 49–97.
[2] See p. 177.
[3] George F. Staunton to F. A. Newsam, 6 July 1933, TNA, HO 144/19199.

gathered in protest. But King's and its legal advisors soon realised that their strategy contained serious flaws. Fixing a distraint order had been relatively straightforward, but to secure payment would require finding local labour and a threshing gang. Keynes later complained that 'unsuitable assets' had been chosen by the bailiffs without his knowledge. The college offered to halt proceedings in return for a reduced tithe payment, but the Waspe family was in no mood to compromise. The college backed down. The Waspes received notification from the county court that the crops were no longer in the custody of the bailiff and the police departed from the farm.[4] The Fascist contingent arrived three days before the end of the affair and had little impact on its outcome. Yet the BUF paper, *The Blackshirt*, claimed that this 'first intervention [had] been markedly successful', implying it was fascist activity that had led 'the titheowners […] to remove the bailiffs and not to proceed with the distraint'.[5]

Over the next few months, Mosley's Fascists intervened in other East Anglian tithe disputes. On 25 August, a group of Blackshirts entered a barn on Delvyns Farm, Gestingthorpe (Essex) and ejected a possession man guarding distrained implements. Events on the farm had been widely covered in the press after charges of unlawful assembly were brought against thirty-six protesters, including officers of the Essex Tithepayers' Association and Lady Eve Balfour.[6] In October, five Fascists occupied a barn at Hall Farm, Fincham (Norfolk), the property of Leonard Mason, vice-chairman of Norfolk Tithepayers' Association. The British Union of Fascists held a march and 'area rally' in the village, with 'detachments' attending from newly formed branches in the region. In November, a group of Fascists occupied another barn, this time for three days on a farm in Kersey (Suffolk), on which six steers and heifers had been impounded by a possession man.[7] In late August, uniformed Fascists joined in a 'barrage of heckling' received by George Middleton when addressing a 'mass meeting' of farmers in Saffron Walden.[8]

During the same period, the British Union of Fascists waged a tithe campaign in Devon and Cornwall. In October Blackshirts set up camp and barricaded a farm near Bideford and in November they picketed two farms near Exeter. The same month, BUF members based in Plymouth pitched a tent on a farm at Trevarrian, near St Mawgan-in-Pydar (Cornwall), keeping watch on distrained produce and farmhouse

4   J. M. Keynes, 'Memorandum on the case of Mrs Waspe,' 2 Mar. 1935 in *Royal Commission on Tithe Rentcharge, Minutes of Evidence*, 561–2; 'Ringshall: Weekend Tithe Scenes', *BuFP*, 12 Aug. 1933.
5   'The Tithe War', *Blackshirt*, 19 Aug. 1933.
6   See pp. 240–2.
7   'Fascists at Fincham Hall', *Lynn News & County Press*, 31 Oct. 1933; 'Extortions of the Tithe Owner', *FW*, 10 Nov. 1933.
8   'Tithe Chief faces Barrage of Heckling', *DHe*, 30 Aug. 1933.

furniture. The most publicised intervention in the region took place in December 1933 in connection with a distraint of bullocks and ewes at a farm in Bickington (Devon). The sale of the sheep at Newton Abbot market was disrupted by Richard Plathen, a BUF 'national political officer' attached to the West Country, and the unsold animals were removed from the market in a bailiff's lorry chased by a carload of Fascists.[9]

The culmination of this phase of BUF activity took place at Wortham (Suffolk) on land owned by Rowland Rash and an adjacent plot owned by his wife, Doreen Wallace. On 5 February 1934, bailiffs impounded fifteen bullocks and 134 pigs, leaving three possession men to guard the stock. The Suffolk and Norfolk tithepayers' associations placed their members on alert, pledging to mobilise against attempts to remove the animals. Amongst posters displayed outside the piggeries was 'a caricature of a bishop and a parson with their hands together, as for prayer, with the words, "Let us Prey".'[10] Contingents of Fascists started arriving on 9 February, mostly from London but with a contingent from King's Lynn. Staunton briefed the Home Office that around forty Blackshirts had dug trenches, felled trees and 'placed an elevator at the entrance [...] and so conducted themselves as an apparently organised force as to cause alarm to His Majesty's subjects'.[11]

The Fascist intervention caused alarm in political circles. John Simon, the foreign secretary, wrote to Sir Patrick Gilmour demanding 'vigorous measures': 'I should like to see not only the ringleaders but some of the followers indicted for malicious damage and conspiracy. [...] A good criminal judge [...] could first give them and their like a proper dressing down and then send them to three months' imprisonment with hard labour.'[12] A strategy 'conference' in the home secretary's office assembled representatives of the security services (MI5), the metropolitan police commissioner, the attorney general and the director of public prosecutions, as well as Home Office ministers and senior civil servants.[13] On 17 February, 100 police officers arrived at Wortham to execute an arrest warrant. Eighteen Blackshirts were detained and taken to a specially convened court to be remanded for a week in Norwich prison. A few days later, the BUF's area organiser, Douglas Gunson, a Norfolk farmer, was also arrested. Early on 22 February, General Dealers arrived

[9] For a detailed account of events in Devon and Cornwall see Gray, *Blackshirts*, 111–34; 'Tithe Distraint', WMN, 14 Dec. 1933; 'Distraint for Tithe', *Exeter & Plymouth Gazette*, 15 Dec. 1933; 'The Tithe War in Mid-Devon, WT, 22 Dec. 1933.
[10] Report of PC David Martin, Feb. 1934, TNA, HO 144/19199.
[11] Staunton to Director of Public Prosecutions, 18 Feb. 1934, TNA, HO 144/19199.
[12] John Simon to Patrick Gilmour, 16 Feb. 1934, TNA, HO 144/19199.
[13] 'Conference held in Home Secretary's room', 19 Feb. 1934, TNA, HO 144/19199.

at Wortham in a convoy of eight lorries to conduct the company's biggest operation. Forty men dismantled the obstacles and levelled the trenches, before collecting the livestock, carrying the pigs in specially constructed crates. A total of 140 police officers had set up cordons at approaches to Wortham and prevented attempts by 'a large crowd [...] to get to the scene'.[14] The following month, Gunson and eighteen other Fascists, including Richard Plathen, appeared at the Old Bailey on charges of 'conspiring to effect a public mischief'. Pleading guilty, they were bound over to keep the peace, the judge accepting they had been 'misguided'. 'I hope that being good fellows, you will remain good fellows,' he told them.[15] The Wortham events became the most publicised episode of the tithe war, widely covered in the regional and national press and by British and American newsreel companies. Doreen Wallace fictionalised the affair in a novel, *So Long to Learn*.[16]

The relationship between fascism and the tithepayers' movement is one of the 'uncomfortable bits' of the tithe war.[17] Opponents of the tithepayers' movement were quick to make capital out of the involvement of Mosley's party. In Devon, those attacking the 'outside influence' of Blackshirts included local NFU officials and the mayor of Barnstable. The local newspaper editor warned his readers that tithepayers were being 'used' by the fascists. In Cornwall, Middleton wrote to the local paper to highlight a speech urging tithe non-payment delivered in Helston by a BUF member 'in uniform'.[18] For their part, NTA leaders issued statements repudiating 'any association with the Blackshirt movement'. After the Fascist activity in East Anglia, Frank Allen wrote to Mobbs to congratulate him for 'disclaiming their intervention'.[19] One history of the tithe war suggests that the stance taken by tithepayers' leaders meant that the BUF's intervention had 'no lasting effect'.[20]

Yet fascist involvement in the tithepayers' campaign should be viewed from a wider perspective than a formal relationship between tithepayers' associations and Mosley's organisation. First, there is the question of the wider influence of fascist and far-right ideologies over the tithepayers' movement. Though a slippery creature to define, fascism can be viewed as an ultra-nationalist and populist movement that seeks 'national rebirth' and the creation of an 'organic community' by purging

---

[14] Mitchell, 'Fascism in East Anglia', 65–74; 'Wortham Tithe "War"', *DiEx*, 23 Feb. 1934.
[15] 'Suffolk Tithe Dispute', *The Times*, 27 Mar. 1934.
[16] Doreen Wallace, *So Long to Learn* (London: Collins, 1936).
[17] Howkins, 'Review of Tithe War'.
[18] 'Mayor's Plea for Tithepayers', *NDJ*, 25 Jan. 1934; 'Tithe Rent Charge', *The Cornishman*, 1 Mar. 1934.
[19] 'Suffolk Tithepayers' Association', *DiEx*, 2 Mar. 1934; 'Ringshall: Weekend Tithe Scenes', *BuFP*, 12 Aug. 1933; Allen to Mobbs, 12 Aug. 1935, Mobbs papers.
[20] Twinch, *Tithe War*, 135.

FIGURE 6. Wortham (Suffolk): police guarding trucks of cattle seized by General Dealers, 22 February 1934 (© Topfoto). The huge operation to execute a distraint on land owned by Roland Rash and Doreen Wallace involved 40 men from General Dealers, arriving in eight trucks, and 140 police. One of the General Dealers' operatives can be spotted behind the police officers.

society of aspects considered 'degenerate' and 'decadent', including an autonomous labour movement and minority rights. But, to be successful, fascist movements must embrace their particular nation's political and cultural traditions and build alliances with other sections of the political right.[21] Martin Pugh has shown how, in inter-war Britain, fascist ideas did not 'always appear as novel or alien, but rather as developments of British thinking' with 'a flourishing traffic of ideas and in personnel between fascism and the Conservative Right'.[22] Regarding agriculture, fascists embraced an agrarian ideology that influenced politics of both right and left and which formed an essential element of national identity. Secondly, inter-war British fascism extended beyond membership of the British Union of Fascists. Some prominent tithepayers' leaders – while not card-carrying members of Mosley's organisation – can be firmly placed within the 'magnetic field' of fascism. Most prominent in this category were Viscount Lymington, president of the NTA between 1930 and 1932, and George Pitt-Rivers, who described himself as 'leader' of the tithepayers' movement in Dorset and surrounding counties.[23]

Agrarianism of left and right

Agrarianism became a social force in many European countries during the first decades of the twentieth century. At root, it expressed a political identity of landowners and farmers shaped in opposition to 'industrial modernity'. It gained sustenance from the particularities of the rural economy, which encouraged the image of a 'rural world' made up of social groups with common interests. Agrarianism most deeply permeated trends on the right, including corporatism, social Catholicism and fascism. Right-wing agrarians railed against bourgeois politicians and the socialist left for undermining the 'leading' position of agriculture and for encouraging a 'rural exodus' of small farmers and agricultural labourers. Stressing a relationship between the 'vitality of the race' and the soil, they championed assumed rural values – strong work ethic, individualism, private property, family values, duty to God – against the 'corrupting' cosmopolitan and materialist influences of the towns.[24] In England, the notion of 'national regeneration' by reviving the nation's

---

[21] The above is drawn from two influential approaches towards fascism: Roger Griffin, *The Nature of Fascism* (London: Routledge, 1993) and Robert O. Paxton, *The Anatomy of Fascism* (London: Allen Lane, 2004).

[22] Martin Pugh, *'Hurrah for the Blackshirts!': Fascists and Fascism in Britain Between the Wars* (London: Pimlico, 2006), 5–6.

[23] Pitt Rivers to Secretary of State, 1 Nov. 1933, TNA, HO 144/19199.

[24] Pierre Barral, *Les Agrariens français de Méline à Pisani* (Paris: Armand Colin, 1968); Pierre Cornu and Jean-Luc Mayaud (eds), *Au Nom de la Terre: Agrarisme et agrariens en France et en Europe du 19e siècle à nos jours* (Paris: La Boutique d'Histoire, 2008).

rural roots acted as the 'common thread' binding together a range of trends on the radical right. Lymington, Pitt-Rivers, the British Union of Fascists, along with prominent ruralists such as Rolf Gardiner, linked the fight against 'judeo-bolshevism' with 'a rural-nostalgic, anti-modernist organicist theme wherein a farming community supporting a native craft tradition would represent an eternal and enduring order'.[25]

Sociologically, the roots of agrarianism were weaker in England than on continental Europe. Concentration of land ownership, the decline of the peasantry and a movement from rural areas towards the towns had begun at an earlier stage. Yet, in the years following the Great War, agrarian notions became embedded in the national psyche. Paradoxically – given his status as a *bête noire* for agrarians – Stanley Baldwin did more than most to establish an imagined countryside as a core element of English identity. 'The sound of the scythe against the whetstone, and the sight of a plough team coming over the brow of the hill […] these are the things that make England,' paeaned the Conservative leader.[26]

While mainly associated with the right, agrarianism shaped outlooks across the political spectrum. Liberals extolled the virtues of a mythical pastoral England. The Liberal Land Committee's Rural Report (1926) opened with Cato the Elder's 'eternal and universal truth' that 'it is from the tillers of the soil that spring the best citizens, the staunchest soldiers'.[27] Socialist agrarianism contained several strands. Some Labour figures drew on the ideas of William Morris and John Ruskin to evoke a 'former golden age […] uncorrupted by the pollution of capitalist industry'. Others presented the Labour Party as the modern-day successor to rural rebels, such as Wat Tyler, John Ball and Robert Kett. Most significantly, during the 1930s Labour undertook a 'remarkable' shift in attitude towards farmers. The party attempted to shake off a previous tradition that viewed agriculture as the 'pampered darling of Conservatives' in order to portray itself as 'the party that best understood' farmers' grievances.[28] Labour's policy lacked coherence. Profoundly influenced by a strand in late nineteenth-century liberalism that viewed land as 'the inheritance of the English people', the party proclaimed the objective of land nationalisation. But, alongside ambiguity over what this meant in practice and how it would be implemented, the policy failed to address the major changes in agricultural land ownership since the Great War:

---

[25] Richard Moore-Colyer, 'Towards "Mother Earth": Jorian Jenks, Organicism, the Right and the British Union of Fascists', *Journal of Contemporary History*, 29, 3 (2004), 353–71.
[26] Stanley Baldwin, 'On England' (1926), cited in Simon Miller, 'Urban Dreams and Rural Reality: Land and Landscape in English Culture, 1920–45', *Rural History* 6, 1 (1995), 90.
[27] Liberal Party, *Land and the Nation*, 5.
[28] Griffiths, *Labour and the Countryside*, 25–50, 219 and 258–9.

the fact that many farmers had purchased their holdings from the big landowners. In reality, as Clare Griffiths explains, the party was 'concerned with the question of how to make capitalist agriculture work more effectively, rather than reconstituting it on socialist lines'.[29]

Agrarian ideology also influenced farm workers' trade unionism. The experience of labourers and farm servants – working long hours on low pay and facing constant insecurity – challenged the vision of harmonious, egalitarian rural societies. But trade unionism faced serious obstacles: hierarchal divisions, master–servant paternalism, variations in hiring systems, relentless victimisation of union activists. Despite continuing localised conflicts, the strength of the unions that emerged in the 1870s had declined significantly by the early years of the twentieth century. After the war, farm workers were barely protected as the depression began to take hold again. Legislation to introduce national insurance did not cover agriculture. Many rural families were forced to uproot to seek employment in the towns, further accelerating the 'rural exodus'. A bitter month-long labourers' strike in Norfolk in 1923 had contradictory outcomes. It was a factor behind the restoration of the Wages Boards, which had been abolished in 1921. But, with up to 2,000 workers victimised for taking part, the strike convinced a section of union leaders that they should seek other ways to defend wages and conditions. Edwin Gooch, who became president of the National Union of Agricultural Workers in 1930, embraced the agrarian notion that workers, farmers and landowners should unite to 'defend agriculture'.[30] The idea of making common cause with employers was not popular amongst many union activists, but Gooch persisted. Farm workers are 'my first concern,' he pledged, 'but not to the exclusion of consideration of the wider needs of the industry'.[31] The agricultural workers' section of the Transport and General Workers' Union, whose secretary was Labour MP George Dallas, adopted a similar position.

Agricultural trade unionists were initially split on the issue of tithe. As the conflict heated up during 1931, farmers' leaders began attempts to impose cuts in the minimum agricultural wage. At the Wages Board in Suffolk, they forced through a reduction from 30s to 28s a week. In Kent, they sought a cut of 2s 6d; in Bedfordshire and Sussex, the figure was 5s. Most belligerent were Norfolk farmers, who at the end of 1932 voted to dismiss up to 6,000 workers, everyone except 'key men', if the Wages Board would not agree to a cut in wages.[32] Some prominent

---

[29] Ibid., 232.
[30] Alun Howkins, 'Gooch, Edwin George (1889–1964)', *ODNB* (2016); Howkins, *Death of Rural England*, 84–5.
[31] 'Bro. Gooch as President of the Norfolk Chamber of Agriculture', *LW*, Sept. 1935.
[32] 'Suffolk Agricultural Wages', *DiEx*, 20 Feb. 1931; 'Suffolk Farm Pay', *DHe*, 31 Mar. 1931; 'The Union in Kent – Good Progress', *LW*, Mar. 1932; 'Executive and the

members of the NUAW pointed to farmers' attacks on wages as reason not to support the tithepayers' movement. At the union's conference in 1932, George Edwards, a legendary figure amongst farm workers, asked rhetorically: '"Who are the leaders of this [tithepayers'] movement?" Why, the very men who last October had told the people to elect the present ramshackle, dishonest, and wicked government'. Tithe was, said Edwards, not 'a workers' question; it was the farmers' and landlords' question.'[33] Gooch rebuked him, arguing that there should not be the 'slightest idea of supporting the farmers as individuals' but they should oppose the 'principle of tithe'. His position gained sustenance from the nonconformist tradition within the union. At the conference, the delegate who moved the resolution denouncing 'the iniquitous burden of tithes' was a Methodist lay preacher.[34]

Gooch gave consistent support to the tithepayers' movement throughout the conflict. In April 1931, he sent a 'letter of solidarity' to the founding meeting of the county federation of tithepayers' associations in Essex.[35] In 1932, the NUAW leader spoke alongside Mobbs at a 'mass meeting' of tithepayers in Norwich, stating it was rare for him to be in so much agreement with farmers.[36] In May 1934, Gooch joined a NTA delegation to lobby ministers and MPs, declaring he was 'pleased to be able to work side by side with the farmers in determined opposition to the present tithe system'.[37] Not surprisingly, tithepayers' leaders welcomed an alliance with the farmworkers' union. 'While farmer and employee are quarrelling over the bones, the tithe collector is running off with the meat,' Mobbs told a meeting in King's Lynn (Norfolk).[38]

The Labour Party's position on tithe evolved more slowly. Party leaders had sided with the titheowners in the debate over the 1925 Tithe Bill and, between 1929 and 1931, the Labour government defended tithe legislation. Though trying to encourage understanding between tithepayers and titheowners, Christopher Addison, the minister of agriculture, could 'hold out no prospect of [...] asking the Government to reopen the question'.[39] The fact that the Bounty's leading official, Middleton, was a former Labour MP, also tarnished the party's reputation.

Against the background of the tithe war, Addison and others on the party's agricultural committee realised that Labour's support for the status quo was

Government: The Wages War', *LW*, Oct. 1931; 'Norfolk Farmers Rebuked', *DHe*, 20 Dec. 1932; Norfolk Farmers' Threat, *Suffolk and Essex Free Press*, 8 Dec. 1932.
33 'Lively discussion upon tithes', *LW*, July 1932.
34 Ibid.
35 'Tithepayers Combine', *ChCh*, 24 Apr. 1931.
36 'Farmers and Tithes', *DiEx*, 4 Mar. 1932.
37 'Westminster deputation', *F&S*, 7 May 1934.
38 'NFU and Tithe', *F&S*, 18 May 1931.
39 'The Tithe Question', *NFU Record*, Apr. 1931, 163–4.

untenable. Yet, as late as 1934, party spokespeople could only promise that Labour was in the process of 'formulating a definite tithe policy'.[40] Debates on tithe at the Labour conferences of 1934 and 1935 brought traditional differences to the surface. Opposing concessions to tithepayers, Ruth Uzzell, a delegate from Oxfordshire and long-standing member of the executive committee of the National Union of Agricultural Workers, said that workers 'knew from bitter experience that whatever the farmer was given, the farmer would continue to squeal [and] would scrap the Wages Board tomorrow if they could'.[41] But another delegate, Mrs G. Bowen-Jones from Cardiganshire, said that on tithe the farm labourer could see 'eye to eye with the farmer' and urged the party to support steps to remove tithe, which was 'wholly alien to the whole ideal of Socialism'. Some delegates spoke in favour of tithe abolition. But Norman Smith, the parliamentary candidate for Faversham (Kent), warned against becoming the instrument of 'unscrupulous and dishonest agitation' against tithe, which would be 'playing into the hands of landowners'.[42] The 1935 Labour conference adopted a tithe policy drawn up by Addison. It proposed an immediate reduction in tithe payments to an amount proportionate to the fall in agricultural prices, followed by a yearly adjustment to take account of further price movements. The policy also proposed the liquidation of tithe through a 'redemption' scheme in which tithepayers would make payments for fifteen years to a 'national land fund'. Labour stressed that its solution of the tithe problem was linked to its programme of land nationalisation. Tithe obligations would be replaced by a 'fair rent system' and clergy in financial difficulty after losing their tithe income would be compensated from the central fund.[43]

Some Labour candidates at the 1935 general election made strong statements against tithe and won support from sections of the tithepayers' movement. Doreen Wallace spoke at meetings alongside the Labour candidate for South Norfolk, Colin Clark. In Lowestoft, she shared a platform with the Labour candidate, Frederick Wise, who condemned 'the whole principle of tithes and promised to stand wholeheartedly with the tithepayers'.[44] But elsewhere the link between tithe policy and land nationalisation created difficulties. When the Labour candidate for Ashford, William Beck, tried to explain his party's position to farmers at a distraint auction in Mersham he was 'severely heckled'. 'You want to take the tithe and everything else we have', shouted one farmer.[45]

40 'Workers' Mass Meeting at Stowmarket', *DiEx*, 26 Oct. 1934.
41 'Workers and Tithe', *F&S*, 8 Oct. 1934.
42 'President joins Labour's Executive', *LW*, Nov. 1935; 'Faversham Candidate and Agitation', *KE*, 11 Oct. 1935.
43 J. S. Middleton, 29 Oct. 1935, Bodleian Special Collections, MS. Addison dep. c. 165.
44 'Townsmen Open War on Tithes', *News Chronicle*, 28 Aug. 1935.
45 'Fireworks at Tithe Sale', *KE*, 8 Nov. 1935.

English Agrarianism and Fascism

On the political right, agrarianism also appeared in varying guises. One strand had its genealogy in late Victorian 'pure squire' Toryism – an aristocratic concept of nationhood that had opposed attempts to widen the social base of the Conservative Party and waged war against liberal and socialist demands for land reform. Between 1893 and 1901, the earl of Winchilsea and his National Agricultural Union sought to organise landlords, farmers and labourers within a single organisation, preserving the traditional tripartite structure of the English countryside. Others, such as Robert Loyd-Lindsay (1832–1901), attempted to popularise a vision of Merrie England – in Loyd-Lindsay's case through the Lockinge Old English Revels, at which his farm labourers would parade in medieval garb.[46] Another strand of agrarianism placed the 'sturdy Yeoman', rather than the big landowner, at the centre of its vision. By the end of the nineteenth century, the idea of promoting a class of owner-occupying farmers to act as a bulwark in defence of private property and against social unrest had become an essential element in Conservative ideology. There was, however, much cross-fertilisation of ideas between the two trends. Though conjuring up images of a pre-industrial past, neither advocated a return to pre-modern methods of farming and were unified by two themes: the 'defence of agriculture' as a foundation for national renewal and the need for strict protectionist measures against foreign imports.[47]

Right-wing agrarianism gained sustenance in the late 1920 and early 1930s as the three main parties struggled with agricultural policy. Conservatives found it hard to shake off responsibility for the 'Great Betrayal', a narrative that took hold in agricultural communities after Griffith-Boscawen announced an ending of guaranteed cereal prices in 1921. Baldwin could be accused of 'appeasing' the towns by prioritising cheap food at the expense of the livelihoods of farmers and their dependents. Agrarians also attacked Labour's policy of land nationalisation and Liberal ideas about 'cultivating tenure' as threats to rural stability and property rights. The Labour and Liberal parties were associated with free trade and could be blamed when, during the 1929–31 government, agricultural prices collapsed while competition increased from food imports.

As the depression took hold, right-wing agrarianism tapped into rural discontent. On 1 March 1930, around 20,000 farmers and farm labourers – for the most part from East Anglia – joined a demonstration in Cambridge around the slogan 'save agriculture'. *The Times* described the protest as 'the biggest of its kind ever held in this country'. The NTA distributed leaflets against tithe on the fringes of the event.[48] Another 'mass assembly'

---

[46] Paul Readman, 'Conservatives and the Politics of Land: Lord Winchilsea's National Agricultural Union, 1893–1901', *English Historical Review*, 121 (2006), 25–69; Readman, *Land and Nation*, 162–70.
[47] Readman, *Land and Nation*, 170–6.
[48] Allen to Mobbs, 25 Feb. 1930, Mobbs Papers.

took place in Salisbury on 5 March, attended by around 10,000 farmers and farm workers from across the south of England, and a 'vast crowd' of 'masters and men' turned out in York on 12 April.[49] Presiding over the rally at Cambridge was the 'typical country squire', Ernest Pretyman, president of the Land Union and former Conservative MP. A man 'informed by a conviction that the old ways were the best',[50] Pretyman argued that the 'millions of pounds' being 'uselessly and harmfully' paid as dole to the urban unemployed should be diverted 'to restore agriculture'. At Salisbury, proceedings were chaired by Henry Somerset, the duke of Beaufort, a descendent of John of Gaunt who had been 'given his own pack of harriers at the age of eleven'.[51] He spoke loftily about 'agriculture as the backbone of English life'. The demonstrations had been organised not by right-wing agrarians but jointly by the NFU and the agricultural workers' section of the Transport and General Workers' Union as 'non-political' displays of unity by the agricultural industry. From the platform, trade union leaders and Labour MPs, including George Dallas and William Taylor, MP for Thetford, spoke against 'unfair' foreign competition and demanded a 'fair price' for cereal production. A letter of support arrived from John Beard, president of the Trade Union Congress. But, advocating the 'sinking of party differences', the labour movement speakers failed to suggest a policy markedly different from that advocated by the right-wing agrarians. Similarly, representatives of the NFU, Edward Morris and Rowland Robbins, made calls for the government to 'take some steps […] to enable arable farmers […] to carry on', but were vague about what these should be.[52]

The rallies received a message of support from Lord Rothermere, proprietor of the *Daily Mail*. He promised that his recently created United Empire Party would – as its first commitment – 'defend agriculture' and reverse the crisis facing farming. Established by Rothermere and fellow press baron Lord Beaverbrook, the United Empire Party was part of a sustained offensive by the Conservative right on Baldwin's leadership. It combined a campaign for tariffs on industrial and agricultural goods with opposition to concessions to the independence movement in India. It proposed making Britain 'self-sufficient', safeguarding the livelihood of farmers by plundering the resources of the empire. Though a short-lived

[49] 'Farmers and Corn', *Yorkshire Post*, 14 Apr. 1930.
[50] Readman, *Land and Nation*, 169.
[51] Raymond Carr, 'Somerset, Henry Hugh Arthur Fitzroy, tenth duke of Beaufort (1900–1984)', *ODNB* (2011).
[52] 'Condition of Agriculture', *The Times*, 3 Mar. 1930; 'Measures to Help Agriculture', *The Times*, 7 Apr. 1930.

phenomenon, it reached 200,000 members, one of whom was the future leader of East Kent Tithepayers' Association, George Christopher Solley.[53]

Beaverbrook and Rothermere were also associated with a more explicitly agrarian project, the establishment of the Agricultural Party. Launched in Norfolk in January 1931, the party grew to 122 branches in twenty-three counties. The driving force was J. F. (Jimmy) Wright, the Norfolk NFU secretary; Rothermere served as honorary president and Beaverbrook acted as a vice-president. Describing itself as 'the political arm of agriculture', the Agricultural Party pledged to oppose 'the industrial complex of politicians […] seeking to override the agricultural interest'. The 'keystone' of its policy was the introduction of duties on 'foreign foodstuffs'.[54] Amongst the party's supporters was Sir William Wayland, Conservative MP for Canterbury – one of the few Conservative MPs to associate himself consistently with the tithepayers' movement. Like the United Empire Party, the Agricultural Party venture was short-lived and by December 1933 was in decline. The National Government's adoption of some protectionist measures and particularly, after his appointment in late 1932, the corporatist policies of the minister of agriculture, Walter Elliot, took the wind from its sails.

Agrarianism was divided over the issue of tithe. Many of those influenced by pure squire Toryism were titheowners as well as landowners, and most viewed the Anglican Church as a foundation stone of the political order and national identity. Big farmers often had similar loyalties. Jimmy Wright, chairman of the Agricultural Party and secretary of Norfolk NFU, was personally close to the bishop of Norwich and also a member of the Bounty's local tithe collection committee.[55] It is interesting that, although their newspapers gave sympathetic coverage to its activities, Beaverbrook and Rothermere took care not to associate directly with the tithepayers' movement. Normally eager to accept public platforms, Beaverbrook turned down requests to speak at meetings on tithe, claiming that he was 'by no means conversant with all the ramifications of the problem'.[56]

Right-wing agrarians portrayed tithe as an obstacle to the recovery of farming and an even greater barrier to the possibility of agriculture becoming once again 'the nation's greatest industry'. But they also used tithe to illustrate the supposed common interests of different strata within agriculture. Tithepayers might be property-owning farmers, either well-off or struggling to eke out an existence, or they could be part of the gentry or

---

[53] 'The Empire Crusade and Agriculture', F&S, 13 Jan. 1930; 'The Empire Crusade', 19 Feb. 1930, Solley Papers, KHLC, EK/U1507/Z3.
[54] J. F. Wright, leaflet July 1932, Beaverbrook Papers, BBK F/19.
[55] See p. 143.
[56] See correspondence (Mar. 1933) about an invitation to address a meeting organised by George Pitt-Rivers. Beaverbrook Papers, BBK F/21.

aristocracy. Moreover, tithepayers could unite with those without a stake in land ownership: tenant farmers and agricultural labourers, the latter attracted by egalitarian arguments as well as promises that relief from tithe would allow improvements in their conditions. In short, tithe could illustrate an 'organic' and unified rural world.

Viscount Lymington and the NTA

Throughout the 1930s, Viscount Lymington (later the ninth earl of Portsmouth) was one of the most prominent representatives of English right-wing agrarianism. Born Gerard Wallop in 1898 and inheriting his first title in 1925, Lymington was elected in 1929 as Conservative MP for Basingstoke. He took the helm of a group of young 'neo-Tories' opposed to the party leader, Stanley Baldwin. Describing him privately as 'a scheming old bladder of stale wind', Lymington attacked Baldwin for being too accommodating to liberalism, too conciliatory to working-class interests, too willing to 'sacrifice' the empire and, most particularly, for failing to champion policies 'to save' agriculture.[57]

Soon after he and his 'stoutest friend', Michael Beaumont, raised the issue of tithe in parliament,[58] Lymington began attending meetings of the NTA and, in July 1930, accepted an invitation from Frank Allen to become the association's president. NTA leaders considered Lymington a major catch. A regular speaker at agricultural gatherings, he won plaudits from commentators for his 'clear-sighted and independent' arguments. Though in many ways an archetypal 'pure squire Tory', Lymington was also an agricultural modernist. His reputation for 'experimental farming' drew visitors from across Britain and abroad to marvel at the innovative techniques employed on his 2,500-acre estate at Farleigh Wallop (Hampshire).[59] In 1938, his book *Famine in England*, a paean to agricultural revival tinged with supremacist, racist and misogynist

---

[57] Philip Conford, 'Organic Society: Agriculture and Radical Politics in the Career of Gerard Wallop, Ninth Earl of Portsmouth (1898–1984)', *AgHR*, 53, 1 (2005), 90. On Lymington, see also Bernhard Dietz, *Neo-Tories: The Revolt of British Conservatives against Democracy and Political Modernity, 1929–1939* (London: Bloomsbury, 2018), 24–7 and 68–73; Dan Stone, 'The English Mistery, the BUF, and the Dilemmas of British Fascism', *The Journal of Modern History*, 75 (2003), 336–58; 'The Far Right and the Back-to-the-Land Movement', in Julie V. Gottlieb and Thomas P. Linehan (eds), *The Culture of Fascism: Visions of the Far Right in Britain* (London: I.B. Tauris, 2004), 182–98; Kian Aspinall, 'Viscount Lymington: The Journey of a fascist "Fellow Traveler"' (unpublished Masters by Research thesis, Canterbury Christ Church University, 2022).

[58] Gerard Wallop, *A Knot of Roots: An Autobiography by The Earl of Portsmouth* (London: Geoffrey Bles, 1965), 110.

[59] 'Lord Lymington and the Agricultural Situation', *Kent & Sussex Courier*, 18 Dec. 1931; 'Visit of South African Farmers', *Hants & Berks Gazette*, 24 July 1931;

overtones, received enthusiastic reviews. Lymington would later become one of the pioneers of the organic farming movement, linking up in 1945 with another stalwart of the tithepayers' movement, Eve Balfour, as a founding member of the Soil Association.[60]

Almost simultaneously with his appointment as NTA president, Lymington – along with Beaumont – joined the English Mistery, a secretive group established by William Sanderson, a 'disaffected freemason' and member of the Imperial Fascist League. Sanderson had chosen the medieval word Mistery to signify a concept of service. The Mistery would be a 'school of leadership' to renew 'the vigour of the English race', a renewal that would take place through the repopulation of the countryside, the re-establishment of 'fine feudal loyalty' between landlords, tenant farmers and labourers, the revival of medieval rural guilds, the abolition of parliamentary democracy and elevation of the monarch 'to his proper position as the political head'.[61] This elitist vision of aristocratic revival was laced with a cocktail of racist, eugenicist and misogynist pseudo-theory. The Mistery outlined a hierarchy of races and argued that miscegenation should be outlawed because sexual relations with 'degenerate people will produce degenerate children'. Members were reminded that 'those whose inferiority is due to bad breeding […] should never be the object of pity' and that it was an 'inexcusable waste of resources to help them in any way without ascertaining that they are attempting to make good their inferiority'.[62]

Although small in numbers, the Mistery attracted some influential figures. Members included the rural revivalist and journalist Rolf Gardiner, the future president of the NFU (1936–37) and minister of agriculture (1939–41) Reginald Dorman-Smith, the future Conservative MP Bryant Godman Irvine and the military personality Major J. F. C. 'Boney' Fuller. Women were not permitted to join. The movement's chief ideologue was Anthony Ludovici, a eugenicist who announced that 'the time has come to recognise the inevitability of violence […] and consciously to select the section or elements of the world or the nation that should be sacrificed'.[63] English Mistery was an example of how a recognisably fascist movement was able to grow out of the British cultural and political environment.

'Kentish Farmers at Farleigh Wallop', *Hants & Berks Gazette*, 27 May 1932. See Cuttings Book of Viscount Lymington, 1931–32, HRO, 15M84/5/13/15.

[60] Philip M. Coupland, *Farming, Fascism and Ecology: A Life of Jorian Jenks* (London: Routledge, 2017), 185–204.

[61] Stone, 'The English Mistery', 338–40; Thomas Linehan, *British Fascism, 1918–39: Parties, Ideology and Culture* (Manchester: Manchester University Press, 2000), 73; English Mistery, *Order of 1930*, no. 2 (London, 1930).

[62] English Mistery, *Order of 1930, no. 5, Rules of Conduct for Companions* (London, 1930).

[63] Cited in Pugh, *'Hurrah for the Blackshirts!'*, 13–14.

The Tithe War in England and Wales, 1881–1936

Lymington became the Mistery's 'Chief Syndic', as well as its candidate for the future 'Lord Protector of the whole country'.[64]

Lymington's position on tithe flowed from his general world view. Many of his arguments coincided with those put forward by leaders of the NTA. Lymington described tithe as 'a tax on food', highlighted its inequities – regional disparities, that the capital value of tithe could be higher than the capital value of land – and attacked 'the anomaly of the countryside paying for a Church established over the whole nation'. He ridiculed the 'quality of present statesmanship' displayed by politicians who argued that the tithe situation would improve 'as soon as agriculture is on its feet again', a dishonest position that failed to understand the deep-rooted nature of the problem.[65]

Yet Lymington's arguments differed from those of others in the NTA leadership in crucial respects. While the tithepayers' movement attacked tithe as a 'medieval tax' unsuited to modern conditions, Lymington railed against the modern conditions that had distorted the medieval tax. For him, the tithe crisis was proof of the wrong course taken by British history in the seventeenth century. The development of ministerial government, the weakening of the power of the monarchy, the Industrial Revolution, which had transformed the central role of land and undermined the position of the aristocracy: all had contributed to the transformation of the nature of property, including tithe, into a system of 'irresponsible ownership'. Tithe had, explained Lymington, become a 'dead possession', a 'chattel property' that no longer imposed duties on its recipients. The 1836 Act and the 1925 'compromise' had consolidated this situation by removing the titheowner from 'the last vestige of direct partnership with the land' and from 'any shadow of dependence on agricultural prosperity'. Lymington could therefore support reforms such as Kedward's proposed Tithe Remission Bill – as it would alleviate the impact of the charge – but he was implacably opposed to calls to abolish tithe. Rather, he had his sights set upon a reactionary rural utopia in which those 'who receive tithe [would] be responsible for the performance of their duties through the bishops to the king as defender of the faith, and [would] be responsible to the people as partners in their prosperity or distresses'.[66]

Lymington resigned as president of the NTA in January 1932. In truth, he had never felt comfortable within the association, often leaving before the end of meetings on account of 'other engagements'. After one session of the national council his diary entry reads: 'Tithepayers Assoc Meeting.

---

[64] Stone, 'The English Mistery', 340.
[65] 'Lord Lymington and the Agricultural Situation', *Sevenoaks Chronicle and Kentish Advertiser*, 18 Dec. 1931; 'Lord Lymington fears for Agriculture', *Sevenoaks Chronicle and Kentish Advertiser*, 15 Dec. 1933.
[66] Lymington, 'Tithe Rent-Charge: An Essay on Property', *The National Review*, Nov. 1932, 577–80.

Gawd'.[67] Lymington opposed the non-payment strategy, arguing that the tithe problem could only be resolved through 'constitutional means'.[68] He was himself a titheowner and his Portsmouth Estate Improvement Company showed little hesitation before applying for court orders to demand payments from tithepaying farmers.[69] His resignation came two weeks before the conference that established a 'united tithepayers' association' committed to 'passive resistance'. A membership-based movement committed to popular protest was an anathema to Lymington's elitist view of society and politics.

Lymington resigned as an MP in 1934, pledging to work outside parliament to find the best way to fight socialism and communism.[70] The same year, he joined the January Club, described by its chairman as a place for people 'for the most part in sympathy with the Fascist movement'.[71] After a split in the English Mistery in 1936, Lymington became leader of a new organisation, English Array (a term recalling medieval troop formations). Proclaiming himself 'the Marshall', Lymington hosted 'camps for officers' at his Farleigh Wallop estate. He travelled to Germany, communicated with Richard Darré, the Reich minister of food and agriculture, and contributed to Nazi publications. In July 1938, he wrote that it was 'absurd to represent the present governments of Germany or Italy as tyrannies'.[72]

Despite his resignation from the NTA, Lymington continued to speak out on tithe, particularly when invited to address meetings of the NFU. Frank Allen remained on good enough terms with him to 'ask for help' in acquiring information when developing policy.[73] In 1933, Lymington began collaborating with another aristocratic fascist to attach himself to the tithepayers' movement, George Pitt-Rivers.

George Pitt-Rivers and the Wessex Agricultural Defence Association

On 8 April 1933, Lymington presided over a debate in the Tithe Barn, a converted theatre standing in the grounds of the manor house belonging to George Pitt-Rivers in Hinton St Mary (Dorset). Journalists noted it was a lively affair. On the platform was George Middleton, who presented a 'calm and courageous' defence of tithe and the activities of Queen Anne's Bounty, and, opposing him, Pitt-Rivers, who argued

---

[67] July 1930, 'Diary of Gerard Wallop, Viscount Lymington, 1930', HRO, 15M84/5/13/11.
[68] 'Tithe denounced as "slavery"', *F&S*, 26 Jan. 1931.
[69] See correspondence about Wield Tithe, HRO, 15M84/E6/4/227.
[70] Lymington (Viscount), 'To the Electors of North West Hants Parliamentary Division', HRO, 15M84/5/13/17.
[71] Pugh, 'Hurrah for the Blackshirts!', 134.
[72] *The Quarterly Gazette of the English Array*, No. 4, July 1938.
[73] 'Bureaucratic Fabian Methods', *Sevenoaks Chronicle and Kentish Advertiser*, 15 Dec. 1933; F. R. Allen to Mobbs, 2 Mar. 1933, Mobbs Papers.

that tithe no longer had 'any relation to the profits of the industry it taxed'. Frank Allen also addressed the audience of 350 or so farmers and agricultural notables, including the duke of Beaufort and Viscount Weymouth (Henry Thynne MP).[74]

A month later, Pitt-Rivers announced the formation of the Wessex and Southern Counties Tithepayers' and Common Law Defence Association. The association's name was later changed to the more manageable Wessex Agricultural Defence Association. An inaugural gathering took place on 24 May, Empire Day, at Larmer Tree Gardens, near Tollard Royal (Wiltshire), pleasure grounds owned by Pitt-Rivers. A rally was addressed by Pitt-Rivers, Frank Allen and Stanley Kidner of the Norfolk Tithepayers' Association. A crowd of around 3,000 were treated to horse jumping, motor-cycle racing and an auction of farm stock to raise funds for the new association. A journalist commented that the leadership of Pitt-Rivers was now 'the mainspring of the tithepayers' organisation in this part of the country'.[75]

Grandson of the pioneering archaeologist, Pitt-Rivers was one of England's biggest landowners, apparently able 'to ride from the Wiltshire border to the sea without going off his own land'.[76] He paid tithe to Queen Anne's Bounty, but was also – in his words – 'a tithe owner, and a not inconsiderable owner of advowsons or livings' (meaning he had rights to nominate clergy to certain parishes).[77] Prominent within the eugenics movement, Pitt-Rivers held notable academic credentials, including fellowship of the Royal Anthropological Institute. Politically, he had been a personality on the extreme right since the early 1920s. An early book railed against the 'Jewish-Bolshevik-Masonic conspiracy' supposedly responsible for the First World War and Russian Revolution. Another warned of destructive consequences if Europeans mixed with 'primitive races', advocating apartheid-type policies in colonised countries.[78] In 1930, Pitt-Rivers became an enthusiastic supporter of the United Empire Party, writing to Beaverbrook to 'bear witness to the general and growing dissatisfaction of the farming community with all existing political parties'.[79] After 1933, he became increasingly enthralled with the ideology and political practice of Nazi Germany. He told his friend Rolf Gardiner that he was studying *Mein Kampf* and 'particularly interested in the beginnings of movements often articulated through the mind of one man'.[80] Feted

[74] 'The Tithe Controversy', WG, 14 Apr. 1933.
[75] 'Wessex Tithe Payers', WG, 26 May 1933.
[76] 'Farming Week by Week', DEx, 23 Apr. 1935.
[77] 'Tithes Meeting at Dorchester', *Dorset County Chronicle & Somersetshire Gazette*, 19 Oct. 1933.
[78] George Henry Lane-Fox Pitt-Rivers, *The World Significance of the Russian Revolution* (Oxford: Basil Blackwell, 1920); *The Clash of Culture and the Contact of Races* (London: Routledge, 1927).
[79] Pitt-Rivers to Beaverbrook, 24 June 1930, GPR, CAC, PIRI 18/1.
[80] Pitt-Rivers to Rolf Gardiner, 19 Aug. 1936, GPR, CAC, PIRI 22/3.

by the Nazi regime, he was invited to lecture in German universities and was received by Hitler while attending the 1937 Nuremburg Rally. On the outbreak of war, Pitt-Rivers' 'fascist and pro-Nazi sympathies' led to his arrest and detention under Defence Regulation 18B.[81]

With some resemblance to the earl of Winchilsea's National Agricultural Union of the 1890s, the Wessex Agricultural Defence Association attempted to unite 'owners of agricultural estates, tenant farmers, owner-occupiers, and agricultural workers'. But Pitt-Rivers' vision of a mobilised rural nation gave pride of place to the yeoman myth. 'The yeomen of England are ready and crying out for leadership,' he told Rolf Gardiner, 'the real England is to be found not in the cosmopolitan Jew-run urban centres but amongst the yeomen and the agricultural workers in the countryside.'[82] Membership of WADA was small, hovering at around 200, increasing to 365 in early 1936.[83] Affairs were tightly controlled by Pitt-Rivers and a handful of associates, mostly wealthy landowners – some of whom, such as Henry Farquharson, were former members of the North Dorset Conservative Party. NTA leaders, including Allen, Mobbs and Doreen Wallace, accepted invitations to speak at WADA events. Yet relations between Pitt-Rivers and the NTA were frosty from the outset. Before publicly announcing its launch in April 1933, Pitt-Rivers met Frank Allen and Roderick Kedward in London to outline the aims of his new organisation. Allen and Kedward 'returned quite dispirited' from the discussion.[84] In Somerset, the Crewkerne and District Tithepayers' Association publicly disassociated itself from WADA.[85] In effect, Pitt Rivers ploughed his own furrow within the tithepayers' movement, keeping a distance from the NTA – though something of a rapprochement would take place in 1936, when his association became a component in the 'United Committee of Protest' that organised the 'Great March' of tithepayers in London.[86]

One issue of dispute with the NTA was Pitt-Rivers' position that titheowners should not receive any compensation after tithe abolition. Pitt-Rivers' case was conditioned by an anti-democratic and anti-modernist ideology. Tithe was, he maintained, neither private nor public property, but a creation of medieval canon law. Its legal position and its rules of

---

[81] Bradley W. Hart, *George Pitt-Rivers and the Nazis* (London: Bloomsbury Academic, 2015); David Renton, 'George Henry Lane Fox Pitt-Rivers (1890–1966)', *ODNB* (2005).

[82] Pitt-Rivers to Rolf Gardiner, 19 Aug. 1936, GPR, CAC, PIRI 22/3.

[83] 'Wessex Tithes Opponents', *Dorset Daily Echo*, 31 Jan. 1934; Evidence by Pitt-Rivers to the Royal Commission, 10 Jan. 1935, 273; 'Decision of Wessex Association', *WG*, 17 Jan. 1936, GPR, CAC, PIRI 18/2.

[84] Allen to Mobbs, 12 Apr. 1933, Mobbs Papers.

[85] Minutes of Executive Committee, Crewkerne & District TPA, 2 July 1935, Dorset Record Office, D491/1.

[86] See pp. 281–3.

recovery had 'been determined by the Statutes of Henry VIII to William III'. And since parliament had no right to legislate on a matter enshrined in canon law, the 1836 Commutation Act was 'unconstitutional'. The collection of tithes was, argued Pitt-Rivers, not only 'un-christian and immoral' but also 'illegal'. As such, there could be no financial recompense for titheowners.[87] This convoluted argument did not impress NTA leaders, who were during the summer of 1933 attempting to develop a practical policy for tithe abolition.

Tensions grew between Pitt-Rivers and the NTA on other issues. Audiences cheered as Pitt-Rivers pledged to protect the jobs and wages of his farm labourers by refusing to pay tithe that had not been 'legally presented'. Newspapers highlighted his principled stance.[88] Yet, as soon as Queen Anne's Bounty started proceedings, Pitt-Rivers quietly and promptly 'paid substantial sums into court'.[89] He also encouraged the NTA to coordinate legal action to challenge the rights of titheowners on aspects of tithe recovery. During 1933–34, lawyers acting on behalf of tithepayers presented six test cases in the courts.[90] In all instances, judges found in favour of the titheowners, leaving the tithepayers' movement with sizeable legal costs. But when the NTA appealed for funds, Pitt-Rivers failed to put his hands in his considerable pockets. Frank Allen commented that those 'who have been most insistent [about taking legal action] have generally borne least of the burden' and 'neither [Pitt-Rivers] nor the organisation he has founded has contributed anything to the costs'.[91]

As the name chosen for his association suggests, Pitt-Rivers' campaign against tithe was part of a wider agrarian project. The fact that the tithe 'burden' was shouldered solely by agriculture was, he argued, because 'the industrial community [had become] too powerful [and] shared too large a part of the wealth of the country'. Tithe abolition would be a step towards 'the restoration of the countryside'.[92] The policy of WADA was not only to attack the principle of tithe but also 'to see that there was a strong section of agriculturists and others who [aimed] to weld themselves into a party to defend agriculture'. His organisation would, stressed Pitt-Rivers, have 'nothing to do with any of the existing political parties'.[93]

---

[87] 'The Tithe Dispute and Justice for the British Agriculture: WADA statement presented by Captain Pitt-Rivers', GPR, CAC, PIRI 14/3.
[88] 'Anti-Tithe Leader's Unpaid Tithe', WG, 20 Oct. 1933.
[89] QAB, Tithe Committee, 25 July 1934, CERC, QAB/2/1/50.
[90] See pp. 243–6.
[91] East Kent Tithepayers' Association, 'Recent Tithe Cases in the Law Courts', 19 May 1934, DWPap.
[92] 'Wessex Tithe Payers', WG, 26 May 1933.
[93] 'Wessex Tithes Opponents', Dorset Daily Echo, 31 Jan. 1935; GPR, CAC, PIRI 3; Pitt-Rivers to Beaverbrook, 24 June 1930, GPR, CAC, PIRI 18/1.

Seeking allies, Pitt-Rivers made overtures to Lord Beaverbrook, who he 'looked upon [...] as a friend'. Beaverbrook congratulated him on 'building up so powerful an organisation' and promised to follow his project 'with close attention', but the press baron was not prepared to pin his colours to Pitt-Rivers' mast.[94] Next, Pitt-Rivers turned to Oswald Mosley. In May 1934, like Lymington he joined the January Club, telling the club secretary that he believed 'the agricultural policy of the WADA [was] consistent with the Fascist agricultural policy'.[95] In September 1934, he invited the BUF leader to Hinton St Mary to address a WADA meeting. Uniformed Blackshirts helped to steward the event, which drew an attendance 'representative of the agricultural community'. Mosley told the gathering that 'fascism welcomed an organisation like WADA which organised the farmers against their foreign masters in London'.[96]

Membership of WADA was drawn from Dorset, Wiltshire, Somerset and Hampshire, but Pitt-Rivers also planned to build a nationwide Agricultural Defence Association by 'pooling efforts' with Rolf Gardiner. He sought to convince BUF-supporting farmers in Cornwall, Devon and East Anglia 'to come in' on the project.[97] In 1933, he linked up with Sir Bowater George Vernon, another aristocratic sympathiser of fascism, who farmed 5,000 acres on the Hanbury Hall Estate, Droitwich (Worcestershire). After announcing he would not pay his tithe, Vernon was invited to serve as honorary president of the Worcestershire Tithepayers' Association.[98] In August 1933, he enlisted Pitt-Rivers' support for the association's campaign against the distraint seizure at Thomas Howard's farm in Tenbury Wells.[99] Pitt-Rivers travelled to Worcester to address a solidarity rally, which was chaired by Vernon. He also fired off letters to the home secretary complaining of the 'illegal' action of the police in facilitating the execution of the distraint order.[100] A few weeks later, Vernon accepted a reciprocal invitation from Pitt-Rivers to take the chair of a big WADA rally in Dorchester.[101] Labelled by journalists as 'the fighting baronet', Vernon became something of a celebrity in the tithepayers' movement. In June 1935, his non-payment stance resulted in a distraint auction of goods and furniture on the

[94] Correspondence between Pitt-Rivers and Beaverbrook, 6 and 7 June 1933, GPR, CAC, PIRI 18/1.
[95] Cited in Dietz, *Neo-Tories*, 161.
[96] 'Wessex Tithepayers Addressed by Sir Oswald Mosley', *WG*, 28 Sept. 1934.
[97] Pitt-Rivers to Rolf Gardiner, 19 Aug. 1936, GPR, CAC, PIRI 22/3.
[98] 'Mr Baldwin and Tithe', *F&S*, 16 Jan. 1933.
[99] See pp. 183–4.
[100] 'Tithe Seizure "Burglary"', *Birmingham Daily Gazette*, 2 Oct. 1933; see file of correspondence in TNA, HO 144/19199.
[101] 'Tithes Meeting at Dorchester', *Dorset County Chronicle & Somersetshire Gazette*, 19 Oct. 1933.

steps of his stately residence. The following month he received 'a great reception' when guest speaker at a tithe auction in Herefordshire.[102] Like Pitt-Rivers, Vernon drew close to Mosley's British Union of Fascists. After expressing publicly his 'great privilege' on hearing the fascist leader at 'a crowded meeting' organised by the Worcestershire NFU, Vernon invited Mosley on several occasions as a guest to Hanbury Hall. He committed suicide in June 1940, seemingly fearful of being arrested under Defence Regulation 18B.[103]

Pitt-Rivers' friendly relations with Mosley's movement led to speculation on whether a 'fusion' would take place between WADA and the British Union of Fascists and whether Pitt-Rivers would stand as a 'Blackshirt candidate' at the 1935 general election. In the event, negotiations between Pitt-Rivers and Mosley's representatives resulted in a 'backroom alliance' under which WADA would stand candidates and 'all fascists within reach' would be 'instructed' to lend their support.[104] 'My Dear Mosley', wrote Pitt-Rivers to the fascist leader, 'I know it is unnecessary for me to assure you of my belief in the cause for which you stand. I firmly believe that you in your wider movement and I in the agricultural world [...] are fighting for the same principles and for the same end.'[105] Pitt-Rivers stood in the North Dorset constituency as an 'independent agriculturalist'. He was well beaten, receiving less than 7 per cent of the vote. Interestingly, the warrant for his detention issued in 1940 referred, alongside his 'pro-German and anti-British views', to his candidature 'as an Independent Anti-Tithe candidate' as evidence of activity in 'furtherance of the objects [of the British Union of Fascists]'.[106]

Mosley and the Tithe War

Mosley launched his 'fascist agricultural campaign' in September 1933 at an open-air meeting at Ashford market (Kent). According to the local press, he was given 'an uninterrupted hearing by a large gallery of farmers'; *The Blackshirt* deemed the event a 'brilliant success'. It is no accident that the Fascists launched their campaign in Ashford, part of the constituency previously represented in parliament by Kedward and generally viewed

---

[102] 'Baronet's Furniture for Tithe', *Daily Mirror* 15 June 1935; 'Tithe Distress Sale', *Kington Times*, 27 July 1935.
[103] 'Fascist Policy for Agriculture', *Tewkesbury Register & Agricultural Gazette*, 7 July 1934; Adrian Tinniswood, *The Long Weekend: Life in the English Country House between the Wars* (London: Jonathan Cape, 2016), 366–7.
[104] 'Dorset and the Next Election', *Southern Times, Weymouth*, 16 Feb. 1935, GPR, CAC, PIRI 3; Hart, *George Pitt-Rivers*, 99–100.
[105] Pitt-Rivers to Mosley, 8 Apr. 1935, GPR, CAC, PIRI 13/1.
[106] Hart, *George Pitt-Rivers*, 148; See Security Service file: TNA, KV 2/831.

as a frontline in the tithe war. Over the next weeks, further 'agricultural meetings' took place in Aylesbury, Colchester, Hitchen and Bedford. In December, Mosley visited Cornwall and Devon, speaking at a meeting in Bodmin and to a crowd of 700 in the Civic Hall, Exeter.[107]

In his speeches, Mosley recited the credo of right-wing agrarianism that 'a healthy and a mighty race must have roots deep in the soil of a native land'. Under fascism, he explained, 'a great system of owner farmers' would provide the backbone of a 'great corporate system', which would increase the purchasing power of the masses and 'restore' the English countryside.[108] He always highlighted the issue of tithe. In Bodmin, he was joined on the platform by Samuel Johns, secretary of the Cornwall Tithepayers' Association. In Exeter, he spoke alongside a farmer's wife from Trevarrian, north Cornwall, outside whose farm Blackshirts were encamped to prevent a distraint seizure.[109]

Mosley's propaganda was attractive to many in and around the tithepayers' movement. With aspirations of business success and, in most cases, hostility to workers' rights, owner-occupying farmers were a natural constituency for the Conservatives. But Fascists could point to the National Government's refusal to reform tithe – as well as the record of the previous Labour government – to illustrate the 'betrayal' of the political classes. Typical of those they sought to attract was E. Thurgood, a keen hare courser who farmed at Epping. 'The 1925 [Tithe] Act had been passed by a Conservative government and for that reason,' he told a meeting of the Epping Tithepayers' Association, 'although a life-long Tory, as was his father before him, he would never vote for that party again.'[110]

In popular memory, the British Union of Fascists is associated with antics by blackshirted thugs and provocative marches through London's East End, rather than with agitation in rural towns and villages. Yet, particularly in its early years, Mosley emphasised the importance of winning support amongst farmers and courted links with landowners.[111] A keen student of far-right movements elsewhere in Europe, he would have known that Mussolini's movement in Italy made a breakthrough when its *squadre* mobilised in support of farmers resisting agricultural workers' trade unionism in the Po Valley (1920–21). He would have been aware that the Nazis achieved their first electoral successes after 1928

[107] 'If fascism comes to power, we shall ... ', *KM*, 30 Sept. 1933; 'Fascist Agricultural Campaign', *The Blackshirt*, 7 Oct. 1933; 'Sir Oswald Mosley', *Bedfordshire Times & Independent*, 13 Oct. 1933; 'Tithe "War" in West', *WMN*, 18 Dec. 1933.
[108] 'Conflict between Town and Countryside', *FW*, 19 Jan. 1934.
[109] 'Tithe "War" in West', *WMN*, 18 Dec. 1933.
[110] 'Tithe Protest at Epping', *ChCh*, 26 June 1931.
[111] On Mosley's agrarianism, see Dan Stone, 'Rural Revivalism and the Radical Right in France and Britain between the Wars', in *The Holocaust, Fascism and Memory* (Basingstoke: Palgrave Macmillan, 2013), 110–22.

by 'turning to the farmers', in particular winning support in Schleswig-Holstein amongst cattle farmers who had been organising tax strikes and protests against banks and middlemen. He might also have followed the more recent activities in France of Henri Dorgères, far-right leader of the Committees of Peasant Defence (known as 'the Greenshirts'). Dorgères achieved notoriety in June 1933 by organising a protest outside a farm in Normandy to obstruct the auction of equipment seized for a farmer's refusal to pay social security contributions. Both the social composition of Dorgères' supporters and the tactics they deployed were remarkably similar to those of the tithepayers' movement in England.[112]

The British Union of Fascists was, of course, late on the scene of the tithe war. The conflict had been raging for over two years before Blackshirts turned up at the Ringshall Farm in August 1933. Up to this point, Mosley had shown little interest in the tithe issue, including during his time as a government minister. Perhaps not surprisingly, then, fascist policy on tithe evolved with some hesitancy. At the time of the Ringshall events, an editorial in *The Blackshirt* explained that it was unable 'at present to set out the detailed policy of the British Union of Fascists on this vexed question'.[113] Policy amounted to a call for a moratorium on tithe payments until the establishment of a parliamentary Select Committee to examine the problem.[114] This came shortly after the NTA had agreed a detailed policy for tithe abolition and rejected calls for an inquiry as an unnecessary prevarication. In November 1933, BUF proposals were still vague. An article in *The Fascist Week* called for a meeting of 'all parties concerned' around 'a British Round Table' – an idea with Arthurian connotations but also pointing towards corporatism – in order to secure 'a temporary adjustment of the worst wrongs which have been inflicted on the unfortunate farmer'. Mosley's party also launched a 'petition to the King', urging him to order that tithes be put on 'a just basis'.[115]

It was not until March 1934 that the British Union of Fascists came out clearly for the abolition of tithe, proposing that lost revenues of the Church should be replaced from general taxation.[116] A comprehensive explanation of BUF policy followed in November 1934. Penned by ideologue Raven Thompson, but clearly influenced by the analyses of Lymington and Pitt-Rivers, it described tithes as an anachronism 'out of keeping with the

---

[112] Robert O. Paxton, *French Peasant Fascism: Henry Dorgères's Greenshirts and the Crises of French Agriculture, 1929–1939* (Oxford: Oxford University Press, 1997), 78–84.
[113] Editorial, *The Blackshirt*, 5 Aug. 1933.
[114] 'The Tithe War', *The Blackshirt*, 19 Aug. 1933.
[115] 'Extortions of the Tithe Owner', *FW*, 10 Nov. 1933; 'Fascists Organising Petition to the King', *FW*, 5 Jan. 1934.
[116] 'Fascism will Abolish Tithes', *FW*, 16 Mar. 1934.

modern world, but completely out of touch with their original purpose', which was the 'healthy principle of service' existing in medieval times. The tithe system had originally been 'a fully fascist conception'. Its 'degeneration and distortion' started at the Reformation and 'the process of decay' was completed by 'the Financial Revolution of recent times'. As a short-term measure, Fascists proposed the revision of the 1925 Act and a return 'to the original commodity basis [of tithe]', though without elaborating on the practicalities of collecting farm produce and stock. Thompson explained that after tithe abolition by a Fascist government, though the Church would not lose money, lay titheowners would receive compensation only in cases of hardship. He concluded his statement with an agrarianist flourish: fascism would 'release' farming 'to lead the way to national regeneration through the healthy vigour of a restored countryside'.[117]

The BUF's relationship with the tithepayers' movement also lacked clarity. Stung by accusations that they were 'poking their nose' into the conflict, the Fascists responded that their members were 'local residents [...] engaged in the agricultural industry' who were 'giving disciplined form to the existing resistance'. The Blackshirts were 'controlling and directing' the protests and farmers were 'accepting willingly the leadership offered'.[118] Many in the tithepayers' movement would have noticed that the remarks ignored the 'leadership' offered over the previous two years by the tithepayers' associations.

While keen to show themselves on the side of farmers, the British Union of Fascists was fearful of accusations that it was stoking up opposition to the national church and supporting actions that threatened law and order. An article in *The Fascist Week* disassociated Fascists from 'outbreaks of violence such have resulted from mobs collecting at farms [during distraint sales]' and stressed that 'fascists take only forms of passive resistance to tithe collection as are legitimate' – another comment that seemed to disparage tactics deployed by the tithepayers' movement. The article coincided with events at Kersey (Suffolk), where six cattle had been impounded by a possession man. Shortly after a group of Blackshirts arrived, the bailiff noticed that the distrained cattle had 'disappeared'. The Fascists denied any responsibility and when the stock was found – mingling with cattle in a field about a mile away – they helped bailiffs to round up the animals. In effect, a desire to prove they were not 'out for trouble' led the Fascists to disrupt the tactics being deployed by local farmers to prevent the distraint sale.[119]

---

[117] Alexander Raven Thompson, 'Fascism and the Tithe Question', *The Blackshirt*, 23 Nov. 1934.

[118] 'The Tithe War', *The Blackshirt*, 19 Aug. 1933; 'Extortions of the Tithe Owner', *FW*, 10 Nov. 1933.

[119] 'Kersey Tithe Diversion', *Suffolk & Essex Free Press*, 9 Nov. 1933; 'Extortions of the Tithe Owner', *FW*, 10 Nov. 1933; Mitchell, 'Fascism in East Anglia', 63–5.

Devon and Cornwall

The British Union of Fascists' intervention in the West Country was more adept. One contributing reason was the later development of the tithe war in the region. The Devon Tithepayers' Association had been established in Newton Abbot in October 1931, but its activity remained relatively low key and, moreover, the association did not immediately adopt a non-payment campaign. Visiting the region in November 1932, Frank Allen was told by members that 'the Devonshire farmer was a law-abiding citizen' and would have 'nothing to do' with an association that 'advocated breaking the law'.[120] But the same month saw the inaugural meeting of the North Devon Tithepayers' Association with leaders committed to the non-payment campaign. Its secretary, Albert Turner, a prominent local Liberal, urged members to follow the example of 'the men of Kent' and stand together by not paying the tithe. Yet, in October 1933, he admitted that most members of the association were still reluctant to take such a stand.[121]

During 1933, however, attitudes amongst West Country tithepayers hardened. In the summer, farmers began to receive summonses for arrears and soon county court sittings were issuing distraint orders, fifty in a single day at Barnstaple. The 'raid' in June by General Dealers at St Pinnock (Cornwall) further raised the temperature.[122] The distraint orders acted as a spur to the tithepayers' movement. The North Devon association doubled its size, reporting 509 members at its annual meeting in January 1934. Local groups and committees were established at well-attended meetings in remote villages. Frank Allen, Roderick Kedward, Harry Roseveare (chairman of Ashford Tithepayers' Association) and George C. Solley travelled from Kent to assist with the campaign.

The first distraint sale in Devon took place in October at Holwell Farm, Buckland Brewer, a hamlet five miles from Bideford. The North Devon Tithepayers' Association had neither the experience nor the mobilising network to organise an effective response. Consequently, an opportunity was left open for the Fascists. Following the example of their comrades in East Anglia, BUF members set up camp at the farm, barricading the entrances, digging trenches and preparing obstacles to block roads. After staying three weeks, they claimed victory when the court registrar temporarily gave up attempts to remove the stock

---

[120] 'Farmers and Tithes, *WMN*, 24 Nov. 1932.
[121] 'Farmers and the Tithe Controversy', *NDJ*, 10 Nov. 1932; 'North Devon Tithe Protest Meeting, *NDJ*, 8 June 1933; 'North Devon Tithe War', *NDJ*, 12 Oct. 1933.
[122] 'Bideford Tithe Case', *NDJ*, 26 Oct. 1933; 'North Devon Tithe War', *NDJ*, 30 Nov. 1933; 'Farmers Rush Auctioneer', *WMN*, 10 June 1933; '"Legal Robbery" Allegation', *WMN*, Tuesday 13 June 1933; 'Secret Raid on Farm', *WMN*, Wednesday 28 June 1933. See p. 183.

FIGURE 7. Fascists at Whitestone (near Exeter), Devon, 29 November 1933 (© Getty Images). After being alerted by the farmer's daughter, the fascists dug a trench across the approach to Hayne Barton Farm, Whitestone in an attempt to prevent bailiffs from seizing two bullocks.

after noticing that most of the distrained crops had 'mysteriously' disappeared. Over the next three months, BUF members organised similar activity at farms in Whitestone (near Exeter), Abbotskerswell, Bickington (both near Newton Abbot) and Alverdiscott (near Bideford). In Cornwall, the occupation of a farm at Trevarrian continued until early January, when bailiffs' attempts to seize furniture failed after the distrained possessions had, as at Buckland Brewer, 'disappeared'.[123]

In the West Country, in contrast to their intervention in East Anglia, the Fascists did not generally substitute themselves for the tithepayers' organisations. They told farmers to strengthen their own organisations. 'You should all become members of the Tithepayers' Association and the Farmers' Union,' urged Ernest Oxland, who had helped to 'defend' Holwell Farm, 'then as one great body, you will be able to stand out against the burden imposed on you'.[124] Some BUF members were embedded within the tithepayers' movement from the outset. Important roles were played by William Down, a livestock farmer from Sampford Peverell, who was chairman of Tiverton Tithepayers' Association, and Frederick Hooper, another Tiverton farmer, who joined the Fascists after previously being in the Conservative Party. The two men shared the platform at meetings in towns and villages throughout Devon.[125] Both would remain committed members of Mosley's movement: Hooper was arrested in 1940 under Defence Regulation 18B while 'half-way through sheering his sheep'.[126] In Cornwall, another enthusiastic Fascist, Samuel Johns, became chairman of Bodmin Tithepayers' Association as well as chairman of the Cornwall Tithepayers' Association when it was established in October 1933.

Leaders of the tithepayers' associations stressed there was 'no connection' between their organisations and the British Union of Fascists.[127] But farmers and farming communities often welcomed the practical support offered against distraint seizures. In some cases, a farmer facing the threat of bailiffs telephoned the local BUF office to ask for assistance. At Whitestone, it was the daughter of one of the tithepayers who contacted the Exeter BUF branch. Always, the Fascist contingent sought agreement for their actions and tactics with

---

[123] Gray, *Blackshirts*, 111–34.
[124] 'Fight Against Tithes', *WT*, 27 Oct. 1933.
[125] In October, Down and Hooper spoke from the top table at a meeting to establish a TPA in Whitestone; in November, they spoke at meetings in Cheriton Fitzpaine and Witheridge. 'Whitestone Farmers Appeal to Government', *WT*, 27 Oct. 1933; 'More Tithe Opposition', *WT*, 17 Nov. 1933; 'Readjustment Appeal to Bishops and Clergy, *WT*, 1 Dec. 1933.
[126] 'The Defence Regulation 18B British Union Detainees List', Friends of Oswald Mosley (2008).
[127] '"Stand Against Tithe Justified"', *WT*, 17 Nov. 1933.

the farmers concerned. After their intervention at Buckland Brewer, a journalist wrote how the Fascists 'had left warm hearts' and 'were most pleasant and tactful both to the local inhabitants and to the many visitors. [...] Mr Brown [the farmer] is happy because he has seen his enemies discomforted.'[128] In his report to the annual meeting of North Devon Tithepayers' Association in January 1934, the honorary secretary, Frederick Chipman, a Labour Party member, said that, though the association had 'not invited' them, it 'gratefully recognise[d] the valuable help that has been given us by the British Union of Fascists'. A fortnight earlier, a group of Fascists had erected stakes and barbed wire around the entrance to Chipman's Alverdiscott farm to prevent the seizure of household furniture and a cow. When criticised by a local newspaper editor, Chipman wrote: 'I am in a burning house, requiring help. The only man willing to give me help wears a black shirt. [...] I ask, what would you do?'[129]

Not only did the West Country Fascists show greater sensitivity towards the tithepayers' movement, they sometimes also demonstrated innovation in terms of tactics. In February 1934, the BUF's 'Devon propaganda officer' issued summonses for animal cruelty against the registrar and bailiffs of Newton Abbot county court and a police inspector. The action related to the aftermath of the aborted auction of ewes and bullocks at Newton Abbot market in December. Though the case was dismissed, the affair generated some positive publicity for the Fascists.[130]

There were, however, contradictory aspects to the BUF's strategy. In January 1934, the leader assigned to the region, Richard Plathen, announced the formation of the British Union of Farmers. Outlining its aims, Plathen said that 'recent developments, particularly in connection with tithe' showed the need for 'a strong organisation which would link together the farmers of the country'. But he struggled to explain why the Fascists wanted to set up a separate – supposedly independent and 'non-political' – organisation alongside the tithepayers' associations and the NFU.[131] Several meetings took place in Devon and Cornwall, all addressed by local Fascists. Samuel Johns became secretary of the new 'union', whilst remaining secretary of Cornwall Tithepayers' Association. Despite attempts by some Fascists in other regions to

---

[128] *Bideford Gazette*, 31 Oct. 1933. Cited in Gray, *Blackshirts*, 117.
[129] *NDJ*, 18 and 25 Jan. 1934; Gray, *Blackshirts*, 127–8.
[130] 'Court Sequel to Tithe Distraint', *The Times*, 21 Feb. 1934.
[131] Meetings took place in Bodmin, Stratton, Helston, Liskeard, Truro and Bideford. 'Tithe Proposals', *WMN*, 4 Apr. 1934; 'Fascist Plans', *WMN*, 22 Jan. 1934.

breathe life into the organisation,[132] the British Union of Farmers was stillborn and quickly forgotten.

The tithe intervention in Devon and Cornwall was heralded as a model at the BUF's London headquarters. With typical hyperbole, *The Blackshirt* declared that 'the successful "war" conducted in "tithe country" [...] has almost converted the whole of Western England to Fascism.' A visit to London in January 1934 by Plathen and a group of Plymouth-based Fascists 'created quite a stir'. They told Mosley's lieutenants about their 'transport section' comprised of 'lorries, motor cars and motor-cycles' and how their activity on tithe had filled 'columns in the local newspapers'.[133] With hopes of repeating the operation, Plathen was immediately reassigned to oversee the BUF's tithe activities in the eastern counties.

'A drowning man clutches at straws'

On 9 February, Plathen arrived with a group of Blackshirts at Rowland Rash and Doreen Wallace's farm in Wortham. Over the next week, the Fascist presence in the village increased to close on fifty. Plathen coordinated an intervention that deployed, though on a greater scale, methods that had been tried and tested in the West Country. During 1933, East Anglian Fascists had tended to turn up at tithe disputes uninvited. At Fincham and Kersey, farmers told journalists that BUF members did not have permission to stay on their property and, more embarrassingly, at Gestingthorpe, the farmer threatened them with proceedings for trespass if they did not depart.[134] In contrast, at Wortham the Fascists acted in tacit agreement with Rash and Wallace. In early February, Wallace's father wrote to the BUF's London headquarters, enclosing newspaper clippings about the distraint and suggesting 'perhaps [...] you may care to take a hand'.[135] In her fictionalised account of events – a book promoted by a BUF newspaper as its 'book of the week' – Wallace narrates how 'a tall young Blackshirt' came to the farmhouse to offer help and very quickly he and the farm's owner Edward (the Rowland Rash character in the novel) were getting on 'like houses on fire'. Later, 'Edward' informs the police that the Fascists were camping 'on the farm

---

[132] 'Fascism and Tithes', *Kington Times*, 13 Apr. 1935.
[133] 'West Country', *The Blackshirt*, 5 Jan. 1934.
[134] 'Fascists at Fincham Hall', *Lynn News & County Press*, 31 Oct. 1933; 'Extortions of the Tithe Owner', *FW*, 10 Nov. 1933; Mitchell, 'Fascism in East Anglia', 63–5.
[135] Mitchell, 'Fascism in East Anglia', 68.

FIGURE 8. Fascists at Wortham, early February 1934 (© Daily Herald Archive / Science & Society Picture Library, Science Museum). (© Daily Herald Archive/Science Museum Group). Demonstrators standing around a trench dug by BUF members to prevent General Dealers and police from removing distrained livestock. The fascists are on the far side of the trench, facing the camera. To their left are journalists and a newsreel crew.

with his permission'.[136] In real life, they were offered lodgings in a house normally occupied by Rash's farm steward.

Plathen's methods at Wortham displayed greater sensitivity towards the tithepayers' movement than previous BUF activity in East Anglia. Rather than acting autonomously, the Fascists worked alongside members of the local community to cut down trees and set up barricades. We are 'here to help you, but at the same time you must help yourself,' Plathen told a crowd of farmers and farm labourers. A police observer reported that 'all seemed quite interested in what he had to say'.[137] The arrest of Plathen and his comrades on 17 February was witnessed by a large crowd mobilised by the tithepayers' associations that had 'poured into the village'. Correctly viewing the police action as preparation for the arrival of General Dealers, those present expressed solidarity with the arrested fascists. A police sergeant described how 'about 800 people' assailed his colleagues with 'booing and shouts of "let the hogs out"' as they made the arrests. The Fascists were set stringent bail conditions, including a commitment from BUF senior leaders that they would withdraw from the Wortham dispute.[138] At their trial the judge imposed a lenient sentence, though his remarks contained an implicit warning that further infractions would be treated more severely.

Fascism put an imprint on the tithepayers' movement throughout 1934. That year saw Mosley make special efforts to court the landed classes and personalities on the Conservative right. An indication of the 'discreet traffic of ideas and personnel' between the fascist and non-fascist right is the sympathetic coverage of BUF activities in right-wing newspapers, most notably Lord Rothermere's *Daily Mail*. In the spring, the 'Mosley Speaks on Agriculture' campaign was relaunched with a series of meetings, including some in tithe war hotspots.[139] The collusion between the Rash-Wallace family and the Blackshirts during the Wortham dispute indicates that many farmers viewed the Fascists as a legitimate part of the tithepayers' movement, even if they might not adhere to the ethos of Mosley's organisation. Speaking at a packed meeting of the Suffolk Tithepayers' Association after the Wortham events, Mobbs acknowledged the sympathy amongst the farming community. After dispelling 'the rumour' that tithepayers' associations were 'linking up with the Fascist movement', he conceded that what 'individual tithepayers do [was] another matter'. To 'enthusiastic applause and a cry of "Bravo"', Mobbs

---

136 'The Book of the Week', *Action*, 12 Mar. 1936; Wallace, *So Long to Learn*, 323–5.
137 PC George Hitchens, 13 Feb. 1934, TNA, HO 144/19199.
138 'Blackshirts Arrested at Wortham', *BuFP*, 24 Feb. 1934; Sergeant William Clarke, Feb. 1934, TNA, HO 144/19199; Mitchell, 'Fascism in East Anglia', 71–2.
139 Pugh, *'Hurrah for the Blackshirts!'*, 146–50; *Grantham Journal*, 5 May 1934; *Herts & Essex Observer*, 16 June 1934; *Lynn News & County Press*, 24 July 1934.

continued: 'A drowning man will clutch at any straw [...] I know of nothing in this country more calculated to encourage the growth of Fascism than the apparent indifference of Parliament to the grievances of the tithepayers.'[140]

Amongst those joining the British Union of Fascists in Suffolk was Charles Westren, a founding member of Suffolk Tithepayers' Association who had in 1932 been at the centre of a well-publicised distraint case.[141] Westren would continue to lead the BUF's agricultural campaign in the region until the end of the decade. Two farmers from Eye also signed up after participating in the Wortham events: George Hoggarth, who joined along with his brother and some friends, and Ronald Creasy, who later became a BUF parliamentary candidate. Both men would be detained under Regulation 18B in June 1940.[142] In Essex, the Fascists recruited P. M. Sloman, who farmed at Greenstead and was an activist in the Colchester Tithepayers' Association. In August 1933, some of Sloman's household furniture had been seized and, in August 1934, a dozen operatives from General Dealers removed two 'freshly-calved' cows from his property. After this, Sloman spoke at Suffolk Tithepayers' Association in support of a resolution moved by Doreen Wallace against 'excessive distraints'. He wrote: 'tithe owners have just distrained on my property for the paltry sum of £9 12s. [...] I think it wants a party such as the Blackshirts to deal with such unscrupulous financial interests in a drastic way.'[143] In Norfolk also, the Fascists exploited grievances over tithe to win support amongst farmers. A famous recruit was Henry Williamson, author of *Tarka the Otter*, who took the deeds of a farm at Stiffkey in August 1936. 'The parasite [that has] worked its way up into the skull of its host, the land of England', was Williamson's description of tithe in his *The Story of a Norfolk Farm*, a book with 'roots in Mosleyite economics and the iconography of fascism and which is elaborated by a protagonist who identifies with Hitler'.[144]

The British Union of Fascists also gained some influence within the tithepayers' movement in East Sussex and Kent. In June, a bailiff guarding distrained cattle on a farm at Icklesham was confronted at around midnight by 'a band of young men wearing the Fascist uniform'. They locked him in a hut and by the time he managed to get free the

---

[140] 'Suffolk Tithepayers Association', *DiEx*, 2 Mar. 1934; 'Wortham Tithe Dispute', *BuFP*, Saturday 3 Mar. 1934.
[141] See pp. 157–8 and pp. 165–6.
[142] Mitchell, 'Fascism in East Anglia', 294–6 and 75–7.
[143] 'Taken for Tithe', *ChCh*, 14 Sept. 1934; 'Tithe Sales by Tender', *DiEx*, 19 Oct. 1934; 'Tithe Owners' Action', *The Blackshirt*, 7 Sept. 1934.
[144] *The Story of a Norfolk Farm* (London: Faber & Faber, 1942), 109; Mark Rawlinson, 'Dead Chickens: Henry Williamson, British Agriculture and European War', in Brassley, Burchardt and Thompson (eds), *English Countryside*, 88–9.

cattle had been driven away.[145] Such activity was organised by Stanley Vincent, the youthful 'political organiser' of the Ashford BUF branch. Vincent became a well-known face at tithepayers' activities. In March 1934, wearing his black shirt, he addressed the annual meeting of the Rye and Northiam Tithepayers' Association, alongside Kedward and Frank Allen.[146] In March 1935, he spoke at a distraint auction at Newchurch on the Romney Marsh, this time sharing the platform with Harry Roseveare, chair of Ashford tithepayers' association.[147]

Elsewhere in Kent, Fascists won recruits within the tithepayers' movement in Elham, including an officer in the association, William S. Wood of Beverage Bottom Farm. Later in the year, Wood stood trial for his part in the 'Battle of the Ducks'. Of greater import was the resignation of Kingsley Dykes, chair of Elham Tithepayers' Association, from the Canterbury Division of the Conservative Party, in which he held a senior post. In a resignation letter which created considerable local waves, Dykes signalled the disaffection of a layer of Conservative-inclined farmers for whom 'the Government had not kept their promises in regard to agriculture'. Shortly afterwards, the fascist press announced that Dykes 'was seriously thinking of joining the British Union of Fascists'.[148]

Mosley's major catch in Kent was George C. Solley, chairman of East Kent Tithepayers' Association and, as a pioneer of the non-payment campaign, well known within the national tithepayers' movement. Solley joined the Fascists in August 1934, soon after General Dealers had seized fifty pedigree sheep and lambs from his Richborough farm. A major political and cultural figure in the region, Solley's enthusiastic endorsement of the BUF normalised fascism for other farmers. In December 1934, while presiding at a special meeting of Canterbury Farmers' Club convened to hear BUF speakers explain their agricultural policy, Solley predicted that 'before another twelve months are past, Fascism will be the party of the day'.[149]

How, then, should the influence of fascism within the tithepayers' associations be evaluated? In fact, the latter part of 1934 marks the highpoint of the British Union of Fascists' influence. During 1935, Mosley placed less emphasis on activity in rural areas. Although continuing his 'agricultural campaign',[150] the Fascists' priority became rallies and marches in big towns and cities. The British Union of Fascists had little

---

[145] 'Cattle Raiding near Hastings', *The Times*, 9 June 1934.
[146] 'Blackshirts and Tithes', *Sussex Express*, 29 Mar. 1934.
[147] 'Police guard rectory and church', *Kentish Express*, 29 Mar. 1935.
[148] 'Tithepayers to Boycott the Church', *Folkestone, Hythe, Sandgate & Cheriton Herald*, Saturday 11 Aug. 1934; 'Conservative Activities', *KE*, 16 Nov. 1934; *The Blackshirt*, 2 Nov. 1934.
[149] 'Tithe Seizure at Sandwich', *DE*, 17 Aug. 1934; 'Fascism comes to Sandwich', *The Blackshirt*, 5 Oct. 1934; 'Farmers meet Blackshirts', *KG*, 8 Dec. 1934.
[150] 'How Fascism would Tackle Agriculture', *The Blackshirt*, 13 Sept. 1935.

to say about the Royal Commission on tithe, which sat during late 1934 and early 1935, and its members were conspicuously absent from the mass tithepayers' demonstration in London in June 1936.[151] Mosley's party had won some significant recruits. Some of its members, including Solley, Hooper and Down, became regular attendees at the NTA national council. But they remained a minority trend and tended to work as individuals rather than as part of an organised BUF grouping.

Fascist influence in the tithepayers' movement extended, of course, beyond the activities of the British Union of Fascists. Some of those who shunned the methods of Mosley's movement saw no problem with collaborating with more 'respectable' adherents of fascism. On a visit to East Anglia in August 1933, George Gill, secretary of Elham Tithepayers' Association, asked for an assurance from local tithepayers' leaders that there was 'no collusion, or collaboration whatsoever [with the British Union of Fascists]'.[152] Yet, two and a half years later, Gill began to work with Pitt-Rivers, closely collaborating with him during the campaign against the 1936 Tithe Bill. After his death, Gill's wife and sons had no compunction in publishing posthumously his *A Fight against Tithes* with 'unrestricted help from Henry Williamson', who had been detained for pro-fascist sympathies under Defence Regulation 18B.[153]

One obstacle for Mosley's organisation was the insistence of tithepayers' associations that they were 'non-political and non-sectarian'. This signalled to tithepayers that they could win if they rejected the type of innately divisive activity associated with the British Union of Fascists. Throughout the tithe war, the tithepayers' movement remained a loose political coalition. One wing – that associated with Kedward – was linked to liberalism and, in the case of some of its adherents, political nonconformism. Despite the British Union of Fascists' campaign in Devon, for example, the leadership of the tithepayers' movement remained in Liberal hands and became associated with the successful campaign by the radical Liberal Richard Acland to win the Barnstaple seat at the 1935 general election.[154]

The other wing was conservative. Sociologically, it was formed for the most part of better-off farmers, some employing a significant number of agricultural workers. A small but influential minority were part of the landed and gentry classes. Many Conservatives shared a right-wing agrarian outlook with fascism: supporting protectionist policies, lamenting the weakened economic and social status of agriculture, and condemning the Tory leadership for prioritising the interests of both workers in the

---

[151] See pp. 281–3.
[152] George Gill to Marjory Allen, n.d. (Aug. 1933), Modern Records Centre, University of Warwick, LAH, MSS.121/F/3/3/16.
[153] Gill, *A Fight against the Tithes*.
[154] 'Fund to Help Tithe "Victims"', *WT*, 22 June 1934.

towns and finance capital. But disaffected Conservatives had a range of political choices. Eve Balfour, for example, contemplated establishing 'a new party [...] for those Conservatives who are dissatisfied with the party and its master, the City'. Though repelled by Mosley's 'ghastly methods; his anti-semitism, his intolerance', Balfour conceded that 'there is much of what Mosley advocates and says that is such good sense'.[155] In Mersham (Kent) a BUF representative turned up at a distraint auction of goods seized from Mr H. R. Hooper, an officer in the local Conservative Party. Despite assuring farmers that they 'had the support of his party', he was greeted with shouts of 'We don't want Mussolini here'.[156]

Doreen Wallace is representative of a section of the tithepayers' movement that prioritised the tithe question over party politics. She explained how 'her alienation from the Conservative Party' had begun 'when she was repeatedly told by the Central Office not to mention tithe'.[157] After her dalliance with their members during the Wortham dispute, she maintained a somewhat ambivalent attitude to relations with the British Union of Fascists. In June 1935, she visited Devon to speak at protests against a series of distraint sales in the county. Two meetings took place near Chulmleigh. At the first, chaired by BUF member William Down, men in 'blackshirt uniforms' distributed fascist leaflets. At the second, the novelist spoke alongside H. B. Hammond, the BUF district officer. She said that although 'the Tithepayers Association had not identified itself with any colour shirt, [...] they were very interested to hear what any political party had to tell them. It would give a ray of hope in the present situation.'[158] Yet, at the 1935 general election, Wallace and some members of the Norfolk Tithepayers' Association gave public support to the Labour Party. Speaking at a Labour meeting in Lopham, she explained that Labour was 'no enemy of the smallholder' and its tithe policy meant 'immediate relief' to tithepayers.[159]

But most of the 'conservative wing' of the tithepayers' movement maintained their party loyalty, even if in a less than enthusiastic manner. Their ties with Conservatism were strengthened by the increasing authority of Walter Elliot, minister of agriculture. A man once close politically to Oswald Mosley, Elliot promised to restore the prestige of agriculture, offered a corporatist partnership to the farming industry and began to make serious efforts to resolve the problem of tithe.

[155] Eve Balfour to Mr Brayshaw, 25 Nov. 1933, cited Gill, 'Lady Eve Balfour', 68.
[156] 'Fireworks at Tithe Sale', *KE*, 8 Nov. 1935.
[157] 'The General Election', *Norfolk & Suffolk Journal*, 15 Nov. 1935.
[158] 'Blackshirts and a Novelist', *WT*, 28 June 1935.
[159] 'Tithepayers' Support', *Yarmouth Independent*, 9 Nov. 1935.

8

Pressures for a Settlement

Elliot and the NFU

Elliot's appointment as minister of agriculture in September 1932 signalled a shift in the National Government's agricultural policy. After winning the general election in October 1931, the Conservative-dominated coalition pursued a more interventionist and protectionist economic policy, but its measures had only a marginal impact on the crisis facing farming. In February 1932, the Import Duties Act imposed a 10 per cent tariff on imports, though foodstuffs were on the list of exemptions. In August 1932, the Imperial Economic Conference in Ottawa failed to reach general agreement on trade and, in the words of the NFU, had 'not formulated a policy for the development of home agricultural interests'.[1] The Wheat Act of 1932 introduced a quota scheme and guaranteed prices for producers, with subsidies financed by a levy on imported flour. But most benefits under the scheme went to a minority of large growers and, even with the subsidy, the price of wheat remained lower than its level in 1930.[2]

Carrying a promise of something new, Elliot was welcomed by politicians of all shades: Baldwin 'rejoiced' at the choice of 'a young man with ability and with enthusiasm'; Lloyd George likened him to a tractor that would 'cut fresh ground'; Harold Laski, the Labour politician, spoke of his 'experimental mind'.[3] The NFU applauded him as 'an able and vigorous champion' of agricultural interests who 'had a thorough grasp of the problems'.[4] Against the background of severe financial depression, Elliot began his ministerial days with expectations that he would become the hoped-for 'saviour' of agriculture.

Elliot was, however, extremely reluctant to enter the tithe minefield. His predecessor, John Gilmour, and other senior figures in the administration had explicitly ruled out changes to the law. Stanley Baldwin – who Elliot

---

[1] 'The Ottawa Agreements', *NFU Record*, Oct. 1932, 5–6.
[2] J. A. Mollet, 'The Wheat Act of 1932', *AgHR*, 8, 1 (1960), 29–30.
[3] Elizabeth M. M. Taylor, 'The Politics of Walter Elliot, 1929–1936' (unpublished PhD thesis, University of Edinburgh, 1979), 198–9 and 205–6.
[4] 'Major Elliot's Task', *NFU Record*, Nov. 1932, 29.

viewed as something of a mentor – had warned that the government would not legislate on the matter.[5] Elliot knew that radical tithe reform would require compensation to the Church from state coffers, which was likely to prompt resistance from the Treasury and others in government. Moreover, his agenda was full enough and he already had battles on his hands over aspects of his agricultural policy within the Cabinet.[6]

Born into a wealthy Lanarkshire farming family, Elliot represented a younger generation of 'progressive' Tories. He was often reluctant to follow conventional Tory dogma, drawing ideas from both the left and radical right. Lecturing at the summer school of the Independent Labour Party in August 1930, Elliot argued that large-scale state intervention was necessary to resolve problems inherent within laissez-faire capitalism. He advocated a state-regulated corporatist system: an economy based on autonomous and self-governing industrial cartels in partnership with the state.[7] At this time, his views were close to those of Oswald Mosley, who he considered 'a friend' and to whose 'salon' he was a frequent visitor. In December 1930, Elliot wrote to *The Times* praising Mosley's 'courage' for issuing – with fifteen other Labour MPs – a 'manifesto' to tackle the economic crisis and restore national spirit. He expressed support for Mosley's programme of 'executive government', selective tariffs, increased state intervention, measures to stimulate the home market and 'inter-imperial planning' to create a captive overseas market. He also collaborated with Mosley in drafting one of the policy statements of the New Party, the organisation that bridged Mosley's transition from the Labour Party to fascism.[8] Elliot was not tempted, however, to follow Mosley's trajectory. He remained committed to the Tories, and particularly loyal to Stanley Baldwin – though this did not prevent an unsuccessful attempt to convince Viscount Lymington, one of the Tory leader's most vehement critics, to become his parliamentary private secretary at the Ministry of Agriculture.[9]

Elliot sought to pull agriculture out of depression by redefining its position within the national economy. Farming should not, he explained, be a 'picturesque survival from pre-industrial times, but a living, organic, and indispensable part of any modern nation's structure'.[10] Central to his strategy was a partnership between the state and farming industry – which

[5] HC Deb., *Hansard*, 22 June 1932.
[6] Taylor, 'Politics of Walter Elliot', 212–18.
[7] Cooper, *British Agricultural Policy*, 160–3.
[8] Walter Elliot, 'Labour MPs' Manifesto', *The Times*, 11 Dec. 1930; 'The National Need', *The Times*, 17 Dec. 1930; Matthew Worley, *Oswald Mosley and the New Party* (Basingstoke: Palgrave Macmillan, 2010), 35–6.
[9] Wallop, *A Knot of Roots*, 124.
[10] Elliot writing in *The Countryman*, Dec. 1933. Cited in Cooper, *British Agricultural Policy*, 166.

meant, essentially, partnership with the NFU. The system would function through a series of 'marketing boards', of the type proposed in 1931 by the Labour minister Christopher Addison. But Elliot's Agricultural Marketing Act of 1933 went further, introducing mechanisms for the self-governing boards to plan the level of agricultural production and restrict imports.[11] 'The boards,' said Elliot, 'must regard themselves as bound closely with the farmers of the country and the NFU. [...] They were "bone of our bone and flesh of our flesh". They were the farmers' own show.'[12]

Relations between the minister and NFU leaders became cordial, both politically and in some cases on a personal level. The NFU had already reversed its principled opposition to marketing boards when, in January 1932, its conference voted narrowly in favour of compulsory membership of a Milk Marketing Board. Senior NFU figures became enthusiastic members of nine boards, including those for milk, potatoes, pigs, wheat, sugar and hops. The partnership was celebrated in November 1933 when Elliot was, along with the Prince of Wales, fêted as guest of honour at the NFU's twenty-fifth anniversary dinner. The union president, B. J. Gates, introduced him as 'the best minister of agriculture the NFU had had to deal with' and assured him of its support 'to the last man and to the last ounce'. Elliot, who stood up to 'a remarkable ovation', was keen to reciprocate, praising 'the Farmers' Union [which] stood out prominently among all the industries of the country'.[13]

The closer relationship with government impacted on the NFU's tithe policy. During 1932 Roland Robbins and Thomas Ryland, the two men most associated with the 1924–25 negotiations and the NFU's reluctance to support tithe reform, withdrew from their leadership roles. They were hostile to the NFU's involvement in the marketing boards, which they viewed as the continuation of 'a scheme dreamt up by a socialist Labour Government'.[14] In their absence, NFU leaders became more sensitive to the problem of tithe. They pressed Elliot on the matter, stressing the union's opposition to the 1925 Act, calling for an inquiry into its operation and demanding immediate legislation to 'alter the basis' of tithe remission.[15]

The NFU leaders' more considered approach towards the tithe issue did not imply a change in their attitude towards the tithepayers' movement. Officials still tried to marginalise the NTA, which was described as 'an irresponsible organisation purporting to speak for tithepayers'.[16]

---

[11] Cooper, *British Agricultural Policy*, 160–1 and 167–9.
[12] 'The Twenty-Fifth Anniversary Dinner', *NFU Record*, Dec. 1933, 57–61.
[13] Ibid., 58–61.
[14] Smith, *From Campbell to Kendall*, 77.
[15] NFU, 'Report of Tithe Committee', 24 Feb. 1933, MERL, SR NFU, AD1/15.
[16] NFU, 'Tithe Committee', 30 May 1933, MERL, SR NFU, AD1/15; NFU, News Sheet, 22 Aug. 1933, MERL, SR NFU P4/A12.

They failed to respond to letters from the NTA offering coordination of policy and activity. But they could not fail to notice that, within the union, demands were growing for a working relationship between the NFU and the NTA. Frank Allen was invited to address NFU events, as, for example, in Salisbury, at a 'large' meeting organised by the South Wiltshire NFU branch.[17] The county branch in Kent, which in June 1932 had condemned the 'unconstitutional methods' of the NTA, passed a resolution demanding that 'the Council of the Union should confer and unite with other organisations, especially the National Tithepayers' Association which [...] is supported by the main body of tithepayers'.[18] Resolutions from other county branches were openly critical of the senior officials. Devon 'protest[ed] against the failure of the Union to fight in the interests of tithepayers as they should have done'. Montgomeryshire expressed 'disappointment at the progress achieved by Headquarters and warn[ed] Headquarters that the county will soon become involved in wholesale tithe disturbances'.[19]

In January 1933, for the second year running, a stormy debate over tithe took place at the NFU annual meeting. Makens Turner, vice-chair of the Suffolk Tithepayers' Association, proposed the formation of a tithe committee to develop and coordinate NFU policy and activity. The committee should be set up 'without delay' and be 'composed mainly of tithepayers'. The idea, for which the NTA had campaigned for over a year, was strongly resisted by the leadership. Outgoing president Mervyn Davies argued that 'it would be folly' to take the tithe question out of the hands of 'men who possess experience' of the NFU national council's 'past activities in the matter'.[20] Delegates rounded on the top table. Catching the mood, the representative from Denbighshire accused senior officials of 'ostrich-like behaviour' and failing 'to feel the pulse of the industry', before adding that '500 farmers in his county [...] were going to defy the law by refusing to pay tithe'. The resolution to establish a tithe committee was passed by 'a large majority [...] amid much cheering'.[21] Four prominent NTA members were successfully nominated to sit on the committee: Albert Mobbs (Suffolk), Vernon Drewitt (Berkshire), Frederick Krailing (Essex) and Harry Roseveare, chairman of the Ashford Tithepayers' Association (Kent) and a close

---

[17] 'Farmers and Tithe', *WG*, 20 Jan. 1933.
[18] NFU Kent, Executive Committee, 1 Feb. 1934, Kent NFU Archives, KHLC, ACC 3654/23.
[19] NFU, 'To Members of the Tithe Committee', 28 Feb. 1934, MERL, SR NFU, AD1/86.
[20] NFU, Minutes of the Annual General Meeting, 18 Jan. 1933, MERL, SR NFU, AD1/77; Note from Mervyn Davies on proposed Tithe Committee, 6 Jan. 1933, MERL, SR NFU, AD1/51.
[21] 'A Tithe Discussion', *F&S*, 23 Jan. 1933.

associate of Roderick Kedward. The majority of the committee was formed of supporters of the NFU leadership, including three senior officials: Mervyn Davies, B. J. Gates and vice-president Stanley Ratcliff, a man whose propensity to travel to London from his thirteen-farm Essex estate in a Rolls-Royce driven by 'his loyal Chauffer' symbolised the NFU's new corporate identity.[22] At the committee's first meeting, the majority voted down a proposal from Mobbs and Roseveare that the union should enter into a 'consultation' with the NTA 'with a view of arriving at a common line' to obtain immediate relief for tithepayers.[23]

'Agitation remains active'

The pressure within the NFU on tithe reflected the growth in the breadth and activity of the tithepayers' movement. In May 1933, the Queen Anne's Bounty office draw up a balance sheet of the 'agitation':

> In Cambridgeshire, Huntingdonshire and parts of Northamptonshire tithepayers' associations have been formed in the larger centres and some of the branches are extremely active and antagonistic. These generally recommend their members to offer 50 per cent and to raise obstruction with regard to payment of the balance. […] In Norfolk and Suffolk […] agitation remains active and the tithepayers' associations are highly organised, branches having been formed in several small market towns. […] In Essex the agitation is active and many landowners who can afford to pay are refusing to do so from a sense of loyalty to their poorer farming neighbours. […] In Kent, where the agitation arose, the Convener thinks that it has to some extent died down largely owing to the willingness of Queen Anne's Bounty to consider cases of hardship and to make concessions. In the county of Berkshire, agitation has spread a little, the convenor attributing this to recent inability to obtain an effective sale against a ringleader owing to legal difficulty. The agitation is very strong in the eastern part of Sussex, and the East Sussex Tithepayers Association has a large membership. […] In Dorset, Hampshire and Wiltshire, the agitation is strong in certain areas, noticeably around Andover, Grimstead and Donhead.[24]

Sources from tithepayers' associations confirm this general picture.[25] Throughout East Anglia, associations reported 'steady progress'. The

---

[22] 'The Twenty-Fifth Anniversary Dinner', *NFU Record*, Dec. 1933, 60; Smith, *From Campbell to Kendall*, 83.
[23] NFU, 'Report of Tithe Committee', 10 Mar. 1933, MERL, SR NFU, AD1/15.
[24] 'Report of joint meeting of Chairmen and Convenors of Area Collection Committees with members of the QAB Tithe Committee'; 'Appendix A, b) Anti-tithe Agitation', 30 May 1933, CERC, QAB/2/1/50.
[25] Much of the information that follows is drawn from *Tithe: A Monthly News Sheet of Current Events and Opinions*, a bulletin published by activists in the

annual meeting of the Norfolk Tithepayers' Association in January 1934 was 'the largest meeting yet held', reporting over 500 members. In Suffolk, membership increased from 506 (in 1932) to 554 in 1934. The number of tithepayers' associations in Kent grew to six, including new groups in Paddock Wood and Tenterden. In East Sussex, the annual meeting of the association covering Rye and district reported an increase in membership from ninety-five to 125. A joint committee coordinated activity across the latter two counties.[26]

The best organised tithepayers' associations began to act as mutual aid societies, providing resources to members threatened with distraint. One to benefit in Suffolk was Charles Westren, who was granted £75 by the executive in recognition of 'how great was the service he was doing the cause of the association'.[27] The Berks, Bucks and Oxon Tithepayers' Association raised funds for a 'Guarantee Fund', which aimed to 'stiffen the back' and 'relieve the mind' of those facing distraint.[28] 'Gift Sales' became a popular method of raising money. Held at markets, these were special auctions conducted by friendly auctioneers, followed by speeches. Venues during 1933 and early 1934 included Oxford, Ipswich, Rye, Norwich, Lyminge (Kent), Liskeard (Cornwall), Barnstaple (Devon) and Oxford. In Oxford, goods on sale included cattle, calves, sheep, pigs, horses, dogs, agricultural machinery and bicycles, as well as items of a more modest nature, such as eggs, butter, flowers and vegetables. The Ipswich sale raised £800 from 600 lots, including a Dartmoor pony named 'tithekicker'.

The new feature of the period was the movement's advance outside its strongholds in eastern and south-east England. In Herefordshire, the tithepayers' association's annual meeting (January 1934) reported a membership of 461, and there were further members in a branch based in Ross, which covered the south of the county. In June 1933, the auction of a bullock on a farm at Upton Bishop attracted 'a large crowd of farmers', who kept up 'a continual and increasing tide of chaff', forcing the auctioneer to abandon the sale before a bid could be made. In Gloucestershire, a county tithepayers' association was established in February 1933 after Frank Allen addressed a meeting in Gloucester. A few weeks earlier, the NFU secretary had instructed members of his executive to stay away from the event because the union was 'diametrically opposed to the tithepayers'

Elham Tithepayers' Association throughout 1934.

[26] Suffolk TPA, Second Annual Report, 26 Feb. 1933, SuRO, GC32/1; 'Report of Annual Meeting of Rye & District Tithepayers' Association', *Sussex Agricultural Press*, 7 Apr. 1933; Suffolk TPA, Members Subscriptions, SuRO, GC32/2; 'A Drag on Agriculture', *KM*, 25 Nov. 1933.

[27] Suffolk TPA Executive, 17 May 1932, SuRO, GC32/1.

[28] Bulletin of Berks, Bucks & Oxon Tithepayers' Association, n.d. (Sept. 1932), Berkshire Record Office, D/Ex 2547/4/6/5.

Pressures for a Settlement

association, which believed in militant methods'. The movement in Oxfordshire received a fillip in June 1933 when farmers from a dozen villages and market towns surrounding the Chiltern Hills mobilised to prevent the auction of ten heifers at a farm in South Weston, near Thame. The auctioneer and bailiff were accompanied by fifteen police officers, but the sale was aborted when the bailiff found that the cows had been mixed with cattle in a neighbouring field, making it impossible to identify which were to be sold. The following year, an auctioneer had greater success when – accompanied by thirty police officers – he offered forty cattle for sale on a farm at Hailey.[29]

In Berkshire, an attempt to distrain on the Wallingford farm of Vernon Drewitt, chair of the regional tithepayers' association, ended with the car of an auctioneer from Reading being 'tarred and feathered'. A large crowd mobilised at the same farm on 1 May 1934 to witness the first successful distraint sale in the county. In Leicestershire, an NTA branch was formed in February 1934 in Harborough with 'cooperation' from the local NFU.[30]

In Shropshire, a federation coordinated activities in sixteen market towns, including Minsterley, Bishops Castle, Westbury, Wellington and Wem. In May, the South Shropshire NFU branch invited Roderick Kedward and R. F. Watkins, a prominent Welsh anti-tithe campaigner, to address a 'special meeting' of members in Kington. In Worcestershire, the campaign began to spread after six farmers in the vicinity of Claines were summoned to the county court for non-payment of tithe due to Sir Offley Wakeman, a baronet and high sheriff of Shropshire. A few months later, a distress order was placed on furniture belonging to one of the farmers, James Philips, who had recently become an activist in the tithepayers' association. After travelling to Claines to conduct the sale, the auctioneer was confronted by a group of men: 'Before I could turn,' he recounted, 'a sheet was dropped over my head and a rope used round my legs and arms […] I was carried a short distance and put in a car.' The unfortunate auctioneer found himself dropped in a country lane on the outskirts of Banbury, some fifty miles away. In his absence, the sale – which attracted a protest demonstration of around 100 people – was cancelled. Five hundred farmers attending an auction in Wyre Piddle, on the banks of the Avon, sent a telegram to Stanley Baldwin calling on him 'to suspend

---

[29] 'Police body guard for auctioneer in Oxfordshire', 27 June 1934, MERL, P FW PH2/T37/22.
[30] 'Farmers and Tithes', *Gloucester Citizen*, 27 Jan. 1933; 'A Tithe Challenge', *F&S*, 26 Feb. 1934; 'No Bids at Tithe Sale', *Kington Times*, 1 July 1933; 'County Tithe Payers to Fight', *Gloucester Citizen*, 23 Feb. 1933; 'Farmers and Tithe', *F&S*, 16 Jan. 1933; 'Tithe Distraint Sale Called Off', *Berks & Oxon Advertiser*, 9 June 1933; 'Tithe Tar', *WG*, 29 Sept. 1933; *Tithe*, Mar. 1934.

all distraint for tithes [...] and to instigate an enquiry into the farmers' grievances'.[31]

The campaign in Somerset coalesced during the winter of 1933–34. A 150-strong meeting addressed by Frank Allen led to the formation of a branch in Crewkerne, which adopted a policy that 'all tithepayers be recommended to withhold payment of tithe and in cases of difficulty to report the circumstances to the association for guidance and advice'.[32] Other groups were established in Yeovil and Chard, while links were built with an association in Beaminster (Dorset). Dorset also saw the formation of the Pitt-Rivers' Wessex Agricultural Defence Association. Tithepayers' associations grew throughout Devon, with particularly strong support around Bideford, Barnstaple, Tiverton and Newton Abbot.[33] The Devon association had links with a group in Wiveliscombe (just over the Somerset border). In October, Roderick Kedward travelled to Cornwall to speak at large meetings in Bodmin and Liskeard and, in January 1934, the Cornish associations came together to form a county federation.

Though rare, there were incidences when the tithe conflict extended beyond agriculture. In the South Yorkshire coalfield, the Thurnscoe Urban District Council, of which most members were miners, passed a resolution to refuse to pay tithe due to Queen Anne's Bounty on land purchased for housing and public buildings. The local official of the miners' union argued that by taking the stance local authorities could 'give support to people suffering [...] the extreme hardship and appalling injustices' of 'this iniquitous Act'.[34] In Suffolk, residents on a new housing estate close to Lowestoft pledged to resist tithe 'by every legitimate means'. They were predominantly working-class men and women whose previous homes had been condemned as unfit for habitation. Tithe due on the land had been divided up between the new housing plots and residents received demands for redemption payments. A protest meeting established the 'Small Property Owners' and Tithepayers' Association', which agreed to affiliate to the NTA. A statement pledged that townspeople would stand 'shoulder to shoulder' with farmers against 'the whole injustice of the tithe system'.[35]

31 'News from All Quarters', *Tithe, A Monthly News Sheet of Current Events and Opinions*, Jan. 1934; 'Tithe Question', *Kington Times*, 3 June 1933; 'Baronet Sues for Tithes', *Birmingham Daily Gazette*, 16 Feb. 1934; 'Auctioneer "Taken for a Ride"', *Warwick & Warwickshire Advertiser*, 4 Aug. 1934; 'Amazing Story of Tithe Kidnapping', *DHe*, 28 July 1934; '500 farmers at tithe sale', *Cheltenham Chronicle*, 24 Mar. 1934.
32 Crewkerne & District Tithepayers' Association, Minutes 1934–35, Dorset History Centre, D491/1.
33 'North Devon Association's First Annual Meeting', *NDJ*, 18 Jan. 1934.
34 'Council's Tithe Revolt', *Leeds Mercury*, 29 Nov. 1933; 'Tithe Charge', *Yorkshire Post and Leeds Intelligencer*, 20 Dec. 1933.
35 'Townsmen Open War on Tithes', *News Chronicle*, 28 Aug. 1935.

FIGURE 9. 'Save Us from these Raiding Priests': demonstration at a distraint sale at Gwersyllt Hall Farm, near Wrexham, 22 February 1933 (© Daily Herald Archive/Science Museum Group). The demonstration saw the first outing of 'The Farmers' Hymn'. A crowd of around 1,000 people forced the auctioneer to abandon the sale.

The conflict also spread into Wales. During 1933, tithepayers' federations functioned in Cardiganshire, Pembrokeshire, Monmouthshire and Denbighshire, where – as in the 1880s – the campaign was strongest. In late January, 300 farmers 'crowded' Ruthin County Court to support forty-four farmers summoned for non-payment.[36] In the following month, on 22 February, 1,000 farmers and their supporters turned out for an auction of goods seized from Richard Edwards, leader of the local tithepayers' association, who farmed at Gwersyllt Hall Farm, near Wrexham. It was the first tithe distress sale in Wales since the 1880s. A journalist reported how the auctioneer was 'surrounded by a crowd of jeering farmers, and interruptions were so frequent that eventually the sale was abandoned'. There was 'much cheering' when the auctioneer pledged not to participate in any more tithe sales 'here or anywhere else'.[37] The demonstration also saw the first outing of 'The Farmers' Hymn', which had been 'composed for the occasion':

> God save us from these raiding priests,
> Who seize our crops and steal our beasts,
> Who pray 'Give us our daily bread'
> And take it from our mouths instead.[38]

The disestablishment and disendowment of the Anglican Church meant that the tithe conflict in Wales had its particularities. Ecclesiastical tithe was collected by the Welsh Church Commission, a secular institution despite its name. Though there were no more 'raiding priests', farmers were acutely aware that a large portion of the Welsh Commission's budget went to service loans taken out to compensate the Church for its endowments and, partly, to provide compensation for parsons whose income had previously derived from tithe. In north-east Wales, the Commission continued to employ the firm of solicitors that had been used by the Church to chase farmers for tithe arrears before disestablishment.[39]

A report from the Welsh Commissioners claimed that the tithe non-payment movement in Wales was 'not indigenous'. Yet, rather contradictorily, it also noted that 'it is not without significance' that the main areas affected 'figured prominently in the Tithe Agitation of the 80s and 90s of the last century'.[40] Indeed, as in the tithe war of the 1880s, the Welsh conflict was coloured by political nonconformism and Welsh

---

36 'Welsh Farmers' Tithe', F&S, 23 Jan. 1933.
37 'Auctioneer's Promise', Western Mail, 23 Feb. 1933. See file (6 Mar. 1933) in TNA, HO 144/19199.
38 'Tithe Sale on Farm', Western Mail, 7 Mar. 1933.
39 Evidence of Mr R. F. Watkins, Denbighshire, *Royal Commission on Tithe Rentcharge, Minutes of Evidence*, 10 Jan. 1935, 303.
40 'Report of the Commissioners of Church Temporalities in Wales, 1933', CERC, ECE/SEC/TITHE/NC/4.

nationalism. R. F. Watkins, who farmed at Ruthin, was a key personality. A supporter of Plaid Genedlaethol Cymru (National Party of Wales, today's Plaid Cymru), Watkins' rhetoric earned him a reputation as a 'firebrand', which led to invitations to meetings and demonstrations in Wales and nearby English counties. In February 1934, he spoke alongside Frank Allen at an 'anti-tithe rally' of 'hundreds of farmers' in Cardigan. In March, he was the star speaker at the distraint auction in Wyre Piddle (see above). Tithepayers were, he told the crowd, 'the youngest organisation fighting against the oldest, the Church' who would 'ground down to the dust, one by one, everyone who stands up [against it]' and when 'a man was down, would stick to him like a serpent'.[41]

The transfer of Welsh ecclesiastical tithes to fund educational and community projects had been one of the demands raised by Liberal leaders of the tithe war of the late 1880s. But support for the demand had not been unanimous, with sections of the movement demanding a major reform of how tithe was calculated and some calling for its total abolition. In the 1930s, resentment remained over the fact that the 'national property' of tithe derived, almost exclusively, from payments by farmers. The NTA argued that just as it was wrong in England to ask a particular section of the population to support a national church, so it was wrong to compel Welsh tithepayers 'to contribute something over and above the common taxation' to finance universities and other cultural institutions. The University of Wales should be 'paid for by all the people according to their means', argued a policy statement.[42]

Tensions between the NFU and the NTA became particularly sharp in Wales. The legacy of the 1880s tithe war meant that the Welsh Committee of the NFU grasped the significance of the tithe issue more acutely than the NFU headquarters in London. Paradoxically, this also made the Welsh leadership more determined not to give any quarter to an autonomous tithepayers' movement. A further complication arose from the fact that the NFU's Welsh leader, Mervyn Davies, was a prominent member of the Anglican Church, serving as a lay preacher and sitting on the governing body of the Church in Wales. Instinctively hostile to the tithepayers' movement, he warned that 'unless some steps were taken [to resolve the conflict] there was a danger that it would not be possible to restrain individuals from taking unconstitutional action'. By December 1933, tithepayers' associations had made sufficient progress to prompt the NFU's Welsh Committee to seek advice from officials in London on ways to deal with 'the efforts now being made by another organisation to establish branches in Wales in connection with Tithe payment'.[43]

[41] 'Anti-Tithe Rally in Wales', *Western Mail*, 19 Feb. 1934; Distraint Sale for Tithes, *Tewkesbury Register and Agricultural Gazette*, 24 Mar. 1934.
[42] NTA Statement, 2 June 1933, quoted in 'Notes on Policy', 3 July 1935, DWPap.
[43] NFU Welsh Committee, 12 Dec. 1933, MERL, SR NFU, AD1/15.

The Tithe (Amendment) Bill

Leaders of the NFU sought to influence government policy on tithe through the Conservative Parliamentary Agricultural Committee (CPAC). Chaired by Sir Joseph Lamb, a NFU member in Staffordshire, the committee included Liberal and Labour 'national' MPs and was an influential presence on the government's backbenches.[44] In May 1932, the NFU had criticised the Conservative Parliamentary Agricultural Committee for failing to end its 'support to the obdurate attitude on the [tithe] question adopted by the minister of agriculture'. So, when in March 1933 the Committee voiced support for the union's demands for an inquiry into the workings of the 1925 Act and for legislation 'to increase the amount of [...] remission of tithe', NFU leaders regarded it as a sign that the tide had turned in parliament in favour of tithe reform. More optimism came when the backbench committee agreed to sponsor an amendment to the 1891 Tithe Act and asked the NFU to draft the legislation.[45]

On 10 March, NFU leaders presented the union's tithe committee with a proposed 'Tithe (Amendment) Bill'. Although they did not acknowledge the fact, it was a watered-down version of Kedward's Tithe Remission Bill. It would amend the 1891 Tithe Act by reducing the ceiling on tithe from two-thirds to one-third of the rental value of land. (Kedward's bill had proposed 15 per cent.)[46] Three of the four NTA members on the tithe committee expressed support for the proposed bill, a stance that prompted the fury of Frank Allen. He told Mobbs, who had remained opposed, that though it contained 'a portion' of NTA policy, 'the bill would fail to satisfy a large section of tithepayers'.[47] A few months later, the Conservative Parliamentary Agricultural Committee agreed to sponsor a Tithe (Amendment) Bill – essentially a watered-down version of the NFU's draft bill – in the House of Commons as a private member's bill. The Committee hoped that Elliot and the government would adopt it, or – at the very least – that the proposed legislation would increase pressure on ministers to introduce measures of their own. Symbolically, the MP chosen to propose the bill was William Spens, who had entered parliament in March after defeating Roderick Kedward in a by-election in the Ashford constituency.

Kedward's failure to win back his Ashford seat was a setback for the NTA. He stood in the election as an 'Independent Liberal', pledging to sit on the opposition benches as a 'constructive critic' of the government. Tithe was a major issue throughout the campaign. Kedward presented himself as someone 'who had given his time and fought the battle, at times

---

[44] *The Times*, 5 Oct. 1931, reported a membership of 138 MPs, a number which would increase substantially after the General Election later that month.
[45] 'Tithe Act Amendment', *F&S*, 5 Mar. 1934.
[46] NFU 'Report of Tithe Committee', 10 Mar. 1933, MERL, SR NFU, AD1/15.
[47] Allen to Mobbs, 17 Mar. 1933, Mobbs Papers.

overwhelmed by scorn and contempt'; Spens, standing on the Conservative ticket, pledged to 'use his influence to get the question reconsidered in a constitutional and proper manner'.[48] Tithepayers' associations sent messages of support to Kedward, hoping he would be returned to parliament 'to fight [their] battles'.[49] But Kedward's prospects were weakened by wider issues, as well as the general decline in support for the Liberal Party. Spens campaigned for a programme of selective tariffs, while Kedward continued to oppose restrictions on trade, an unpopular policy in farming communities. Kedward also faced an energetic challenge from the Labour Party, whose candidate, William Beck, reminded voters of his Liberal opponent's support for the National Government in 1931.[50] Labour, which had not stood a candidate in the 1931 general election, polled 18.4 per cent, while Kedward saw his vote fall from 41 to 34 per cent.

The election campaign left Spens in little doubt about the strength of feeling over tithe in east Kent. Moving the Tithe (Amendment) Bill on 26 July, he spoke of 'a growing movement against the payment of tithe, in the form of passive resistance, [...] auction sales made completely abortive [and] agents of tithe owners making forays under cover of dawn – reminiscent of border forays in the Middle Ages'.[51] The bill proposed to make tithe remission automatic, rather than requiring an application to the county court as under the 1891 Act. But, in an unsuccessful attempt to win ministerial support, the Conservative Parliamentary Agricultural Committee had adopted, rather than the NFU's proposal of remission once tithe reached one-third of the value of land, an alternative suggestion from the Central Chamber of Agriculture that substituted the higher figure of one-half. As a result, the NFU distanced itself from the bill. The NTA rejected it out of hand. How to respond to the NFU's initial draft may have led to differences amongst leaders of the association, but all were united in their opposition to Spens' bill. Allen wrote to *The Times* to criticise it, contrasting the more favourable provisions of Kedward's Tithe Remission Bill. Local tithepayers' associations described it as 'hopelessly inadequate and wrong in principle'.[52]

The NTA's response to the bill reflected a change of policy within the association. In January 1931, the association had rejected tithe abolition as an immediate practical policy, adopting instead the aim of outlawing 'excessive tithe' by campaigning around Kedward's bill. In June 1933, the NTA Council reversed this position. It agreed that prioritising the aim

---

[48] 'Prospect of Lively By-election Fights', *KM*, 4 Mar. 1933.
[49] 'County Tithe Payers to Fight', *Gloucester Citizen*, 23 Feb. 1933; Suffolk TPA, Minutes of Second Annual Meeting, 28 Feb. 1933, SuRO, GC32/1.
[50] 'Four-Cornered Fight in Kent By-Election', *KM*, 25 Feb. 1933.
[51] HC Deb., *Hansard*, 26 July 1933.
[52] F. R. Allen, 'Tithe Remission Bill', *The Times*, 14 Aug. 1933; 'Tithe Payers' Protest', *Hampshire Telegraph & Post*, 6 Oct. 1933.

of tithe remission was now 'inadequate as an expression of the views of tithepayers as a body'.[53] The objective of the NTA now became, in the words of Frank Allen, 'the alteration of the law so as to bring the tithe system to an end'.[54]

Based on measures introduced in 1903 to phase out tithe in Denmark, the new policy advocated the government buy out the titheowners and contribute to a compensation package to secure the life interests of clergy who derived income from tithe. Tithepayers would make annual payments to the state for around twenty years, but their level would be regulated by the principles of the Tithe Remission Bill, meaning that tithe would be around one-half of its previous level.[55] It was in many senses an insightful policy, anticipating elements of the (far less radical) Royal Commission's report that would be published in 1936. Some in the tithepayers' movement disagreed with the new policy. Michael McCreagh argued that the NTA's priority should remain focused on the 'restriction of excessive tithe' and 'the passing of the Tithe Remission Bill'. He began to criticise the NTA for its 'defiant attitude'. Defiance, he said, was 'no substitute for reason [and] creates hostility instead of understanding'.[56] As leader of the Tithe League and editor of *The Tithepayer*, McCreagh reflected the views of some landowners, who were concerned about the level of tithe but either supported, or remained ambivalent over, the principle of tithe.[57]

Three reasons underpinned the NTA's policy shift. First, the tithepayers' movement had spread into areas in which tithe was relatively light. In these regions, the measures outlined in the Tithe Remission Bill would have little, if any, impact on the level of tithe demands. Yet farmers still held grievances over the permanent setting of tithe at £105 and over compulsory redemption at prices in excess of tithe's market value. Secondly, the development of specialised forms of agriculture – poultry farming, fruit for canning – had led to significant investments of capital, which tended to increase the value of land and would, accordingly, decrease the amount of remission offered by the bill. These tithepayers, concluded the NTA, thought it 'unfair that the position of the titheowners should be improved by the expenditure of the tithepayers' capital'.[58] Finally, and most significantly, the policy shift reflected a radicalisation of the tithepayers' movement. Seizures of stock and furniture, the intransigence of government and Queen Anne's Bounty, the heavy-handed

---

53 Statement agreed at NTA National Council, 22 June 1933; NTA, Notes on Policy, 3 July 1935, DWPap.
54 'Suffolk Tithepayers' Association', *DiEx*, 2 Mar. 1934.
55 NTA, 'Resolution of Council, 5 April 1930' (the date is an error – the meeting took place in 1933), KHLC, EK/U1276/B4/105.
56 'A Defiant Attitude', *The Tithepayer*, Jan. 1937.
57 *The Tithepayer*, July 1935, 1.
58 NTA, 'Resolution of Council'.

activities of General Dealers and the mobilisation of large numbers of police not only heightened a sense of bitterness but had the effect of raising the stakes of the conflict. A few years earlier, most in the tithepayers' movement had probably viewed tithe as primarily a financial problem, but the experience of the conflict had led many to consider its history and to draw the conclusion that it was the nature of tithe that was at the root of the problem. As the NTA council put it, many tithepayers 'are now declaring that the only result which would satisfy them [...] would be the abolition of the tithe altogether. Some evidently feel that the arbitrary and shifty methods of the titheowners, especially Queen Anne's Bounty, would justify their being deprived of the tithe altogether.'[59] For the NTA leaders, 'victory' was no longer a more generous scheme of tithe remission but achieving the removal 'once and for all [...] the shackles' of a charge with 'no moral foundation'. In early 1930, Kedward had argued that such an objective would be unable to win broad support, but his rhetoric at demonstrations and meetings had become progressively radical, at times recalling that of Albert Bath, fifty years earlier:

> We have drawn the sword [...] and it is never to be sheaved until victory is completely ours. [...] They have driven us to the only method by which success must ultimately come. [...] There is no other way but to [...] fill up every County Court in the land with orders which it is impossible for them to execute and that when they bludgeon one man down you will come to his aid and lift him up again. I think if we pursue that course, we shall win through.[60]

The law of contempt

As it radicalised, the authorities increasingly used the law to try to thwart the tithepayers' movement. In January 1933, during his meeting with Primrose (representing General Dealers), Sir Ernley Blackwell (the assistant under-secretary of state at the Home Office) promised that the government would encourage 'proceedings against the persons responsible for organising the opposition'. He referred to steps recently taken against leaders of the Hunger Marches and spoke of taking a similar hard-line approach against the tithepayers' movement. 'It should not be difficult,' he said, 'to obtain evidence against those responsible for collecting a mob whose purpose is by forcible means to prevent the legal removal of goods.'[61] In November 1932, 3,000 police and 800 special

[59] Ibid.
[60] 'Anti-Tithe Demonstration at Diss', *DiEx*, 2 Mar. 1934. See also Kedward's speech published in Wallace, *The Tithe War*, 146–57.
[61] General Dealers Limited. Memorandum of interview with Sir E Blackwell, 18.1.33, CERC, ECE/SEC/TITHE/GD/5.

constables had mobilised to prevent the unemployed workers' movement presenting a petition to parliament. When violence broke out, forty-two demonstrators were arrested and, subsequently, four leaders of the movement were imprisoned, including the 76-year-old Tom Mann.[62]

In comparison with their handling of working-class protest movements, the authorities treated the farmers' activists in a gentler fashion. At first, the strategy was to bring contempt proceedings against those disrupting distraint proceedings. In March 1933, the aborted auction at Gwersyllt Hall Farm (Denbighshire) was considered a serious setback by both titheowners and the Home Office (see above). Representatives of General Dealers had travelled to the auction with the attention of bidding, but the size of the crowd forced the company to keep a low profile. In an affidavit, one of its representatives claimed that the auctioneer had warned that 'if he was proposing to bid, he felt alarmed for his safety'.[63] After the auction, Blackwell advised Primrose to apply to the courts for a Rule Nisi 'to show cause why [Edwards, the farmer] should not be committed for contempt of court'. The two men 'hoped that [the outcome would] result in proving an effective deterrent'.[64] The Rule Nisi was granted in a divisional court on 6 March and made absolute in the High Court on 20 March. But the judges agreed to leave the writ 'on the table' for a week to give Edwards time to settle his tithe, which – facing possible imprisonment – he did, along with paying considerable costs and his own legal bill.[65] At the Home Office, the outcome was viewed as extremely encouraging. A note suggested that the case 'may have considerable effect in putting an end to tithe disturbances' and agreed to recommend that Queen Anne's Bounty and Ecclesiastical Commissioners should threaten tithe resisters with 'similar action'.[66]

Yet the next attempted use of contempt law was not so successful. It concerned events at Delvyns Farm, Gestingthorpe (Essex), owned by Margaret Gardiner (a farm which in August 1933 saw an intervention from the British Union of Fascists). On 22 May 1933, a buyer from Wales, accompanied by a solicitor, a bailiff and a small group of men with a lorry, arrived to collect goods and produce that had been distrained for tithe of £48 6s owed to the local rector. Their arrival had been anticipated by the Essex Tithepayers' Association and, when the buyer's party entered the barn in which the stock had been impounded, they were followed by sixty people, while another 200 demonstrated outside. According to an affidavit from the solicitor, the crowd did not allow the buyer to check the goods and

---

[62] Peter Kingsford, *The Hunger Marchers in Britain 1920–1940* (London: Lawrence & Wishart, 1982), 129–65.
[63] 'Contempt Alleged', *Gloucester Citizen*, 7 Mar. 1933.
[64] R. Primrose to Sir Ernley Blackwell, 6 Mar. 1933, TNA, HO 144/19199.
[65] 'Law Report March 6', 'Law Report, March 20' and 'Law Report, March 27', *The Times*, 7, 11 and 28 Mar. 1933.
[66] 'File on Edwards case 6.3.33'. TNA, HO 144/19199.

insisted that he accept a cash payment as settlement. When this was refused, he and the bailiff were 'struck by rotten eggs' and became worried that 'grave bodily injury' might be inflicted on them. Police arrived 'to rescue' the party, who had been 'imprisoned' in the barn for nearly three hours.[67] Prompted by the Home Office, the rector began legal proceedings and on 31 May the King's Bench ordered a Rule Nisi for contempt against Gardiner and two leaders of the Essex Tithepayers' Association, Frederick Krailing and Frederick Smith, who were accused of 'interfering with and inciting others' to obstruct a court order. Yet two months later (25 July), three High Court judges discharged the Rule Nisi on the basis of insufficient evidence.[68] The ruling provoked the fury of Sir John Gilmour, the home secretary. He told his officials that 'when so glaring a case occurs of intimidation and obstruction, I think that recourse should be had to every available procedure for the purpose of making it well known to farmers that conduct of this sort is punishable by law.'[69] Following his cue, police identified thirty-six demonstrators and charged them with unlawful assembly. Those charged were members of the Gardiner family, the two officers of the Essex Tithepayers' Association and thirty local farmers, including Evelyn Balfour, who had recently been elected to the executive of the Suffolk Tithepayers' Association.[70] In early July General Dealers, accompanied by a contingent of forty police officers, had seized eight cows from her farm despite, in the words of the police report, '100 people there doing what they could to frustrate our efforts'.[71]

In November, the presence of 'Lady Eve' in the dock at Essex County Assizes helped to ensure that the Gestingthorpe trial received extensive coverage in the national press. Most publicity was sympathetic to the farmers, the *Daily Express* even establishing a 'defence fund'.[72] Twenty-nine defendants, including Balfour, were acquitted by order of the judge for lack of evidence. Amongst the seven found guilty were three members of the Gardiner family and the two officers of the Essex Tithepayers' Association. In bringing in the guilty verdicts, the jury 'strongly recommended the defendants to mercy'. In his summing up, the judge denounced 'the evil thing' by which people 'take the law into their own hands and should by collective numbers coerce people against whom they think they have a grievance'. Sentencing, he expressed

---

[67] 'The Tithe War', *BuFP*, 10 June 1933.
[68] 'Law Report, July 25', *The Times*, 26 July 1933.
[69] Note by Gilmour in file on 'Tithe Distress at Delvyns Farm, Gestingthorpe', TNA, HO 144/19199.
[70] Suffolk TPA, Minutes of Second Annual Meeting, 28 Feb. 1933, SuRO, GC32/1.
[71] George Staunton to F. A. Newsam, 6 July 1933, TNA, HO 144/19199.
[72] 'Harvest Interrupts a Tithe War Charge against 36 Farmers' & '36 Farmers on Unlawful Assembly Charge', *DEx*, 2 Aug. and 10 Oct. 1933.

'considerable sympathy' for the Gardiner family but reserved barbed words for the 'ringleaders' of the tithepayers' association, who were 'interfering in matters in which they themselves had no actual interest'. In terms of sentence, however, he was lenient: all seven defendants were bound over for two years against the sum of £10.[73]

Legal quagmire

The judiciary's role in the tithe war was not without its contradictions. Judges were often outspoken in condemning 'unconstitutional behaviour' and the influence of 'agitators'. In the High Court and Court of Appeal, a series of judgements interpreted the law in ways that enhanced the rights of titheowners and restrained opportunities for the tithepayers' movement to hamper the recovery process. Yet, other judges – particularly those in county courts – expressed sympathy for tithepayers, stating apologetically that their role was to uphold the law, not to defend its rationality. Some judges were bold enough to criticise openly the government's handling of tithe. At the annual dinner of the Norwich, Yarmouth and Lowestoft Chamber of Commerce, Judge Herbert-Smith proposed a toast to the minister of agriculture, who was present as a guest speaker. He told Elliot that the tithe question had 'assumed alarming proportions'. The men on whom he was having to serve distraint orders were 'smarting under a feeling that they were not getting fair play' and the issue was 'eating like a canker into the social life of this part of the country'.[74] Magistrates were sometimes even more explicit in showing affinity with tithepayers. When in September 1933 those arrested for participating in the protest at Gestingthorpe appeared for committal proceedings at Castle Hedingham Police Court, one of the six justices on the bench told them that he and his colleagues 'had been placed in a very unhappy position in hearing this charge against our friends and neighbours'.[75]

During 1933, county courts granted a total of 7,174 distraint orders to titheowners, on top of 5,865 the previous year. In comparison, in the years before the Great War the figure had averaged at around 600.[76] Many county court judges expressed frustration over problems the large number of distraint applications were presenting for the running of their courts. They began to scrutinise the paperwork accompanying distraint applications and on a number of occasions refused to issue orders on account of errors or technicalities. One embarrassing case for Queen Anne's Bounty was when Judge Randolph at Wallingford County Court

[73] 'Tithe Dispute Case', *The Times*, 7 Nov. 1933.
[74] 'Judge's Tithe Pleas to Minister', *Suffolk & Essex Free Press*, 29 Mar. 1934.
[75] '36 Farmers for Trial after Tithe Scene', *DEx*, 6 Sept. 1933.
[76] 'Statement of Evidence submitted by the Lord Chancellor's Office', *Royal Commission on Tithe Rentcharge, Minutes of Evidence*, 627.

Pressures for a Settlement

twice threw out an application for an order against Vernon Drewitt, chairman of the Berks, Bucks & Oxon Tithepayers' Association. Queen Anne's Bounty's documentation had included incorrect field numbers and a demand for tithe on land owned by another farmer. After ridiculing Drewitt's defence that tithe was 'legalised robbery', the judge went on to describe Queen Anne's Bounty's request for a distraint order as 'legalised robbery of another kind'.[77] The Queen Anne's Bounty office lamented that 'in normal times' demands for court orders against tithepayers had often contained 'small inaccuracies – or even big ones' and this 'seldom had serious results'. But now 'the anti-tithe people are supplied with funds and with adequate legal advice, and are carefully watching our every move with a view to opposing us if the smallest chance be given.'[78]

In fact, titheowners had far greater access to funds and legal expertise than the tithepayers' movement, as well as a history of recourse to litigation.[79] During 1933, Queen Anne's Bounty, the Ecclesiastical Commissioners and King's College, Cambridge instructed lawyers to challenge a series of county court rulings in the High Court and Court of Appeal. The cases well illustrate the archaic nature of tithe law: barristers and judges found themselves citing not only case law from *Halsbury's Laws of England*, but also referring to pages from the Book of Leviticus in the Old Testament. On one occasion, the court debated the significance of a Statute passed during the reign of Henry III and how to translate the Norman French expression *Bestes ke gaignent sa terre*.[80]

Six test cases were eventually settled – all in favour of the titheowners. A case in October 1934 was over whether or not titheowners were entitled to apply for a second distress when a sale of seized goods failed to raise sufficient funds to cover the tithe. The litigation concerned events at Hyde Farm near Fordingbridge (Hampshire). In October 1932, bailiffs had impounded three ricks of hay from the farm and, after 'anti-tithe activity' made an auction impossible, the hay was put out for sale by tender. Despite having a value of £150, the highest bid was only £10, and that was from Tom Spicer, the farmer who owed the tithe. In November 1933, the titheowners – King's College, Cambridge and Queen Anne's Bounty – went to court for a second distraint order. The application was rejected by judges in county courts in Ringwood (January 1934) and Bournemouth (April), on the basis that the 1891 Tithe Act did not provide

---

[77] 'Wallingford Tithe Case', *Berks & Oxon Advertiser*, 19 May 1933; 'Wallingford County Court', *Berks & Oxon Advertiser*, 19 May 1933.
[78] QAB, 'Appendix B. Procedure for recovery' and 'Appendix A. General remarks', 30 May 1933, CERC, QAB/2/1/50.
[79] 'Legal Records', CERC, QAB/5.
[80] 'Law Report, Oct 13', *The Times*, 14 Oct. 1933; 'High Court of Justice', *The Times*, 30 Nov. 1933.

for more than one distress.[81] Elsewhere, however, county courts were making contradictory rulings: in June 1934, a second distress was ordered on the farm owned by Roderick Kedward, after a sale of seized goods raised only £32 of the £100 owed to the Ecclesiastical Commissioners.[82] Hearing the case at the Court of Appeal was Lord Justice Henry Slesser, who – it will be remembered – had, while a Labour MP during the parliamentary debate on the 1925 Tithe Bill, spoken strongly in defence of the clergy's 'absolute right to tithe'. Since then, Slesser had moved further to the right, condemning the 1926 General Strike and speaking out against women's rights, before being appointed by Ramsay MacDonald in 1929 to the Court of Appeal.[83] Announcing his judgement in favour of the titheowners, Slesser noted Spicer's membership of 'an organisation for opposing the payment of tithes and for preventing the sale of goods taken in distress', and added that 'if that were a correct statement of its objects [the tithepayers' association] was nothing more than an illegal organisation and a conspiracy to break the law'.[84]

Another dispute settled in the Court of Appeal centred on whether tithepayers were entitled to receive notice from titheowners of intention to distrain. The case concerned attempts by Queen Anne's Bounty to collect tithe from Ernest Thorne of Coombe Bissett (Wiltshire). In February 1933, bailiffs entered his farmhouse without warning and placed a distress order on items of furniture. The county court judge granted an application to sell the furniture by tender, but Thorne won an appeal in the divisional court, which ruled that the 1836 and 1891 Tithe Acts stipulated ten days' notice of distraint. When the case reached the Court of Appeal in March 1934, judges ruled that there was no obligation to serve notice. Slesser was again on the bench, but the senior judge on this occasion was Master of the Rolls, Sir Ernest Pollock, brother of a prominent member of the Queen Anne's Bounty tithe committee, the bishop of Norwich, Bertram Pollock.[85]

The third test case also arose from the Thorne distraint: whether or not household contents could be seized for tithe non-payment. Titheowners knew that the threat to seize furniture was probably the most effective way to pressurise a farmer to pay. The police also encouraged the practice: it was logistically easier to support operations to remove sideboards and chairs than those to remove livestock or crops. But distress orders on furniture were controversial, often leading to unfavourable publicity for the Church. The tithepayers' movement

[81] 'Tithe Rent Tangle', *WG*, 20 Apr. 1934.
[82] 'Second Distress in Tithe Cases', *The Times*, 5 June 1934.
[83] S. M. Cretney, 'Slesser [*formerly* Schloesser], Sir Henry Herman (1883–1979)', *ODNB* (2008).
[84] 'Court of Appeal', *The Times*, 19 Oct. 1934.
[85] 'Law Report, 12 Mar., *The Times*, 13 Mar. 1934.

protested vigorously that they were not only unethical but unlawful, because tithe related historically to the fruits of the land and not to personal effects. In October 1933, the High Court settled the issue by ruling that titheowners were entitled to 'distrain anything that was on the land and which was not specifically exempt by some statute', a definition that included property within a farmhouse.[86]

The fourth legal dispute arose over whether or not tithepayers were entitled to protection against 'oppressive distress'. The NTA argued that those facing distress for tithe non-payment should possess the same rights as tenants facing distress for rent arrears. Under the 1601 Poor Law Act certain items were 'privileged' from distress, including clothes, bedding and, most significantly, 'tools or implements of trade'. In November 1933, three farmers from Kent (one from Kingsnorth, two from New Romney) sued the county court bailiff for serving a distraint order on working horses, milking cows and sheep. Their lawyers claimed that the animals were 'privileged' from distress because other goods and implements on the farms were available at the time.[87] A High Court judge found that the distraint on one of the horses, which had been pulling a cart at the time, was wrong under common law. But he rejected the substance of the farmers' case, deciding that on all other matters the bailiffs had acted legally. He ruled that distress for non-payment of tithe could not be compared to landlord's distress and that 'the rule of law laid down in the ancient statutes did not apply to it'.[88]

The two final issues settled in the High Court arose from decisions made by A. F. Clements, a judge on the Kent circuit who had on several occasions expressed empathy for the tithepayers' cause. In November 1932, he told farmers crowded into a session of Canterbury county court that 'it was a great pity' that 'some sort of moratorium' could not be arranged with the titheowners.[89] During 1933, Clements voiced concern at the 'piling up' of unexecuted distress orders in the courts under his jurisdiction. Considering applications for 180 orders in early May at Ashford county court, he complained that the accumulation of orders had created an inordinate amount of work and there was 'not the staff to deal with them'. 'It was,' he said, 'becoming impossible, owing to the number of cases, to administer the law.'[90]

The judge began to turn down applications on two grounds. First, he ruled that the 1836 and 1891 Tithe Acts stipulated that applicants could recover only tithe that was due in a two-year period before the distress.

[86] 'Law Report, Oct 12' and 'Law Report, Oct. 13', *The Times*, 13 and 14 Oct. 1933.
[87] 'Tithe test actions brought by three Kent farmers', *KM*, 2 Dec. 1933.
[88] 'High Court of Justice', *The Times*, 30 Nov. 1933.
[89] 'Elham Farmers and the Tithe', *DE*, 11 Nov. 1932.
[90] 'The Tithe War', *DE*, 5 May 1933; 'Judge and Tithe Cases', *Daily Telegraph*, 3 May 1933.

Arrears of more than two years were accordingly not recoverable. This decision threatened to undermine an essential element of the Bounty's collection strategy. The 'hard cases' policy of investigating farmers' circumstances meant inevitably a delay, normally of several months but sometimes longer. In addition, Queen Anne's Bounty had twice (in June 1931 and May 1932) put a halt on enforcing distress orders while it reconsidered its strategy – a decision that had created further delays in the recovery process. By the end of 1933, the majority of farmers participating in the non-payment campaign would have owed tithe going back further than two years. The Bounty complained that, in Kent alone, the judge's ruling meant it would not be able to recover outstanding tithe in around 1,100 cases. The test case involved a tithepayer who owed a total of one and a half years' tithe in the period before October 1931. Clements had granted a court order for payment in May 1932, but in November 1933 he refused Queen Anne's Bounty's request that it be enforced, ruling that it was outside the time limit. The High Court heard the case in January 1934 and overturned the judge's decision. The court ruled that the reference to two years in the Tithe Acts stipulated a ceiling on the quantity of tithe that could be recovered during a distress, rather than limiting the time after which a distress could be ordered.[91]

A second ruling by Judge Clements posed more problems for the titheowners' recovery strategy. In November 1932, he insisted that applications for orders in his courts should include the names of bailiffs who would enforce the distress. He announced that the court registrar would no longer appoint bailiffs because, first, it had become 'impossible owing to the number of cases' and, secondly, because hostility to tithe meant that 'they could not get a man to act as bailiff unless he had wider protection'.[92] On 19 May 1933, Clements turned down thirty-five distress orders from Queen Anne's Bounty for failing to provide names of bailiffs. 'Unless, and until the titheowners bring before me some person approved and able and willing to carry out the Court's order, I shall refuse to exercise my discretionary power in all cases,' he told the court.[93] The High Court heard an appeal from Queen Anne's Bounty on 27 July. Lawyers for Clements explained the problems arising from 664 unexecuted distress orders for unpaid tithe in courts on his circuit. The High Court judges 'sympathised very much' with his position but ruled that the Tithe Acts stipulated that county court judges had no alternative but to make the orders when requested.[94]

[91] 'Law Report, Jan. 30', *The Times*, 31 Jan. 1934.
[92] 'Tithe Agitation will Stop', *Whitstable Times and Tankerton Press*, 6 May 1933.
[93] 'Judge Refuses Tithe Order', *Folkestone Herald*, 20 May 1933.
[94] 'High Court of Justice', *The Times*, 28 July 1933.

Pressures for a Settlement

Blockage in the recovery system

On 12 October 1933, Middleton gave an optimistic briefing on the tithe situation to the archbishop of Canterbury. Three factors had, he suggested, led to an 'improvement' in tithe collection: a stabilisation in wheat prices, the 'hard cases' policy, and the action taken by General Dealers, which had been utilised against '106 cases of flagrant defiance [and] had no failure'. Middleton argued that the Church should continue to resist calls for legislation, which were arriving not only from the farming lobby but also from figures in the justice system. Policy 'must still be to deal with individual cases rather than change the present law', he told the archbishop.[95]

Middleton deployed a fair amount of sophistry to make his case. Certainly, the total amount of tithe coming into the Bounty's coffers had increased (by around 7.5 per cent) and, equally true, this increase was largely a result of the investigation policy. Between the summer of 1932 and October 1933, Queen Anne's Bounty had 'investigated' 3,150 'hard cases' and, by offering concessions of 10 or sometimes 20 per cent, managed to reach agreement with 1,400 farmers. But included in the total collected was a substantial backlog of arrears from those farmers who made payments after an investigation. Moreover, while 1,400 farmers agreed to settle under the 'hard cases' policy, 1,750 (a majority) had failed to do so, despite in most cases being offered a concession.[96]

Particularly uncomfortable for Middleton were the criticisms of the efficacy of the 'hard cases' policy arriving from those in the front line of tithe collection. The Bounty's collection convenor for Norfolk reported that 'the policy adopted ha[d] not brought the money in as expected'. The convenor for Kent said that 'although in large numbers of cases a concession has been offered, the response has not been satisfactory.' Collectors in Berkshire, Oxford, East Sussex, Wiltshire and Dorset reported 'the failure of response in many cases to offers of concession', which they put down to 'the policy of the tithepayers' association'. The convenor for Cambridgeshire argued that the 'hard cases' policy was playing into the hands of the tithepayers' movement, warning that applications for concessions were 'being made in large and rapidly increasing numbers' and would 'if not checked […] paralyse efficient collection'.[97] A Queen Anne's Bounty 'position paper' admitted that tithe arrears were still

---

[95] 'Tithe Situation 12th October 1933. Statement by Mr George Middleton at Queen Anne's Bounty', LPL, Lang 71.
[96] Ibid.
[97] Queen Anne's Bounty, Report of joint meeting of Chairmen and Convenors of Area Collection Committees with members of the QAB Tithe Committee, 30 May 1933, Appendix A, c) Investigation of Cases of Hardship, QAB Tithe Committee, 30 May 1933, CERC, QAB/2/1/50.

increasing because of the 'belief on the part of many occupying owners that the recovery of tithe by process of law had broken down'.[98]

Middleton's claims about the success of General Dealers were also exaggerated. There is little doubt that the imminent threat of its deployment often encouraged farmers to settle. Between January 1933 and November 1934, the control committee handed the company the files of 369 non-payment cases.[99] Of these, 218 farmers paid their tithe before a distraint sale was enacted, often after receiving a concession.[100] Yet the successes achieved by General Dealers represent a fraction of the task at hand. In January 1933 there were 2,495 unexecuted orders for recovery of tithe owed to Queen Anne's Bounty. By the end of June, the number had risen to 4,902 and by May 1934 it had increased further to 5,557. Kent was the county with the highest number of unexecuted orders (1,232), followed by Suffolk (1,224) and Essex (815). There were significant numbers (over 100) in Sussex, Norfolk, Hampshire, Devon, Berkshire, Wiltshire, Cambridgeshire, Shropshire, Oxfordshire and Herefordshire.[101]

From a propaganda viewpoint, the high-profile distraint seizures had often been counterproductive. Rather than encouraging tithepayers to settle their debts, as was the intention, they served to galvanise support for the tithepayers' movement. For example, the Wortham operation in February 1934 had technically and logistically been a total success: sufficient stock was seized to cover the outstanding tithe and the rights of the titheowner were 'vindicated'. Yet, in reputational terms, the affair was a disaster. Throughout east Suffolk and south Norfolk, middle-class voices expressed disgust at the behaviour of Queen Anne's Bounty. Eric Wolton, a lay reader and chair of the parochial church council in Burgate, said that 'coming from a church-loving family he [had] never dreamt the church would allow such methods to be put into operation'. He had written to the rural dean and bishop 'telling them what he thought of the treatment meted out to Mr Rash'.[102]

Middleton placed the blame for the 'very numerous outstanding tithe orders' on failings by the county courts and their officials. He argued that the lord chancellor's office should tighten the rules of recovery and provide more support to court officials to ensure that they were able to

---

[98] 'Tithe: The Views of Queen Anne's Bounty', 31 July 1933, CERC, ECE/SEC/TITHE/GD/5.

[99] 'Tithe Situation 12th October 1933. Statement by Mr George Middleton ', LPL, Lang 71.

[100] Cases approved by the Control Commission (QAB or EC cases) for release of orders for recovery of tithe rentcharge. Position reached 2 November 1934, CERC, ECE/SEC/TITHE/GD/5.

[101] 'Tithe: The Views of Queen Anne's Bounty', 31 July 1933, CERC, ECE/SEC/TITHE/GD/5; 'Statement of Evidence submitted by the Lord Chancellor's Office', *Royal Commission on Tithe Rentcharge, Minutes of Evidence* , 622.

[102] 'Wortham Tithe "War"', *DiEx*, 23 Feb. 1934.

fulfil their duty. To support his case, he asked the directors of General Dealers, Captain Parlour and Major Miller, to prepare a report of problems involving court officials, bailiffs and possession men.[103] Failings in four areas were identified. The first was a tendency for bailiffs employed by the courts to seize 'unsuitable goods when suitable goods were available'. Nine examples were given, including: 'the worst cows out of a herd [being] seized' (Donhead St Mary, Wiltshire); 'pigs seized without their troughs (Wortham, Suffolk); 'grain seized without the bags in which it was contained (Ubbeston, Suffolk); 'cow seized uncleaned after calving' (Pluckley, Kent); 'ricks of unsaleable course hay in the middle of a growing cornfield seized' (West Grinstead); 'chaff-cutter no better than scrap iron seized' (Bryngwyn, Ceredigion). Often, the value of seized stock and possessions failed to cover the amount in the court order.

A second problem was the widely differing interpretations of recovery law. Difficulties signalled included: delays because 'the wife and children of the landowner claimed the goods belonged to them'; 'trouble' because 'animals seized were not properly marked' or 'properly impounded with the result that they strayed or were moved'; and 'questions [...] with regard to the feeding and watering of animals impounded'. In short, the report concluded, 'county court officials do not as a rule seem to have a clear idea of the law relating to distress for tithe'.

The third issue was more fundamental. According to Parlour and Miller, many bailiffs were simply 'unsuitable for their task'. The problem was not just their general 'lack of knowledge' but in 'about a third of the cases, the relationship between the distraining officer and the owner of the land upon which the distraint was levied was, to say the least of it, friendly'. As a result, they tended to follow 'blindly the suggestions, often quite unsuitable' made by the tithepayer.[104] One example given was of a part-time official who worked also as 'a dealer in old clothes, his customers largely comprising of farmers' wives'. The report advocated a 'central staff of skilled officers who could be temporarily attached as and when required to particular Courts'.

The final issue was the role of 'possession men' – agents appointed by the court registrar to watch over impounded stock during the period between the execution of distraint and the stock's sale and removal from the farm. Paid 7s a day (a little more than a farm labourer), sleeping in barns and outhouses and often known to the farmer whose goods they were guarding, theirs was an unglamorous and unpopular role. Often, possession men were at the receiving end of ridicule from the local community or became the focus of protests. Sometimes, the stock they were guarding vanished from under their nose. In Frittenden (Kent), the local press reported an

---

[103] 'Draft Report by Captain Parlour and Major Miller', n.d. (1934), CERC, ECE/SEC/TITHE/P9.
[104] Ibid.

'amazing midnight happening' at Parsonage Farm: 'The village street was blocked with cars, and fifty farmers descended on [the] farm [...] Shadowy figures with sacks glided by [...] The pigs and bullocks, which had been impounded for tithe, disappeared ... and nobody knows where they are!'[105] In such cases, animals marked for removal would be mixed with other livestock, sometimes on the farm of a neighbouring farmer, making it difficult for the authorities to ascertain which had been marked for sale.

On rare occasions, pranks aimed at possession men got out of hand. In June 1932 at the Wingham petty sessions, a farmer and three young farm labourers pleaded guilty to assault and incitement to assault after an incident on a farm at Great Mongeham (Kent). Speaking of 'a most cowardly and brutal attack on a defenceless man', the prosecutor described how the possession man had been sitting in the scullery when the men came in and 'placed a scarf around his neck'. They 'took him through the yard, into the cowshed, across the road and there they were disgusting enough to throw him into a cesspool'. When the unfortunate man emerged 'with clothing ruined', the farmer, Frederick Solley, a committee member of the East Kent Tithepayers Association, told him 'You are lucky to have got off with what you have got'.[106] Parlour and Miller cited another case in Devon:

> Two men were put in possession and for several days stuck to their post though surrounded by a crowd of about 100 farmers and sympathisers who although they did not actually molest them did everything possible to make their position untenable; they prevented sleep by constantly rotating a milk can containing weights; the room they occupied was constantly entered, windows opened, fire made to smoke, feed and water supplies were cut off. Eventually the men were forced to abandon the distress.

The report recommended that 'sufficient numbers' of possession men should be recruited and provided with police protection: they should be 'carefully selected', 'not drawn from the locality' and receive a more appropriate remuneration.[107]

The General Dealers' report formed the basis of a policy document drawn up by titheowners (Queen Anne's Bounty, Ecclesiastical Commissioners, Welsh Church Commissioners, Oxford and Cambridge tithe-owning colleges and representatives of private titheowners). Sent to the lord chancellor's office, it argued for urgent action to reinforce the rules surrounding tithe recovery, clearer guidance and more effective training for court staff and bailiffs and measures to obtain 'more

[105] 'Midnight Swoop on Kent Farm', KM, 31 Mar. 1934.
[106] 'Tithe Bailiff Thrown in Cesspool', DE, 17 June 1932.
[107] 'Draft Report by Captain Parlour and Major Miller', n.d. (1934), CERC, ECE/SEC/TITHE/P9.

suitable possession men'. The titheowners were, however, careful not to suggest legislation. To do so would have undermined their contention that the 1925 Act had been 'a permanent and final settlement' of the tithe problem. 'The solution of the problem of the effective collection of tithe rentcharge lies almost wholly with the County Courts and their officials,' they argued.[108]

The lord chancellor had drawn different conclusions. Sankey viewed the issue as one of archaic laws that had proved impotent when faced with a mass non-payment campaign. Tithe law was, he argued, 'cumbrous and expensive' and 'bristled with points of doubt', with no fewer than fifty-eight county court rules affecting the recovery procedure. Most particularly, the 'peculiar' practice of distress was not fit for purpose. The series of cases in the High Court and the blockages in the county court recovery system confirmed the necessity of modernising tithe law. Sankey began to lobby Elliot for legislation that would make tithe a personal liability, rather than a charge linked to a particular piece of land. Debts for tithe should be treated in the same way as debts to banks or other lenders, which meant courts would have power to impose bankruptcy or even imprison someone who owed tithe. The idea of personal liability was, of course, nothing new. It had been a component of the unsuccessful tithe bills introduced by Salisbury in 1887 and 1888. For the lord chancellor, its introduction was now urgent because 'organised opposition had brought the execution and administration of the law temporarily into contempt' and created a threat to 'the maintenance of law and order in our country'.[109]

Elliot seeks a compromise

Elliot faced, therefore, pressure from two directions. On one side, the lord chancellor and senior figures in the judiciary lobbied for 'modernisation' of tithe recovery legislation, arguing that existing law was arcane and, most urgently, that the tithepayers' non-payment campaign had created a legal logjam.[110] On the other, the tithe issue risked poisoning crucial aspects of his wider agricultural policy, particularly the partnership with the NFU. Feeling the weight of the tithepayers' movement, the NFU had made the establishment of an inquiry into the operation of the 1925 Tithe Act and 'its amendment on equitable lines' one of its top six policy priorities. It had

---

[108] 'Draft Memorandum to the Lord Chancellor', n.d. (1934), CERC, ECE/SEC/TITHE/P9.

[109] 'Statement of Evidence submitted by the Lord Chancellor's Office, *Royal Commission on Tithe Rentcharge, Minutes of Evidence*, 620–23; Lord Chancellor speaking in the House of Lords, 17 Apr. 1934.

[110] Lord Chancellor speaking in the House of Lords, *Hansard*, 17 Apr. 1934.

also won support for these demands from the Conservative Parliamentary Agricultural Committee and the Central Land Association.

Although previously resisting calls to intervene, Elliot drew the conclusion that the case for new legislation had become overwhelming. During October and November 1933, he held meetings with delegations from the NFU, Conservative Parliamentary Agricultural Committee and CLA. He also received representatives of the titheowners (Queen Anne's Bounty, Ecclesiastical Commissioners, Welsh Church Commissioners and Oxford and Cambridge titheowning colleges).[111] By the New Year, the minister had sketched 'a short bill' to provide 'immediate relief' on tithe to farmers in the most financial difficulty – effectively by adapting the provisions in Spens' private member's bill. In order to make the concessions palatable to titheowners, he agreed to adopt the lord chancellor's proposals to make tithe a personal debt. In private discussions with Middleton, he promised to resist the idea of a public inquiry and gave a commitment that his legislation would avoid any radical 'uprooting of the 1925 Act'.[112]

Elliot's decision to sponsor legislation was a setback for the Church and a personal defeat for Middleton. Queen Anne's Bounty had opposed any reopening of the 'final' settlement of 1925. It had suggested that its 'hard cases' policy could deal with farmers facing genuine hardship, pointed to 'the improving position' of tithe collection and predicted that the tithe problem would be resolved as agriculture pulled out of depression. Meeting with the archbishop of Canterbury to formulate the Church's response, Middleton explained that Elliot had been forced to act because he 'could no longer resist the pressure, not only of tithepayers but of the Central Chamber of Agriculture, the Farmers' Union [...] and of many Conservative MPs for some modification of the tithe position'. But the two men decided it would be unwise to oppose the principles behind the bill. They recognised that the minister was seeking a compromise and agreed that the Church should focus efforts on ensuring that the legislation did not lead to 'unwarrantable sacrifices to the titheowners'.[113]

The biggest concern for the Church was the trigger point Elliot was proposing for tithe remission. The minister had told NFU leaders that he was minded to accept their policy of one-third of land value (replacing the two-thirds in the 1891 Act). The Church lobbied hard to prevent a ceiling on tithe at that level, which would, according to Middleton, have the 'very serious' effect of reducing tithe income by one-tenth. After further deliberations between Middleton and Cosmo Lang, the Bounty's

[111] NFU, Tithe Committee, 12 Dec. 1933, MERL, SR NFU, AD1/15.
[112] George Middleton to archbishop of Canterbury, 3 Mar. 1934; Cosmo Lang, 'Memorandum. Tithe', 7 Mar. 1934, LPL, Lang 71.
[113] QAB, Report of Special Meeting of the Tithe Committee, 7 Mar. 1934; Middleton to the Minister of Agriculture, 13 Mar. 1934, CERC, QAB/2/1/51.

tithe committee agreed to inform the ministry that in order to 'have [the Church's] goodwill' the figure should not be set below one-half. But it also agreed to let Elliot know that it was prepared to accept a compromise figure of two-fifths, which would be its 'utmost limit'.[114] Elliot went back to consult senior officers of the NFU. Without delay, they signalled their acceptance of the compromise and promised to support the bill.

The Cabinet discussed and agreed the bill at its meeting on 21 March 1934. The first of two clauses would grant remission at two-fifths of land value and simplify the process by which tithepayers could apply for remission, making it obtainable through a certificate from the tax authorities rather than through the county court. The second clause would end the system of distraint by making tithe a personal debt. The lord chancellor spoke strongly in favour of the bill, stressing the necessity of repairing the 'failure of the law' in the face of organised opposition. But some in the Cabinet were sceptical about prospects for a successful 'compromise'. These included Edward Wood (now known as Lord Halifax), who as minister of agriculture had steered the 1925 Act through parliament. Elliot conceded that his proposals would 'not satisfy the extremists concerned in the tithe agitation' and predicted further demands for a public inquiry. But he was optimistic about the bill's prospects, telling the Cabinet that 'informal conversations [...] with leading representatives of the more moderate element represented by the NFU and the CLAs [had led him] to believe that these proposals would be accepted as a reasonable contribution'.[115]

The tithepayers' movement was quick to mobilise against the bill. A special meeting of the NTA national council (7 April) described it as 'indefensible, both morally and economically': the alteration of the level for remission would benefit only a small proportion of tithepayers and the change to the laws of recovery was 'entirely foreign to the nature of tithe'. By turning tithe into a personal debt, the bill 'placed tithepayers in an even worse position than they are now'. Protest meetings were organised around the country, including in Sandwich, Tenterden, Shrewsbury, Southminster, Saffron Walden, Wisbech, Lincoln and several towns in Wales. In Ipswich, a 'mass protest meeting' was organised jointly between the Suffolk Tithepayers' Association and the Suffolk NFU. A large rally in Diss condemned the bill as 'an insult to the intelligence' of British farmers. In Hereford, 1,000 farmers made 'threats to the government if the tithe bill [was] not withdrawn'.[116]

[114] Cosmo Lang, 'Memorandum. Tithe', 7 Mar. 1934, LPL, Lang 71; QAB, Report of Special Meeting of the Tithe Committee, 7 Mar. 1934, CERC, QAB/2/1/51.
[115] Cabinet Meeting, 21 Mar. 1934, TNA, CAB/23/78/11; 'Tithe Rentcharge. Memorandum by the Minister of Agriculture and Fisheries', 16 Mar. 1934, TNA, CAB/24/248/10.
[116] 'Tithe Bill protest', DiEx, 27 Apr. 1934; 'New Bill "Indefensible"', F&S, 9 Apr. 1934; 'Demand for Withdrawal of the Bill', F&S, 16 Apr. 1934.

The four NTA supporters on the NFU's tithe committee challenged the union leadership's commitment to the bill by tabling a resolution to demand that union should 'refuse to accept' it. The resolution also reaffirmed the union's call for 'an impartial inquiry into the whole incidence of tithe', adding that 'in the meantime' tithe should be limited to 'one-tenth of the rental value of land'. NFU national officials were determined to face down the NTA's arguments, prompting a major clash at the tithe committee on 13 April. Stanley Ratcliff, now president of the union, moved a long amendment, welcoming the bill as a 'response of the Government to the representation made by the NFU in favour of the provision of immediate relief'. The amendment withdrew the union's demand for an inquiry and, in relation to the clause transforming tithe into a personal debt, called simply for 'satisfactory assurances' about its operation. Ratcliff claimed the bill should be viewed as a stepping-stone for further legislation to amend the 'injustices of the 1925 Act'. The tithe committee passed his amendment by six votes to four (the NTA members).[117]

Leaders of the NFU had, once again, miscalculated the mood on tithe amongst their members. There were 'heated' exchanges at the national council on 19 April as representatives from heavily tithed regions expressed disbelief that the tithe committee had abandoned the demand for an inquiry and had lent support to legislation which was 'mainly for the benefit of tithe-owners'.[118] 'It's selling ones birth right for a mess of pottage,' said the delegate from East Sussex. Even self-declared 'moderates' warned that the proposed stance was 'dangerous' as it would do 'a great deal to foment agitation'. Supporting the bill 'would do more harm to the union than anything that had ever been done,' said the Wiltshire representative. Resolutions and letters sent from branches to NFU headquarters pressed a similar message. The Worcestershire branch warned that 'the passage of such a measure would result in a definite revolt on the part of tithepayers in this county who up to now have acted constitutionally'. The Devonshire branch, which had previously been critical of the NTA, decided 'to ask the Tithepayers' Association to join with [them] in a protest meeting'. The NFU leadership defended its position by stressing that it 'had got to retain a negotiating relationship with the government'. Yet, by a three-to-one majority, the national council agreed to refer back the tithe committee's report and survey the views of the membership before taking a decision on the union's attitude towards the bill.[119]

The result of the consultation was decisive. NFU county branches rejected the bill by a majority of thirty-nine to nine. The national council

---

[117] NFU Tithe Committee, 13 Apr. 1934, MERL, SR NFU, AD1/16.
[118] 'NFU Faces a Tithe Crisis', *F&S*, 23 Apr. 1934.
[119] Meeting of the Council of the Union, *NFU Record*, May 1934, 181–4; Ratcliff, Davies, Joyce to county branches, 23 Apr. 1934, MERL, SR NFU, AD1/87; 'The Tithe Bill', *Exeter & Plymouth Gazette*, 13 Apr. 1934.

instructed officials to inform the minister of agriculture that the union was 'opposed to the bill in its entirety' and renewed the demand 'for an inquiry into the operation of the tithe acts'.[120] In 1925, the government had proceeded with the Tithe Bill in despite of the NFU's opposition. A decade later, the union's evolving partnership with the Ministry of Agriculture and its influence with the Conservative Parliamentary Agricultural Committee meant its position could not be ignored. Moreover, the Central Chamber of Agriculture and the CLA – which had a considerable number of adherents in the House of Lords – had also shifted their positions and were now opposing the bill.[121]

The government also faced difficulties from the Church. While the archbishop of Canterbury continued to express support for 'an agreement', important sections of the clergy were not so willing to accept the compromise. It is 'all in favour of the tithepayer at the expense of the titheowner,' the archdeacon of Dorset told an assembly of clergy at Wimborne Minster.[122] The *Church Times* described the bill as 'an injustice [...], a thoroughly bad bill, which pleases nobody and ought not to please anybody'. Making tithe a personal debt could, the paper suggested, act as a double-edged sword: 'The tithe situation is already quite sufficiently difficult and unpleasant for the Church without the promising attempt of the new bill to make it more unpleasant and create fresh difficulties.'[123] Cosmo Lang began to have second thoughts about the extent of support the Church should offer the bill. He asked Middleton to consider the possibility of a Church-sponsored amendment during the committee stage to stipulate a time limit on 'the concession made to the tithepayer'.[124] *The Times* noted the government's dilemma: 'It cannot be denied that the reception given to the measure has been more critical than favourable. [...] The passions both of tithepayers and of titheowners have been so roused that the bill cannot be left to stand upon the fact that their criticisms largely cancel each other out.'[125]

Announcement of a Royal Commission

By the beginning of May, Elliot knew his proposed legislation faced serious problems. 'It [had been] hoped,' he wrote in a memorandum to the Cabinet, 'that the bill would attract the large body of moderate opinion which exists in such bodies as the CLA and the NFU, and

---

[120] NFU Tithe Committee, 10 May 1934, MERL, SR NFU, AD1/16; 'Meeting of the Council of the Union', *NFU Record*, June 1934, 209.
[121] '"Drop Tithe Bill"', *F&S*, 30 Apr. 1934.
[122] 'Dorset Archdeacon's Visitation', *WG*, 25 May 1934.
[123] *The Church Times*, 20 Apr. 1934.
[124] Rev. Alan Don to Middleton, 24 Apr 1934, LPL, Lang 71.
[125] 'The Tithe Bill', *The Times*, 24 Apr. 1934.

enable them to dissociate themselves definitively from the extremists. This objective has not been achieved.'[126] In an attempt to save the bill, Elliot decided to concede the demand for an inquiry into tithe, hoping that the announcement would defuse the opposition. He was still adamant that the bill should proceed, arguing that its withdrawal 'would be a great surrender to agitators. It would not only involve loss of prestige to the Government but there is every reason to believe it would encourage intensification and spread of resistance during the holding of the enquiry.'[127] Church leaders were particularly insistent that the bill should go ahead. Cosmo Lang informed Earl De La Warr, parliamentary secretary to the Ministry of Agriculture, that an inquiry 'would be a lesser evil than the stimulus of agitation which would result from the bill being dropped or an enquiry promised without the bill'.[128]

Yet it quickly became clear that Elliot's promise of an inquiry would not be enough to regain the support of the NFU, or even to guarantee the bill's passage through parliament. Moreover, the announcement posed new problems. Given the bill's provisions would inevitably be scrutinised by an inquiry, should they be time-limited, and if so for how long? On 30 May, the Cabinet appointed a committee, chaired by the prime minister, to decide the bill's fate. Its membership also included the chancellor of the exchequer, an indication that the government was beginning to accept that a resolution of the tithe controversy would involve a contribution from the public purse. The committee decided to withdraw the bill and prepare 'wide terms of reference' for an inquiry. The decision was ratified by the Cabinet on 6 June and announced in the House of Lords the following day. A Royal Commission would 'inquire into and report upon the whole question of tithe rentcharge in England and Wales and its incidence, with special reference to stabilised value, statutory remission, powers of recovery, and methods and terms of redemption'.[129]

The withdrawal of the bill served to wrong-foot Church policymakers. Only a week earlier, Middleton had told a conference of tithe area collection agents that the governors of Queen Anne's Bounty would 'object strongly' to an inquiry if the bill were to be dropped by the government.[130] Yet, immediately after the announcement, the bishop of Norwich (a member of the Queen Anne's Bounty tithe committee) told the House of Lords he 'was glad to hear' news of a Royal Commission

[126] 'Memorandum by Minister of Agriculture. Tithe Rentcharge', 4 May 1934, TNA, CAB/24/249/12.
[127] Ibid.
[128] 'Tithe', note by Cosmo Lang, 1 May 1934, LPL, Lang 71.
[129] Cabinet. Meeting of Ministers on the Tithe Bill, 30 May 1934, NA CAB/24/249; Cabinet, 6 June 1934, TNA, CAB/23/79/8.
[130] QAB, Report of Meeting of Representatives of Area Collection Committees with members of Tithe Committee, 29 May 1934, CERC, QAB/2/1/51.

and urged it should be set up without delay.[131] Middleton complained to Cosmo Lang about the 'blessing' bestowed on the inquiry by the bishop: 'The terms of reference open up alarming possibilities and it seems to me that while we must of necessity put on a bold front publicly it is foolish not to admit inside our own counsels that the withdrawal of the bill and the granting of an inquiry is a set-back.'[132]

The NTA had not campaigned for an inquiry but for immediate legislation to resolve tithe grievances. Nevertheless, it welcomed the announcement of the Royal Commission, while also warning that such inquiries were invariably used to shelve difficult questions and there were good reasons to think that the present one might not be an exception. The NTA stressed the need to maintain and strengthen the tithepayers' movement. Around the country, affiliated associations raised demands for a moratorium on tithe collection pending the outcome of the Commission. Frank Allen issued a statement on behalf of the East Kent Tithepayers' Association calling for tithe to be set as a 'token payment' of 20 per cent and the recovery of tithe arrears to be restricted to 50 per cent of the due amount. In north Devon, a large meeting of farmers called for a moratorium on all tithe payments. In Shropshire, the tithepayers' association recommended its members pay only 50 per cent while waiting for the inquiry's recommendations.[133]

For the titheowners, these developments seemed to confirm their fear that the dropping of the bill and the announcement of an inquiry would give renewed impetus to the non-payment campaign. The Queen Anne's Bounty tithe committee warned that the government's actions 'would be regarded as a victory for the more subversive sections amongst those opposed to the payment of tithe, and it might be found that what was a rapidly improving position might once more become a bad one'. The archbishop of Canterbury raised similar concerns in the House of Lords and received an assurance from De La Warr that the law would be fully enforced.[134] Faced with the possibility of 'increased resistance' by tithepayers, an emergency meeting of Queen Anne's Bounty, attended by convenors of area collection committees, agreed an eight-point plan: collection policy would be 'tighten[ed] up'; investigations of 'hard cases' and the granting of concessions of up to 15 per cent would continue, but arrears would not be allowed to accumulate; and legal proceedings would

---

[131] HL Deb., *Hansard*, 7 June 1934.
[132] Middleton to Cosmo Lang, 9 June 1934, LPL, Lang 71.
[133] 'The Royal Commission', *Tithe*, No. 5, July 1934; 'While the Commission Sits', *F&S*, 18 June 1934; 'Tithepayers Call for Moratorium', *WT*, 15 June 1934; Middleton to Cosmo Lang, 19 June 1934, LPL, Lang 71.
[134] HL Deb., *Hansard*, 28 June 1934.

not be delayed in cases where there was no obvious hardship.[135] Meeting on 20 July, the control committee passed a further fifty-four cases for recovery action to General Dealers. The minutes bely the Bounty's public promise of sympathetic treatment of farmers facing financial hardship: 'The investigator is of the opinion that distraint would put him out of business,' reads the report on a tithepayer in Woodbridge (Suffolk), '[but he] makes no suggestions whatsoever for payment and merely reiterates his inability to pay. Distraint seems the only remedy.' Another report, on a farmer in Minster (Kent), reads: 'The case is one of considerable hardship and the landowner's position is very acute. [...] Distraint would probably put [him] out of business [...] On the other hand, there seems to be no other way in which the tithe could be recovered.'[136]

The same day, a delegation of titheowners (Queen Anne's Bounty, Welsh Church Commissioners, university tithe-owning colleges, Christ's Hospital and the private titheowner the earl of Malmesbury) met the lord chancellor. Informing him that there were over 2,000 outstanding distraint orders, the delegation demanded special measures to ensure that the law was enforced, stressed the need to train more bailiffs and possession men, and argued for the appointment of twelve 'advisory officers', who would be 'specially experienced in the matter of recovery for distraint'. It also insisted that titheowners' recovery plans should be supported by the 'sufficient use of police assistance'.[137] The lord chancellor pointed out that the issue was 'a matter of high politics on which he might have to consult other members of the government', but he promised that 'anything practicable to facilitate and strengthen the administration of the law had his entire sympathy'. As far as the titheowners were concerned, there would be no 'truce' in the tithe war during the sitting of the Royal Commission.

---

[135] QAB, Report of Emergency Meeting of Conveners of Area Collection Committees, 18 June 1934, CERC, QAB/2/1/51.
[136] Controlling Committee, 20 July 1934, CERC, ECE/SEC/TITHE/GD5.
[137] W. G. Hannah, 'Deputation and Memorandum to the Lord Chancellor, 20 July 1934, CERC, QAB/2/1/51.

9

The Royal Commission

The Royal Commission held its first public session on 25 October 1934. In the chair was Sir John Fischer Williams, a 'staunch Liberal' and lawyer of international repute on account of his role on the Reparations Commission arising from the Treaty of Versailles. Sitting alongside him were Lord Cornwallis, the prominent 'agriculturist' and former Conservative MP, who had previously expressed concern at the 'heavy and unfair burden of tithe',[1] Sir Leonard James Coates, a legally trained former civil servant, and Sir Edward Robert Peacock, former director of the Bank of England. The final commissioner was Sir John Edward Lloyd, professor of history at the University of Wales, president of the Welsh Language Society and, as chair of the federation of Welsh Congregationalist churches, a prominent nonconformist. The Commission's membership, along with its broad terms of reference, promised a forensic scrutiny of all aspects of the tithe problem.[2] Twenty public sessions were held, the last on 21 March 1935. Oral testimony was taken from fifty individuals, mostly representatives of institutions and associations. A further twenty-one statements were submitted, though their authors did not give verbal evidence. The submissions and transcripts of the public sessions were published in twenty-one dense volumes.[3]

Public sessions

The sessions were divided into five broad tranches of evidence. Senior civil servants appeared first. Officials from the Ministries of Agriculture and Health outlined the history and functioning of tithe legislation; those from the Board of the Inland Revenue explained titheowners' liability for rates and other taxes. Next came professional associations with a stake in landownership, including land agents, auctioneers and chartered surveyors. Given they were either public servants or offering services

---

[1] See p. 156.
[2] J. L. Brierly, 'Sir John Fischer Williams (1870–1947)', *ODNB* (2004); Robert Thomas Jenkins, 'Sir John Edward Lloyd', *Dictionary of Welsh Biography* (2001).
[3] *Royal Commission on Tithe Rentcharge, Minutes of Evidence.*

to both titheowners and tithepayers, these first witnesses maintained an air of neutrality, though occasionally signalling that they regarded elements of the tithe system as 'anachronisms'.[4] The third tranche of submissions, which came primarily from organisations linked to the agricultural industry, began to discuss solutions to the tithe problem. Represented by Joshua Steed (whom we met in Chapter 5), the Central Chamber of Agriculture proposed that tithe should become a land tax collected by the state and limited to one-third of the value of the tithable land. The CLA's representatives, two Conservative landowners, Clifton Brown MP and Lord Hastings, argued that the government should issue bonds to buy out titheowners and recover the money from tithepayers through a charge on land, payable for a specified number of years. A similar proposal came from the Land Agents' Society. Questions from the Commissioners signalled that some kind of compulsory redemption scheme was likely to receive their serious consideration.[5]

Officials of the NFU, including Davies and Ratcliff, appeared on 23 November. Their submission had prompted more tithe controversy within the NFU and another row between national officers and supporters of the National Tithepayers' Association. After the government's announcement of the Commission, Ratcliff decreed that the tithe committee should be reorganised and made up only of members of the national council. The decision effectively purged the four NTA supporters, who had, a few weeks earlier, called out senior officials for 'welcoming' Elliot's Tithe Bill. Reconstituted, the tithe committee agreed to prepare a submission that was, in its own words, 'a constructive policy'.[6]

In fact, the submission from the NFU was not only one of the briefest to be presented to the Commission but one of the most cautious. It contained no critique of the principle of tithe and argued explicitly that the charge should continue. Under the union's plans, tithe would revert to a variable amount linked to the price of corn, though limited to one-third of the value of tithable land. The submission opposed any form of compulsory redemption, arguing for a voluntary scheme facilitated by state-backed loans. It promised that 'the titheowner would once more be put in the position he had occupied through the course of history – a partner linked with the recurrent prosperity and adversity of agriculture'. The NFU officials also hedged their bets. While arguing for the continuation of

[4] Evidence of the Ministry of Agriculture and Fisheries & Ministry of Health and Board of the Inland Revenue, 25 Oct. 1934, 1–45; Evidence of the Incorporated Society of Auctioneers, & Land Property Agents, 9 Nov. 1934, 86–94.
[5] Evidence submitted by the Central Chamber of Agriculture, 26 Oct. 1934; Central Landowners' Association and Land Agents' Society, 7 Dec. 1934, 46–62 and 177–203.
[6] NFU, General Purposes Committee, 20 June 1934, MERL, SR NFU, ADI/16.

tithe, they anticipated that the Commission was likely to recommend a scheme to extinguish it. If that were to be the case, they argued that redemption payments by tithepayers should not be a personal liability and should be repaid to the state, rather than collected by Queen Anne's Bounty. But, to illustrate their 'constructive' approach, they proposed that tithepayers should make payments of a 'reasonable' amount for a period of around fifty years.[7]

NFU branches attacked the 'autocratic' purging of the tithe committee and criticised the union's submission as 'not strong enough'.[8] Mobbs urged the national council to reject an 'entirely inadequate' document that aimed 'to go back to a basis [for the continuance of tithe] that existed one hundred years ago'. He argued that the NFU's proposals for tithe redemption seemed 'more concerned about the income of the ecclesiastical tithe owner than […] the amount the tithepayer was going to continue to pay'.[9] Given its miscalculation of the members' mood when offering support to Elliot's Tithe Bill, the NFU leadership's approach might seem surprising. But foremost in the minds of senior officers was the rapidly developing corporate relationship between the NFU, government and state. 'If the Union were not moderate on this question, they would be throwing away their golden opportunity,' argued J. W. Pye, chair of the Kent branch and part of the delegation to the Commission. In reply to Mobbs, Pye argued it was necessary to 'take the line of compromise' and not 'go before the Commission with a one-sided case […] that did not realise justice on either side'.[10]

In contrast to those of the NFU and CLA, the NTA's submission challenged the principle of tithe, arguing that titheowners' claims were 'inferior morally, economically and legally to the interest of agriculture and to claims for contractual debts'. Presented by a delegation that included Mobbs, Kedward and Allen, the submission was comprehensive in content and five times longer than the NFU's, offering an interpretation of tithe history since the Anglo-Saxon monarchies and a detailed examination of the principles behind the 1836 Commutation Act. A memorandum, drawn up by the association's 'legal advisor', Edward Iwi, outlined the evolution of tithe recovery law since 1836. In addition, Allen submitted a personal statement, after which he was questioned individually on account of his 'very long' experience of working for 'both titheowners and tithepayers'. The NTA's submission reiterated the policy adopted by the association in 1933. It proposed the abolition of tithe through the advance by government or loan company of £31.5 million

---

[7] Evidence submitted by the NFU, 23 Nov. 1934, 115–16.
[8] Criticisms from Norfolk and Hereford branches: 'Union's Tithe Attitude', *F&S*, 30 July 1934; 'NFU's Tithe Evidence', *F&S*, 10 Dec. 1934.
[9] 'November Council Meeting', *NFU Record*, Dec. 1934, 59–61.
[10] Ibid.

(equivalent to ten years' tithe) to buy out the titheowners. Tithepayers would repay the amount over twenty years at 3 per cent interest, though the sum payable would not exceed 15 per cent of the tithable land's annual value. Members of the Commission showed interest in the principle of the scheme but baulked at its radical nature. It would, claimed Fischer Williams, give 'the titheowner something like 30 per cent of his present income [and] involve a very drastic reduction in the value of [his] property'.[11]

The NTA's submission opened the tranche of evidence drawn from various components of the tithepayers' movement. During five sessions, the Sanctuary Buildings in Westminster heard vivid accounts of the 'tithe war'.[12] Joseph Swales, a Norfolk farmer, told how he had been forced to sell his holding after being pursued by bailiffs for tithe owed by neighbours and previous owners. Evelyn Balfour outlined how General Dealers had arrived at her farm with seven lorries and fifty police officers to take her wheat. She gave examples of operatives of General Dealers 'roughly handling' farmers and animals in other 'excessive tithe distraints'. Leonard Mason of Fincham (Norfolk) described how he had witnessed a bailiff sitting in a barn for a week 'waiting for an opportunity to get into the house to seize the furniture [...] of a poor man with a daughter and wife ill upstairs'. It is the 'sort of thing that makes socialists of people and is very bad for the countryside,' he bemoaned.[13] Members of tithepayers' associations endorsed the arguments in the NTA's submission. W. H. Harvey and Frederick Smith (Essex) argued that the whole 'parasitic' system was 'an obsolete and unnecessary survival of medieval times'. George C. Solley (East Kent) rejected the idea that the tithepayers' campaign had been 'instigated by nonconformists': he had been 'brought up in the Church of England but [...] been turned away by [its] callous disregard of our unfortunate plight'. Representing Welsh tithepayers, R. F. Watkins argued that the time was 'opportune to write the last page of [tithe] history in England and Wales'.[14]

The Commission also heard from representatives of the aristocratic wing of the tithepayers' movement: George Pitt-Rivers, who led a large delegation from the Wessex Agricultural Defence Association; Michael McCreagh, who spoke on behalf of his Tithe League, and the Worcestershire landowner and fascist sympathiser George Vernon, who announced that he represented 'the opinion and sentiments of all classes in the countryside, from the Bishop to the Blacksmith, and the man who

11 Evidence submitted by the National Tithepayers' Association & Evidence submitted by Mr F. R. Allen, Canterbury, 6 Dec. 1934, 136–69 and 170–6 (140); 'Tithe Inquiry', *The Times*, 7 Dec. 1934.
12 Evidence submitted on 20 and 21 Dec. 1934, 10, 11 and 25 Jan. 1935, 204–379.
13 Ibid., 313, 335 and 334.
14 Ibid., 255, 372 and 286.

The Royal Commission

is drilling my wheat'.[15] Amongst others to appear were the Quakers, who outlined objections to tithe on 'religious principle', and the Liberation Society, now a shadow of its nineteenth-century self. Its delegate, Wilfred J. Rowland, replied several times that he had 'not thought out things sufficiently', making him the most unconvincing witness to appear before the Commission.[16]

The final seven public sessions were devoted to evidence from titheowners.[17] George Middleton led the Queen Anne's Bounty delegation and later reappeared to represent the Ecclesiastical Commissioners. Continuing to argue that the 1925 Act had been a 'permanent and final settlement' and that the subsequent fall in the price of produce 'could not justify' any alteration, he maintained that the tithe problem would recede as agriculture moved out of depression.

The Commission proved to be an uncomfortable experience for Middleton. Some of the evidence criticising clerical titheowners vexed him to such an extent that he challenged witnesses to the Commission outside its formal sessions. He wrote to Ratcliff, the NFU president, to demand the withdrawal of his statement – 'so completely at variance with the facts' – that the Ecclesiastical Commissioners had 'compelled' tenants to buy their farms in the aftermath of the Great War. Despite Middleton's threat of 'formal action', Ratcliff doubled down, providing letters from farmers to prove his point, and – to avoid embarrassment – the 'tithe chief' quietly let the matter drop.[18] Middleton was particularly indignant at evidence from tithepayers about the activities of General Dealers. 'We are accused of employing gangs of roughs to go about the country breaking open the gates and doors of law-abiding citizens and behaving generally as hooligans,' he complained, while emphasising his 'reasonable approach' to tithe collection. Yet Middleton struggled to explain how the establishment of General Dealers was not 'in spirit an infringement of the law', which forbade a titheowner tendering in respect of his own tithe.[19] Under questioning, he came close to admitting that General Dealers was an appendage of Queen Anne's Bounty and other titheowners. 'When [tithe]owners decided that the only way in which they could protect their interests was by securing that there should be a purchaser on a sale by tender, it obviously became their business to take such steps as were open to them to create such an organisation,' he explained. But, after Middleton's reassurance that General Dealers was 'a separate legal entity', the Commissioners were not inclined to probe

---

[15] Ibid., 205.
[16] Ibid., 309.
[17] Evidence submitted on 7, 8, 21 and 22 Feb. 1935, 7, 8 and 21 Mar. 1935.
[18] Correspondence between George Middleton & Stanley O. Ratcliff, 28 Dec. 1934–Jan. 1935, CERC, ECE/SEC/TITHE/NC/4.
[19] Evidence of the Governors of Queen Anne's Bounty, 435–8.

any further. Secrecy surrounding the financing of General Dealers, the subterfuge deployed to separate 'the Company' from the Church and the functioning of the 'Control Commission', on which Middleton played the main role, remained secure.

Evidence presented by representatives of the 'lower' clergy drew conflicting conclusions. The Churchmen's Defence Union reiterated its support for the tithe system, maintaining that 'any concessions [...] would show that the Church was liable to intimidation by threats of violence'. Its submission had been prepared by E. W. R. Peterson, son of Edward Peterson, who had died the previous October after devoting a lifetime to championing the rights of clergy to tithe.[20] Submissions from the Lower Houses of the Convocations of Canterbury and York also spoke of the serious consequences for the living standards of incumbent clergy if there were to be any reduction in the value of tithe. But other sections of the clergy stressed the need to find a settlement 'on honourable and fair terms to both parties'. Canon Brocklehurst outlined the 'ill-effect [of the] agitation on the spiritual work of the Church'. It was necessary to avoid 'ever again going through the stress of the last five years', he pleaded. A clergyman from Lincolnshire also favoured 'a compromise, in which no one party can claim a victory', pointing out that 'the other property of the Church [would] be ample to provide a living wage [for tithe-owning clergy]'.[21]

The bursars of Oxford and Cambridge colleges spoke on behalf of a group of lay titheowners, with Eton and Christ's Hospital public schools and Guy's and St Bartholomew's hospitals amongst those expressing support for their proposals. The bursars spoke against any concessions to tithepayers, who had 'greatly benefitted' from the legislation of 1918 and 1925. Yet they also argued for the abolition of the tithe system through 'an immediate state purchase', under which titheowners would receive cash or government stock. The details of their scheme – no reduction in income, but reductions of rates and land tax – were very favourable to titheowners.[22]

The penultimate public session considered evidence from John Maynard Keynes, who chose to appear in a personal capacity rather than as part of the delegation from the Cambridge colleges.. The economist's reputation, along with his first-hand experience of the tithe issue, lent special weight to his submission. Earlier in the tithe war, Keynes had taken a hard line when confronted with the non-payment campaign, criticising Queen Anne's Bounty for making too many concessions to tithepayers,

[20] Evidence of the Churchmen's Defence Union, 593; 'Mr E. W. I. Peterson', *The Times*, 8 Oct. 1934.
[21] Evidence of Rev. Canon Brocklehurst & Rev F. H. Roach, 497 and 513.
[22] Evidence of the Bursars on behalf of the University and Colleges of Oxford and Cambridge, 519–72.

supporting the creation of General Dealers and calling in its help in the high-profile case of Mrs Waspe (Ringshall, Suffolk). By 1935, however, he had drawn the conclusion that 'a general and drastic' reform of the tithe problem was necessary. Keynes refuted arguments from Queen Anne's Bounty and the Ecclesiastical Commissioners that the tithe problem would be resolved as agriculture recovered. He also rejected the notion that it could be 'cleared away' by adjustments to the existing system or by granting more relief to tithepayers, a suggestion implicit in the NFU's submission. Such measures, said Keynes, would not resolve 'the popular discontent with the system, the worry and expense and friction and bad temper generated, and the scandalous inadequacy of the existing law and practice'. What was required was 'a winding up of the whole system in its present form'. Keynes proposed a scheme to abolish tithe by issuing government stock to titheowners, noting that 'several important bodies representing different interests' had already suggested such to the Commission. But whereas most of the other schemes benefited one side of the conflict at the expense of the other, Keynes wanted to do 'substantial justice both to the titheowners and to tithepayers'.[23] Repayments by tithepayers would be set at £109 10s for seventy-six years (the length of tithe designated by the 1925 Act), with payments capped at two-fifths the value of land. Compensation to clerical and lay titheowners would be based on £85 10s and £62 10s respectively (per £100 of tithe), a figure less than current net entitlements. Keynes considered his scheme a good compromise. It might be 'considered by representative tithe owners as unnecessarily generous to tithepayers', he opined.[24] Yet tithepayers were not convinced and were quick to point out that – though technically tithe was to be 'abolished' – their payments would remain high and continue for another three generations. As the Commission finished taking public evidence in March 1935, most commentators and protagonists anticipated that Keynes' scheme would provide the basis of its recommendations, but it was certain that controversy would continue over the details.

No truce in the war

While the Royal Commission was taking evidence and beginning its deliberations, attitudes hardened on both sides of the 'tithe war'. Fears from within the Church that the Commission might lead to 'increased resistance' by tithepayers proved to have substance. 'What you anticipated has come to pass', the dean of Hereford told Middleton, suggesting that farmers were postponing payments in the hope of favourable recommendations from the Commission.[25] The Bounty's tithe

[23] Evidence of J. M. Keynes, 8 Mar. 1935, 573–5.
[24] Ibid., 574.
[25] Dean of Hereford to Middleton, 6 Aug. 1934, CERC, ECE/SEC/TITHE/NC/3.

committee recorded a fall in 'total collections' in the year starting March 1935. Particular concerns were raised at the drop of income from the west of England, where the impact of the agricultural depression had begun later. In the face of complaints from within the clergy that collectors were being 'far too lenient with some of the tithepayers', Queen Anne's Bounty was determined to apply the 'full enforcement' of the law while the Commission completed its work.[26]

The result was another round of well-publicised distraint seizures, accompanied by the now customary response from the tithepayers' movement. On the edge of the Malverns, 'a great gathering of tithepayers' attended an auction of thirteen cattle at the farm of Thomas Howard in Tenbury Wells in February 1935; in July 1935 another large crowd turned up at an auction of ten dairy cows in Leysters (Herefordshire). In Suffolk, an auction in Rushmere attracted 'farmers from Suffolk, Norfolk and Essex, together with practically the whole of the inhabitants from the immediate district'. Kedward told the crowd that 'the tighter they turn the screw and use the bludgeon, the more will the old spirit of resistance rise to stop them'.[27] In November 1934, a demonstration at the auction of two pairs of bullocks seized by the Tiverton county court bailiff from the Devon farm of BUF member William Down attracted 'a large attendance of farmers'. The spring and summer of 1935 saw a wave of distraint sales in Devon, including at Romansleigh, West Down, Georgeham, Berrynabor and Chumleigh. Kedward, Allen and Doreen Wallace travelled to the West Country to speak at protest rallies. In Cornwall, the centre of attention was attempts by bailiffs to impound ten cattle on a farm in St Columb Major. For several days, farmers played cat-and-mouse with possession men, moving the cattle in the middle of the night. Events culminated with a 'mass protest meeting' and 'gift sale' in the market square, at which Doreen Wallace was guest speaker. Posters proclaimed: 'Damnable Toryism. Tithe War proceeding'.[28]

Kent became once again the hottest spot in the tithe war. Spens, MP for Ashford, wrote about 'tithe trouble' being 'particularly bad' in his district. He complained that 'something of a "drive" is going on at the

[26] W. G. Hannah, 'Epitome of Report as to a) the increased flow of tithe moneys and b) the desirability of special efforts with respect to tithe arrears', May 1935, CERC QAB/2/1/52; QAB Tithe Committee, 22 Apr. 1936 and 27 Jan. 1936, CERC, QAB/2/1/53; 'Clergy and Tithes', *Wiltshire Times & Trowbridge Advertiser*, 25 May 1935.

[27] 'Church and Tithe', *Yarmouth Independent*, 6 July 1935.

[28] 'Tithe Auction Sale', *Kington Times*, 23 Feb. 1935; 'Tithe Distress Sale', *Kington Times*, 27 July 1935; 'Auction to Pay Tithe', *Exeter & Plymouth Gazette*, 16 Nov. 1934; 'North Devon Distraint Sale', *Exeter & Plymouth Gazette*, 23 Aug. 1935; 'Tithe Sale', *Exeter & Plymouth Gazette*, 26 July 1935; 'Challenge to Bishop', *WT*, 16 Aug. 1935; 'Cornish Tithe War Moves' and 'Tithe War at St Columb', *WMN*, 19 and 20 Nov. 1934.

moment [...] as regards the collection of tithe' and sales were 'deeply inflaming feeling' even amongst 'many moderate people'.[29] Throughout 1934 and 1935, the control committee targeted prominent figures in the East Kent tithepayers' movement. In August 1934, General Dealers seized fifty pedigree sheep from the farm of George C. Solley, chair of East Kent Tithepayers' Association. In December, it was the turn of George Gill, secretary of Elham Tithepayers' Association. Bailiffs and 'a considerable number of police' arrived at his farm to take two cows, which were sold to General Dealers.[30] But it was a series of distraint seizures involving some elderly farmers that particularly stoked anger. An 85-year-old in Mersham had his home 'stripped' of furniture. 'I have paid tithe for 60 years [and] have taken moderate views in the past, but this has made me one of the militant farmers in the movement,' the farmer, William Powell, told a journalist. Several weeks later, bailiffs visited a farm in Kingsnorth, near Ashford, to seize eight bullocks and household furniture, including tables, chairs and a piano, from a 75-year-old farmer and 'his invalid wife'.[31]

In 1935, a series of auctions and sales by tender took place on the Kentish Weald and the Romney Marsh. In March, the first of two distraint auctions took place at Court Lodge Farm in Ruckinge, a holding owned by Archibald Waddell. After an auction of two sows and four bullocks, over 100 people protested outside the village rectory, 'marching' on the lawn and banging the door, while others created something of a scandal by going into the church to toll the bell.[32] Farmers on the Romney Marsh also took their message directly to local clergy. After thirty police turned up to supervise two auctions in Newchurch, farmers marched to the church and a deputation from the tithepayers' association asked to speak to the rector. Striking a conciliatory note, Canon Lampen told farmers he 'was of the opinion that there should be a truce between all parties until the report of the Royal Commission was published'.[33] But there would be no truce. More angry scenes took place at auctions on two farms in both Pluckley and Mersham.[34] In November, 'fireworks were exploded' during a further sale in Mersham, where twenty-nine pedigree sheep, two cows, eight sows, a boar and fifteen pigs were seized.[35]

A prominent feature of the tithepayers' movement during this period was the increased visibility of women. Press reports of demonstrations to obstruct General Dealers at Kedward's farm in September 1934 highlighted

---

[29] Spens to Denman, 30 Apr. 1935, CERC, ECE/SEC/TITHE/RC2/3.
[30] 'Tithe Seizure at Sandwich', *DE*, 17 Aug. 1934; *KG*, 8 Dec. 1934.
[31] 'Bailiffs Strip Home of Farmer of 85', *DHe*, 16 July 1934; 'Bailiffs Get New Orders', *News Chronicle*, 16 Oct. 1934.
[32] 'Tithe demonstration at a Rectory', *The Times*, 16 Mar. 1935.
[33] 'Police guard Rectory and Church', *Kentish Express*, 29 Mar 1935.
[34] 'More Tithe Seizures', *KG*, 15 Mar. 1935; 'Tithe Distraint', *KE*, 3 May 1935.
[35] 'Tithe sale incidents', *DE*, 8 Nov. 1935.

the presence of farmers' wives and daughters. 'Women lie in Path of Raiding Lorries', headlined the *Daily Herald*; in the *News Chronicle* the banner read: 'Women and Girls in Tithe Fight'.[36] The same week in Suffolk, journalists reported that women took part in 'scuffles' with a 'large force' of police after General Dealers arrived in seven lorries to seize wheat from Hannah Waspe's farm in Ringshall, scene of a fascist intervention in 1933.[37]

The confiscation by bailiffs of household furniture and possessions also drew women into the movement. A case in July at Potter Heigham (Norfolk) gained wide publicity. A reporter for the *Daily Express* described how 'the house looks as if it had been overrun by burglars [...] the floors are bare, stripped of every inch of carpet, the walls are bare, stripped of mirrors and pictures. Lying about in scattered heaps are the articles taken out of the drawers of the seized furniture.'[38] After the seizure, local women organised to raise funds to allow the distraught farmer's wife to repurchase her possessions. A similar occurrence took place in October after bailiffs had 'emptied' three rooms of a house in Shelfanger (Norfolk), a distraint executed despite a report to the titheowners' control committee that the case was 'undoubtedly one of hardship'.[39]

In November 1934, Doreen Wallace and Evelyn Balfour organised a meeting in Norwich to establish a Women's Tithepayers' Association, of which Wallace became president. The new association's declared purpose was to organise farmers' wives and daughters to take 'steps to defend their homes from the bailiffs'.[40] Wallace had on several occasions made an appeal to farmers' wives to join the movement, though recognising – as she did in a speech at Southminster (Essex) – that 'often women folk disliked the [tithe] system but for social or religious reasons did not wish to identify themselves with the movement'.[41] For some, the presence of a strong female advocate for the tithepayers' cause was distasteful. After a speech in Dorchester, a certain A. J. Mayne, chartered surveyor and agent for the Weymouth Bay Estate, felt obliged to write to the home secretary. Complaining that Wallace had 'advocated open resistance to the law,' he advised the minister that 'if this bitch had six months [in prison] it might prevent a repetition in Dorset of the scenes of mob violence which have taken place in other counties.'[42]

36   *DHe* & *News Chronicle*, 7 Sept. 1934.
37   'Wheat Seized Near Stowmarket', *DiEx*, 14 Sept. 1934; '100 Police at Tithe Raid', *DHe*, 11 Sept. 1934.
38   Cited in *Tithe*, No. 5, Aug. 1934.
39   'Norfolk Women Tithepayers', *DiEx*, 9 Nov. 1934; 'Women Rally to Tithe Victim', *Reynold's Newspaper*, 22 July 1934; 'Tithe Distraint at Shelfanger', *DiEx*, 19 Oct. 1934; Controlling Committee, 20 July 1934, CERC, ECE/SEC/TITHE/GD5.
40   'Women Plan Resistance', *News Chronicle*, 16 Oct. 1934.
41   'Speech by Lady Novelist', *ChCh*, 4 Aug. 1933.
42   A. J. Mayne to Home Secretary, 21 Oct. 1933, TNA, HO 144/19199.

Effigy burning

Another characteristic of this phase of the tithe war was the occurrence at distraint sales of mock trials and 'executions' of effigies of titheowners. In June 1932, villagers in Hooe (East Sussex) had burnt a likeness of the local titheowner, Lord St Audries,[43] but this had been an isolated incident in an earlier stage in the tithe war. During 1935 and early 1936, parading and burning effigies became a common feature at tithepayers' demonstrations. A well-publicised incident occurred on 5 April 1935 when, after an abortive distraint sale of nine cows on Kedward's Westwell farm, 200 people marched around the fields carrying effigies of Queen Anne and 'the Arch of Cant', a barely disguised representation of the archbishop of Canterbury. A journalist wrote:

> The figures were placed on a huge bonfire [...] and pelted with mud and stones, while flames rose 50 feet high amid the bursting of fireworks, derisive cheers, and the singing of 'Keep the Home Fires Burning'. [...] A mock inquest held on the effigies afterwards [found] that they 'had met a just death for robbery with violence on the farms and small-holdings of England'.[44]

A few days later, a similar event took place after at a tithe sale in the village of Standlake (Oxfordshire), on the edge of the Cotswolds. A parade led by 'a mock bishop riding a horse draped in red cloth' carried effigies of Queen Anne and the archbishop of Canterbury bearing the inscription 'Parasites of British agriculture, past and present'. The two effigies were then 'burned at the stake'.[45]

Most of the 'ceremonies' involved representations of Queen Anne. In Chilsworthy, near Holsworthy (north Devon), her effigy bore the inscription: 'To the Flames with her. Away with the tithe – we only want British justice'.[46] At Rushmere (Suffolk), it was 'burned on a bonfire bearing the placard "Queen Anne is dead"'.[47] But the same ritualised 'justice' was administered also to representations of living collectors and defenders of tithe. Ire from the tithepayers' movement towards George Middleton increased after the 'tithe chief' received a knighthood in the June 1935 birthday honours. In March 1936, an auction of nineteen bullocks on Rowland Rash's farm at Wortham was followed by a 'procession nearly a quarter mile long [...] to a huge bonfire':

[43] See pp. 178–9.
[44] 'Fireworks at Tithe Sale', *DHe*, 6 Apr. 1935; 'Tithe Bonfire in Kent', *The Listener*, 10 Apr. 1935; 'Effigies burned at Tithe Sale', *The Times*, 6 Apr. 1935.
[45] 'Fireworks and Mock Bishop at Tithe Sale', *Western Daily Press*, 10 Apr. 1935; 'Insults Galore at Sale by Order of the Court', *Berks and Oxon Advertiser*, 12 Apr. 1935.
[46] 'Burning "Queen Anne"', *Devon and Exeter Gazette*, 26 June 1936.
[47] 'Tithe Sale at Rushmere', *Eastern Daily Press*, 1 July 1935.

FIGURE 10. Effigy of 'Queen Anne' before being burnt at a tithe sale at Standlake, Oxfordshire, 9 April 1935. The 'Archbishop of Canterbury' suffered a similar fate. A 'mock bishop' officiated the ceremony, which was accompanied by singing and an accordion player (Daily Herald Archive, © Getty Images).

The Royal Commission

Those in front carr[ied] effigies of Queen Anne and General Dealers Ltd, also satirical caricatures concerning the archbishop of Canterbury and Sir George Middleton. Amid derisive cheers, explosion of fireworks and the singing of Rule Britannia, the effigies were fixed to a wooden cross on top of the fire and pelted with stones and clods as the flames soared up to a great height.[48]

In the New Forest hamlet of Hyde (Hampshire), villagers hanged and burnt effigies representing Cambridge collegiate titheowners. A journalist reported how the 'gallows were erected immediately in front of the [auctioned] hayrick, and on these the effigies were hung, among cheers of the crowd. Mr E. V. K. Parsons, chairman of the local branch of the National Tithepayers' Association performed the duties of hangman.'[49]

Rituals of community justice within agrarian protest movements have a long history. They extended earlier traditions of folk justice, administered usually against violators of patriarchal imperatives and community norms: adulterers, people living out of wedlock, those suspected of wife or child cruelty, 'promiscuous' women, but also swindlers, informers and the like. In varying local customs, the accused would be mocked and humiliated, and sometimes they or their effigy paraded on a pole or ladder. In a classic text, E. P. Thompson describes how in the eighteenth century 'the symbolism of public execution irradiated popular culture':

> The elaborate effigies of the offenders which were carted or ridden through the community always ended up with a hanging or a burning [...] In extreme cases a mock funeral service was conducted over the effigy before a 'burial'. [...] To burn, bury or read the funeral service over someone still living was a terrible community judgement.[50]

In the nineteenth century, those resisting the enclosures of common land carried effigies on poles before ripping them apart or, in one incident, hanging a representation of a landowner from a tree in the churchyard and setting it on fire. During the Rebecca riots in Wales, ritualised justice took the form of the *Ceffyl Pren* (wooden horse), a frame on which effigies were paraded to the accompaniment of a cacophony of noise.[51] The tradition continued into the Welsh Tithe War of the 1880s, which was marked by the display of effigies and the 'rough music' of 'tithe horns'. The tithe conflict of the 1880s in England also saw isolated

---

[48] 'Wortham, The Tithe Storm Centre', *Yarmouth Independent*, 21 Mar. 1936.
[49] 'Tithepayers' Protest', *WG*, 24 Apr. 1936.
[50] E. P. Thompson, 'Rough Music Reconsidered', *Folklore*, 103, 1 (1992), 7.
[51] Graham Seal, 'Tradition and Agrarian Protest in Nineteenth-Century England and Wales', *Folklore*, 99, 2, (1988), 155, fn60, 167; Williams, *The Rebecca Riots*, 53–6; Lowri Ann Rees, 'Paternalism and rural protest: The Rebecca riots and the landed interest of south-west Wales', *AgHR*, 59, 1 (2011), 36–60.

cases of effigy burning, as for example in Warnford (Hampshire).[52] But the incidents linked to the tithe war of the 1930s are a rare example of an inter-war social movement deploying folkish notions of popular justice. By the early twentieth century, effigy burning had become less common, with the exception of activities around 5 November.[53]

As well as serving 'terrible community judgements' on living people, the tithepayers' demonstrations drew from a tradition that satirised 'ill-assorted marriages' – relationships that 'affronted neighbourhood opinion [that could] ensue in effigy burning and ran-tanning'.[54] In April 1936, a crowd gathered for the second year running in Fressingfield (Suffolk) to attend a tithe auction at Gissings Farm. In February 1935, farm workers had paraded an effigy of Queen Anne adorned with the sign 'Q A B General Stealer'. In 1936, after the distraint sale, the tithepayers' association auctioned a 'little black pig with a white clerical collar' to raise funds to compensate the farmer. The crowd was then invited to 'a wedding' on a neighbouring field in which a bonfire had been prepared with 'a stake' in a prominent position and, from the farm buildings, workers arrived with effigies of a bridegroom and bride.[55] Queen Anne wore 'a necklace of barbed wire' and her fiancé was a likeness of one of the directors of General Dealers. The marriage service was conducted by Mobbs, who ordered that, instead of being wed, the couple should be burnt at the stake. 'The bottom half of the bride was quickly burnt away and, amid cheers, […] the figures perished in the roaring flames'.[56]

The effigy burnings caused consternation within the Church. Middleton sent a protest to the Gaumont film company after footage of the burning of the 'Arch of Cant' was featured on newsreels in London cinemas. The company agreed to withdraw the item 'out of courtesy to the archbishop'. After the effigy burning at Fressingfield, Rev. G. T. Wilkes, a clergyman often willing to engage in public debate with the tithepayers' movement, condemned 'an act of indecency, which would cause the public to see the immorality of the tithe warfare'.[57] At the Chilsworthy auction, the burning prompted 'strong protests' from a woman who praised the charitable work of the local church.[58]

---

[52] See pp. 61–2.
[53] Philip J. Gooderson, 'Aspects of the Decline of English Rough Music and Effigy-burning and the Transformation of the Fifth of November in the Nineteenth and Twentieth Centuries', *International Journal of Regional and Local History*, 16, 2 (2021), 94–110.
[54] Thompson, 'Rough Music', 12.
[55] 'Tithe Sale at Pressing Field', *DiEx*, 15 Feb. 1935; Tithe Sale at Fressingfield', *Yarmouth Independent*, 4 Apr. 1936.
[56] 'Tithe Sale at Fressingfield', *Yarmouth Independent*, 4 Apr. 1936.
[57] Ibid.
[58] 'Burning of Effigy', *WMN*, 23 June 1936.

The effigies indicated a hardening of attitudes amongst activists in tithepayers' associations. But they had implications for the campaign's wider appeal. The movement's strength had derived from its 'non-sectarian' nature, as well as its ability to unite farmers opposed to tithe on principle with a wider section more concerned at the 'excessive' nature of the charge. Symbolic attacks on representatives of the Church and administrators of tithe highlighted not only the movement's 'nonconformist' tinge but also that its target was the tithe system rather than its functioning.

The Commission's proposals

The Royal Commission's report was considered by the Cabinet on 27 November 1935, after several weeks' delay caused by the general election of 15 November. The chancellor of the exchequer, Neville Chamberlain, and the minister of agriculture, Walter Elliot, urged that the report should not be made public without an accompanying statement of government policy. Recognising that the Commission's recommendations had 'consequences of importance both financially and politically to the State, Local Authorities and the Church', they warned that immediate publication would lead 'agitation for suspending proceedings for the recovery [...] of tithe [to] be greatly strengthened'. Elliot was, however, keen on the report's basic recommendation, which provided opportunities for the state to strengthen its ties with the agricultural industry.[59] The Cabinet agreed to postpone publication and appointed a committee of senior ministers to formulate the government's position. Chaired by Chamberlain, the committee was effectively led by Lord Halifax (Edward Wood), who as minister of agriculture had steered the 1925 Tithe Bill through parliament.[60]

The Royal Commission had, in fact, produced two reports. A majority statement, supported by all commissioners with the exception of Sir Leonard Coates, drew much of its argument from the submission of John Maynard Keynes.[61] It advocated that the state should pay off titheowners 'on fair terms' and collect from tithepayers the amount they 'could properly be asked to pay'. Implicitly rejecting the Bounty's contention that tithe was 'a mere money payment', the report recognised the 'general feeling that tithe rentcharge is a payment whose history makes its continuance unsuitable to the circumstances of the present day'. It concluded:

---

[59] Walter Elliot, HC Deb., *Hansard*, 29 June 1936.
[60] Memorandum by the Chancellor of the Exchequer and the Minister of Agriculture, 22 Nov. 1935, TNA, CAB/24/257/30; Cabinet, 27 Nov. 1935, TNA, CAB/23/82/17.
[61] One member of the Commission, Lord Cornwallis, died in September 1936 before the finalisation of its work, though he had signalled his support for the majority position.

We believe that the complete abolition of the system is the only satisfactory method of dealing with its inherent and ineradicable difficulties and is a measure urgently needed in the interests not only of all persons directly concerned, whether tithepayers or titheowners, but also of the country as a whole.[62]

The majority report proposed that titheowners should receive £70 million of government stock at 3 per cent interest. It suggested that this was an attractive offer, as titheowners would no longer face costs of collection, land tax or rates and would have the 'improved security' of a gilt-edged stock. But, in return for these advantages, there would be significant reductions in net income. Members of the clergy, whose tithe had previously been collected by Queen Anne's Bounty, would receive an estimated £75 12s, instead of £93 15s; ecclesiastical corporations would see a reduction from £82 15s to £67; lay titheowners a drop from £65 10s to £52. The Commission recommended reduced payments for tithepayers. Instead of paying ecclesiastical tithe at £109 10s and lay tithe at £105, they would be liable for annuity payments of £91 11s 2d (the average tithe per annum between 1837 and 1916), which would be collected by the Inland Revenue. The recovery process would become the same as for other debts; in other words, tithepayers would be personally liable in the event of non-payment. Annuity payments would continue for forty years. (Keynes had recommended payments for seventy-six years.) In addition, payments on agricultural land would be capped at one-third of the value of land.[63]

The Commission's terms of reference had not included the question of extraordinary tithe, the additional charge on hops, fruit and market gardens that had been transformed by the 1886 Act into an 'annuity' – a permanent charge calculated at 4 per cent of the tithe's capital value at the time of the Act. By reducing and fixing payments by farmers and growers, the 1886 settlement had succeeded in calming the 'extraordinary tithe war' of 1881–86. But, by the 1930s, grievances over extraordinary tithe had re-emerged, particularly in Kent. A first source of injustice arose from the decline in acreage devoted to hop production, reduced from 70,000 in 1886 to 18,000 in the early 1930s. Yet growers remained liable for annuities on the land that was no longer cultivating hops. A second source was the provisions of the Hop Marketing Scheme (1932). In order to prevent 'overproduction', the scheme placed restrictions on the acreage and quantity of hop production. This meant that some growers were prevented from producing the crop on which they were paying the extraordinary tithe annuities. Recognising the continuing 'misunderstandings and considerable discontent' over extraordinary tithe,

[62] Royal Comm, 22–7.
[63] Ibid., 28–48.

the Commissioners recommended that the annuities should be included within their general scheme to 'extinguish' tithe.[64]

The 'minority report' from Sir Leonard Coates proposed a settlement more favourable to tithepayers. Extremely critical of arguments from Queen Anne's Bounty, Coates pointed out that only one-tenth of the Church's income from tithe found its way to the poorer clergy. He noted that in recent years income from investments held by the Church had increased by a sum higher than the total due from tithe. The Church, he argued, rather than being compensated generously by the general taxpayer, should 'rearrange' its finances to protect the income of clergy. Coates proposed that tithepayers should pay annuities of £80 for a forty-year period (instead of the £91 11s 2d suggested in the majority report).[65]

The Cabinet committee welcomed the Commission's general recommendations but objected to important details. Its first concern was over Church finances. 'We cannot overlook,' said Neville Chamberlain, 'the equitable claim of the Church to consideration on account of the heavy loss of income.'[66] The committee agreed to engage in 'confidential consultation' with Church leaders over the impact of the proposals. The second concern was the 'very large additional liabilities' for rural local authorities, who would lose income from rates paid on tithe. The Commission had argued that, since previous legislation had 'complicated the problem' in relation to rates, there was 'a strong case' for the state to make up potential losses for local authorities. This was rejected by Chamberlain, who insisted that the loss of rate income – estimated at between £650,000 and £700,000 per year – should be covered in the monies raised from tithepayers.[67] In order to compensate losses to the Church and the shortfall in rates, the Cabinet's tithe committee proposed to extend repayments by tithepayers from forty to sixty years. It agreed a further delay to the publication of the report while consultations took place. Negotiations with local authorities led quickly to an agreement for annual lump sums from the Treasury to compensate their losses. Negotiations with Church authorities proved more difficult.

Secret consultations

In late December and early January 1936, Lord Halifax sent two 'strictly confidential and secret' communications to the archbishop of Canterbury enclosing the Commission's report and an outline of the government's

---

[64] Royal Comm, 63; Evidence of NFU, 127.
[65] Ibid., 77–107.
[66] Cabinet, Committee on Tithe Rentcharge, Report, 21 Feb. 1936, TNA, CAB/24/260/14.
[67] Cabinet, Royal Commission on Tithe Rentcharge, Statement by His Majesty's Government, 25 Feb. 1936, TNA, CAB/260/15.

proposals. Cosmo Lang passed the documents to Middleton to seek an opinion, informing Halifax that tithe was a subject 'on which my poor brain refuses to work'.[68] In fact, the archbishop had closely followed the different stages of the conflict, often expressing concern at its impact on Church finances but becoming increasingly worried about the reputational damage being inflicted on the Church.

The radicalisation of the tithe war in the Canterbury diocese, including the burning of his effigy at Westwell, had focused Cosmo Lang's mind. In the wake of the publicity surrounding the 'Battle of the Ducks', the archbishop had written to Spens, MP for Ashford, asking for 'a personal and friendly talk' about the situation. 'I am greatly troubled by the increasing tension between the tithe-payers and the tithe-owners, particularly the clergy in the district of Ashford, as well as elsewhere,' he told the MP.[69] The two men met on 20 October 1934 and discussed the submission prepared for the Royal Commission by Canon Brocklehurst, which argued for an 'honourable and fair' settlement.[70] Cosmo Lang started to advocate such a compromise. In January 1936, he told Halifax that, though 'the loss which the clerical tithe-owners would receive either through the Report or the Memorandum would be very considerable', they would be 'well advised to submit to some measure of sacrifice' in order to reap the 'benefits' of putting an end to tithe.[71]

Yet Middleton was flabbergasted at the Royal Commission's recommendations. Meeting the archbishop on 15 January, he claimed the measures would mean 'the expropriation [...] of about 20 per cent of the Church's tithe redemption and they were 'so largely of a confiscatory nature' that they had 'seriously to be combated'. Lang could not ignore the opinion of the Church's most senior lay official. 'I'm sorry to say,' he noted to himself, 'that [Middleton] regards the proposals [...] as gravely unsatisfactory.' Lang delayed a detailed response to Halifax, informing him that the loss of income 'to be borne by the clerical titheowners, so many of whom are already so impoverished' was a 'heavy price to pay' for tithe redemption. Middleton began to work on alternative proposals and started discussions with Treasury officials to seek concessions.[72] Meanwhile, the archbishop's attention to the tithe question was distracted by his duties surrounding the death of King George V.

By late January, the government's delay in publishing the Commission's report had become a political problem. It was common knowledge that the

[68] Halifax to Cosmo Lang, 19 Dec. 1935 and 8 Jan. 1936, Lang to Middleton, 11 Jan. 1936, LPL, Lang 71.
[69] Lang to Spens, 11 Oct. 1934, LPL, Lang 71.
[70] Lang to Brocklehurst, 20 Oct. 1934, LPL, Lang 71.
[71] Lang to Halifax, 12 Jan. 1936, LPL, Lang 71.
[72] George Middleton, 'Secret Memorandum, Tithe Rentcharge: Commission's Scheme of Extinguishment', 20 Jan. 1936; Private note, Cosmo Lang 15 Jan. 1936; Lang to Halifax, 15 Jan. 1936, LPL, Lang 71.

document had been in its hands for over two months and ministers feared awkward questions when parliament reconvened in early February.[73] In addition, a 'momentary indiscretion' by Cosmo Lang encouraged speculation about a backroom deal being struck between the government and Church. Attending a service on 13 January in Great Mongeham, near Deal (Kent), the archbishop was confronted by members of the East Kent Tithepayers' Association. Asked whether he had seen a copy of the report, Lang let slip that he had indeed, but could not divulge its contents because 'it is at present entirely secret'. The tithepayers' campaign made capital out of the affair. Kedward found it 'almost unbelievable that the report should be in the possession of the Chairman of Queen Anne's Bounty before it had been communicated to parliament'.[74] NFU leaders informed Elliot of the many 'letters and resolutions' from branches protesting that the archbishop had been sent the report 'without a corresponding act of courtesy being extended to the NFU'.[75]

After a 'confidential conversation' on 6 February with Halifax, who 'fully appreciated' the Church's difficulties, Lang forwarded a response to the government's proposals.[76] Drawn up by Middleton, the paper argued that the loss of income on clerical tithe should be restricted to 10 per cent and that there should be 'full compensation' for incumbent clergy. To fund this, the paper advocated that the annuity paid by tithepayers should be raised from the suggested £91 11s 2d to £97 15s with repayments continuing for seventy-five years, rather than the sixty or forty suggested respectively by the government and Royal Commission. Negotiations took place between Middleton and Chamberlain, who ruled out the proposals as impractical, on the basis they amounted to major changes to the Commission's recommendations. The chancellor agreed, however, that the government would hand the Church an additional £2 million lump sum 'for the relief of existing interests'.[77]

The government finally published the Royal Commission's report along with its White Paper on 27 February.[78] It promised to treat the question as 'an urgent matter' and introduce a bill in parliament in the coming weeks. The Cabinet had recognised that 'the proposals would

---

[73] Halifax to Cosmo Lang, 30 Jan. 1936, LPL, Lang 71.
[74] 'Tithepayers and the Archbishop', *East Kent Times*, 18 Jan. 1936.
[75] NFU, Parliamentary, Press & Publicity Committee, 18 Feb. 1936; NFU Welsh Committee, 18 Feb. 1936, MERL, SR NFU, ADI/18.
[76] Cosmo Lang to Middleton, 6 Feb. 1936, LPL, Lang 71.
[77] 'Secret Memorandum: Tithe Rentcharge', 3 Feb. 1936; Lang to Halifax, 8 Feb. 1935; Middleton to Lang, 19 Feb. 1936, LPL, Lang 71.
[78] Cabinet, Committee on Tithe Rentcharge, Report, 21 Feb. 1936, TNA, CAB/24/260/14; Cabinet, Royal Commission on Tithe Rentcharge, Statement by His Majesty's Government, 25 Feb. 1936, TNA, CAB/24/260/15.

be attacked and criticised, both by the tithepayers and the titheowners'. The Church authorities 'would certainly not accept what was now contemplated as a fair and reasonable solution', but, nevertheless, they were committed to supporting the broad lines of the settlement. Tithepayers were expected to object to annuity payments becoming a personal liability and the extension of the payment period from forty to sixty years. But, predicted Elliot, it was likely that 'moderate opinion' would prevail and tithepayers 'would not press their objections to the point of wrecking the new proposals'.[79] In short, the government was taking a calculated risk that its bill would be viewed as an acceptable compromise, which would neutralise serious opposition on both sides.

Elliot's assessment of the Church's position proved accurate. Statements from Queen Anne's Bounty were sprinkled with bullish rhetoric, predicting dire consequences for the clergy, cuts in the Church's pension scheme and shortage of funds to maintain cathedrals and their dedicated staff.[80] The Rev. H. Gathorne Crabtree, chair of the Church Assembly's tithe committee, told *The Times* that the government's scheme would 'cripple the Church'.[81] Another member of the Church Assembly, Lord Hugh Cecil, condemned it as 'theft' and 'an immorality'.[82] Yet, behind the scenes, the archbishop of Canterbury urged that, while it was necessary to press 'legitimate criticisms', the Church should not 'lend the Government to suppose that we are so opposed to the [...] scheme that it would be wise to drop it'. Canon Brocklehurst appealed to clergy publicly: '[If] complaints and unkind criticism [are carried too far], the Government may say a pest to both your houses. This may give some satisfaction to anti-tithe agitators, but it spells ruin for us clergy.'[83]

The government published its bill at the beginning of May. It stipulated that the final six-month instalments of tithe would be fixed at £91 11s 2d and collected by titheowners on 1 October 1936.[84] It also gave details of a scheme to deal with arrears, which would be collected by an Arrears

[79] Cabinet, 26 Feb. 1936, TNA, CAB 23/83/11.
[80] The Tithe Report. Effect on the Church. Preliminary Memorandum by Queen Anne's Bounty, 28 Feb. 1936, Lang 71; Special Meeting of QAB Tithe Committee, 2 Mar. 1936, CERC, QAB/2/1/53.
[81] H. Gathorne Crabtree, 'Church and the New Proposals', *The Times*, 12 Mar. 1936.
[82] Hugh Cecil, 'Harshness to the Church', *The Times*, 18 Mar. 1936; HC Deb., *Hansard*, 13 May 1936.
[83] Cosmo Lang to Middleton, 4 Mar. 1936, LPL, Lang 71; Rev. George Brocklehurst, *The Times*, 25 Mar. 1936.
[84] The Bill covered most aspects of tithe, including extraordinary tithe, but some anomalies remained. Parishes in the City of London continued to collect tithe rentcharge until 1947, when the City Corporation (under the City of London (Tithes) Act 1947) issued £1 million of 3 per cent stock to cover the Church's revenue.

The Royal Commission

Investigation Committee with powers to reduce debts in cases of hardship. A conference of Church institutions expressed 'alarm and misgiving' at these details.[85] Middleton told government representatives that, if they were not modified, 'Church authorities would feel bound to oppose the bill and that he himself would have to discontinue the negotiations forthwith'. But when the government offered the Church a further £732,000 lump sum and stipulated that non-agricultural tithe (a small proportion of the total) would continue to be collected at £105, Middleton advised that 'it would be desirable to accept [the concessions] rather than to oppose the passage of the bill and incur the risk of the bill being dropped.'[86] W. G. Whittingham, the bishop of St Edmundsbury and Ipswich and a member of the Bounty's tithe committee, told his diocesan conference that 'the bill is broadly on fair grounds [and] affords a prospect of bringing to an end a long-existing source of contention.'[87] In private, Middleton began to concede that public warnings about the financial consequences of the settlement had been exaggerated. A 'strictly confidential' document circulated by the Bounty to the Church hierarchy explained that losses 'may be made up in the course of time by the sale and re-investment of the Government stock'.[88] Another document prepared for the Ecclesiastical Commissioners argued that the government scheme 'seems really a good one and [...] in the long run advantageous. Political developments in the future would hardly result in obtaining a better scheme.' Policy should be 'reluctant acceptance combined with negotiation on detail'.[89]

Yet divisions within the Church remained and some senior figures pushed for more concessions. The bishop of Norwich, another member of the Queen Anne's Bounty tithe committee, argued for the extension of payments by tithepayers from sixty to sixty-eight years.[90] William Temple, now archbishop of York, criticised the 'indecent haste' with which a settlement was being forced through. The Church's approach had been too conciliatory, he argued. In reply, the archbishop of Canterbury told Temple that he had 'little idea of the degree of agitation and irritation which at one time was centred in my own diocese and spread to districts like Essex, Berks, and Suffolk'. If the bill were withdrawn, he explained,

[85] Joint meeting of QAB Tithe Committee with representatives of the Ecclesiastical Commission, the two House of Convocations, Central Board of Finance and Church of England Pensions Board, 28 Apr. 1936, CERC, QAB/2/1/53.
[86] Memorandum of Interview with Mr E. L. Mitchell, Ministry of Agriculture and H. Gatliff, Treasury, 24 Apr. 1936, QAB/2/1/53; Joint Meeting of QAB Tithe Committee with representatives of the Ecclesiastical Commission, the two Houses of Convocation, Central Board of Finance and Church of England Pension Board, 1 May 1936, CERC, QAB/2/1/53.
[87] 'The Tithe Proposals', *BuFP*, 11 Apr. 1936.
[88] W. G. Hannah, 'The Tithe Bill', 24 June 1936, LPL, Lang 72.
[89] 'The Tithe Report' (n.d.), CERC, ECE/SEC/TITHE/L/6/1.
[90] B. Norwich, 'Settlement of Tithe', *The Times*, 12 Mar. 1936.

the 'disastrous' result would be 'a general strike [...] against the payment of the Tithe as would [make] the position of the Church in many country districts almost impossible'.[91]

Queen Anne's Bounty attempted to coordinate a joint response between clerical and lay titheowners to the government's proposals. It convened a series of 'informal conferences' attended by representatives of Oxford and Cambridge colleges, public schools (Eton, Charterhouse, Christ's Hospital) and charitable institutions, including St Bartholomew's Hospital. But hopes of a united front of titheowners quickly dissipated.[92] The Oxford bursars urged strident opposition to the government's proposals, which they claimed would 'permanently reduce the funds available in Oxford for education and learning'.[93] Led by Geoffrey Radcliffe, bursar of New College, they proposed that clerical and lay titheowners lobby together for an increase in repayments by tithepayers to £97 15s, continuing over a seventy-five-year period – the position argued by Queen Anne's Bounty in January and February. 'The Church authorities should not give any undertaking to leave the bill unopposed,' insisted Radcliffe.[94] Middleton argued that such a position was not 'practical' and that the Church should 'concentrate most strongly' on prioritising 'the existing interests of the tithe-owning clergy'. This prompted blunt words from the Oxford titheowners.[95] The Church is 'busy looking after itself', noted a briefing paper; 'we should act as far as possible with the Church, but should not consent to be pushed practically out of sight.'[96] Even more frustrating for the Oxford bursars was the lack of solidarity from the Cambridge colleges. Acting as their spokesperson, Keynes argued that 'there was no alternative to acceptance of the terms now available': whatever the 'many possible criticisms of the scheme, it would be undesirable to take any action which might lead to its abandonment'.[97]

The 'Great London March'

The government had believed that, though its proposals would not 'satisfy the views of extremists' in the tithepayers' associations, the reduction of payments to £91 11s 2d would be enough to placate 'moderate' sections

---

[91] William Temple to Cosmo Lang, 4 June 1936; Cosmo Lang to William Temple, 7 June 1936, LPL, Lang 72.
[92] Informal Conference of Tithe-Owners, 3 Mar. 1936, CERC, QAB/2/1/53.
[93] Scheme of the Oxford Bursars, 27 Mar. 1936, CERC, QAB/2/1/53.
[94] Informal Conference of Tithe Owners, 29 Apr. 1936, CERC, QAB/2/1/53.
[95] Informal Conference of Tithe Owners, 27 Mar. 1936, CERC, QAB/2/1/53.
[96] Scheme of the Oxford Bursars, 27 Mar. 1936, CERC, QAB/2/1/53.
[97] Informal Conference of Tithe Owners, 29 Apr. and 3 Mar. 1936, CERC, QAB/2/1/53.

of the farming community.[98] Though the assessment was broadly correct, opposition to the bill from the tithepayers' movement gathered momentum as the debate developed. As with the 1934 bill, pressure from the movement forced the NFU to reverse its initial supportive stance and express opposition to the proposed legislation.

The NTA's campaign against the bill highlighted the sixty-year period of annuities, the threat of bankruptcy or imprisonment for debts, and the 'inadequate reduction' in tithepayers' payments. It pointed out that if payments were to be linked to the current price of corn, they would be £80 – or £71, excluding the war-time wheat subsidy – rather than £91 11s. The association also attacked plans to collect arrears, arguing that 'in many cases [they] should either be cancelled entirely or settled by the State'.[99] Kedward characterised the bill as the government's attempt to make tithe 'not smell so rank' but still 'strap it to the shoulder of the [farming] industry for the next 60 years'.[100] Tithepayers' associations held protests against the bill in Elham (27 May), in Norwich (30 May) and at a series of distraint sales. The Norwich rally assembled a broad political coalition. Speaking on the platform alongside Doreen Wallace, Mobbs and Solley were agricultural workers' leader Edwin Gooch and William Whiteley MP, the Labour Party's chief whip. Receiving warm applause, Whiteley explained how, as 'a socialist and a miner', he had been brought up to fight 'for justice for all citizens'.[101]

The tithepayers' campaign culminated on 24 June with a 'Great London March' organised by the 'United Committee of Protest against the Tithe Bill'. Chaired by George Gill, secretary of Elham Tithepayers' Association, the Committee drew together the NTA, the Norfolk Women's Tithepayers' Association, McCreagh's Tithe League and George Pitt-Rivers' Wessex Agricultural Defence Association. Front-page newspaper articles described 'a three-mile procession of 5,000 farmers, farm labourers, dairymaids, landgirls, farmers' wives and friends'. Photographs highlighted the 'many picturesque characters in medieval garb'.[102] For the agricultural press, it was an 'event without parallel in recent years', though *The Times* thought it 'foolish' and 'ill-judged'.[103] Prime Minister Baldwin refused to meet a delegation that waited several hours to lobby him at 10 Downing Street.

[98] 'An End of Tithe', *The Times*, 28 Feb. 1936. 'Tithe Grumbles', *The Times*, 16 Mar. 1936.
[99] NTA, 'Government's Tithe Proposals, 1936', 25 Mar. 1936, DWPap.
[100] 'Wortham, The Tithe Storm Centre', *Yarmouth Independent*, 21 Mar. 1936.
[101] 'March on London', *Yarmouth Independent*, 6 June 1936.
[102] '5,000 Farmers' Protest March Through West End', *News Chronicle*, 25 June 1936; 'The Farmers Mobilise', *Daily Sketch*, 25 June 1936.
[103] 'Mr Baldwin Incenses Tithe-payers', *F&S*, 29 June 1936; 'A Foolish Demonstration', *The Times*, 27 June 1936.

FIGURE 11. Rev. Roderick Kedward addressing the crowd in Hyde Park after the 'Great London March', 24 June 1936 (© Topfoto).

The Royal Commission

The speakers who addressed the crowd from four platforms in Hyde Park represented different shades on the political spectrum. Alongside leaders of the tithepayers' movement – including Kedward, Mobbs, Pitt-Rivers and Frank Allen – were politicians of the left, Sir Richard Stafford Cripps MP, and Andrew MacLaren MP, and of the right, particularly the prominent Kentish Conservative Sir John Prestige. The BUF had no organised presence, though at least one of its members, George C. Solley, spoke in Hyde Park. Pitt-Rivers helped to shape much of the demonstration's agrarian identity, including its description as 'a mass meeting of the yeoman tithepayers of England'. The organising committee adopted Pitt-Rivers' suggestion of a 'petition to the King', asking the monarch to exercise the royal prerogative to refuse assent to the government's bill. After the event, the text was circulated to tithepayers' associations to gather signatories. Whilst most farmers signed to express their opposition to the bill, the WADA leader had wider motives in addressing Edward VIII. With others on the extreme right, he was encouraged by the king's sympathies for authoritarian rule and Nazi Germany and believed that, by overruling parliament, the sovereign might become, in the words of one right-wing newspaper, the British equivalent of the 'strong men of destiny in Italy and Germany'.[104]

The NFU declined an invitation to participate in the 'great march'. Its leaders had 'welcomed' the Commission's report and the Government's White Paper as 'a complete vindication of all the union has said on the tithe question'. While criticising the extension of payments to sixty years and personal liability for tithe debt, the union announced it was 'not prepared to oppose the bill being given a second reading'. It would accept it 'under protest […] to secure an immediate measure of relief for tithepayers'.[105] Once again, the NFU leadership's position was conditioned by its relationship with government, which had evolved into one akin to a devoted partner in a fractious marriage. At the union's AGM in January, Elliot had received an ovation after speaking of mutual 'comradeship, trust and goodwill'.[106] In May, a high-powered NFU delegation met Baldwin. Reassuring him of their 'full support' for the government's agricultural policy, they also reported 'disappointment and anxiety' amongst farmers that agriculture was not being 'accorded its proper place in the economic life of the country'. Yet, amongst their long list of grievances, tithe did not warrant a mention.[107] An editorial in the *Farmer &*

---

[104] *Saturday Review*, cited in Pugh, 'Hurrah for the Blackshirts!', 242.
[105] 'Farmers' Attitude', *The Times*, 29 Feb. 1936; NFU Tithe Committee, MERL, SR NFU, AD1/18, 6 Mar. 1936; NFU, Report of Tithe Committee, 11 May 1936, MERL, SR NFU, ADI/18; *NFU Record*, June 1936, 215; NFU News Sheet, 23 Mar. 1936, MERL, SR NFU P4/A16.
[106] 'Annual General Meeting of the Union', *NFU Record*, Feb. 1936, 120–1.
[107] 'The Deputation to Mr Baldwin', *NFU Record*, June 1936, 219–20.

Stockbreeder – possibly written but certainly inspired by NFU-sponsored MP Sir Joseph Lamb – explained that a government defeat on tithe should be avoided as it could lead to 'the end of the promised agricultural policy of the Wheat Act, beet-sugar subsidy, cattle subsidy, bacon quotas'. 'Tithe is important,' it continued, 'but it is not the whole agricultural problem, and it is the whole problem that has to be kept in mind.'[108]

As with the 1934 bill, the NFU's attitude to tithe legislation stirred unrest in its ranks. At the April National Council, two officers of Suffolk Tithepayers' Association, Mobbs and Makens Turner, rounded on national officials. The policy 'was another illustration of the way the troubles of tithepayers had been handled by the Farmers' Union,' complained Makens. 'Let down by N.F.U.', headlined the *Farmer & Stockbreeder*.[109] In a consultation of county branches, sixteen out of twenty-eight responses urged the union to oppose the legislation. On the eve of the London march, the national council made an about-turn and voted to reject the bill. Reluctantly, officials issued a statement calling on the government to withdraw the legislation because of 'grave dissatisfaction that exists in farming circles'.[110] The NFU's opposition had been decisive in forcing the withdrawal of the 1934 bill. Yet this time no one was under any illusion that its stance would make any difference. Reginald Dorman-Smith, NFU president and Conservative MP, told the council he would vote against the final reading of the bill in parliament. But he explained there was 'no hope whatever that the Government would withdraw the bill'. Sir Joseph Lamb warned that voting down the bill 'would mean a defeat of the Government [...] on a major bill [which] would mean that the Government would say they would have to go to the country or resign'.[111] Supporters of the tithepayers' movement described the NFU's position as 'a sop' that 'only toed the line at the last moment'.[112]

The 1936 Act

The Baldwin administration was determined to push the legislation through parliament at speed. Despite significant increases in the Labour vote at the November 1935 general election, the government had a majority of over 260 and a major rebellion on its benches would be required to defeat the bill. Guaranteeing parliamentary time for its progress, the government introduced a Financial Resolution to restrict the possibility of MPs moving amendments to the bill's more controversial elements.

---

[108] 'Tithe and Agricultural Policy', *F&S*, 6 July 1936.
[109] *NFU Record*, May 1936, 190–1; '"Let down by N.F.U"', *F&S*, 1 June 1936.
[110] *NFU News Sheet*, 22 June 1936, NFU P4/A16; 'June Council Meeting', *NFU Record*, 237–40.
[111] *NFU Record*, July 1936, 'June Council Meeting', 240.
[112] 'Was NFU to Blame?', *F&S*, 20 July 1936.

The Royal Commission

The Labour and Liberal Parties both opposed the bill. Eleven years earlier, Labour had voted against the 1925 Tithe Bill, but this time its arguments were pitched from a markedly different direction. Some Conservative MPs teased Labour for its 'remarkable' change: 'The Socialist party [is] seeking the plaudits of the dukes and earning the maledictions of the deans,' mocked junior agricultural minister Herwald Ramsbotham. In fact, Labour was attempting to show it was a 'true friend' of farmers. The party proposed the reduction of tithepayers' annuity payments to £80 (the position advocated in Coates' Minority Report) and the continuation of payments for fifteen years (rather than forty) with a suggested possible compromise of eighteen or twenty years. It also adopted the NTA's position that all tithe arrears should be wiped. In the debates, Labour MPs quoted from leaflets issued by tithepayers' associations and read out letters from struggling smallholders. Andrew MacLaren, who had spoken at the Hyde Park rally, hoped that tithepayers would 'do everything' to make implementation of the bill 'an impossibility'.[113] The Liberal position was, in the words of Richard Acland, one of the party's spokespeople, 'less drastic than that put forward by the Labour Opposition'. It proposed a reduction of payments by tithepayers to the value of tithe on the open market – less than in the government's scheme but higher payments for a longer period than Labour's. Liberals representing Welsh constituencies were aggrieved that Welsh farmers would contribute towards the £2 million granted to the Church of England, despite the disestablishment of the Church in Wales.[114]

Ministers were aware that there was little enthusiasm for the bill on the government's benches. They also recognised considerable disquiet over their use of a Financial Resolution to restrict debate. But they were confident that, while many of the government's MPs were expressing 'grave misgivings' at its 'imperfect' nature, they would vote for the bill as 'the fairest compromise' that could be devised.[115] Some Conservatives spoke forcibly in support of the legislation, including Howard Clifton Brown, who had in October 1932 represented the CLA at the meeting to establish General Dealers Ltd. Others sought a more favourable settlement for titheowners. Ralph Assheton, MP for Rushcliffe, proposed that payments by tithepayers be extended to sixty-eight years, the position advocated by the bishop of Norwich. Hugh Cecil, Conservative MP for Oxford University, entertained the House with a speech denouncing the bill as 'wicked', an 'immorality' for 'partial disendowment of the Church'. His address was almost identical to the one he had made during

---

[113] Rt. Hon. C Addison, 'Report and Recommendations of the Agricultural Sub-Committee, May 1936; HC Deb., *Hansard*, 29 June 1936.
[114] HC Deb., *Hansard*, 29 June 1936; Henry Haydn Jones, HC Deb., *Hansard*, 13 May 1936.
[115] 'Tithe Bill To-Day', *The Times*, 13 May 1936; Edward Ruggles-Brise, HC Deb., *Hansard*, 29 June 1936.

the debate on the 1925 tithe legislation. The National Labour MP and Church Commissioner Richard Denman also borrowed from the 1925 debate, using arguments made by Labour's then spokesperson Josiah Wedgwood, to describe the bill as a 'gift to landowners'. A larger group of government-supporting MPs urged more concessions for tithepayers. Dorman-Smith warned that opposition to the bill by farmers was 'still on the upgrade' and Colin (Mark) Patrick, MP for Tavistock, argued that grievances amongst tithepayers would 'persist in a chronic and acute form'.[116] On a vote on an amendment to relax some of the available powers to recover arrears, the government's majority was reduced to three.[117] Yet, on the Third Reading, only six Conservatives and one National Liberal voted with Labour and the Liberals to oppose the bill. One was the NFU president, Dorman-Smith; the others represented constituencies in hot spots of the tithe war.[118] There were also a number of abstentions. A Labour MP accurately described the government's benches as 'a very rebellious and mutinous crew' who had 'come to heel' after being 'threatened with the yard arm'.[119]

On 29 June, the Tithe Bill passed through the House of Commons on a vote of 251 to 128. After some minor amendments from the House of Lords, a new Act entered the statute book on 31 July 1936. Throughout the debate, MPs on all sides of the House had warned that the legislation could not provide a lasting settlement. Even Elliot, the minister of agriculture, conceded that the Act may only be a 'step on the road' towards a solution, rather than 'the final solution'. From the Labour front bench, Albert Alexander warned of a continuing 'spirit of resistance among tithepayers'.[120] Yet, while grievances and a great deal of bitterness remained amongst leading protagonists on both sides, the passing of the 1936 Act marked for all intents and purposes the conclusion of the Tithe War.

---

[116] HC Deb., *Hansard*, 13 May and 29 June 1936.
[117] 'The Tithe Bill', *The Times*, 27 June 1936.
[118] Government supporters opposing the bill were the Conservatives Henry Burton (Sudbury), Somerset de Chair (Norfolk South West), Dorman-Smith (Petersfield), Patrick (Tavistock), Pierse Loftus (Lowestoft) and William Wayland (Canterbury), and the National Liberal Edgar Granville (Eye).
[119] Frederick Bellenger, HC Deb., *Hansard*, 29 June 1936.
[120] Walter Elliot and Albert Alexander, HC Deb., *Hansard*, 29 June 1936.

10

Aftermath

The Tithe War came to a somewhat messy end, neither side feeling satisfied with the outcome. Titheowners maintained that the 1936 Act, while 'liberating' them from the unpleasant task of collecting tithe, was – in the words of the archbishop of Canterbury – 'more for the relief of the tithepayer' and would 'inflict real hardships on the titheowners'.[1] Tithepayers argued that, though their payments were reduced by around 17 per cent, tithe continued to exist, albeit 'in another form'. The National Tithepayers' Association pledged to continue their fight 'by all constitutional means'.[2]

The Tithe Redemption Committee began to collect tithe annuity payments on 1 April 1937. Simultaneously, titheowners received compensatory government stock and, in the case of Queen Anne's Bounty, a cash payment to provide for the 'existing interests' of incumbent clergy. Drawing expertise from 'churchmen' with ties to the City of London, the Queen Anne's Bounty tithe committee began to trade stock and invest monies with 'very satisfactory' results. In effect, the Bounty's role was transformed from tithe collector to fund manager, a change that would encourage the merger in 1948 with the Ecclesiastical Commissioners to form the Church Commissioners.

The end of its tithe-collecting responsibilities posed some practical problems for the Church. The first was what to do with the considerable number of Queen Anne's Bounty staff employed to collect and administer tithe. The problem was resolved when the Treasury offered the Bounty's employees positions with the Tithe Redemption Commission without loss of pay or pension rights. The redeployment provided the government with a ready-made, experienced team to collect tithe annuities, though tithepayers would soon notice that they were being chased for payments by the same people who had previously collected for the Church.[3]

The future of General Dealers proved a trickier challenge. The company's final accounts showed that it had cost titheowners £24,597 14s 3d over four

---

[1] HL Deb., *Hansard*, 7 July 1937.
[2] 'Tithepayers resist Bill', *DHe*, 30 July 1936; East Kent Tithepayers' Association, Report for the Year 1936, 4 Feb. 1937, KHLC, EK, U1276/B4/105.
[3] QAB Tithe Committee, 11 Jan. 1937 and 24 Nov. 1937, CERC, QAB/2/1/54; QAB Tithe Committee, 22 July 1936, CERC, QAB/2/1/53.

years (equivalent to around £2 million in 2023).[4] Its contract was terminated on 31 March 1937, but, to avoid unwelcome scrutiny, the titheowners agreed there should be no 'formal winding up'; instead, General Dealers Ltd. was to simply 'fade away'. In a statement that would have to remain secret, Queen Anne's Bounty paid tribute to the 'very valuable services' rendered by its managing directors: 'but for the highly efficient manner in which [their] work had been done, the recovery of tithe rentcharge through the County Courts might have broken down completely.'[5] Yet Captain Parlour and Major Miller wanted more than warm words and demanded a golden handshake. They claimed they were 'morally entitled to receive something' as they had 'never failed to get the goods away [despite] the organised difficulties and personal danger with which they were faced'.[6] Some on the control committee expressed sympathy for their case. But in February 1938, Queen Anne's Bounty turned down their requests, recommending to the governors that no further payments to General Dealers could be justified.[7]

While managing to avoid damaging publicity over General Dealers, the Church could not sidestep embarrassment over the Archbishops' Tithe Compensation Fund. Launched in October 1937 by the archbishops of Canterbury and York, the fund sought contributions from tithepayers 'who had entirely different feelings' than the agitators leading the tithepayers' movement. Throughout the summer, members of the Central Board of Finance had argued that many 'important' landowners were opposed to the end of tithe and prepared to continue making payments at the old rate.[8] After a consultation of bishops, only a few of whom expressed misgivings, the fund was launched. 'Our hope is,' wrote Cosmo Lang and William Temple, 'that through the gifts of many whose lands have for centuries contributed tithe […], the cause of religion may be maintained and set forward.'[9] A first batch of 72,000 letters was posted to tithepayers in October 1936. Within days, Lambeth Palace was inundated with 'returned empties', many of them containing less than friendly remarks. The fund's administrator wrote to Cosmo Lang's chaplain: 'Would you express to His Grace my regret […] for the "horror" with which […] His Grace viewed the litter in his hall! I have telephoned the Post Office and asked them to be sure that such returned packets are sent

[4] £19,851 came from QAB, £2,705 from the EC and £2,040 from the Welsh Commissioners. Letter from Deacon & Co, Tithe Recovery Control Committee, 3 Dec. 1936, CERC, ECE/SEC/TITHE/GD/2.
[5] QAB Tithe Committee, 1 Feb. 1937, CERC, QAB/2/1/54; Tithe Recovery Control Committee, 3 Dec. 1937, CERC, ECE/SEC/TITHE/GD/2.
[6] Primrose to Middleton, 10 Nov. 1937, CERC, ECE/SEC/TITHE/GD/2.
[7] QAB Tithe Committee, 7 Feb. 1938, CERC, QAB/2/1/55.
[8] Lord Selborne to Canon Partridge, 11 May 1936, CERC, ECE/SEC/TITHE/L/6/1.
[9] 'Archbishops and Tithe' and Cosmo Cantuar, William Ebor, 'Voluntary Tithe', *The Times*, 12 Oct. 1936.

here and not to Lambeth.' But he also wanted to reassure the archbishop that 'the "abuse" has not been as violent as one might have expected… [though] such phrases as "robber" occur pretty frequently.' During the next few weeks, the Fund received sixty-eight donations totalling £1,595. Most came from two large contributions: £500 from Imperial Chemicals Ltd and £420 from a well-heeled woman in Cheltenham. Cosmo Lang's chaplain wrote: 'Speaking privately, His Grace cannot but think that the result of the Appeal so far is very disappointing.'[10]

'Fighting with half a membership'

As the curtain fell on the Tithe War, each opposing side found themselves mourning the sudden death of their most prominent protagonist. In March 1937, a wave of emotion swept members of the tithepayers' movement at the passing of Roderick Kedward at the age of 55. The NTA collected subscriptions to erect a monument to their 'beloved leader', who had 'killed himself in the task of bettering the lot of the people'. Carved out of Cornish granite, the Kedward Memorial was unveiled in June 1938 at a ceremony attended by activists from around the country.[11] Today, it stands in a corner of Ashford Market. Later in 1938, the 62-year-old George Middleton collapsed in the presence of the archbishop of Canterbury. Commenting on his role in the Tithe War, an obituary in *The Times* credited Middleton for saving 'a position in danger of being lost without cause to factious agitators', work that had 'tak[en] its toll of his strength'.[12]

After Kedward's death, Doreen Wallace became chair of the NTA; Edgar Granville, MP for Eye, was appointed national president; Frank Allen continued to coordinate activities and communications. In 1938, the NTA Council agreed a new constitution, which pledged to 'protest strongly against the unjust provisions of the Tithe Act 1936 and the enforced payment of tithe in any form'. Its declared aim was 'the total abolition of tithe'.[13] But appeals to activists to revive branches received a disappointing response. 'I have spent a good deal of time on tithe but unfortunately, against my advice, the tithepayers of this area have closed

---

[10] Meeting of Representatives of Area Collection Committees with Members of the QAB Tithe Committee, 29 July 1936, CERC, QAB/2/1/53; Lord Selbourne to Canon Patridge, 11 May 1936; CERC, ECE/SEC/TITHE/L/6/1; Tithe Appeal. Epitome of Replies from Dioceses, Aug. 1936, LPL, Lang 72; 'Archbishops and Tithe', *The Times*, 12 Oct. 1936; R. M. B. Mackenzie to Rev A. Sargent & Sargent to Mackenzie, 28 Oct. 1936, LPL, Lang 72.

[11] 'Rev. R. M. Kedward Cremated', *KE*, 19 Mar. 1937; 'Memorial to Tithe-Leader', *KE*, 10 June 1938.

[12] *The Times*, 26 Oct. 1938.

[13] NTA, Proposed Basis of Association, 14 July 1938, Dorset Record Office, D491/8.

up and branches [in] Yeovil, Chard, Beaminster and at Taunton are all gone dead,' reported one former local leader; 'I am far from satisfied with the 1936 Tithe Act, but it seems to me extremely doubtful whether it is possible, for the present at any rate, to make a live political issue out of this matter,' wrote another.[14] For Doreen Wallace, looking back on the period, 'the 1936 Act [...] was not a win; it ended in a compromise [but] it satisfied our National Tithepayers' Association. [...] We were still fighting with half a membership.'[15]

Nevertheless, the tithe controversy persisted, albeit with less intensity. One factor was the continuing impact of the agricultural depression. After stabilising in the mid-1930s, prices of important agricultural produce fell sharply during 1938. Farmers in East Anglia highlighted the impact of a drop of almost a quarter in the price of barley. Rallies in Ipswich and Norwich expressed anger at the complacency in the face of 'the serious plight of the agricultural industry' of prime minister Neville Chamberlain and William Morrison, who had succeeded Elliot as minister of agriculture. Organised by Mobbs, now the leader of Suffolk NFU, the Ipswich rally called for 'a united front of all agricultural industries' and voted to oppose candidates of the National Government who did not support a policy of agricultural revival. In early February 1939, around a thousand East Anglian farmers marched through London around the slogan 'Save Agriculture and Save Britain'.[16] Against the background of falling prices and a feeling of general 'agricultural decline', tithe annuity payments remained a grievance for many farmers. In June 1939, a tithe conference organised by the NFU passed an NTA-inspired resolution demanding 'immediate steps towards the total abolition of tithe', given the 'inability of many tithepayers to meet demands [...] owing to falling prices of agricultural products'. Though refusing to endorse the resolution, the NFU parliamentary committee agreed to lobby ministers for the 'alleviation of the burden of tithe annuity payments'.[17]

Arrears built up during the conflict also kept the tithe issue alive. Queen Anne's Bounty and other titheowners had made special efforts to apply for recovery orders in the county courts before the deadline at which collection powers were transferred to the Tithe Redemption Committee.[18] Consequently, distraint seizures instigated by titheowners continued for some time after the 1936 Act came into force. The Kentish Weald was once again a hot spot. In October 1936, the *Daily Mirror*

---

[14] Replies to letters sent out by R. Whitlock, Dorset Record Office, D491/8.
[15] Wallace to Kinn McIntosh, 9 May 1976, DWPap.
[16] 'Suffolk Farmers' Strong Protest', *Suffolk & Essex Free Press*, 12 Jan. 1939; 'Farmers March Through London', *DHe*, 2 Feb. 1939.
[17] Correspondence of NFU Tithe Conference, 1 June 1939, Dorset Record Office, D491/8; 'NFU and Tithe', *KE*, 30 June 1939.
[18] QAB, Tithe Committee, 1 Feb. 1937, CERC, QAB 2/1/54.

featured the seizure of furniture and stock from the Ruckinge farm of Archibald Waddell, a founding member of the East Kent Tithepayers' Association. In December, a ram and three cows were sold at an auction in Mersham and, the same month, General Dealers removed two cows and a calf from the Pluckley farm of Ebenezer Haffenden, another veteran of the conflict. Two weeks later, Haffenden and a group from the local tithepayers' association interrupted Sunday service in the parish church. Arriving during the *Te Deum*, they protested the vicar's support for tithe distraints before marching out, slamming the door behind them.[19] In January 1937, Ashford county court issued 230 recovery orders in favour of Queen Anne's Bounty and other titheowners. According to the local press, it 'was the largest number ever dealt with at Ashford in one day, and believed to be a record for the country'.[20]

After April 1937, the Tithe Redemption Committee became responsible for arrears, a substantial sum of around £550,000, not counting debts pursued separately by the titheowners.[21] Tithepayers had the right to have their cases heard by an Arrears Investigation Committee, which had powers to reduce or cancel the debt after a review of their ability to pay.[22] But the process contained many pitfalls. By applying for remission, tithepayers gave up the legal right to object to a titheowner's claim. At hearings, evidence relating to their financial position could be challenged by representatives of the titheowners, and there were penalties for 'frivolous' claims.[23] Tithepayers also found that that the interpretation of the law on remissions was stacked against them. The Act had stipulated that annuity payments should be capped at one-third of the value of the land, but the Tithe Redemption Committee and later the Inland Revenue included farmhouses, workers' cottages and other buildings when calculating the value, thereby ruling out many claims for remission.

Most farmers arranged to pay their arrears, but some continued a campaign of passive resistance. In March 1938, the Redemption Committee sent bailiffs to Wortham to confiscate Roland Rash's car and to nearby Yaxley to seize pigs from another farmer. In November, in Devon, animals and wagons belonging to William Down, a member of the British Union of Fascists, were auctioned near Tiverton. In March and April 1939, bailiffs removed livestock from a number of East Anglian farms, including at Stow Bedon (Norfolk) and Wattisfield (Suffolk). When pigs were auctioned in the market square at Attleborough (Norfolk),

---

[19] 'And they call it ... Queen Anne's Bounty', *Daily Mirror*, 30 Oct. 1936; 'Tithe Concession Principle', *KE*, 11 Dec. 1936; 'Farmers interrupt Church Service', *Sevenoaks Chronicle and Kentish Advertiser*, 25 Dec. 1936.
[20] '230 Tithe Orders', *KE*, 5 Mar. 1937.
[21] Harry Crookshank, HC Deb., *Hansard*, 23 June 1939.
[22] NTA, 'Tithe Act, 1936: What is to Happen after 1 April 1937?' DWPap.
[23] QAB, Tithe Committee, 28 June 1938, CERC, QAB 2/1/54.

'scores of East Anglian farmers greeted every bid with ironical cheers'. A parade around the town concluded with a speech from Mobbs, who declared with misplaced optimism the start of 'a series of demonstrations in the eastern counties'. In July, the trustees of Great Sampford Baptist Church (Essex) appeared at Saffron Walden county court and offered to go to prison rather than pay tithe for 'doctrines of which we do not approve'.[24] Doreen Wallace also announced she was 'ready to go to prison', a statement that made headlines in the national press.[25] The Tithe Redemption Committee successfully applied to make her bankrupt and, in July 1939, a large crowd assembled in Wortham to witness the auction of Wallace's possessions. After the sale – at which all 201 lots were purchased by Mobbs – Wallace was 'carried shoulder high [and] a huge bonfire, in which was burnt a copy of the 1936 Tithe Act, was ignited'. The novelist announced that the sale meant 'her husband, three children, and two maids, will sleep on the floors of their bedrooms'.[26]

Some tithe agitation continued during the war. The NTA wrote to senior ministers arguing for a moratorium on annuity payments in order to remove an obstacle to food production. The Ashford Tithepayers' Association publicised cases of 'threatening letters' sent by solicitors employed by the Tithe Redemption Committee and the 'multitudinous issue' of court orders against farmers. After receiving a delegation of tithepayers from East Sussex, the archbishop of Canterbury, William Temple, reported that 'there is still strong feeling among many farmers and members of the agricultural community against the payment of Tithe [and] that this feeling is still directed against the Church.'[27]

Yet this wartime agitation represents the last embers of the tithe conflict. In the two decades following the Second World War, the tithe controversy and increasingly its memory faded away against the background of the 'second agricultural revolution'. Technological innovation – tractors, combine harvesters, factory farming methods – larger and more capital-intensive holdings and, crucially, a corporatist deal between state and industry that surpassed Elliot's pre-war partnership with NFU leaders all underpinned a period of prosperity and price stability for farmers.

24 'Tithe Distraints at Wortham', *DiEx*, 25 Mar. 1938; 'Occasional Notes', *NDJ*, 1 Dec. 1938; 'Tithe Distraints on Three Farms', *Eastern Daily Press*, 25 Mar. 1939; 'Farmers Parade a Town', *Evening News*, 6 Apr. 1939; 'Gaol rather than pay tithes', *Daily Telegraph*, 25 July 1939.
25 'Woman ready for prison in Tithe dispute', *DMa*, 27 Mar. 1939; 'Novelist ready to go to jail for her Tithes', *DEx*, 27 Mar. 1939; 'Authoress may lead "War" on Tithes', *News Chronicle*, 27 Mar. 1939; 'Ready to go to Prison', *Daily Mirror*, 27 Mar. 1939.
26 'A Tithe Sale', *F&S*, 25 July 1939; 'Will Sleep on Floor after Tithe Sale', *DMa*, 17 July 1939.
27 Ashford Tithepayers Association, 13 Oct. 1941, Dorset Record Office, D491/8; William Temple to TRC, 11 May 1944, LPL, W. Temple 48.

Historians draw parallels between the post-war years and the 'high farming' era of the mid-nineteenth century.[28] In short, farmers, particularly those in the arable regions of eastern and southern England, experienced a 'good war' and an even more propitious peace. By 1950, Wallace and Allen had begun steps to wind up the NTA.[29] 'We meet with a good deal of apathy here,' wrote Wallace, 'farmers have been doing too well […] and have forgotten what Tithe may mean in less prosperous times.'[30]

Seeking an explanation for the decline of the tithepayers' movement, Allen spoke of the NTA's error in 'laying too much stress' on the impact of the agricultural depression. 'I did see the mistake, but [only] when it was too late to revise our policy,' he contended, 'we should have stuck solely to the point that the tithe was (and is) an unfair tax, whatever the state of agriculture.'[31] Yet Allen's analysis overlooks the fact that the movement had drawn strength from its ability to link those opposed to tithe on principle with others whose primary objective was to mitigate its negative consequences, both for individual farmers and for the wider fortunes of agriculture. As during the tithe conflicts of the nineteenth century, the tithepayers' movement of the 1930s was a coalition. Radicals of varying shades of right and left campaigned alongside conservative-minded 'tribunes' of the farming community, who emphasised their respect for property and national institutions. The movement was influenced by a deep-rooted radical tradition that viewed tithe as a symbol of privilege and injustice but also by an agrarian ideology that pervaded right-wing politics throughout the inter-war years.

The social change rooted in the new agricultural revolution transformed both wings of the tithepayers' movement. As the number of small farmers and agricultural labourers declined, villages that had been battlefields in the Tithe War began to lose their identity as agricultural communities. In Norfolk before the war, 44 per cent of the male working population had been involved in agriculture; by 1970, the figure had fallen to 13 per cent. As Howkins outlines, 'in counties of East Anglia [and this applies also to other centres of the Tithe War], a powerful tradition of village self organisation, which included the nonconformist chapel, friendly societies and trade unions […] began to disintegrate.'[32] Simultaneously, more farmers adopted a business identity, albeit of a very particular kind, speeding up a process that was already well advanced. While becoming increasingly disconnected from the wider village community, farmers formed a 'tightly interlocking and rather inward-looking social network' comprised of 'NFU meetings, farmers' clubs, agricultural shows, shoots

---

[28] Newby, *Country Life*, 188.
[29] Allen to Miss Puplett, 9 Oct. 1950, Dorset Record Office, D491/9.
[30] Doreen Rash to Puplett, 28 Mar. 1947, Dorset Record Office, D491/9.
[31] Allen to Puplett, 5 Jan. 1954, Dorset Record Office, D491/9.
[32] Howkins, *Death of Rural England*, 164 and 173.

and rural Conservative Party functions'.[33] For them, tithe was just another item on the balance sheet, one that became increasingly insignificant through the effect of inflation and, more importantly, increases in the value of land.

A few veterans of the tithepayers' movement could not reconcile themselves to such changes. In November 1952, Archibald Waddell, now aged 77, served seven days in Canterbury prison for failure to comply with a court order to pay annuity arrears of £12 8s. It was, he said, 'his last chance to show the younger generation [...] that it is the principle of the thing that matters, and what it is to fight tithe'. He was 'bitterly disappointed with the attitude of young farmers today who say they might as well pay tithe as pay extra income tax'.[34]

As for Frank Allen, he remained 'as busy as ever' offering legal advice and administrative services to tithepayers. 'It is not the kind of business I would have preferred,' he wrote in 1954, 'I would much rather be working to get rid of tithe altogether.' The former Canterbury Cathedral tithe collector and NTA organiser also turned his attention to the movement's historical significance:

> I have a considerable assembly of books, pamphlets and other documents which during the years when we were most active I collected in different parts of the country. [...] I think that this collection may be unique. What I would like to do would be to deposit the whole lot in some public institution with a covering statement, so that they and it could be used by some future historian who wished to give a detailed account of matters agricultural in this Country during the Depression which followed the 1914–1918 War. I do not think that any historian worthy of the name could entirely ignore the efforts of the Tithepayers Associations.[35]

His leading role in the tithe war largely forgotten, Allen – the gatekeeper turned poacher of this story – died in relative obscurity in 1961. Unfortunately, it appears that his 'assembly' of documentation is lost.

---

[33] Newby, *Country Life*, 98–9.
[34] 'Kent Farmer Committed to Prison' and 'Why Farmer Waddell Went to Jail', *KM*, 14 Nov. and 5 Dec. 1952.
[35] Allen to Puplett, 3 Apr. 1954, Dorset Record Office, D491/93.

Conclusion: A 'Curious Rural Revolt'?

In June 1976, Denzil Davies, minister of state for the Treasury in the Labour government, announced that tithe annuity payments would cease after October 1977, rather than continuing until 1996. The next finance bill would make the necessary amendments to the 1936 Tithe Act. Several factors prompted the decision. As prosperity returned to farming during the 1950s and 1960s, a significant number of tithepayers had 'redeemed' their annuities – that is, paid off their future commitments with a lump sum. Together with inflation, this meant that the costs of collection and administration of the annuities now outweighed the total amounts received. In addition, the Treasury held sufficient funds to service the remaining redemption stock.[1] Quite simply, it was no longer financially prudent to collect tithe annuities. The announcement of an end to the vestiges of tithe prompted no debate and hardly any publicity. Politicians, journalists and historians failed to mark the last rites of an institution that had, for centuries, formed an essential element of social and political life, and which had for much of its history been marked with contention.

The nature and manifestations of tithe disputes through the ages were conditioned by the political and social relations of the day. In the late medieval period, tensions over tithe between Church and state signalled an argument over sharing the spoils of power and privilege. After the Reformation, 'small-scale resistance' by tithepayers became, in many regions, a normal occurrence of village life. At various times, those seeking to 'turn the world upside down' – Diggers and Levellers during the English Civil War, early Quakers, Radicals inspired by revolutionary France – tried to fashion a more fundamental challenge to tithe. The 'tithe war' outlined in this book needs therefore to be placed in historical perspective.

Perhaps the first curiosity of this 'curious rural revolt' is that it should have happened at all. In most European countries, the legal requirement to pay tithe was abolished or reformed out of existence during the 'long nineteenth century', often as a result of revolutionary or liberal nationalist upheaval. In France, *la dîme* was swept away by the 1789 Revolution; in Spain, *el diezmo* was abolished in 1841, after a 'liberal' victory over

---

[1] HC Deb., *Hansard*, 17 June 1976; Evans, *Contentious Tithe*, 166–7.

attempts to resurrect an absolute monarchy – the population in several regions having waged 'mass tithe strikes' in protest at clerical support for the royalist 'enemy';[2] in Hungary, *o dézsma* was a casualty of the 1848 Revolution, the 'springtime of the people'; in Italy, the Church finally lost its rights to *la decima* in the aftermath of the Risorgimento. Britain's more gradualist route to modernity meant that tithe survived in England and Wales, albeit after 1836 transformed into a cash payment. It is a paradox that, despite – or rather because of – its early agricultural and industrial 'revolutions', the 'home of capitalism' chose to cling to a range of medieval practices and institutions, including tithe.

In the early nineteenth century, the ruling elites and their Tory political representatives had viewed demands for tithe reform as a revolutionary challenge, first to the state – as they threatened to undermine the position of the Established Church – and, secondly, to property rights. Leading agriculturalists and the parliamentary Whigs, despite viewing it as an anachronism, also accepted tithe's legitimacy as a form of property. A Whiggish compromise, the 1836 Tithe Commutation Act attempted to remove the worst excesses of the system while protecting the interests of titheowners. In consequence, it failed to resolve the clash of conflicting interests surrounding tithe and, by introducing the principle that tithe should be regulated through parliamentary legislation, served to entwine the tithe problem further into the fabric of politics and the state. A century later, leaders of the NTA, quite correctly, pointed to the Act's 'unjust provisions, errors and omissions' as the root of tithepayers' grievances.[3]

In 1841, fears that a challenge to property rights could undermine social order also led to a gradualist approach to the abolition of copyhold.[4] As with tithe, this vestige of medieval land tenure endured well into the twentieth century. Copyholders were finally 'emancipated' from manorial obligations by the Law of Property Act of 1922, which – after a delay – became law on 31 December 1925. Though copyholders became freeholders, the process was not complete. Lords were entitled to compensation for the loss of interest on their property and lengthy negotiations and delays meant that some copyholders were not fully 'emancipated' until the 1950s. The issue of tithe can be viewed, therefore, as part of a history of long persistence and slow death of medieval institutions.

Once the 1836 Tithe Commutation Act was passed, it was inevitable that demands for further reform would pose serious difficulties for government, political parties, state institutions and the legal system, without forgetting the Church and elitist educational institutions. Indeed,

[2] Mark Lawrence, *The Spanish Civil Wars: A Comparative History of the First Carlist War* (London: Bloomsbury Academic, 2017), 74.
[3] 'Report of the Council of the National Tithepayers' Association', 11 May 1925, London School of Economics, Special Collections.
[4] See pp. 21 and 25–6.

Conclusion: A 'Curious Rural Revolt'?

the painful attempts of the Salisbury government (1886–92) to pass tithe legislation – six bills in almost as many years – indicate the deep-rooted nature of the tithe imbroglio. So too, does the botched 'settlement' of 1925: during the debate in parliament, only a few rare voices questioned the basic principle of tithe. By the early 1930s British politics had realigned. But all parties – Conservative, Labour and Liberal – were wrong-footed by the outbreak of the tithe war. Right up until 1935, a near consensus existed amongst politicians of all major political shades that abolition of tithe remained off the agenda. Also telling, but perhaps more understandable, is the way all wings of the Church continued to defend an archaic institution. Some of the most vehement pro-tithe protagonists – including George Middleton – had come from a 'Christian socialist' background. Instead of sensing the damage tithe posed to the Church's reputational standing in a rapidly changing world, they resurrected the idea, originally proposed by E. W. I. Peterson and Lord Grey in 1890, of forming a private company to resist 'illegal combinations of tithepayers'. Amongst lay titheowners, the bursars of Oxford and Cambridge Colleges were some of the most belligerent. It is striking that a liberal and far-sighted academic such as John Maynard Keynes was one of the first to utilise the services of General Dealers, before later suggesting ways to resolve the conflict.

The tithe war – and this gives rise to a second 'curious' feature – was fought, perhaps inevitably, with arguments and methods that appear as hallmarks of another age. Titheowners spoke of securing 'vindication' of their 'rights' and 'entitlements', opposing reforms of tithe as 'confiscation'. Parallels can be drawn between the arguments and language used during the debates around the 1936 Tithe Act and those deployed over the Commutation Act a century earlier.[5] For their part, tithepayers called tithe 'an attack on the rights of the freeborn Englishman', a theme of nonconformism since the seventeenth century.[6] They described their campaign as 'passive resistance', words used during the Irish tithe revolt of the 1830s and again in the Kentish and Welsh campaigns of the 1880s. Though related to modern ideas of civil disobedience, passive resistance signals non-cooperation, rather than open defiance. Some find its roots in medieval political theory; others connect it to the Enlightenment doctrine of John Locke; etymologists find the first recorded use of the term in 1819.[7] During the inter-war years, passive resistance would have been associated in the historical memory with the campaign by nonconformists against the 1902 Education Act. While the tithepayers' movement deployed methods honed during tithe conflicts of the nineteenth century, some

---

[5] Evans, *Contentious Tithe*, 167.
[6] Howkins, 'Review of Tithe War'.
[7] John Morrow, *History of Political Thought* (London: Palgrave, 1998), 355–70; Michael Randle, *Civil Resistance* (London: Fontana, 1994), 19–51.

aspects of the campaign looked further back: parades and burning of effigies recall pre-modern forms of protest. Right-wing agrarians spoke of returning to a 'healthy', medievalist model of tithe, undiluted by the 'decay' of the modern world. In 1936, the Hyde Park rally was publicised as an assembly of 'the yeoman tithepayers of England', some participants turning up in medieval costume.

So, the tithepayers' movement feels out of place when viewed alongside other inter-war popular protests, which are primarily associated with 'the forward march of labour' – strikes led by trade unions, marches by unemployed workers, street demonstrations against fascism – and cloaked with the ideology of the political left. Yet, despite its arguments and methods, the tithepayers' movement also does not fit the social model of rural protests of the nineteenth century, which were generally based around agricultural labourers or tenant farmers.

The movement was conditioned by a particular and relatively short-lived conjuncture in the history of the social structure of agriculture. Following the Great War, a continuing decline in numbers working on the land coincided with the break-up of the tripartite template of landlords, tenants and labourers. Within this state of flux, new relationships began to form. Most significantly for the topic of this book, a burgeoning class of owner-occupying farmers sought to assert its identity and interests. Eventually, this class would form the basis of a corporate partnership between government and farming industry, a process initiated by Elliot during the 1930s and reaching fruition after the Second World War. The NFU became the farming industry's voice in this relationship, while also gaining a reputation for pursuing the interests of owner-occupying farmers. Yet, the NFU had its origins as an organisation of primarily tenant farmers. In 1924–25, during the negotiations that led to the 1925 Act, its leaders failed to grasp the significance of the tithe problem for those farmers who had recently purchased their holdings. Later, during the early 1930s, a different set of leaders continued to keep a distance from the tithepayers' movement, fearing support for its activity would undermine their relationship with the National Government and, particularly, the Ministry of Agriculture. This left a vacuum for the emergence and growth of the NTA. Despite limited resources, a single-issue pressure group succeeded in mobilising thousands of farmers.

This brings us to a final 'curious' aspect of the conflict: the diverse, and rather strange, political coalition that surrounded the tithepayers' movement. The campaign around tithe of the 1880s had drawn support from a peculiar alliance of Welsh nationalists, Liberals, nonconformists, Conservative agriculturalists and a number of aristocratic Conservatives, such as Lord Brabourne. The composition of politics in the 1930s was different. As it reached a climax, the tithepayers' campaign won support from Liberals, the Labour Party and Communist MP Willie Gallagher, as

Conclusion: A 'Curious Rural Revolt'?

well as the British Union of Fascists and other shades of the far right. At the time, the National Government appeared politically stable and financially competent, strengthened by damaging splits in the Labour and Liberal Parties. But it was struggling to deal with structural problems, signalled most clearly by continuing mass unemployment and vast variations in social conditions, including in rural areas. In these circumstances, tithe acted as an issue to combine opponents of the National Government, despite their ideological differences.

The broad political support for the movement also reflects its cross-class nature. Tithepayers were not a homogeneous social group. Some farmed small or middling holdings, often having had no alternative than to buy out their landowners. Some retained an anti-landlord mentality and, in certain regions, were influenced by a tradition of Liberalism and nonconformism. Others – as property owners – held aspirations to climb the social ladder and were politically inclined towards Conservativism and open to ideologies of the extreme right. Some tithepayers were already at the top of the rural hierarchy, managing large concerns and employing significant numbers of agricultural workers. This group included the long-standing 'yeoman' class of gentleman farmers. Some aristocratic landowners also attached themselves to the movement, articulating grievances at their reduced status in modern society. At the opposite end of the class spectrum, agricultural labourers viewed the campaign against tithe as serving their interests, despite sensing antagonisms with their tithe-paying employers. Yet, regardless of class differences and varying political motives, a 'social unity' bound together the tithepayers' movement, an identity rooted in specific features of rural society and economy. In this sense, the characteristics of the tithepayers' movement can be interpreted as an English manifestation of agrarianism.

In his book on tithe commutation, Evans emphasises the role played in the inter-war tithe campaign by farmers at the top of the social hierarchy. He talks of a 'situation […] ripe for theatrical exploitation [with] playing to the gallery from the better-off farmers'.[8] There is an element of truth in this remark. 'Better-off' farmers often acted as local spokespeople of the tithepayers' movement, reflecting the 'authority relationships' that mark rural communities. But noting their prominent role should not contradict observations of a broad social cohesion and solidarity within the tithepayers' movement. 'I am a member of the tithepayers' association and I intend to leave the matter in their hands,' was the regular reply by tithepayers – whether small, middling or large farmers – when asked by the Bounty's 'investigators' to pay their tithe.[9] Similarly, the 'theatrical' nature of activities around auctions and distraint seizures does not detract

---

[8] Evans, *Contentious Tithe*, 166.
[9] Tithe Recovery Controlling Committee, 29 Jan. 1934, CERC, ECE/SEC/TITHE/GD/5.

from their seriousness. Those making up the crowds were conscious that an element of 'theatre' could help secure publicity and embarrass the government and Church.

The tithe war was a remarkable historical event. It led directly to the 1936 Tithe Act, which resolved a problem that had been contentious for centuries. By stipulating that the Treasury should buy out tithe and issue annuities, the Act also enhanced farmers' corporate relationship with the state. Along with other measures of the time – marketing boards, tariffs, subsidies, tax exemptions – the legislation can be viewed as one of the foundation stones for the 'second agricultural revolution'.[10] The 'war' was remarkable also because tithe abolition had not been a project of any section of the political elite. A movement of owner-occupying farmers – a group without reputation for militant activity – faced down resistance from titheowners and the authorities, as well as opposition from official representatives of the farming industry, to force the government into a major policy reversal. At times, it was a bitter conflict. Refusing to pay tithe was not without risk. Some farmers faced losses of stock or household property. Those joining protests could face fines or threats to their freedom.

In November 1934, eighteen men – farmers, farmers' sons and farm labourers – faced trial at the Kent assizes for their part in the 'Battle of the Ducks'.[11] They initially faced conspiracy charges, though these were dropped on the eve of the trial. Seventeen defendants pleaded guilty to riotous assembly; thirteen were bound over and four 'ring leaders' received fines of £10. The judge told them that 'but for their assurance not to repeat such conduct, he would have sent them to prison'.[12] Yet the defendants were unrepentant. While awaiting trial, one of them, David Gill, spoke about the wider significance of their actions to his mother: 'His point of view', she wrote, 'has always been that you may go on talking forever and nothing happens, but do something and people sit up and take notice – hence the Royal Commission – a direct result not of talk but of direct action. It is the highest duty of a citizen to resist bad laws.'[13]

Though a 'curious' example, the tithe war reveals how, as with other aspects of modernity, the collective engagement of ordinary men and women has been the most powerful driver of democratic reform and social progress.

[10] Cooper, *British Agricultural Policy*, 216.
[11] The charges against one of the nineteen arrested had been dropped.
[12] 'Four £10 Fines in Tithe Raid Case', *DE*, 23 Nov. 1934; Mrs Sarah Shorey Gill, Nov. 1934; Modern Records Centre, University of Warwick, LAH, MSS.121/F/3/3/6.
[13] 'Mrs Sarah Shorey Gill, Nov. 1934; Modern Records Centre, University of Warwick, LAH, MSS.121/F/3/3/6.

SOURCES AND BIBLIOGRAPHY

Archival sources

Berkshire Record Office
Papers of Castle Family (Home Farm, Charlton)

Bodleian Special Collections
Christopher Addison papers

Canterbury Cathedral Archives
Chapter meetings (1911–25)
George Bell, diary (1924–27)
Tithe files (1910–40)
Tithe letter books (1919–34)

Church of England Record Office
Secretary to the Ecclesiastical Commissioners: Tithe (1887–1947)
Queen Anne's Bounty, minute books (1925–47)

Churchill Archives Centre
George Pitt-Rivers papers

Doreen Wallace papers (private collection)

Dorset Record Office
National Tithepayers' Association, Crewkerne, Dorset & Salisbury branches archive (1934–54)

Essex Record Office
Dedham Grammar School and other charities: Correspondence and papers relating to administration and collection of tithe rentcharge

Hampshire Record Office
Gerard Vernon Wallop papers

Sources and Bibliography

Kent History and Library Centre
Charles Petley papers
County Courts (Hythe, Maidstone, Romney): Proceedings under Tithe Act, 1893–1942
National Farmers Union Kent Branch
Solley & Co papers

Kingsley-Dykes papers (private collection)

Lambeth Palace Library
Cosmo Lang papers
Edward Benson papers
William Temple Papers

London School of Economics, Special Collections

Mobbs, A. G., papers (private collection)

Modern Records Centre, University of Warwick
Lady Allen of Hurtwood papers

Museum of English Rural Life (Reading)
Records of County (Central) Landowners' Association
Records of NFU
Records of National Union of Agricultural Workers

The National Archives
Cabinet Papers
Home Office (HO): Reports on Tithe Conflicts in 1880s and 1930s
Royal Commission on Tithe Rentcharge 1934: Minutes and Papers

North East Wales Archives
Tithe War Album, 1886–90

Parliamentary Archives
Beaverbrook papers

Suffolk Record Office
Papers of Suffolk Tithepayers' Association

Sources and Bibliography

Official documents and publications

Hansard, particularly parliamentary debates on tithe, 1830–36, 1880–91, 1918, 1925, 1929–36.
Report from the Select Committee on Tithe (Rent-Charges), House of Commons, 22 July 1881.
Report of an Inquiry as to Disturbances connected with the Levying of Tithe Rentcharge in Wales, (London: HMSO, 1887).
Report of the Royal Commission on Tithe Rentcharge in England and Wales (London: HMSO, 1936).
Royal Commission on Redemption of Tithe Rentcharge in England and Wales, Minutes of Evidence (London: HMSO, 1892)
Royal Commission on Tithe Rentcharge, Minutes of Evidence (London: HMSO, 1934–36)
Tithe Acts, 1836, 1846, 1891, 1918, 1925, 1936.

Newspapers

This study has made extensive use of the national and local press accessed through the following databases (details are found in the footnotes):

The British Newspaper Archive (British Library)
Daily Mail Historical Archive (Gale)
Mirror Historical Archive (Gale)
The Telegraph Historical Archive (Gale)
The Times Digital Archive (Gale)
UK PressOnline (Digitorial Ltd)

Contemporary books, articles and pamphlets

Balfour, Lady Eve, *What is all this about Tithe?* (Stationers' Hall, 1933).
Brocklehurst, George, *Tithes and Tithe Rentcharge* (New Romney: Bale & Co, 1911).
Brown, Robert, Jr. 'Tithes in England and Wales', *Political Science Quarterly*, 7, 2 (1892), 244–57.
Cobbett, William, *Manchester Lectures in support of his Fourteen Reform Propositions* (London: Bolt-Court, Fleet Street, 1832).
Everett, Robert Lacey, *Tithes: Their History, Use, and Future* (London: James Clarke & Co, 1887).
Farquharson, Henry R., 'The Case for the Tithe-Payer', *The National Review*, 15, 18 (1890), 545–54.
Garratt, G. T., *Agriculture and the Labour Party* (London: Fabian Society, 1929).
Gill, George, J. *A Fight Against the Tithes* (Haslemere, 1952).

Inderwick, Frederick Andrew, *Taxes on Agriculture: The Extraordinary Tithe on Hops, Fruit and Market Gardens: Speech at the Market Hall, Rye, October 1880* (London: National Press Agency, 1880), LSE Selected Pamphlets.

Kent and Sussex Tithepayers' Association, *Facts and Incidents of an Unequal Struggle* (Ashford, 1950).

Le Fanu, William R., *Queen Anne's Bounty: A Short Account of its History and Work* (London: Macmillan, 1921).

Liberal Party, *The Land and the Nation: Rural Report of the Liberal Land Committee, 1923–25* (London: Hodder and Stoughton, 1926).

Liberal Party, *We Can Conquer Unemployment: Mr Lloyd George's Pledge* (London: Cassell, 1929).

Lymington, Viscount, *Horn, Hoof and Corn: The Future of British Agriculture* (London: Faber & Faber, 1932).

Percival, Edward France (ed.), *The Foundation Statutes of Merton College* (Oxford: William Pickering, 1847).

Prothero, R. E., *The Anti-Tithe Agitation in Wales* (London: The Guardian, 1889).

Squire, W. H. and E. W. I. Peterson, *Tithe Rentcharge Recovery Bill, 1890, with notes and criticisms* (London: Chant & Griffith, 1891).

Tithe: A Monthly News Sheet of Current Events and Opinions, bulletin published by activists in the Elham Tithepayers' Association (1934).

The Tithepayer (1931–1938)

Wallace Doreen, *So Long to Learn* (London: Collins, 1936).

——, *The Portion of the Levites* (London: Ernest Benn, 1933).

——, *The Tithe War* (London: Victor Gollancz, 1934).

Wallop, Gerard, *A Knot of Roots: An Autobiography by The Earl of Portsmouth* (London: Geoffrey Bles, 1965).

Whitland, Rev. W. Thomas, *The Anti-Tithe Movement in Wales: Its Justice, Morality, and Legality* (Llanelly: South Wales Press, 1891).

Williamson, Henry, *The Story of a Norfolk Farm* (London: Faber & Faber, 1942).

Visual sources

'Boxted Hall Farm Scenes' (1925), East Anglian Film Archive

'England's Tithe War', dir. Harry Watt (1936), BFI Screen Online

Secondary sources

Adams, Norma, 'The Judicial Conflict over Tithes', *English Historical Review*, 52, 205 (1937), 1–22.

Adams, R. J. Q., 'Sir Arthur Sackville Trevor Griffith-Boscawen (1865–1946)', *Oxford Dictionary of National Biography* (2008), https://doi.org/10.1093/ref:odnb/59306.

Sources and Bibliography

Aparicio, Gema and Vicente Pinilla, 'The Dynamics of International Trade in Cereals, 1900–1938', *Sociedad Española de Historia Agraria*, 1504 (2015).

Armstrong, Alan, 'Agriculture and Rural Society', in Nigel Yates (ed.), *Kent in the Twentieth Century* (Woodbridge: Boydell Press, 2001), 59–116.

Arnold, Rollo, 'The "Revolt of the Field" in Kent, 1872–1879', *Past & Present*, 64 (1974), 71–9.

Aspinall, Kian, 'Viscount Lymington: The Journey of a fascist "Fellow Traveler"', unpublished Masters by Research thesis, Canterbury Christ Church University (2022).

Barral, Pierre, *Les Agrariens français de Méline à Pisani* (Paris: Armand Colin, 1968).

Beaken, Robert, *Cosmo Lang: Archbishop in War and Crisis* (London: I.B. Tauris, 2012).

Beckett, J. V. (revised), 'John Christian Curwen (1756–1828)', *Oxford Dictionary of National Biography* (2007), https://doi.org/10.1093/ref:odnb/37334.

Best, G. F. A., *Temporal Pillars: Queen Anne's Bounty, The Ecclesiastical Commissioners and The Church of England* (Cambridge: Cambridge University Press, 1964).

Boswell, Laird, 'Rural Society in Crisis', in Nicholas Doumanis (ed.) *The Oxford Handbook of European History, 1914–45* (Oxford: Oxford University Press, 2016), 243–60.

Boyce, D. George, 'William Waldegrave Palmer, second earl of Selborne (1859–1942)', *Oxford Dictionary of National Biography* (2008), https://doi.org/10.1093/ref:odnb/35373.

Brace, Laura, *The Idea of Property in Seventeenth-Century England* (Manchester: Manchester University Press, 1998).

Brassley, Paul, Jeremy Burchardt and Lynne Thompson (eds), *The English Countryside between the Wars: Regeneration or Decline?* (Woodbridge: Boydell Press, 2006).

Brierly, J. L. (revised), 'Sir John Fischer Williams (1870–1947)', *Oxford Dictionary of National Biography* (2004), https://doi.org/10.1093/ref:odnb/36926.

Brigden, Roy, 'George Baylis (1846–1936)', *Oxford Dictionary of National Biography* (2020), https://doi.org/10.1093/ref:odnb/50158.

Bristow, Edward, 'The Liberty and Property Defence League and Individualism', *The Historical Journal*, 18, 4 (1975), 761–89.

Brock, M. G. and M. C. Curthoys (eds.), *The History of the University of Oxford, Vol. VI, Part One, Nineteenth-Century Oxford* (Oxford: Clarendon Press, 1998).

Brown, Jonathan, 'Agricultural Policy and the National Farmers' Union, 1908–1939', in J. R. Wordie (ed.), *Agriculture and Politics in England, 1815–1939* (Basingstoke: Macmillan, 2000), 178–98.

Sources and Bibliography

Burchardt, Jeremy, *Paradise Lost: Rural Idyll and Social Change since 1800* (London: I. B. Tauris, 2002).

Burrin, Philippe, 'La France dans le champ magnétique des fascismes', *Le Débat*, 32 (1984/5), 52–72.

Cannadine, David, *The Decline and Fall of the British Aristocracy* (London: Yale University Press, 1990).

Carr, Raymond, 'Henry Hugh Arthur Fitzroy Somerset, tenth duke of Beaufort (1900–1984')', *Oxford Dictionary of National Biography* (2004), https://doi.org/10.1093/ref:odnb/31700.

Charlesworth, Andrew (ed.), *An Atlas of Rural Protest in Britain, 1548–1900* (Abingdon: Routledge, 2018).

Chase, Malcolm, 'Gerard Vernon Wallop, ninth earl of Portsmouth (1898–1984)', *Oxford Dictionary of National Biography* (2009), https://doi.org/10.1093/ref:odnb/59347.

Collins, E. J. T., 'Rural and Agricultural Change', in E. J. T. Collins (ed.), *The Agrarian History of England and Wales, Vol. VII, 1850–1914* (Cambridge: Cambridge University Press, 2000), 72–223.

Conford, Philip, 'Organic Society: Agriculture and Radical Politics in the Career of Gerard Wallop, Ninth Earl of Portsmouth (1898–1984)', *Agricultural History Review*, 53, 1 (2005), 78–96.

Cooper, Andrew, F., *British Agricultural Policy 1912–36. A Study in Conservative Politics* (Manchester: Manchester University Press, 1989).

Cordle, Celia, *Out of the Hay and into the Hops: Hop cultivation in Wealden Kent and Hop Marketing in Southwark, 1744–2000* (Hatfield: University of Hertfordshire Press, 2011).

Cornu, Pierre and Jean-Luc Mayaud (eds) *Au Nom de la Terre: Agrarisme et agrariens en France et en Europe du 19e siècle à nos jours* (Paris: La Boutique d'Histoire, 2008).

Coupland, Philip M., *Farming, Fascism and Ecology: A Life of Jorian Jenks* (London: Routledge, 2017).

Cox, Graham, Philip Lowe and Michael Winter, 'The Origins and Early Development of the National Farmers' Union', *Agricultural History Review*, 39, 1 (1991), 30–47.

Cretney, S. M., Sir Henry Herman Slesser [formerly Schloesser] (1883–1979)', *Oxford Dictionary of National Biography* (2004), https://doi.org/10.1093/ref:odnb/65525.

Davies, Russell, *Secret Sins: Sex, Violence and Society in Carmarthenshire, 1870–1920* (Cardiff: University of Wales Press, 2012).

Davis, John, 'John Lloyd (1833–1915)', *Oxford Dictionary of National Biography* (2006), https://doi.org/10.1093/ref:odnb/47861.

Dawson, Michael, 'The Liberal Land Policy, 1924–1929: Electoral Strategy and Internal Division', *Twentieth Century British History*, 2, 3 (1991), 272–90.

Dietz, Bernhard, *Neo-Tories: The Revolt of British Conservatives against Democracy and Political Modernity, 1929–1939* (London: Bloomsbury, 2018).
Dunbabin, J. P. D., 'Finance since 1914', in Brian Harrison (ed.), *The History of the University of Oxford, Volume VIII, The Twentieth Century* (Oxford: Clarendon Press, 1994).
——, *Rural Discontent in Nineteenth Century Britain* (New York: Holmes & Meier, 1973).
Ernle, Lord (Rowland Prothero), *English Farming, Past and Present*, 6th edn (London: Heinemann, 1961).
Evans, Eric J., *The Contentious Tithe: The Tithe Problem and English Agriculture, 1750–1850* (London: Routledge & Kegan Paul, 1976).
——, 'Some Reasons for the Growth of English Rural Anti-Clericalism c.1750–c.1830', *Past & Present*, 66 (1975), 84–109.
——, 'Tithes 1640–1750', in Joan Thirsk (ed.), *Agricultural Change: Policy and Practice: 1500–1750* (Cambridge: Cambridge University Press, 1990), 216–32.
——, *Tithes and the Tithe Commutation Act 1836* (London: Bedford Square Press, 1978).
Fisher, J. R., 'The Farmers' Alliance: An Agricultural Protest Movement of the 1880s', *Agricultural History Review*, 26, 1 (1978), 15–25.
Flynn, Andrew, Philip Lowe and Michael Winter, 'The Political Power of Farmers: An English Perspective', *Rural History* 7, 1 (1996), 15–32.
Gash, Norman, *Aristocracy and People: Britain 1815–1865* (London: Edward Arnold, 1979).
Gill, Erin, 'Lady Eve Balfour and the British Organic Food and Farming Movement', unpublished PhD thesis, Aberystwyth University (2010).
Gooderson, Philip J., 'Aspects of the Decline of English Rough Music and Effigy-burning and the Transformation of the Fifth of November in the Nineteenth and Twentieth Centuries', *International Journal of Regional and Local History*, 16, 2 (2021), 94–110.
Grant, Wyn, *Pressure Groups and British Politics* (Basingstoke: Macmillan, 2000).
Gray, Todd, *Blackshirts in Devon* (Exeter: The Mint Press, 2006).
Green, E. H. H., *The Crisis of Conservatism: The Politics, Economics and Ideology of the British Conservative Party, 1880–1914* (Abingdon: Routledge, 1995).
Green, Ewen, 'No Longer the Farmers' Friend? The Conservative Party and Agricultural Protection, 1880–1914', in J. R. Wordie (ed.), *Agriculture and Politics in England, 1835–1939* (Basingstoke: Macmillan Press, 2000), 149–77.
Griffin, Carl J., *Protest, Politics and Work in Rural England, 1700–1850* (London: Palgrave Macmillan, 2014).

Sources and Bibliography

——, *The Rural War: Captain Swing and the Politics of Protest* (Manchester: Manchester University Press, 2012).
Griffin, Roger, *The Nature of Fascism* (London: Routledge, 1993).
Griffiths, Clare V. J., *Labour and the Countryside: The Politics of Rural Britain, 1918–1939* (Oxford: Oxford University Press, 2007).
Grimley, Matthew, 'Bertram Pollock (1863–1943)', *Oxford Dictionary of National Biography* (2014), https://doi.org/10.1093/ref:odnb/35561.
——, *Citizenship, Community and the Church of England: Liberal Anglican Theories of the State between the Wars* (Oxford: Clarendon Press, 2004).
Harrison, Melissa, *All Among the Barley* (London: Bloomsbury, 2018).
Hart, Bradley W., *George Pitt-Rivers and the Nazis* (London: Bloomsbury Academic, 2015).
Hastings, Paul, 'Radical Movements and Workers' Protests to c1850', in Frederick Lansberry (ed.), *Government and Politics in Kent, 1640–1914* (Woodbridge: Boydell Press, 2001), 95–138.
Higgins-McHugh, Noreen, 'The 1830s Tithe Riots', in William Sheehan and Maura Cronin (eds), *Riotous Assemblies: Rebels, Riots & Revolts in Ireland* (Cork: Mercier Press, 2011), 80–95.
Hill, Christopher, *Change and Continuity in 17th-Century England* (New Haven, CT: Yale University Press, 1991).
——, *The World Turned Upside Down: Radical Ideas During the English Revolution* (London: Penguin, 1991).
Hobsbawm, Eric, *Industry and Empire* (London: Penguin, 1999).
Hobsbawm, Eric and George Rudé, *Captain Swing* (London: Phoenix Press, 2001).
Holderness, B. A. and G. E. Mingay, 'The South and South-East', in E. J. T. Collins (ed.), *The Agrarian History of England and Wales, Vol. VII, 1850–1914* (Cambridge: Cambridge University Press, 2000).
Horn, Pamela, *The Tithe War in Pembrokeshire* (Fishguard: Preseli, 1982).
Howell, David W., 'The Land Question in nineteenth-century Wales, Ireland and Scotland: a comparative study', *Agricultural History Review*, 61, 1 (2013), 83–110.
Howkins, Alun, *The Death of Rural England: A Social History of the Countryside Since 1900* (London: Routledge, 2003).
——, *Reshaping Rural England: A Social History, 1850–1925* (London: Routledge, 1992).
——, 'Edwin George Gooch (1889–1964)', *Oxford Dictionary of National Biography* (2016), https://doi.org/10.1093/ref:odnb/46448.
——, 'Review of Tithe War, 1918–1939. The Countryside in Revolt by Carol Twitch', *Agricultural History Review*, 53, 2 (2005), 260–1.
Jackson, Patrick, *Harcourt and Son: A Political Biography of Sir William Harcourt, 1827–1904* (Madison, NJ: Fairleigh Dickinson University Press, 2004).

Jacob, W. M., *The Clerical Profession in the Long Eighteenth Century, 1680–1840* (Oxford: Oxford University Press, 2007).

James, Margaret, 'The Political Importance of the Tithes Controversy in the English Revolution, 1640–60', *History*, 26, 101 (1941), 1–18.

Jenkins, Robert, 'Sir John Edward Lloyd (1861–1947)', *Dictionary of Welsh Biography* (2001), https://biography.wales/article/s2-LLOY-EDW-1861

Kain, Roger, 'Tithe as an Index of Pre-Industrial Agricultural Production', *The Agricultural History Review*, 27, 2 (1979), 73–81.

Kain, Roger and Hugh C. Prince, *The Tithe Surveys of England and Wales* (Cambridge: Cambridge University Press, 1985).

Kingsford, Peter, *The Hunger Marchers in Britain 1920–1940* (London: Lawrence & Wishart, 1982).

Lawrence, Mark, *The Spanish Civil Wars: A Comparative History of the First Carlist War* (London: Bloomsbury Academic, 2017).

Le Roy Ladurie, Emmanuel, *Tithe and Agrarian History from the Fourteenth to the Nineteenth Centuries: An Essay in Comparative History*, translated by Susan Burke (Cambridge: Cambridge University Press, 1982).

Lee, Geoffrey, 'The Tithe rentcharge: a pioneer in income indexation', *Accounting, Business & Financial History*, 6, 3 (1996), 301–13.

Lee, Robert, *Rural Society and the Anglican Clergy, 1815–1914: Encountering and Managing the Poor* (Woodbridge: Boydell Press, 2006).

Linehan, Thomas, *British Fascism, 1918–39: Parties, Ideology and Culture* (Manchester: Manchester University Press, 2000).

Lowe, Philip and Maryvonne Bodiguel (eds), *Rural Studies in Britain and France*, translated by Henry Buller (London: Belhaven, 1990).

Lynch, Patricia, *The Liberal Party in Rural England: Radicalism and Community* (Oxford: Oxford University Press, 2003).

Maiden, John G., 'English Evangelicals, Protestant National Identity, and Anglican Prayer Book Revision, 1927–1928, *Journal of Religious History*, 34, 4 (2010), 430–45.

Miller, Simon, 'Urban Dreams and Rural Reality: Land and Landscape in English Culture, 1920–45', *Rural History* 6, 1 (1995), 89–102.

Mingay, Gordon, 'British Rural History: Themes in Agricultural History and Rural Social History', in Philip Lowe and Maryvonne Bodiguel (eds), *Rural Studies in Britain and France* (London: Belhaven, 1990), 76–89.

Mitchell, Andrew, 'Fascism in East Anglia: The British Union of Fascists in Norfolk, Suffolk and Essex, 1933–1940', unpublished Phd thesis, University of Sheffield (1999). Available at: http://etheses.whiterose.ac.uk/3071/

Mollet, J. A., 'The Wheat Act of 1932', *Agricultural History Review*, 8, 1 (1960), 20–35.

Moore, Simon, 'The Agrarian Conservative Party in Parliament, 1920–1929, *Parliamentary History*, 10, 2 (1991), 342–62.

Sources and Bibliography

Moore-Colyer, Richard, 'Towards "Mother Earth": Jorian Jenks, Organicism, the Right and the British Union of Fascists', *Journal of Contemporary History*, 29, 3 (2004), 353–71.

Morgan, Kenneth O., *Rebirth of a Nation: Wales, 1880–1980* (Oxford: Oxford University Press, 1982).

——, *Wales in British Politics, 1868–1922* (Cardiff: University of Wales Press, 1980).

Morrow, John, *History of Political Thought* (London: Palgrave, 1998).

Newby, Howard, *Country Life: A Social History of Rural England* (London: Cardinal, 1987).

——, *The Deferential Worker: A Study of Farm Workers in East Anglia* (London: Allen Lane, 1977).

——, *Green and Pleasant Land? Social Change in Rural England* (Harmondsworth: Penguin, 1980).

Newby, Howard, Colin Bell, David Rose and Peter Saunders, *Property, Paternalism and Power: Class and Control in Rural England* (London: Hutchinson, 1978).

Norman, Edward R., *Church and Society in England, 1770–1970: A Historical Study* (Oxford: Oxford University Press, 1976).

Orwin, C. S. (revised by H. C. G. Matthew), Edward Strachey, first Baron Strachie (1858–1936)', *Oxford Dictionary of National Biography* (2004), https://doi.org/10.1093/ref:odnb/36336.

Overton, Mark, *Agricultural Revolution in England: The Transformation of the Agrarian Economy, 1500–1800* (Cambridge: Cambridge University Press, 1996).

Paxton, Robert O., *The Anatomy of Fascism* (London: Allen Lane, 2004).

——, *French Peasant Fascism: Henry Dorgères's Greenshirts and the Crises of French Agriculture, 1929–1939* (Oxford: Oxford University Press, 1997).

Pitt-Rivers, George Henry Lane-Fox, *The Clash of Culture and the Contact of Races* (London: Routledge, 1927).

——, *The World Significance of the Russian Revolution* (Oxford: Basil Blackwell, 1920).

Pittman, Susan, 'John Wood & Family: Fruit farmers of The Mount, Crockenhill, Kent', (Darenth Print & Design, 2020). Available from Crockenhill Parish Council Office, Crockenhill Village Hall, BR8 8LT.

Pugh, Martin, *'Hurrah for the Blackshirts!': Fascists and Fascism in Britain Between the Wars* (London: Pimlico, 2006).

——, *We Danced All Night: A Social History of Britain Between the Wars* (London: Vintage, 2008).

Randle, Michael, *Civil Resistance* (London: Fontana, 1994).

Rawlinson, Mark, 'Dead Chickens: Henry Williamson, British Agriculture and European War', in Paul Brassley, Jeremy Burchardt and Lynne Thompson, *The English Countryside between the Wars: Regeneration or Decline?* (Woodbridge: Boydell Press, 2006), 87–101.

Readman, Paul, 'Conservatives and the Politics of Land: Lord Winchilsea's National Agricultural Union, 1893–1901', *English Historical Review*, 121 (2006), 25–69.

——, *Land and Nation in England: Patriotism, Nation Identity, and the Politics of Land, 1880–1914* (Woodbridge: Boydell Press, 2008).

Reay, Barry, 'Quaker Opposition to Tithes, 1652–1660', *Past & Present*, 86 (1980), 98–120.

Reed, Matthew, *Rebels for the Soil: The Rise of the Global Organic Food and Farming Movement* (London: Earthscan, 2010).

Rees, Lowri, Ann, 'Paternalism and rural protest: The Rebecca riots and the landed interest of south-west Wales', *Agricultural History Review*, 59, 1 (2011), 36–60.

Reid, David P., 'The Tithe War in Ireland, 1830–1838', unpublished PhD thesis, Trinity College, Dublin (2013).

Renton, David, 'George Henry Lane Fox Pitt-Rivers (1890–1966)', *Oxford Dictionary of National Biography* (2005), https://doi.org/10.1093/ref:odnb/75512.

Reynolds, Jaime, 'The Fighting Parson', *Journal of Liberal History*, 48 (2005), 32–8.

Ricardo, David, *On the Principles of Political Economy and Taxation* (Cambridge: Cambridge University Press, 2015).

Richter, Donald, 'The Welsh Police, the Home Office, and the Welsh Tithe War of 1886–91', *Welsh History Review*, 12, 1 (1984), 50–75.

Roberts, Andrew, *Salisbury: Victorian Titan* (London: Faber & Faber, 2012).

Roberts, M. J. D., 'Pressure-Group Politics and the Church of England: the Church Defence Institution 1859–1896', *Journal of Ecclesiastical History*, 35, 4 (1984), 560–82.

Royal, Susan, 'John Foxe's 'Acts and Monuments' and the Lollard Legacy in the Long English Reformation', unpublished PhD thesis, Durham University (2014).

——, *Lollards in the English Reformation: History, Radicalism and John Foxe* (Manchester: Manchester University Press, 2020).

Seal, Graham, 'Tradition and Agrarian Protest in Nineteenth-Century England and Wales', *Folklore*, 99, 2 (1988), 146–69.

Sheail, John, 'The White Paper, "Agricultural Policy", of 1926: its context and significance', *Agricultural History Review*, 58, 2 (2010), 236–54.

Shepherd, June, *Doreen Wallace (1897–1989), Writer and Social Campaigner* (New York: Edwin Mellen Press, 2000).

Simpson, Paula, 'The Continuum of Resistance to Tithe, c. 1400–1600', in Robert Lutton and Elisabeth Salter (eds), *Pieties in Transition: Religious Practices and Experiences, c1400–1640* (London: Ashgate, 2007), 93–108.

——, 'Custom and Conflict: Disputes over Tithe in the Diocese of Canterbury, 1501–1600', unpublished PhD thesis, University of Kent, 1997.

Smith, Guy, *From Campbell to Kendall: A History of the NFU* (Wellington: Halsgrove, 2008).

Smith, Paul, 'Salisbury, Robert Arthur Talbot Gascoyne-Cecil, third marquess of Salisbury (1830–1903)', *Oxford Dictionary of National Biography* (2011), https://doi.org/10.1093/ref:odnb/32339.

Sokol, Mary, 'Jeremy Bentham and the Real Property Commission of 1828', *Utilitas*, 4, 2 (1992), 225–45.

Steele, David, *Lord Salisbury: A Political Biography* (Abingdon: Routledge, 1999).

——, 'Roundell Palmer, first earl of Selborne (1812–1895)', *Oxford Dictionary of National Biography* (2004), https://doi.org/10.1093/ref:odnb/21210.

Stone, Dan, 'The English Mistery, the BUF, and the Dilemmas of British Fascism', *The Journal of Modern History*, 75 (2003), 336–58.

——, 'The Far Right and the Back-to-the-Land Movement', in Julie V. Gottlieb and Thomas P. Linehan (eds), *The Culture of Fascism: Visions of the Far Right in Britain* (London: I.B. Tauris, 2004), 182–98.

——, 'Rural Revivalism and the Radical Right in France and Britain between the Wars', in *The Holocaust, Fascism and Memory* (Basingstoke: Palgrave Macmillan, 2013), 110–22.

Tallett, James S., *The Tithe War in the Oxford Area. The final years 1924–1936 as portrayed in correspondence and editorials in the Press* (Oxford: J. S. Tallett, 2006).

Tarver, Anne, 'The Due Tenth: Problems of the Leicestershire Tithing process, 1560–1640', *Transactions, Leicestershire Archaeological and History Society*, 78 (2004), 97–107.

Taylor, Elizabeth M. M., 'The Politics of Walter Elliot, 1929–1936', unpublished PhD thesis, University of Edinburgh (1979).

Taylor, Iain, 'Pressure Groups, Contested "Land-Spaces" and the Politics of Ridicule in Sevenoaks, Kent 1881–85', *Journal of Victorian Culture*, 21, 3 (2016), 322–45.

Thompson, E. P., 'Rough Music Reconsidered', *Folklore*, 103, 1 (1992), 3–26.

Tinniswood, Adrian, *The Long Weekend: Life in the English Country House between the Wars* (London: Jonathan Cape, 2016).

Turner, M. E., 'Agricultural Output, Income and Productivity', in E. J. T. Collins (ed.), *The Agrarian History of England and Wales, Vol. VII, 1850–1914* (Cambridge: Cambridge University Press, 2000), 224–320.

Twinch, Carol, 'Roderick Morris Kedward, 1881–1937', *Bygone Kent*, 24, 7 (2003), 642–51.

——, *Tithe War 1918–39: The Countryside in Revolt* (Norwich: Media Associates, 2001).

Whetham, Edith H., *The Agrarian History of England and Wales, Vol. VIII, 1914–1939* (Cambridge: Cambridge University Press, 1978).

Sources and Bibliography

Williams, David, *The Rebecca Riots: A Study in Agrarian Discontent* (Cardiff: University of Wales Press, 1986).

Williamson, Philip, 'James Edward Hubert Gascoyne-Cecil, fourth marquess of Salisbury (1861–1947)' *Oxford Dictionary of National Biography* (2014), https://doi.org/10.1093/ref:odnb/32338.

Worley, Matthew, *Oswald Mosley and the New Party* (Basingstoke: Palgrave Macmillan, 2010).

INDEX

Abbotskerswell (Devon)   216
Abingdon (Berkshire)   131
Acland, Richard   223, 285
acts of parliament (relating to tithe)   *see* Ecclesiastical Tithe Rentcharge (Rates) Act (1920), Extraordinary Tithe Redemption Act (1886), Rating and Valuation Act (1925), Tithe Act (1846), Tithe Act (1891), Tithe Act (1918) Tithe Act (1925), Tithe Act (1936), Tithe Commutation Act (1836), Tithe Commutation Acts Amendment with respect to Market Gardens (1873), Tithe Rentcharge (Rates) Act (1899), Welsh Church (temporalities) Act (1919), Welsh Church Act (1914)
Addison, Christopher
  and Labour Party tithe policy   197–8
  as minister of agriculture   125–6, 227
  in negotiations on tithe   135–6, 153–4, 175
agrarianism   11, 59, 121, 194–201, 208, 211, 213, 223, 283, 293, 299
agricultural labourers   *see* agricultural workers
agricultural marketing boards   9n.30, 116, 125, 226–7, 274, 300
agricultural workers
  and tithepayers' movement   15, 22–3, 39, 40, 41, 42, 51, 61–2, 196–8, 250, 272, 281, 300
  and trade unionism   31–2, 35–6, 39, 117, 200
  wages and conditions of   85, 86, 96–7, 121, 196
  see also   Kent and Sussex Agricultural Labourers' Union, National Agricultural Labourers' Union, National Union of Agricultural Workers
Agriculture Act (1920)   87, 96, 99, 199
agriculture
  cereal prices   27, 86, 96, 109, 117, 199, 200
  depression in   3, 19, 24, 31–2, 60, 72, 74, 108, 117, 126, 161, 226, 266, 290, 293–4
  'golden age' of   30, 31, 195
  imports   108, 199, 225, 227
  QAB reports on   151–2, 156, 172–3, 252, 263
  social relations in   23, 64–5, 76, 86–7, 95–6, 199, 298
  see also   agricultural workers, corporatism, protectionism, Ministry of Agriculture
Alexander, Albert   9n.27, 286
Allen, Frank R.
  and East Kent Tithepayers' Association   127–8, 257
  and launch of NTA   101, 103–4
  and Royal Commission   261–2
  as Canterbury Cathedral Tithe Agent   81–4, 89, 90
  as NTA secretary   119, 120, 132, 145, 162–3, 185, 192, 202, 205, 236, 289, 293–4
  at protest meetings   127–8, 170–1, 214, 222, 228, 230, 232, 235, 266, 283
  in negotiations   136, 160–1
  policy on tithe reform   123–4, 157, 237–8
  relations with WADA   206–8
Althorp, Lord   13–14, 25, 28
Alverdiscott (Devon)   216, 217

Index

Andover (Hampshire)   58, 61, 229
Anglesey   51, 56
Anti-Extraordinary Tithe
  Association   3, 11, 38–9, 42–3, 45–6, 62, 123
Anti-Tithe League (Wales)   49–50, 51, 53, 69
annuities   97, 274–5, 281, 287, 295, 300
apportionments   26, 84
Arch, Joseph   32, 35
archbishop of Canterbury   147
  effigies of   69, 127ji
  see also   Benson, Edward; Davidson, archbishop Randall; Howley, archbishop William; Lang, archbishop William Cosmo; Temple, archbishop William
Archbishops' Tithe Compensation Fund   288–9
aristocracy   18, 64–6, 86, 98–9, 110, 201–2, 204
  as tithepayers   8, 68, 155, 201–2
arrears in tithe payments   27, 47, 67–8, 71, 74, 82, 149, 154, 162, 164, 174, 234, 246, 247, 285, 286, 290
  Arrears Investigation Committee   278–9, 281
Ash (Kent)   127
Ashford (Kent)   xvi, xviii, 12, 136, 142, 236, 267, 276
  county court   129, 157, 245, 291
  market   119, 210, 289
  parliamentary constituency   122–3, 128, 142, 198, 236
  tithepayers' association   214, 222, 228, 292
Assheton, Ralph   285
Astins, Percy   116
Attleborough (Norfolk)   291
auctioneers   38, 137, 230, 234, 240
  reports of violence against   40, 42–3, 61, 140–1, 178–9, 231
Auctioneers' and Estate Agents' Institute   119, 136
auctions   3, 11, 30, 55, 156, 167, 206, 237, 299
  protests at   38–43, 49, 51, 58–60, 61, 118, 127, 134–7, 140–1, 143–5, 178–9, 183, 198, 209–10, 212, 217,

222, 224, 230–1, 234, 235, 240, 266–7, 269–70, 272, 291–2
QAB and   152–4, 157–8
see also   auctioneers, gift sales
Aylesbury (Buckinghamshire)   211

bailiffs   58, 130, 217, 262
  execution of court orders   xvi, 6, 119, 127, 134–5, 178, 180, 189–90, 191, 213, 216, 266–8, 291
  orders by titheowners   41–2, 47, 51, 0, 53, 54–5, 56
  powers of   71, 74, 243–5, 246
  training of   249, 250, 258
  see also   emergency men, possession men
Baldwin, Stanley   195, 199, 200, 202, 225–6
  and NFU   100, 107, 283
  and tithepayers' demands   5, 231–2, 281, 284
Balfour, Evelyn   130–1, 190, 203, 224, 241, 262, 268
baptists   34, 35, 292
Barham (Kent)   13–14, 15, 84, 127
Barking (Suffolk)   133
Barnes, George   93
Barnstaple (Devon)   214, 223, 230, 232
Barr, James   111
Barton Stacey (Hampshire)   119–20
Bath Albert   35–6, 38–9, 43, 59, 61–2, 239
Baylis, George   60–1, 62, 79
Beaminster (Dorset)   232, 290
Beard, John   200
Beaumont, Michael   121, 202–3
Beaumont-cum-Mose (Essex)   185
Beaverbrook, Lord (Max Aitken)   200–1, 206, 209
Beck, William (W. J.)   198, 237
Becke, Major Jack   184
Bedfordshire   35, 36, 58, 62, 196
Bell, Canon Allen   96
Bell, Rev. Dr George   83–4
Benson, Edward, archbishop of Canterbury   46–7, 55, 65–6, 68, 74, 76–7, 78
Berks, Bucks and Oxon Tithepayers' Association   131–2, 230, 242–3

316

Index

Berkshire 3, 5, 68, 141, 173, 182
  NFU in 124, 125n.48, 126
  tithe collection in 247, 248
  tithepayers' campaign in 35, 38, 49, 60, 62, 102, 130–1, 185, 228, 229, 231
  see also Wallingford
Berrynabor (Devon) 266
Bickington (Devon) 191, 216
Biddenden (Kent) 42–3, 56
bishop of Norwich *see* Pollock, Bertram
bishop of St Edmundsbury and Ipswich *see* Whittingham, rt. rev. Walter
Bishops Castle (Shropshire) 231
Blackwell, Sir Ernley 182, 239–40
Blewitt, Ralph 145
Blomfield, Arthur 104
Bluecoat School *see* Christ's Hospital
Board of Agriculture *see* Ministry of Agriculture
Bodmin (Cornwall) 211, 216, 232
Body, Rev. Bernard 60–1
Bolton, Thomas 33n.8, 35–6, 38, 45–6, 62, 77
Boughton Aluph (Kent) 157
Bournemouth 243
Brabourne Lord *see* Knatchbull-Hugessen, E. H., first baron Brabourne
Braintree (Essex) 130
Brister, Sidney 184
British Sugar (Subsidy Act 1925) 117
British Union of Farmers 217–18
British Union of Fascists xv, 6, 11, 128, 185–6, 190–4, 210–24
  see also British Union of Farmers; Mosley, Oswald
Brocklehurst, Rev. George 89, 90, 156, 264, 276, 278
Bryngwyn (Ceredigion) 249
Buckinghamshire 58, 62, 131–2, 141, 230
Buckland Brewer (Devon) 214, 216, 217
Bude (Devon) 171
Burgate (Suffolk) 248
Burrows, Alfred 119, 123, 129, 145–6

Bury St Edmunds (Suffolk) 108, 116, 129
Butcher, G. 135
Butler, Philip J. 133
Butterworth, Alfred 61, 79
Buxton, Noel 97–8, 100, 116, 121–2, 124–5

Caernarvonshire 50, 51, 53
Cambridge 130, 162, 172, 199–200
Cambridge, University of
  and Royal Commission 264, 280
  as titheowner 1, 73, 78, 98, 136, 148, 168, 174–5, 177, 183, 189, 243, 250, 252, 271
  MPs for 20, 109–10
  see also Clare College, Jesus, King's, Magdalene, Trinity College
Cambridgeshire 5, 29, 38, 130, 132–3, 182, 229, 247, 248
  see also Cambridge
Canterbury 12, 17, 83, 104, 118, 119, 128, 137, 151, 180–1, 201, 222, 245, 294
  see also Canterbury Cathedral
Canterbury Cathedral 81–5, 89, 103, 155
Canvey Island (Essex) 58, 130, 133–4, 150
Captain Swing riots xv, 7, 22–3
Cardiganshire 5, 50, 78, 198, 234
Carne Rasch, Frederic 60, 62
Catterick Bridge (Yorkshire) 183
Cautley, Sir Henry 109
Cave, George 113
  see also lord chancellor
Cecil Robert, first Viscount Cecil of Chelwood 94
Cecil, Lord Hugh (1st Baron Quickswood) 87, 110, 278, 285
Cecil, James Gascoyne, (Viscount Cranborne) 73, 78
Cecil, Robert Gascoyne-, third Marquess of Salisbury *see* Salisbury, Lord
Central Chamber of Agriculture 32, 70, 159–60, 252, 255, 260
Central Landowners' Association 97–9, 101, 102, 105, 107, 136, 161, 175, 252, 255, 260–1, 285

Index

Chamberlain, Joseph   64, 66, 108n.122
Chamberlain, Neville   106, 256, 273, 275, 277, 290
Chambers of Agriculture   136, 162
  see also   Central Chamber of Agriculture
Chard (Somerset)   232, 289–90
Charterhouse School   2, 280
Chelmsford (Essex)   116, 119, 129, 132, 187
Chelmsford Cathedral   156
Chelmsford, bishop of (rev. Henry Wilson)   187–8
Childers, Hugh   46
Chilsworthy (Devon)   269, 272
Chiltern Hills   5, 131, 231
Chipman, Frederick   217
Chipping Norton (Oxfordshire)   131
Cholsey (Berkshire)   185
Christ Church, Oxford   54–5, 174, 175, 179
Christ's Hospital (Bluecoat School)   2, 174, 258, 264, 280
Christian Order in Politics Economics and Citizenship (COPEC)   111
Chulmleigh (Devon)   224
Church (of England) in Wales   2, 3, 49, 53–5, 78, 88–9, 94–5, 234–5
Church Committee for Defence and Instruction   94
Church Defence Institution   34, 47, 55, 65, 68, 69, 71, 72, 94
Church of England
  and demands for disestablishment   3, 15, 33–4, 60, 87–8
  and proposals for tithe reform   9, 15, 18, 20–2, 90–1, 296–7
  and rates on tithe   79, 93–4
  and Royal Commission   275–7
  and tithe legislation   25, 28, 46–7, 68, 70–3, 91–2, 106–7, 113, 115–16, 252–3, 255–6, 278–80
  Central Board of Finance   93, 97, 288
  Church Assembly   89, 151, 153, 156, 158
  Convocation of Canterbury   41, 88, 89, 96, 155
  House of Laity   138
  income from tithe   1, 16
  negotiations on tithe   97–100
  see also   archbishop of Canterbury, Church (of England) in Wales, Ecclesiastical Commissioners, parochial clergy, Queen Anne's Bounty
Church of Ireland   24, 34, 54
Church Property Defence Association   see Churchmen's Defence Union; Tithe Rent-Charge Owners' Union
Churchill, Winston   106, 119
Churchmen's Defence Union   57n.35, 137, 144, 153, 158, 171, 264
  See also E. W. I. Peterson
Claines (Worcestershire)   231
Clare College, Cambridge   177
Clark, Colin   198
Clarke, Thomas   140
Clements, A. F.   245–6
Clergy Defence Association   55, 56
Clifton Brown, Howard   174–5, 260, 285
Clinton, Lord (Charles Hepburn-Stuart-Forbes-Trefusis)   97, 98, 100–1, 107
Coates, Sir Leonard James   259, 273, 275, 285
Cobbett, William   15–16
Cockerham (Lancashire)   150–1
Colchester   124, 129, 131, 133, 145, 211, 221
Collings, Jesse   33, 64, 66
Commissioners of Church Temporalities in Wales   see Welsh Church Commissioners
congregationalists   104, 179, 259
Conservative Party   87–8, 199, 225, 293–4
  and agriculture   8, 9, 100, 115
  and demands for tithe reform   3, 14, 41
  and landed property   32–3
  and the Church   34, 87–8
  and tithe legislation   45–6, 63–6, 68–9, 71–3, 75, 105–9, 285–6
  and tithepayers' movement   60–2, 116, 121, 128, 142, 237, 297

Index

see also Baldwin, Stanley; Conservative Parliamentary Agricultural Committee; Salisbury, Lord
Conservative Parliamentary Agricultural Committee   109, 236–7, 251–2, 255
Cooke, J. H.   135
Coombe Bissett (Wiltshire)   244
Cooper, George   43
copyhold   21, 25–6
corn laws   13, 23, 27
Corn Production Act (1917)   85, 89, 90, 96
corn rent   148
Cornwall   5, 29–30, 35, 183, 190, 192, 209, 211, 214, 216, 217–18, 230, 232, 266
Cornwallis, Fiennes, 1st Baron Cornwallis (Lord Cornwallis)   156, 259, 273n.61
corporatism   5, 194, 201, 211–12, 224, 226, 261, 292, 298, 300
Cotswolds   5, 269
county courts   67, 68, 70–1, 74, 76, 137, 145, 152, 163, 183, 190, 214, 231, 237, 239, 242, 244–6, 248–9, 251, 253, 288, 290
  Ashford   xvi, xviii, 127, 129, 137, 157, 245, 291
  Bournemouth   243
  Canterbury   245
  Deal   129
  Hythe   117–18, 141, 179–81
  Ipswich   157
  Newton Abbot   217
  Ringwood   243
  Ruthin   234
  Saffron Walden   292
  Salisbury   157
  Stowmarket   133
  Sudbury   135
  Tenbury   184
  Tiverton   266
  Wallingford   242–3
Court of Appeal   46, 242–6
Crabtree, rev. H. Gathorne   278
Cranborne, Viscount   73, 78
Creasy, Ronald   221

Crewkerne and District Tithepayers' Association   207, 232
Cromwell, Oliver   18–19
Crump, William E.   135
Crundale (Kent)   104
Curwen, John   20

Dallas, George   121, 124, 136, 196, 200
Darré, Richard   205
Davidson, Randall, archbishop of Canterbury   83, 87, 88–9, 90–1, 113, 147
Davies, Denzil   295
Davies, Mervyn   228, 229, 235, 260
De La Warr, Earl (Herbrand Sackville)   2, 256, 257
de Rothschild, James   124
Deacon & Co (Solicitors)   176, 187
Deal (Kent)   xv, 129, 277
Denbighshire   5, 49, 51, 1 p53, 56, 62, 228, 1 m234, 240
Denman, Richard   286
Denmark, tithe reform in   238
Devon   5, 86–7, 92, 98, 177, 224
  fascists in   11, 190–1, 192, 209, 211, 214–18, 1 k223, 266
  NFU branch   105, 228, 254
  tithepayers' campaign   49, 59, 62, 145, 171, 230, 232, 248, 250, 257, 269, 291
Dibdin, Sir Lewis   90, 91n.45
Dickson, Rev. H. G.   71
Didcot (Berkshire)   131
dissenters   *see* baptists, congregationalists, free churches, methodists, nonconformists, quakers
distraint (distress)
  distraint for rates   47, 119
  execution of orders   xvi, xvii, 29, 30, 39, 43, 53, 54, 55, 58, 61, 141, 152–4, 163–4, 189, 193, 232, 234, 258, 266, 290
  law of   27, 28, 67, 70, 74, 242–6, 249, 251, 253
  on household possessions   127, 134, 135, 178, 183–4, 216, 217, 221, 231, 244, 262, 267, 268
  orders in county courts   117, 179, 214

319

Index

protests at sales   11, 38, 40, 42, 49, 51, 56, 59–60, 78, 157, 190–1, 198, 209, 211, 213, 222, 224, 233, 240, 269–72, 281, 291, 299
unexecuted orders   166, 188, 247–50
distress law   *see* distraint
Donhead St Mary (Wiltshire)   229, 249
Dorchester   209, 168
Dorman-Smith, Reginald   203, 284, 286
Down, William   216, 216n.125, 223, 224, 266, 291
Downing, Sir Stanford
  and General Dealers   174–5, 176, 177, 184, 187
  and policy on tithe   88, 89, 96–8, 99, 99n.75, 100, 107n.117
  on QAB tithe committee   149, 152, 155, 160
Drewitt, Vernon   126, 131, 228, 231, 243
Dyke, Rev. Edwin   41
Dykes, Kingsley   117–18, 179, 181, 222

East Kent Agricultural Association   13, 15
East Kent Tithepayers' Association   xv, 127–30, 137, 201, 222, 250, 257, 262, 267, 277, 291
Ecclesiastical Commission[ers]   xviii, 21, 49n.1, 88, 147, 149, 151, 155, 158, 159, 287
  and General Dealers   167–8, 174–6, 184, 186–7, 250
  and Royal Commission   263, 279
  and tithe redemption   90, 96
  as tithe collector   xvi, 1, 54, 56, 129, 135, 163, 240, 243, 252
  distraint by   35, 53, 164–6, 244
Ecclesiastical Tithe Rentcharge (Rates) Act (1920)   93, 103–4, 119
Edwards, George   197
Edwards, Richard   234, 240
effigies (of titheowners)   51, 62, 178–9, 269–73, 276, 298
Egerton, Wilbraham (Lord Egerton de Tatton)   55
Elham (Kent)   xv, xvii, 16, 117–18, 130, 179–82, 222, 223, 229n.25, 267, 281

Elliot, Walter   5, 201, 224, 225–7, 252–3
  and judiciary   242, 251
  and NFU   236, 261, 283, 292, 298
  and Royal Commission   255–6, 273, 277, 278, 286
Ellis, Tom   56
Elmley, Viscount (Lygon, William)   124, 131
Elmsett (Suffolk)   157–8, 165
emergency men   56–7
English Civil War   18, 295
English Mistery   203–4, 205
Epping (Essex)   129, 211
Ernle, Lord   *see* Prothero, Roland
Essex   3, 5, 49, 62, 102, 116, 119, 124, 126, 129–30, 141, 165, 170, 266, 268, 292
  fascist activity in   190, 221
  NFU in   126, 143, 229
  tithe collection in   57, 76, 153, 154–5, 156, 159, 166, 173–4, 177, 185, 248, 279–80
  see also Blomfield, Arthur; Essex Tithepayers' Association; Occupying Owners' Association; Gestingthorpe
Essex Tithepayers' Association   131–2, 133–4, 145, 197, 228, 240–1, 262
Essex Tithe Reform Association   58, 60
Eton College   2, 174, 264, 280
Evans, Samuel   75
Everett, Robert Lacey   34
Ewyas Harold (Herefordshire)   185
Exeter (Devon)   25, 190, 211, 1 k216
extraordinary tithe   3, 11, 27, 31, 35–48, 148, 274–5, 278n.84
Extraordinary Tithe Redemption Act (1886)   31, 45–8, 148, 274
Eye (Suffolk)   73, 109, 116, 129, 221, 286n.118, 289

Fair Tithe Association   58, 60–1
Fakenham (Norfolk)   133
Farleigh Wallop (Hampshire)   202, 205
farm workers   *see* agricultural workers
farmers   *see* Farmers' Alliance, National Union of Farmers, owner-occupying farmers, tenant farmers, yeoman farmers

320

Index

Farmers' Alliance   31, 32, 35–7, 38, 42, 65, 68, 99
Farmers' Tithe Defence League (Wales)   51
Farquharson, Henry Richard   66
Farquharson, Henry Frank   207
fascism, fascists   8, 11, 122, 192–4, 209, 211, 213, 223, 226, 298
  see also British Union of Fascists; English Mistery; Lymington, Viscount; Pitt-Rivers, George
Fisher, Herbert (H A L)   109
Flint, John   29
Fordingbridge (Hampshire)   243
Framlingham (Suffolk)   129
free churches   112, 171
  see also baptists, congregationalists, methodists, quakers
Fressingfield (Suffolk)   272
Frittenden (Kent)   249–50
Fuller, Major J. F. C.   203
Fuller-Acland-Hood, Alexander, second baron St Audries   178–9, 269

Gallagher, Willie   298
Gardiner, Margaret   240–1, 242
Gardiner, Rolf   195, 203, 206–7, 209
Gardner, Herbert   60, 69, 75, 76
Gardner, Rev. J. L.   41
Gates, B. J.   227, 229
Gee, Thomas   53
General Dealers Ltd
  activities of   xvi, xviii, 11, 182–5, 189, 191–2, 214, 220, 221, 222, 239, 241, 262, 263, 267–8, 291, 297
  control(ling) committee   248, 258
  effigies of   271, 272
  financing of   186–8, 264, 287–8
  plans to launch   78, 168, 174–6, 177, 264–5, 285
  recovery problems   240, 247–50
George, Henry   33, 110
Georgeham (Devon)   266
Gestingthorpe (Essex)   190, 218, 240–1, 242
gift sales   230, 266
Gill, George   130, 179–80, 181–2, 223, 267, 281

Gilmour, Sir John   136, 141, 225, 241
Gilmour, Sir Patrick   191
Gladstone, William E.   32, 34, 37, 45, 46, 66, 73, 75
Gloucestershire   5, 102, 122, 172, 230–1
Goddard, Arthur   145
Gooch, Edwin   196–7, 281
Granville, Edgar   116, 122, 124, 125, 131, 286n.118, 289
Gray, Charles   60, 62, 71, 75
Great Bardfield (Essex)   58
Great Mongeham (Kent)   250, 277
Great Sampford Baptist Church (Essex)   292
Greenstead (Essex)   221
Grey, Charles, second earl Grey   21
Grey, Henry George, third earl Grey   72–3, 76–7, 78, 168, 297
Griffith-Boscawen, Sir Arthur   94–5, 96, 98, 100–1, 105–6, 174
Grimstead (Wiltshire)   229
Grove, Thomas   69
Groves, Arthur   133–4
Guilford, earl of   13
Guinness, Walter   108, 116
Gunson, Douglas   191–2
Guy, Theophilus   29
Guy's Hospital   2, 58, 264
Gwersyllt Hall Farm (Denbighshire)   1 m234, 240

Haberdashers, Worshipful Company of   174
Hacheston (Suffolk)   178
Haffenden, Ebenezer   126–7, 137, 291
Hailey (Oxfordshire)   231
Halesworth (Suffolk)   129
Halifax, Lord   see Wood, Edward, first earl of Halifax
Halstead (Essex)   118
Halstead (Kent)   35, 38, 40
Hammond, H. B.   224
Hampshire   2, 5, 23, 35, 42, 49, 58, 60, 61–2, 82, 102, 119–20, 145, 173, 174, 202, 209, 229, 243, 271–2
Hamstreet (Kent)   137
Hannah W. G.   148–9, 153n.24, 154n.28, 157n.39, 163–4, 166, 184, 279n.88

Index

Harcourt, William   45, 66, 75–6
Harvey, W. H.   135–5, 262
Hatherden (Hampshire)   61
Haughley (Suffolk)   130
Hayman, Rev. Henry   57
Hemyock (Devon)   59
Henry VIII, King   17
Hereford Cathedral   xv, 230
Herefordshire
  agricultural depression in   172
  tithepayers' campaign in   5, 62, 185, 210, 230, 248, 266
Hereward Wake, Sir   175
Hertfordshire   57, 102, 124, 125n.48, 166, 174, 211
Hicks Beach, Sir Michael   73–5
High Court   240, 241, 242–6, 251
High Laver (Essex)   58
Hinton St Mary (Dorset)   170, 205, 209
Hitchen (Hertfordshire)   211
Hoare, Sir Samuel   93
Hoggart, George   221
home office, home secretary   xviii, 43, 45–6, 90, 106, 137, 138, 141–2, 182–4, 189, 191, 209, 239–41 268
Hooe (Sussex)   178–9, 269
Hooper, Frederick   216, 223
Hooper, H. R.   224
hops, tithe on   27, 36–7, 45, 274–5
Hothfield, Lord   122, 123
house tithe   148
Howard, James   36, 37
Howard, Thomas   184, 209, 266
Howley, William, archbishop of Canterbury   14n.4, 22
Hughes, Edward   14
Hughes, Frederick   137, 148, 153
Hundon (Suffolk)   152, 183
Huntingdonshire   172, 229
Huntingfield, Lord (William Vanneck)   109
Hutchinson, Captain G. T.   175
Hyde (Hampshire)   243, 271
Hythe   117–18, 141, 179–81

Icklesham (Sussex)   135, 137, 140, 152, 154, 221
incumbent clergy   *see* parochial clergy
Iden (Sussex)   164, 182

Inderwick, Frederick   37–8, 41, 45, 46
Inskip, Thomas   138
Ipswich (Suffolk)   33, 129, 130, 132, 157, 164, 165, 170, 230, 253, 290
Irish land reform, influence of   21–2, 24, 32–4, 36, 54, 56, 66, 73, 297
Irvine, Bryant Godman   203
Iwi, Edward   261

Jasper More, Robert   62
Jesus College, Cambridge   177, 183
Johns, Samuel   216, 217
Jones, James   134–5
JoynsonHicks, William   106
judiciary   *see* county courts, Court of Appeal, High Court, lord chancellor, magistrates

Kedward, Rev. Roderick   12, 104, 122–3, 223, 289
  and Royal Commission   261, 277, 281
  and tithe non-payment   xvi–xviii, 129, 239, 241
  as MP   124, 136, 142, 210, 236–7
  as NTA leader   82, 145, 185, 207
  at tithe protests   128, 131, 135, 137–8, 156, 214, 222, 231, 232, 266, 1 *r* 1 283
Kent   1, 3, 5, 11–12, 16, 17, 18, 22–4, 28, 63, 104, 109, 156, 198
  agricultural conditions in   76, 173, 196
  distraint protests   138, 139, 140–1, 157, 179–82, 245–6, 250, 266–8, 269
  extraordinary tithe   27, 31, 35–43, 274
  fascist activity   210, 221–2, 224
  NFU in   143, 228, 261
  tithe collection   57, 82, 117, 152, 153–5, 159, 162, 163, 185, 229, 247–8, 249, 258
  tithepayers' campaign   59, 62, 93–4, 102, 119, 122, 214, 230, 237, 300
  see also East Kent Agricultural Association; East Kent Tithepayers' Association
Kent and Sussex Agricultural Labourers' Union   32, 39
Kenyon, George   69
Kersey (Suffolk)   190, 213, 218

Index

Keynes, John Maynard   106, 109
  and Royal Commission   264–5, 273, 274, 280
  as tithe collector   174, 177, 189–90, 297
Kidner, Stanley   131, 163, 206
King's, Cambridge   106, 174, 177, 189–90, 243
King's Lynn (Norfolk)   191, 197
Kingsnorth (Kent)   137, 245, 267
Knatchbull, Michael, fifth baron Brabourne   128
Knatchbull-Hugesson, E. H, first baron Brabourne   45n.63, 63, 69, 298
Knight, Frank and Rutley   119
Krailing, Frederick   228, 241

Labour Party   87, 100
  and agricultural policy   7, 115–16, 195, 199, 200, 211, 227
  and tithe policy   6, 8–9, 92, 93, 97, 109–11, 1978, 285–6, 295, 297
  and tithepayers' movement   217, 224, 237, 281
Lamb, Sir Joseph   109, 113, 236, 284
Lamplugh, Rev. David   47–8
Land Agents' Society   136, 259–60
land nationalisation   33, 100, 112, 195, 198, 199
Land Settlement Facilities Act (1919)   86–7
Land Union   97, 98–9, 101–2, 105, 107, 200
land tax   86, 90–1, 99, 148, 260, 264, 274
  see also   League of Taxation of Land Values
landlord class   *see* aristocracy
Lang, William Cosmo, archbishop of Canterbury
  and Queen Anne's Bounty   167–8
  and tithe conflict   xviii, 9, 57, 155–6, 158, 247, 288–9
  and tithe legislation   252, 255–7, 275, 276–7, 278–9
Lansbury, George   111–12
Laski, Harold   225
Lawther, Will   141
lay impropriators   *see* lay titheowners

lay titheowners   2, 17, 20, 29, 36, 54, 58, 78, 89, 95, 98–9, 99n.75, 178–9, 264, 280
  and General Dealers   174–5, 177, 189–90, 297
  tithe due to   92, 106–7, 109, 113, 117, 138, 213, 265, 274
  see also   public schools, University of Cambridge, University of Oxford, Welsh Church Commissioners
Le Fanu, William   90–1, 92, 148
League of Taxation of Land Values   110
Leicestershire   17, 172, 231
Leighton, Stanley   47, 55, 69n.94
Lewis, Oswald   124
Leysters (Herefordshire)   266
Liberal Party   8, 159
  and Farmers' Alliance, 32, 35–6, 45
  and political nonconformism, 34, 79, 88, 126
  and rural policy   33–4, 115–16, 195, 199
  and tithe legislation
    1836 bill   28
    1891 bill   66–7, 68–9, 71, 73–4, 75–6
    1918 bill   92
    1925 bill   109, 111–12
    1930 remission bill   124
    1936 bill   285–6
  and tithepayers' campaigns   59–60, 61, 77, 103, 104, 108, 131, 214, 223, 299
  and tithe war in Wales   53–4, 56, 58, 94, 235
  see also   Kedward, Rev. Roderick; Whigs
Liberal Unionists   97, 98–9, 101, 102, 105, 107, 200
Liberation Society   34, n, 72, 263
Liberty and Property Defence League   63
Liskeard (Cornwall)   217n.131, 230, 232
Litherland, Henry   29
Little Chart (Kent)   137
Little Maplestead (Essex)   104

323

Index

Llanarmon-yn-Iâl (Denbighshire) 49, 51, 53, 54n.21
Llangwm (Denbighshire) 53
Lloyd George, David 53, 86, 99, 110, 112, 225
Lloyd, John 62–3, 77, 79
Lloyd, Sir John Edward 259
Long Melford (Suffolk) 118, 163
Longmore, Sir Charles 92
Lopham (Norfolk) 224
lord chancellor, lord chancellor's office 113, 142, 193, 250–2, 258
Lower Wallop (Hampshire) 23
Lowestoft (Suffolk) 120, 198, 232, 286n.118
Loyd-Lindsay, Robert 199
Ludovici, Anthony 203
Lygon, William (Viscount Elmley) 124, 131
Lyminge (Kent) xv, 230
Lymington, Viscount (ninth earl of Portsmouth) 11, 170, 194–5, 202–5, 209, 212, 226
as MP 121–2
as NTA leader 124, 129, 136, 145

MacDonald, Ramsey 5, 97, 136, 169, 244
MacLaren, Andrew 283, 285
Macmillan, Rev. John, bishop of Dover 155
Magdalene college, Cambridge 177
magistrates xv, 29, 40, 43, 53, 56, 128, 242
Maidenhead (Berkshire) 131
Maidstone (Kent) 32, 39, 43
Malmesbury, fifth earl of (James Harris) 2, 178, 258
Manafon (Montgomeryshire) 57
market gardens, tithe on 27, 31, 37, 274
Marriot, John H. 176
Mason, Leonard 190, 262
McCreagh, Michael Christopher 119–20, 123, 127, 160, 238, 262
Meiford (Montgomeryshire) 54
Mersham (Kent) 39, 198, 224, 267, 291
Merton College, Oxford 16, 179

methodists xvi, 22, 53, 89, 122, 171, 197
Middleton, Sir George k p197, 297
and effigies 269–71, 72
and General Dealers 174–6, 184, 187
and Royal Commission 256–7, 263–4, 276–7, 279–80
as chair of QAB tithe committee xviii, 9, 167–72, 173, 188, 190, 192, 205, 247–8, 265
death of 289
Miers, Henry 57
miners 51, 53, 232
Ministry of Agriculture 90, 91–2, 96, 98, 100–1, 103, 136, 226, 252–3, 255, 256
Minster (Kent) 258
Minsterley (Shropshire) 231
Mitchell G. J. 145
Mobbs, Albert G. 10
and fascism 192, 220–1
and NFU 143–4, 228–9, 236, 261, 284, 290
as NTA leader 120, 123–4, 126, 131, 160, 171, 197, 207, 261, 283, 292
as Suffolk tithepayers' leader 130, 132–4, 272
Mochdre (Montgomeryshire) 53
Molyneux, Rev. Henry 29
monarchy and tithe 19, 147, 150, 204, 212, 283
Monkton (Kent) 41
Monkton (Pembrokeshire) 57
Monmouthshire 126, 234
Montgomeryshire 5, 49, 54, 56–7, 228
Morris, Edward 200
Morrison, William 290
Mosley, Oswald 209–12, 220, 222, 224, 226
see also British Union of Fascists
Mussolini, Benito 122, 211, 224

National Agricultural Labourers' Union 32, 35
National Agricultural Union 199, 207
National Farmers' Union 5, 200, 290, 292, 298
and tithe legislation 107–9, 113–14, 115, 236–7, 281, 282–6

324

Index

and Royal Commission 142, 255, 260–1, 263, 277
in negotiations 98–101, 136, 146, 159, 161–2
relations with NTA 105, 115, 120–1, 123–4, 126, 132, 143–4, 201, 230, 235
relations with government 93, 225, 227–9, 251–3
National Tithepayers' Association 118–20, 136, 145–6, 287, 290, 293–4, 298
and tithe legislation 105–7, 253–4, 257, 281
and tithe nonpayment xvi, 127–9, 222, 245
formation of 81, 84, 92, 101–5
policy of 123–4, 160–1, 237–9, 261–2, 289–90
relations with fascists 192, 194, 202, 207–8, 218–24
relations with NFU 5, 120, 125–6, 142–4, 227–9, 231, 235–6, 260, 290
National Union of Agricultural Workers 196–7, 198, 281
New College, Oxford 118, 179–82, 280
New Romney (Kent) 245
Newbury (Berkshire) 131
Newchurch (Kent) 222, 267
Newman, Robert 20
Newsam, Frank xviii, 189
Newton Abbot (Devon) 191, 214, 216, 217, 232
Nicholls, George 108
nonconformism, nonconformists 3, 41, 123, 293
and tithepayers' campaign 15, 22, 104, 108, 111, 112, 223, 262, 273, 297, 298–9
in Welsh tithe war 50, 53–4, 234, 259
political nonconformism 34, 58–9, 63, 76, 89, 94, 111, 112, 126, 197, 297
see also baptists, congregationalists, free churches, methodists, quakers
Norfolk 5, 124, 141, 293
agricultural conditions 173, 290
agricultural workers 117, 196

distraint seizures 157, 262, 266, 268, 291
fascist activity in 190, 191, 221
NFU in 105, 124, 143, 201, 261n.8
tithe as an issue in 18, 23, 197, 198, 229
tithe collectors 57, 153, 155, 177, 182, 247, 248
tithepayers' associations in 38, 130, 131–2, 133, 163, 165, 191, 206, 224, 230, 281
North Devon Tithepayers' Association 214–17, 232
see also Devon
Northamptonshire 124, 172–3, 229
Norton, Robert 45–6
Norwich (Norfolk) 130, 131, 191, 197, 230, 268, 281, 290
Norwich Union Life Insurance Society 2, 174

occupying owners' associations (Essex, Suffolk) 118
orchards *see* extraordinary tithe
owner-occupying farmers 11
and tithepayers' movement 102, 104, 118, 130, 155
as a class 64–5, 76, 114, 116, 199, 211, 298, 300
increase in numbers 8, 87, 96, 99, 177
liability for tithe 28, 68, 70, 80, 86, 89, 117–8
Oxford, University of 98, 109–10, 120, 135–6, 148, 168, 181–2, 252, 297
and Royal Commission 264, 280
tithe collected by 1–2, 179
see also Cecil, Lord Hugh; Christ Church; Merton College; New College
Oxfordshire 62, 131, 141, 143, 198, 231, 248, 269, 1 q j
titheowners 37, 53, 183
Oxland, Ernest 216

Paddock Wood (Kent) 230
Palmer, Roundell *see* Selborne, first earl of
Palmer, William *see* Selborne, second earl of

325

Index

Parlour, Captain William 176, 185, 186, 249–50, 288
parochial clergy xvi, 82, 88–9, 206
 and tithe reform 25, 68, 73, 79, 92–3, 96, 111, 255, 264, 274, 275, 277–8, 287
 as tithe collectors 1, 22, 57, 91, 104, 106, 147–8, 151, 155, 187–8, 238
 as tithepayers 61
 in Wales 2, 49, 51, 54–5, 94
 relations with tithepayers 9, 17, 18, 23, 35, 41, 46–7, 156, 158, 170–1, 185, 266–7, 272, 276
Parry, John 53, 54n.21, 62–3
Parsons, E. V. K. 271
Partridge, Canon Frank 98, 106, 153, 158
passive resistance 5, 24, 80, 126–7 133, 163, 173, 175, 188, 205, 213, 237, 291, 297
Patrick, Colin (Mark) 286
Peacock, Sir Edward Robert 259
Peel, Sir Robert 14, 15, 25
Pembroke, Cambridge 177
Pembrokeshire 5, 49, 50, 51, 57, 234
Perks, Roberts 122
Peterson, Edward Whit'tred Iltyd (E. W. I.) 43, 56–7, 76, 78–9, 113, 153, 171, 297
Peterson, E. W. R. 144, 264
Peterson, Rev. William 42–3
petitions on tithe 13, 18, 20, 25, 43, 47, 73, 212, 283
Philips, James 231
Philips, Rev. George 78
Picton, James 76
Pitt-Rivers, George 11, 170, 194, 195, 205–10, 212, 223, 232, 262, 281, 283
Plathen, Richard 191, 192, 217, 218, 220
Pluckley (Kent) 84, 126, 249, 267, 291
Plumptre, John 14
police 239, 250, 258
 and distraint sales xviixix, 119, 137–8, k m14p–2, 153, 165–6 179, 180–2, 231, 241, 242
 and fascists 191–2, 209, 217, 218–20
 and General Dealers 182–4, 188, 189–90, k s2m, 262, 267, 268

chief constables 53, 56, 138, 140–1, 184, 189
 in Welsh tithe war o, 33, 56
Pollock, Bertram, bishop of Norwich 9, 149, 152, 160, 170, 201, 244, 256, 279, 285
Pollock, Sir Ernest 149–50, 244
Pontfaen (Pembrokeshire) 51
possession men xvi, 141, 189, 190, 191, 213, 249–51, 258, 266
Potter Heigham (Norfolk) 268
Powell, William 267
Prestige, Sir John 283
Pretyman, Ernest 97–9, 100–1, 200
Primrose, Reginald 175, 176, 182, 184, 239–40
private detectives 180–1
protectionism 99–100, 121, 199, 201, 223, 225
Prothero Rowland, first baron Ernle 72, 91, 96
public schools 2, 58, 61, 109, 110, 174, 258, 264, 280
Pye, J. W. 261

quakers 19, 22, 29–30, 263, 295
Queen Anne's Bounty
 and distraint orders 134, 137, 140, 152–4, 157, 166, 242–5, 258, 265–6, 291
 and General Dealers 174–5, 184–6, 248, 250, 287–8
 and hard case policy 156, 159–62, 247
 and Royal Commission 256–7, 257, 263–4, 277–80
 area collection committees 143, 173, 201
 as tithe collector xvi, xviii, 1, 3, 147, 90, 106, 113, 115, 118, 150–1, 155, 158, 232, 240
 in negotiations 136, 252
 officials of 90, 92, 147–9, 167–8, 169, 170–1, 187–8, 197, 205
 reports of 229
 tithe committee 9

Radcliffe, Geoffrey 280
Radcliffe, Sir Frederick 9, 98

326

Index

as chair of QAB tithe committee, 149, 152–3, 158, 160
  resignation of 167–8
Ramsbotham, Herwald 285
Rash, Rowland 6, 9, 131, 191, 218, 220, 248
Rash, Doreen *see* Wallace, Doreen
Ratcliff, Stanley 229, 254, 260, 263
rates on tithe 17, 27, 45, 82, 83, 92, 109, 110, 148, 151, 259, 264, 274–5
  negotiations about 97, 100, 102, 106
  see also Ecclesiastical Tithe Rentcharge (Rates) Act (1920); Tithe Rentcharge (Rates) Act (1899)
Rating and Valuation Act (1925) 108
Rawlinson, John 109
Reading (Berkshire) 35, 58, 60–1, 131, 185
Rebecca riots 50, 271
redemption *see* tithe redemption
Rees, Beddoe 112
Rew, Sir Henry 81, 92, 101, 102–4, 107, 119
Ricardo, David 19–20
Rice, Edward Dennis 127
Rice, Edward Royd 13–14
Ringshall (Suffolk) 189–90, 212, 265, 268
Ringwood (Hampshire) 243
Robbins, Rowland 100–1, 105, 120–1, 125, 144, 200, 227
Robinson, Sydney 116
Romansleigh (Devon) 266
Romford (Essex) 130–1
Romney Marsh (Kent) 185, 222, 267
Roseveare, Harry 214, 222, 228–9
Ross (Herefordshire) 230
Rothermere, Lord (Harold Sidney Harmsworth) 200–1, 220
Royal Commission on Tithe Rentcharge (1936)
  announcement of 255–6
  demands for 107, 121–2, 142, 162, 212, 222–3, 227, 236, 251, 253–4, 257
  government response 275–6, 284–6
  hearings of 259–64
  proposals 273–4

  titheowners' response 277–9
  tithepayers' response 280–1, 282, 283–4, 300
royal commissions
  agriculture (191920) 87
  land in Wales (1896) 50n.1
  real property (1828) 21
  tithe redemption (1892) 75, 79
  see also Royal Commission on Tithe Rentcharge (1936)
Royal Institution of Chartered Surveyors 136, 259
Ruckinge (Kent) 136–8, 267, 290–1
rural exodus, fear of 31, 65, 194, 196
  see also agrarianism
ruralism 100
  see also agrarianism
Rushmere (Suffolk) 266, 269
Russell, Ernest 176
Russell, John, first earl Russell 24–5, 28–9
Ruthin (Denbighshire) 56–7, 234
Rye (Sussex) 37, 129, 164–5, 182–3, 222, 230
Ryland, Thomas 100–1, 105, 227

Sackville, Herbrand, ninth Earl De La Warr 2, 256, 257
Saffron Walden (Essex) 58n.36, 60, 129–30, 170–1, 190, 253, 292
Salisbury, Lord (Robert Gascoyne-Cecil) 28, 32, 34, 46, 58
  and tithe legislation 3, 50, 63–70, 73–4, 79, 251, 297
Salisbury (Wiltshire) 132, 157, 171, 199–200, 228
Sampford Peverell (Devon) 216
Sanders, Sir Robert 97
Sanderson, William 203
Sandwich (Kent) xv, 63, 127–8, 129, 222n.149, 253
Sankey, John, first Viscount Sankey 250–2, 258
  see also lord chancellor
Saxmundham (Suffolk) 129
Selborne, first Earl of (Roundell Palmer) 55, 66, 72–3, 78
Selborne, second Earl of (William Palmer) 56, 138, 167–8, 174

Index

Shadingfield (Suffolk) 163
Shadoxhurst (Kent) 137
Shelfanger (Norfolk) 143, 157, 268
Shepherdswell (Kent) xvi–xix, 182
Shepperson, Ernest 109
Shropshire 5, 62, 124, 125n.48, 172, 184, 231, 248, 257
Simmons, Alfred 32, 39
Simon, John 191
Sittingbourne (Kent) 39, 129
Slesser, Lord Justice Sir Henry 111, 244
Sloman, P. M. 221
Small Property Owners' and Tithepayers' Association (Lowestoft) 232
Smarden (Kent) 43, 123
Smith, Frederick 241, 262
Smith, Norman 198
Smyth, John 20
Soames, Arthur 116
Society of Friends *see* quakers
Soil Association 203
Solley, Frederick 250
Solley, George Christopher xv, 127–9, 137, 201, 214, 222, 223, 262, 267, 281, 283
Somerset 5, 124, 172, 178, 207, 209, 232, 286n.118, 289–90
Somerset, Henry, tenth duke of Beaufort 200, 206
South Caernarvonshire Anti-Tithe League 53
South Weston (Oxfordshire) 231
Southminster (Essex) 253, 268
Spencer, John, third Earl Spencer *see* Althorp, Lord
Spens, William 236–7, 252, 266–7, 276
Spicer, Tom 243–4
St Bartholomew's Hospital 2, 264
St Columb Major (Cornwall) 266
St John's, Cambridge 177
St Minver (Cornwall) 35
St Pinnock (Cornwall) 183, 214
Stafford Cripps, Sir Richard 283
Standlake (Oxfordshire) 269, 1 q j
Stanhope, Arthur, sixth Earl Stanhope 41
Staunton, George 189, 191, 241n.71

Steed, Joshua Owen 118, 163, 260
Steeple Gidding (Cambridgeshire) 29
Stelling Minnis (Kent) 118, 137, k ɯ s 140–1, 154, 157, 167
Stevens, Charles 49n.1, 54, 56
Stevenson, Francis 73–4
Stiffkey (Norfolk) 221
Stoke-by-Clare (Suffolk) 134–5, 152, 178
Stourmouth (Kent) 185
Stow Bedon (Norfolk) 291
Stow, James 40
Stowmarket (Suffolk) 129, 133, 190n.40
Strachey Edward, first baron Strachie 112
Stradishall (Suffolk) 157
Strutt, Charles 60
Sudbury (Suffolk) 135, 189, 191, 241n.71
Suffolk 5, 19, 232
  agricultural conditions 23, 173, 196
  distraint seizures 134–5, 152, 157, 163, 165–6, 178, 183, 249, 266, 268, 269, 272, 291
  fascist activity in 189–92, k s2 ɪɜ, 221
  NFU in 120, 124, 228, 253, 290
  tithe as an issue in 34, 73, 108, 109, 116, 118, 248
  titheowners 229, 258
  see also Mobbs, Albert G.; Suffolk Tithepayers' Association; Wallace, Doreen
Suffolk Tithepayers' Association 129, 130–1, 132, 133–4
Sussex 3, 5
  agricultural conditions 173, 196
  distraint sales 135, 137, 140, 144, 164–5, 178–9,182–3, 221, 260, 269
  extraordinary tithe 27, 31, 35, 37–40, 40n.43, 45
  titheowners 57, 153, 154, 247, 248
  tithepayers' associations 59, 62, 129, 141, 229, 230, 292
Swales, Joseph 262

Taunton (Somerset) 289–90
Taylor, William 200

328

Index

Temple, William, archbishop of Canterbury   87, 169, 279–80, 288, 292
tenant farmers   13, 15, 21, 22, 23–4, 32, 42, 65, 85–6, 112, 123
  and Farmers' Alliance   31, 32, 36
  and NFU   99, 102, 298
  and tithe law   27, 45–6, 68, 69, 70, 71, 73, 74, 79, 89, 263
  in Wales   50, 53, 58
Tenbury Wells (Worcestershire)   183–4, 209, 266
tender, sales by   133, 157–8, 163–4, 167, 178, 179, 243, 244, 263, 267
Tenterden (Kent)   82, 230, 253
Thompson, Raven   212–3
Thorne, Ernest   244–5
Thornton-Miller, Major Geoffrey   176, 185, 249–50
Thurnscoe Urban District Council   232
Thynne Henry (Viscount Weymouth)   206
Tithe (Amendment) Bill (1933)   236–7, 252
Tithe Act (1846)   29, 91
Tithe Act (1891)   50, 74–8, 79–80, 85, 243–4
  remission clause   103, 118, 124, 152, 236–7
Tithe Act (1918)   83n.11, 91–2, 95, 98–9, 101, 102–4, 106, 107, 111, 113, 126, 148, 179, 264
Tithe Act (1925)   108–14, 177, 179, 211, 251
Tithe Act (1936)   284–6, 289, 290, 292, 295, 297, 300
tithe as national property   33, 54, 58–9, 63, 66–7, 75, 77, 94, 95, 235
Tithe Commutation Act (1836)   xvi, 3, 9, 24–9, 208, 261, 296–
Tithe Commutation Acts Amendment with respect to Market Gardens (1873)   37–8
Tithe Composition (Ireland) Act (1823)   22
Tithe League, The   120, 238, 262, 281
tithe on fish   24, 29–30, 148, 150–1
Tithe Owners' Union   92, 113, 137
  see also   Churchmen's Defence Union, Tithe Rent-Charge Owners' Union
Tithe Question Association   54n.21, 62–3, 73, 75–6, 77, 79
Tithe Redemption Committee   289, 290–1, 292
tithe redemption   13, 14, 48, 148
  and 1836 Tithe Commutation Act   28
  and 1918 Tithe Act   83, 90–1. 103
  and 1925 Tithe Act   97, 100–1, 102, 106, 109
  and Royal Commission   256, 260–1, 276
  proposals for   36, 37, 42, 63, 67, 70, 73, 75, 79, 198, 238
  see also   annuities, Extraordinary Tithe Redemption Act (1886), Tithe Act (1846), Tithe Redemption Committee
Tithe Remission Bill (1930)   123–4, 125–6, 127, 132, 142–3, 152, 161, 204, 236, 237, 238
Tithe Rentcharge (Rates) Act (1899)   79, 93
Tithe Rent-Charge Owners' Union   57, 72, 76, 78
  see also   Churchmen's Defence Union, Tithe Owners' Union
titheowners   2–3, 15, 17, 19–20, 26–7, 35, 58, 70–2, 74–6, 98, 135–6, 168, 174–5, 182, 188, 242–3, 250–1, 252, 258, 263–5, 274, 280, 287–8
  see also Cambridge, University of; Ecclesiastical Commissioners; General Dealers; lay titheowners; Oxford, University of; Queen Anne's Bounty; Tithe Rent-Charge Owners' Union, Welsh Church Commissioners
Tithepayer, The   238
tithepayers   xvi, 1, 2–3, 17, 26, 33, 37, 49–50, 59–60, 69, 77, 86, 135, 145, 179, 299–300
tithepayers' associations   *see* Anti-Extraordinary Tithe Association, Anti-Tithe League (Wales), Fair Tithe Association, East Kent Tithepayers'

Index

Association, National Tithepayers'
Association, occupying owners'
associations (Essex, Suffolk),
Small Property Owners' and
Tithepayers' Association
(Lowestoft), Suffolk TIthepayers'
Association, Tithe League, Tithe
Question Association, Women's
Tithepayers' Association
Tiverton (Devon)   59, 171, 216, 232, 266, 291
Toppesfield (Essex)   58
Transport and General Workers' Union   196, 200
Trevarrian (Cornwall)   190–1, 211, 216
Trinity College, Cambridge   174, 177
Trustram Eve, Sir Herbert   165
Turner, Albert   214
Turner, Makens   228, 284
Turnour Edward, sixth earl of Winterton   174
Tuting, Rev. Dr W.C.   92–3
Tyman, John   40

Ubbeston (Suffolk)   249
United Empire Party   200–1, 206
Upton Bishop (Herefordshire)   230
Uzzell, Ruth   198

Vanneck William, fifth baron Huntingfield   109
Vernon, Sir Bowater George   209–10, 262
Vincent, Stanley   222

Wace, very rev. Henry   82
Waddell, Archibald   267, 291, 294
Wakeman, Sir Offley   231
Wallace, Doreen   131, 198, 207, 221, 266, 268, 281, 289–90, 293
  and BUF   191–2, 218, 220, 224
  as writer   6, 82
Wallingford (Berkshire)   130, 131–2, 183, 231, 242–3
Wallop, Gerald   *see* Lymington, Viscount
Warnford (Hampshire)   61–2, 272
Waspe, Hannah   189–90, 265, 268
Watkins, R. F.   231, 234–5, 262

Wattisfield (Suffolk)   291
Webster, Richard   71
Wedgwood, Josiah   110–11, 286
Wellington (Shropshire)   231
Welsh Church Act (1914)   2, 79, 88
  see also Church (of England) in Wales
Welsh Church (temporalities) Act (1919)   2, 94–5
  see also Church (of England) in Wales
Welsh Church Commissioners   94–5, 98, 234–5, 250, 252, 258
  and General Dealers   174–6, 184
Welsh Land, Commercial and Labour League   *see* Anti-Tithe League
Welshpool (Montgomeryshire)   54
Wem (Shropshire)   231
Wessex Agricultural Defence Association (WADA)   205–10, 232, 262, 281, 283
Wessex and Southern Counties Tithepayers' and Common Law Defence Association   *see* Wessex Agricultural Defence Association
West Down (Devon)   266
West Grinstead (Sussex)   249
Westbury (Shropshire)   231
Westren, Charles   157–8, 165–6, 221, 230
Westwell (Kent)   xvi, xvii, 122, 137, 267, 269, 276
Weymouth, Viscount (Henry Thynne)   206
Wheler, Sir Granville   109
Whigs   13, 14, 15, 20, 21, 24–5, 32, 33, 63, 66, 296
Whiteley, William   281
Whitestone (Devon)   1, 16–17
Whittingham, rt. rev. Walter, bishop of St Edmundsbury and Ipswich   150, 155, 156, 279
Whittome, Hester   178
Wickford (Essex)   131–2
Wilkinson, Ellen   95
Williams, Llewellyn   92
Williams, Sir John Fischer   259, 262
Williamson, Henry   221, 223
Wilson, Cecil   111

Index

Wiltshire
 agricultural depression in 173
 distraint sales 157, 244
 NFU in 228, 254
 tithepayers' campaign 5, 62, 69, 132, 145, 229, 247, 248, 249
 WADA activity 206, 209
Winchilsea, Earl of 13, 104, 199, 207
Winchester Cathedral 54, 150
Winchester College 2, 58, 61, 174
Wingfield, John 35
Winstanley, George 18
Winterslow (Wiltshire) 132
Winterton, sixth Earl of (Edward Turnour) 174
Wise, Frederick 198
Witney (Oxfordshire) 131
Wiveliscombe (Somerset) 232
Wolmer, Lord (Roundell Cecil Palmer) 138, 188
Wolmer, Viscount (William Palmer) *see* Selborne, second Earl of
Wolton, Eric 248
women in tithepayers' movement xv, 51, 56, 61, 130, 166, 267-8
 see also Balfour, Evelyn; Wallace, Doreen
Women's Tithepayers' Association 268, 281
Wood, Edward, first earl of Halifax 93n.53, 105-6, 113, 253, 273, 275-7
Wood, William S. 222
Woodbridge (Suffolk) 34, 178, 258
Woodhams, Arthur 127, 129
Woods, William 61-2
Worcestershire 5, 172, 183-4, 209-10, 231, 235, 254, 266
Worth (Kent) 162
Wortham (Suffolk) 131, 191-2, 218-21, 224, 248, 249, 269-71, 291, 292
Worthington-Evans, Sir Laming 106, 113
Wright, J. F. (Jimmy) 143, 201
Wyre Piddle (Worcestershire) 231, 235

Yaxley (Suffolk) 291
yeoman farmers 8, 23, 65, 68, 69, 76, 199, 207, 283, 298, 299
Yeovil (Somerset) 232, 290

Boydell Studies in Rural History

The Real Agricultural Revolution:
The Transformation of English Farming, 1939–1985
Paul Brassley, David Harvey, Matt Lobley and Michael Winter

Agricultural Knowledge Networks in Rural Europe, 1700–2000
Edited by Yves Segers and Leen Van Molle

Landless Households in Rural Europe, 1600–1900
Edited by Christine Fertig, Richard Paping and Henry French

Agriculture, Economy and Society in Early Modern Scotland
Edited by Harriet Cornell, Julian Goodare and Alan R. MacDonald